ild in Ontario

The State of the Child in Ontario

edited by
Richard Barnhorst and Laura C. Johnson

The Child, Youth and Family Policy Research Centre

Toronto
OXFORD UNIVERSITY PRESS
1991

Oxford University Press, 70 Wynford Drive, Don Mills, Ontario M3C 1J9

Toronto Oxford New York
Delhi Bombay Calcutta Madras Karachi Petaling Jaya
Singapore Hong Kong Tokyo Nairobi Dar es Salaam
Cape Town Melbourne Auckland

and associated companies in
Berlin Ibadan

Canadian Cataloguing in Publication Data

Main entry under title:

The State of the child in Ontario
Includes bibliographical references and index.
ISBN 0-19-540826-8

1. Children – Ontario – Social conditions.
2. Child welfare – Ontario. I. Child, Youth and
Family Policy Research Centre.

HQ792.C3S73 1991   305.23′09713   C91-093344-8

Contents

Acknowledgements

The Child, Youth and Family Policy Research Centre wishes to thank the members of *The State of the Child* Advisory Committee for the time and expertise they contributed to this project:

William Avison
Centre for the Study of Health and Well Being
University of Western Ontario

Julie Foley
Family Counselling Centre
Sarnia, Ontario

Ralph Garber
Child, Youth and Family Policy Research Centre, President; Faculty of Social Work, University of Toronto

Ben Gottlieb
Department of Psychology
University of Guelph

Julie Mathien
Early Childhood Education
Toronto Board of Education

Jeffrey Patterson
Social Planning Council of Metropolitan Toronto

Suzanne Ziegler
Toronto Board of Education

The production of *The State of the Child in Ontario* has been a major undertaking involving the generous assistance of a great many individuals and organizations. While the following acknowledgements identify many of these individuals, there are undoubtedly significant omissions. To all of these people, we express appreciation for their assistance.

The Centre wishes to acknowledge the contributions made by the following people in the form of obtaining data, reviewing draft chapters, and more generally helping to define the scope and form of the project:

Philip Abrahams, Municipality of Metropolitan Toronto
Carol Appathurai, Children's Services Branch, Ontario Ministry of Community and Social Services
Denise Avard, Canadian Institute of Child Health
Heather Barker, Child Care Branch, Ontario Ministry of Community and Social Services
Nancy Beauchamp, Ottawa Council for Low Income Support Services
Ellen Bobet, Medical Services Branch, Health and Welfare Canada
Monica Boyd, Department of Sociology, University of Western Ontario
Richard Bradley, Child Care Branch, Ontario Ministry of Community and Social Services
Satya Brink, Canadian Centre for Management Development
Lola Bratty, Child Care Branch, Ontario Ministry of Community and Social Services
Daryle Buffalo, Quantitative Analysis and Socio-Demographic Research, Indian and Northern Affairs Canada
Mary Anne Burke, Canadian Social Trends, Statistics Canada
Joel Clodman, Strategic Planning, Ontario Ministry of Community and Social Services
Diane Cresswell, Ontario Association of Children's Aid Societies
James Cummings, Department of Curriculum, Ontario Institute for Studies in Education
M. Dalley, Missing Children's Registry
Errol De Lima, Management Operations and Review Section, Ontario Housing Corporation
Peter Dewdney, housing advocate
Tony Doob, Centre for Criminology, University of Toronto
Martin Dooley, Department of Economics, McMaster University

Kay Eastham, Child Care Branch, Ontario Ministry of Community and Social Services

Margrit Eichler, Department of Sociology, Ontario Institute for Studies in Education

Jonathan Ellison, Statistics Canada

John Engeland, Research Division, Canada Mortgage and Housing

Terry Fagen, Social Housing Programs Branch, Ontario Housing Corporation

Nathan Gilbert, Laidlaw Foundation

Josephine V. Glaser, Management Information Systems, Consumer and Corporate Affairs Canada

Robert Glossop, The Vanier Institute of the Family

Lothar Goetz, Canadian Centre for Justice Statistics

Tom Goff, Indian and Northern Affairs Canada

Sylvia Goldblatt, Sylvia Goldblatt and Associates

Dorothy Gonsalves-Singh, Research Services, Ontario Ministry of the Attorney General

Ben Gottlieb, Department of Psychology, University of Guelph

Cyril Greenland, Easter Seal Research Institute

Morley Gunderson, Department of Economics, University of Toronto

Michelle Harding, Premier's Council on Health Strategy, Ontario Ministry of Health

Stephen Hawkins, Research and Information Analysis Unit, Ontario Ministry of Colleges and Universities

Polly Hill, Polly Hill Associates

Lorna Hurl, School of Social Work, McMaster University

Terry Irwin, Housing Supply Policy Section, Ontario Ministry of Housing

Susan Kaukonen-Low, Housing Field Operations, Ontario Housing Corporation

Jeff Kenedy, Quantitative Analysis and Socio-Demographic Research, Indian and Northern Affairs Canada

Suzanne Klein, Ontario Ministry of Labour

N.M. Lalu, Population Research Laboratory, University of Alberta

Gilles Y. Larocque, Quantitative Analysis and Socio-Demographic Research, Indian and Northern Affairs Canada

Roslyn Lawrence, Ontario Ministry of Skills Development

Donna Lero, Department of Family Studies, University of Guelph

John Lewko, Laurentian University

Colin Maloney, Toronto Catholic Children's Aid Society

Nancy Mandell, Department of Sociology, York University

Anne Martin, Ontario Ministry of Skills Development

Mary McConville, Ontario Association of Children's Aid Societies

Craig McKie, Statistics Canada, Department of Sociology and Anthropology, Carleton University

Henry McLeod, Catholic Children's Aid Society

Peter Morden, Children's Aid Society of Metropolitan Toronto

Sharon Moyer, The Research Group

Peter Nasmith, Ontario Court of Justice

Michael Nix, Ontario Ministry of Community and Social Services

Irene Nowakowski, Ontario Ministry of Treasury and Economics

Dan Offord, Department of Psychology, McMaster University

Karen Oster, Play and Learn

Sally Palmer, Department of Social Work, McMaster University

Angela Pearson, Programs Administration, Ontario Housing Corporation

Alan Pence, National Day Care Research Network, University of Victoria

Pang Poon, Labour Market and Research, Ontario Ministry of Labour

Shirley Post, Hospital for Sick Children

Marg Rapport, Ontario Ministry of Labour

Marg Reitsma-Street, Nipissing University College

Jeffrey Reitz, Department of Sociology, University of California

Carla Resor, Ontario Ministry of Labour

Marcia Rioux, G. Allan Roeher Institute, York University

Bruce Rivers, Metropolitan Toronto Children's Aid Society

Judy Rodegard, Statistics, Ontario Ministry of Treasury and Economics

Jane Rogers, Children's Services Branch, Ministry of Community and Social Services

David Ross, social policy consultant

Sandra Scarth, Children Services Branch, Ontario Ministry of Community and Social Services

Victor Severino, Child Care Branch, Ontario Ministry of Community and Social Services

Paul Siemens, Child Care Branch, Ontario Ministry of Community and Social Services

Richard Shillington, Tristat Resources Limited

Loren Simerl, Social Policy and Research Section, Ontario Housing Corporation

Ed Slugocki, Ontario Ministry of Treasury and Economics

Kathy Nixon Speechley, Child Health Research Institute, University of Western Ontario

Terry Sullivan, Premier's Council on Health Strategy, Ontario Ministry of Health

Maria Svoboda, Information Analysis and Consultation Unit, Ontario Ministry of Education

Angie Szuch, Community Health and Support Services, Ontario Ministry of Community and Social Services

Thomas R. Taylor, Business and Finance Branch, Ontario Ministry of Education

George Thomson, Ontario Ministry of Labour

Denise Van Herk, Residential Rehabilitation Assistance Program, Canada Mortgage and Housing

Frank Wagner, Physical Disabilities Policy Unit, Ontario Ministry of Community and Social Services

Brian Weagant, Justice for Children

Cheuk Wong, Ontario Ministry of Treasury and Economics

Suzanne Ziegler, Research Department, Toronto Board of Education

The editors would like to thank the authors for the time and effort they have spent preparing and revising their chapters for publication.

Special credit goes to the numerous people who are responsible for turning a collection of statistical data into the present volume. Sally Livingston at Oxford University Press edited the manuscript with great care, and it was a pleasure to work with her. Marie Bartholomew and her colleagues in Oxford's art department translated our vague ideas into an effective graphic design. Richard Teleky, Managing Editor at Oxford, provided initial support for this project and continued stewardship to make sure it really happened.

Lee Marks, Office Manager of the Centre, has seen this project through from initial proposal to final manuscript. To her has come the formidable responsibility of keeping track of ever-changing tables and text, translating back and forth from disk to hard copy. She has managed this task with care and good humour, and we acknowledge this important task with gratitude.

The work of the Child, Youth and Family Policy Research Centre is supported by the Government of Ontario, through the Ministry of Community and Social Services. In addition, a grant to support this State of the Child project has been provided by the Laidlaw Foundation. The Centre gratefully acknowledges this support. The conclusions and opinions expressed in this volume are those of the authors, and do not necessarily reflect the views of any organizations that have provided funding for the Centre or its research activities

Richard Barnhorst
Laura C. Johnson

Introduction

We are a society increasingly concerned about our children. Business leaders question whether Ontario's workforce will have the necessary skills to compete in a rapidly changing, highly technological global economy. Policy-makers ask whether existing financial and social support systems for the elderly will be maintained by young people comprising a decreasing percentage of the population. Parents are apprehensive lest their children lack an adequate education. The news media direct public attention to youth violence and child abuse. Child poverty is an acknowledged scandal in our affluent Ontario society.

At the international level, there is also rising concern about the status of children. Canada has played a prominent role in promoting international children's issues, in helping to draft the United Nations Convention on the Rights of the Child, and in chairing the 1990 UN International Summit on Children. Countries ratifying the Convention will be obligated to report periodically on the condition of children in their society. *The State of the Child in Ontario* report is designed to provide the kind of information needed to fulfil this obligation.

The State of the Child in Ontario serves as a benchmark in assessing the well-being of Ontario children and youth. It describes and analyses trends in social indicators pertaining to children's issues: sociodemographic characteristics of their families; their housing; their economic circumstances; their child care arrangements; their health; the child welfare and juvenile justice systems; and their experiences in school and at work. The Child, Youth and Family Policy Research Centre hopes that this collection of information — the first attempt to provide a comprehensive picture of the conditions of children in Ontario — will be a useful resource for policy-makers, researchers, service providers, advocates, and others concerned with the welfare of children and youth.

The Child, Youth and Family Policy Research Centre views this as the first of several such reports. Updates as new data become available would monitor the status of children in Ontario and assess the availability and quality of policy-relevant data.

The information presented in *The State of the Child in Ontario* raises important policy and research issues. For example:

- In light of the increase in mother-led, lone parent families, and the association between divorce and child poverty, what are the public and private responsibilities for child support?
- Should Ontario be moving to integrate child-care and education programs? The report reveals an apparent trend in this direction: 50% of the licensed child-care spaces created since 1983 are located in schools.
- Although the number of children in the care of Children's Aid Societies (CAS) has dropped by almost one-half since 1971, there are still about 5000 children in permanent, long-term CAS care. Little is known about the needs and experiences of these children and the long-term impact of such care. This kind of information is essential to ensure a quality of life comparable to that of Ontario children who have not been removed from their homes and families.
- Why does an Ontario child's opportunity to attend special education classes vary considerably from region to region and between public and Roman Catholic schools? How can the school drop-out rate of about 33% be lowered?
- Youth labour force participation, especially among teenagers, has been increasing steadily over the last decade. Is the high level of part-time work among high school students desirable, or should it be discouraged?

- Why is Ontario's rate for the average number of young offenders in custody and pre-trial detention double the rates of Quebec and British Columbia? Sentencing patterns in Ontario indicate a shift toward sending more youths to custody but for shorter periods of time. Is this consistent with the intention of the Young Offenders Act? Should judges be more clearly directed by legislation or sentencing guidelines?
- Over half of all persons in non-senior households living in 'core housing need' (i.e., crowded, physically inadequate accommodation) are children and youth. What is the long-term impact of growing up in such conditions? What steps should be taken to improve housing for these young people?
- In children's health marked economic and racial disparities exist. Canadian data indicate that poor children are two times more likely to die in their first year of life than are children of upper-income families. During the first year of life, native infants in Ontario are five times more likely to die than are their non-native counterparts. What policy initiatives are needed to address these imbalances?
- The limited information available suggests that children's race and economic circumstances are also related to the quality of their housing, their experiences in school and at work, and the likelihood of their involvement with the child welfare and juvenile justice systems. Research and policy analysis cutting across these areas, and keeping racial and economic factors in clear focus, are needed.

Although *The State of the Child in Ontario* raises policy and research issues, it purposely does not advocate particular policy solutions. Instead, it is designed to provide a factual foundation for informed public policy discussion and analysis. It attempts to clarify what is known, and not known, in key areas, and to highlight areas in which data collection is inadequate. One measure of the success of this endeavour will be the extent to which various community organizations utilize these data in policy planning and advocacy.

There is increasing recognition that policy-makers, researchers, and advocates must take a broad, coordinated approach to children's policy issues. Thinking beyond the boundaries of a single government department, academic discipline, or service sector is important in addressing children's issues, particularly when public resources are so limited. We hope that this book will facilitate such multi-disciplinary, inter-ministerial policy work.

While this report is the first of its kind to be produced in Canada, we were guided by several notable U.S. reports, in particular those from the states of New York, Illinois, and California. Researchers responsible for the production of these reports proved extremely helpful in both raising and clarifying complex methodological issues. Their experiences and their reports helped us to develop the Ontario framework for the project, to make decisions on data collection, and to provide direction to the contributors.

It is our understanding that, at the time of writing, several other Canadian jurisdictions are initiating research on the status of their child populations. It is hoped that these various groups will adopt some of the approaches and conventions employed in the present report and that, ultimately, we will have comparable data on the status of children across Canada.

It is our belief that the development of social policies to support children requires solid, child-based information, and to the extent possible this report uses the child as the point of reference. Given a choice between family-, household-, or child-based information, the child was used as the unit of analysis. In some instances (e.g., family income) child-based data are not meaningful. In these circumstances, and where child-based statistics are simply unavailable, other units have been used.

Whenever possible, comparisons are made between current circumstances and those prevailing at least ten years ago. Census data provide the most reliable source of information on numerous indices. The Census years 1976, 1981, and 1986 thus become key reference points in the present document. Whether or not data were available had a major influence on content and the kinds of comparisons that could be made. Several chapters present data in summary form for Ontario as a whole, along with subtotals for the Greater Toronto Area (Metropolitan Toronto, and the regions of Peel, Halton, Durham, and York) with a total population of some 3.8 million. There are also chapters where data are presented for smaller areas or regions. In some instances data were available at only a local level. In other instances, the analysis of a particular issue relies on regional or interprovincial comparisons. On occasion national-level data are presented, either for comparative purposes or because these were the only available data.

Much of the information presented in *The State of the Child in Ontario* was obtained through special tabulations of data from Statistics Canada and other sources. Where possible, these data were obtained for individual Census Divisions or counties within the province. While the published version of *State of the Child* presents the data in summary form, the Child, Youth and Family Policy Research Centre plans to develop a data base making county-level data available to local communities.

We considered devoting separate chapters to particular groups of children, e.g., disabled, native, visible minorities, and children in poverty, but concluded that it was preferable to integrate the limited information available on these groups into more general chapters. This approach permits easier comparison of the circumstances of these children with those of other children in such areas as health, housing, education, child welfare and juvenile justice.

Finally, this project has impressed upon us the need for improved data collection in Ontario. In nearly every area covered by this report there is insufficient information available to provide the basis for sound policy and planning for children in Ontario. Effective policy development requires a coordinated, inter-ministerial data collection process, not only to describe the current situation, but also to identify trends in the circumstances of children and the impacts of the various systems that serve children. No such data collection process yet exists in Ontario.

List of Contributors

Richard Barnhorst is a lawyer and Executive Director of the Child, Youth and Policy Research Centre, Toronto, Ontario. Formerly, he held senior policy positions with the Ontario Government where he played a key role in the development of Ontario's Child and Family Services Act. He has written and taught in the areas of children's law and family law.

Laura C. Johnson is a sociologist and Research Director of the Child, Youth and Family Policy Research Centre, Toronto, Ontario. Her areas of research and publication include social policy issues related to parental employment, child care and youth employment.

Nicholas Bala is Professor at the Faculty of Law at Queen's University, Kingston, Ontario. He has written extensively on family and children's law, specializing in issues related to juvenile justice and child abuse.

Michael Boyle is Associate Professor in the Department of Psychiatry at McMaster University, Hamilton, Ontario. His training is in social work and epidemiology and biostatistics. His current area of research interest is the epidemiology of childhood psychiatric disorders.

Paddy Colfer completed his university training in Dublin and Edinburgh, and has taught sociology at the Universities of Dublin, York (Toronto), and Calgary. He has published a number of journal articles in social theory and analysis with the Ontario Ministry of Community and Social Services.

Christine Kluck Davis is a principal of Social Data Research Limited. Her main research interest lies in the promotion of integrated community supports for individuals in need. She completed her postgraduate training in sociology at McMaster University, Hamilton, Ontario.

Margaret Denton is Assistant Professor, Department of Sociology at McMaster University, Hamilton, Ontario. She is President of Social Data Research Limited. She has done research monographs, and refereed journal articles and book chapters on education and related topics.

Alfred A. Hunter is Professor and Chair of the Department of Sociology at McMaster University. He is a former public school teacher and teacher educator. He has written books, monographs, and articles on education, work and inequality.

John Kenewell is a lawyer and has worked at Justice for Children, a community legal clinic. He presently is a Senior Policy Advisor for the government of Ontario.

Harvey Krahn is Director of the Population Research Laboratory and Associate Professor of Sociology at the University of Alberta. His main research interests are in the sociology of work. Since 1985 he has been involved in a longitudinal study of the transition from school to work in Toronto, Sudbury, and Edmonton. Prior to his academic career, he worked as a child-care worker in Ontario.

Andrew Mitchell is a Program Director at the Social Planning Council of Metropolitan Toronto. His primary area of expertise is socio-demographic analysis. He obtained his M.A. in Industrial Relations from the University of Toronto.

Norman Park received his Ph.D. in Psychology from the University of Toronto. He is the founder and President of Norpark Computer Design, Inc., a social research consulting firm. He has done research in a variety of areas including child care, education, housing, and transportation.

Nico Trocmé is a doctoral candidate at the University of Toronto, Faculty of Social Work. He has written on the subjects of permanency planning, joint custody, and family services to visible minorities. He worked for six years as a social worker in child welfare and children's mental health services.

CHAPTER ONE

Ontario's Children and Families:
A Demographic Overview

Highlights

- There were 3.4 million children and youth in Ontario in 1986. This number is expected to rise gradually to approximately 3.5 million in the year 2011 and fall gradually thereafter.
- As a proportion of the Ontario population, children and youth have been declining since the early 1970s, and will continue to do so despite the modest increase in numbers expected in the short term.
- The overall dependency ratio in Ontario is low by historical standards, but will increase as the growth in the elderly population compensates for the decline in the numbers of children and youth.
- The level of fertility in Ontario, and Canada, has declined dramatically. Currently it is stable at below replacement levels, as it is in all Western industrialized countries. The level of fertility is one of the most important factors governing future population growth (or decline).
- The population of Ontario is increasingly concentrated in the urban areas of southern Ontario, specifically the fringe area of Metropolitan Toronto and the Ottawa-Carleton region.
- One in five children in Ontario is raised with no siblings.

- Lone parent families constitute 12% of all families in Ontario. Blended or reconstituted families are also increasingly common as divorce and remarriage become more frequent.
- Fifteen per cent of children in Ontario live with a lone parent.
- Almost one half of all divorces in Ontario involve children.
- In 1984, 18,500 children in Ontario experienced a divorce.
- The sources of new immigrants to Ontario have diversified. Europe formerly provided most new immigrants. Asia now provides 41% of new immigrants to Ontario.
- Visible minority and aboriginal children compose 13% of Ontario's 3.4 million children and youth.
- Visible minority children and youth are concentrated in Ontario's urban areas.
- Aboriginal children and youth are concentrated in the north and southwest, but significant numbers live in the Metropolitan Toronto region.
- There are approximately 180,000 francophone children and youth in Ontario, over 5% of the total population aged 0 to 24 years. They are concentrated in the north and southeastern regions of the province.

Introduction

A demographic overview of the population of children and youth, and their families, provides a necessary context for the discussion of issues that will follow in subsequent chapters: the economic circumstances of families and children, health, housing, and labour market experiences, among others. The size of the population of children and youth, their age characteristics and geographic location, their racial characteristics and family circumstances, greatly influence their prospects in a variety of areas: the number of siblings they will have; whether they will have lone parents or multiple sets; whether they will experience economic stress, discrimination, and unemployment, to name only a few.

This chapter attempts to set out that context by describing these general characteristics of the population of Ontario's children and youth: their numbers and the age structure of the population, now and in the future; where they live; the

This chapter was prepared by Andrew Mitchell.

role of immigration; numbers of visible minority and aboriginal children; numbers of francophone children; and changes in family circumstances.

The importance of these trends lies in their application to public policy. The test of public policy is the extent to which it responds to the new social realities that are emerging. While political discourse stresses the importance of 'investing in children', the development of newer family supports such as workplace child care and parental sick leave has lagged. And while society contains a variety of supports and social programs designed to benefit families with children — income security programs, human services and labour market programs — they often seem slow to adapt to the new social realities.

I Numbers of Children and Youth

The most remarkable fact about Ontario's population of children and youth is that it has been rapidly declining. In 1986 there were approximately 3.4 million children and youth (those aged 0 to 24 years) in the province according to the last Census. This figure was 112,000, or about 3%, lower than in 1981, and more than 6%, or 222,000, lower than in 1971, when the number of children and youth was near its maximum of 3.6 million (see Table 1.1).

Moreover, the *proportion* of the Ontario population aged

0 to 24 years has declined even more rapidly after reaching its peak in 1971 at approximately 47%; by 1986 it had fallen to 37%. Figure 1.1 illustrates this long-term decline, dividing the population into three groups: the aged (65 years plus); children and youth (0 to 19 years); and the 'productive' age group (20 to 64 years).

Population Projections

Current projections indicate that the number of children and youth aged 0 to 24 years will begin to grow again modestly between 1991 and 2011, from its current 3.4 million to approximately 3.5 million in 2011.[1] This is the result of the 'baby-boom echo'. as the last members of the baby-boom generation begin to form families and have children of their own.

Different parts of the child and youth population will grow and decline at different points in the future, with different implications for public policy. As Figure 1.2 illustrates, the number of children aged 0 to 14 has fallen by 340,000 from the peak of 2.2 million in 1971. Projections indicate that their numbers will grow 12%, from the current figure of just over 1.8 million to slightly over 2 million, by 2001 and decline thereafter. The same pattern, with a time lag of 10 to 15 years, will occur among 15- to 24-year-olds, whose numbers reached a peak at 1.6 million in 1981, and will first fall 10% from their current 1.5 million to approximately 1.4

Table 1.1
Population aged 0 to 14 by five-year age groups
Ontario, 1951–2011

Age group	1951	1961	1971	1981	1986	1991[a]	2001[a]	2011[a]
				(000's)				
0–4	514.7	740.2	637.3	593.0	631.4	702.1	657.4	631.1
5–9	399.3	674.5	783.5	617.3	608.2	652.8	705.4	640.2
10–14	325.3	593.1	787.7	676.3	629.9	635.0	727.9	681.7
15–19	315.7	436.9	713.4	808.9	689.2	665.3	689.4	739.9
20–24	352.3	386.9	674.1	789.7	814.6	746.6	692.2	782.7
Total	1,907.3	2,831.6	3,596.0	3,485.2	3,373.3	3,401.8	3,472.3	3,475.6

[a]**Projection.** Projections make 'medium' assumptions on fertility, mortality, and migration: that is, fertility constant at 1.68 births per woman, increasing male life from 73.5 years in 1986 to 78.3 years in 2011; female life expectancy will rise from 79.1 years in 1986 to 84.5 years in 2011. Net migration to Ontario will remain high until early 1990s and then stabilize at 48,000 per year.

Sources: Ontario Ministry of Treasury and Economics, 'Ontario Statistics', various years.

Figure 1.1: Population by age group, Ontario, 1901 - 2011

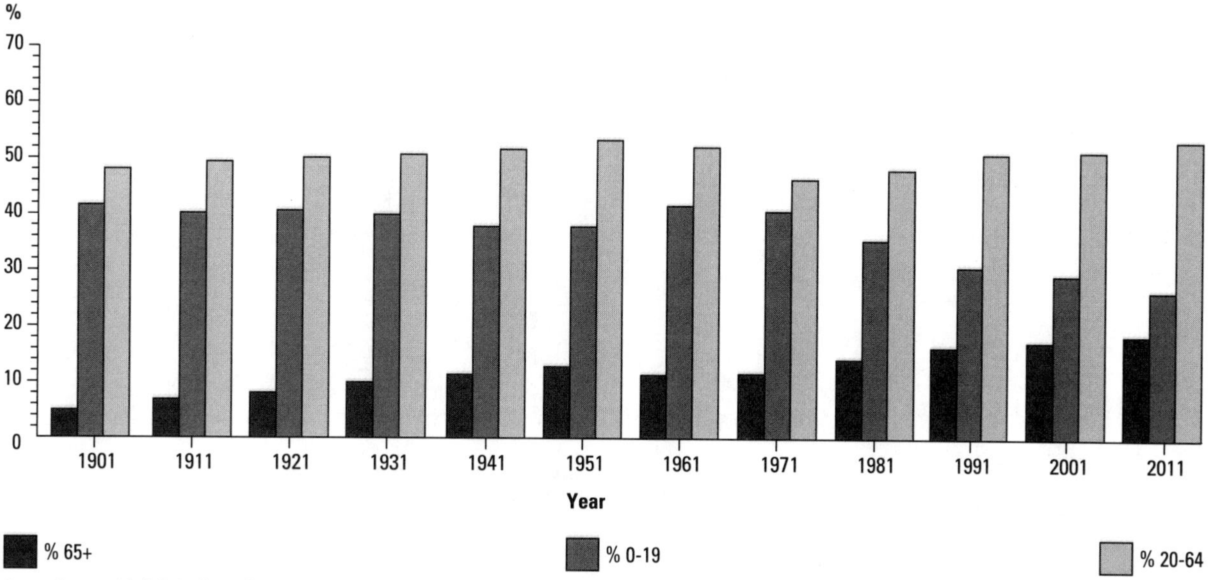

%

[Bar chart showing population by age group for Ontario from 1901 to 2011, with three bars per year: % 65+, % 0-19, and % 20-64. Y-axis ranges from 0 to 70%, X-axis shows years from 1901 to 2011 in 10-year intervals.]

Year

■ % 65+   ■ % 0-19   ▢ % 20-64

Source: Demographic Bulletin, *Ontario Population Projections to 2011* (Toronto: Ontario Ministry of Treasury and Economics, January 1989).

million in 1996, and then increase 12% to over 1.5 million again in 2011.

The Ontario population aged 0 to 4 declined until around 1981 and then began growing; it will peak in 1991 at slightly over 700,000, declining to approximately 631,000 in 2011 (see Table 1.1). As this group ages and enters elementary school, the potential client group for infant child care will shrink and there may be a shift in emphasis towards after-school care.

Similarly, the elementary school population (aged 5 to 13) reached its low point in 1986. Between 1986 and 2001 it will increase, peaking in 2001 at around 1.4 million.

Following this pattern, the population aged 14 to 18 will 'bottom out' in the early 1990s and peak again around 2006. The entry of the 'baby-boom echo' into secondary education will coincide with the retirement of large numbers of teachers originally hired in the expansion of the educational system to educate the baby-boom generation. The population of those 18 to 24 will bottom out in the mid-1990s and rise thereafter.

However, as Figure 1.1 illustrated, despite the slight increase in the numbers of children and youth in the near future, the share of population accounted for by those under

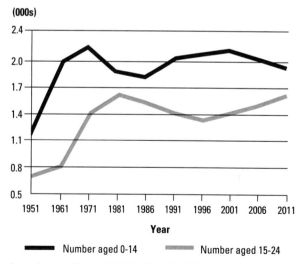

Figure 1.2: Number of 0-to-14 and 15-to-24 year-olds, Ontario, 1951-2011

(000s)

Year

▬▬ Number aged 0-14   ▬▬ Number aged 15-24

Source: Census and Demographic Bulletin, *Ontario Population Projects to 2011* (Toronto: Ontario Ministry of Treasury and Economics), January 1989.

Figure 1.3(a):   Population age structure, Ontario, 1901

Figure 1.3(b):   Population age structure, Ontario, 1961

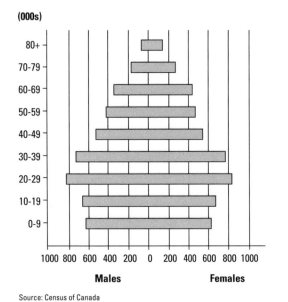

Source: Census of Canada

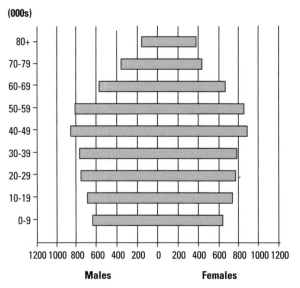

Source: Census of Canada

Figure 1.3(c):   Population age structure, Ontario, 1986

Figure 1.3(d):   Population age structure, Ontario, 2011

25 years of age will continue to decline because of the still larger numbers of aging baby boomers moving into the upper age groups.

A standard tool used by demographers for depicting these trends graphically is known as a population pyramid. Figure 1.3 (a)–(d) shows the shape of the population pyramid for Ontario at four different dates: 1901; 1961, at the peak of the baby boom; 1986; and a projection for 2011. Societies with a high rate of fertility and a rapidly growing population have large numbers of young people and relatively fewer older people. As fertility declines, this characteristic profile changes to reflect greater numbers of middle-aged and older people.

In 1901 the age distribution of Ontario had the pyramid shape characteristic of all high-fertility countries: broader at the bottom, in the younger age groups. In 1961 the pyramid was somewhat less pronounced, with larger numbers in the middle and upper age groups, and the bulge of the baby boom visible in the 0-to-9 and 10-to-19 age groups. By 1986 the bulge corresponding to the baby boom in the age group 20-to-39 was quite pronounced, with smaller numbers of children and youth. By the year 2011 we will have achieved an age structure similar to that which already exists in many Western European countries.

Earlier it was shown that the proportion of the population made up of children and youth has been declining since the early 1970s, and that the actual *number* of children will increase in the short term and decline again early in the next century. To examine the impact of the declining number of children and youth on public policy, it is common to calculate the dependency ratio.[2] These measures are only crude indicators of dependency at best; some people leave school for work earlier than others, while others may retire early or work past the normal retirement age. Still, dependency ratios are a useful guide to changes in the changing relationship between the so-called 'productive' and 'dependent' components of the population. As Figure 1.4 shows, throughout this century, and particularly during the baby boom, dependency ratios have been significantly higher than either those of the 1980s or those projected for the 1990s and the early twenty-first century.

The decline in overall dependency will continue until 2011, when the growth in the elderly population will overtake the decline in the young, and the dependency ratio will begin to

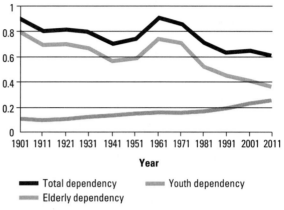

Figure 1.4: Dependency ratios, Ontario, 1901-2011[a]

Legend:
— Total dependency
— Youth dependency
— Elderly dependency

[a] Dependency-population aged 0-19 and 65+ / population aged 20-64.
Source: Table 1.1 data

increase again. Significantly, youth dependency is projected to continue declining, and the dependent population will increasingly be made up of those over the age of 65. The overall dependency ratio will reach levels comparable with those of the baby-boom era after 2026.

Regional Population Shifts

The population of Ontario is growing in some regions and declining in others, thereby altering the regional distribution of the population. Between 1981 and 1986 the population of the north fell by 1.5%, the rural south was stable, and the rural central region grew by about 6% (the provincial average). The rural east grew by 4% — less than the provincial average.[3]

As shown in Figure 1.5, the large urban areas, such as Ottawa/Carleton and the fringe area of the Toronto region, grew rapidly over the same period — 11% and 20% respectively — although Metropolitan Toronto itself grew by less than 3%. The rest of the urban south grew by less than the provincial average, with the exception of the Kitchener-Waterloo Regional Municipality.

Implications

In a low-fertility, high life-expectancy country such as Canada, the gradual aging of society is inevitable. Many

Figure 1.5:   Population growth by region, Ontario, 1981-1986

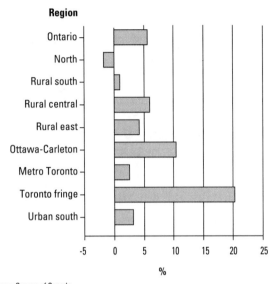

Source: Census of Canada

Western European countries such as West Germany, France, and Sweden already have age distributions similar to those shown in Figure 1.3(d), which Canada and Ontario will have in 25 years.

Of the three factors that influence the size and shape of the population — fertility, migration, and mortality — it is the level of fertility that has the most impact on the age structure of the population in the very long term. Changes in the level or age structure of immigration can affect the age structure, albeit in a more limited way, in the mid- to long term (50 to 100 years). In addition, the average life expectancy is projected to continue increasing, partly because of decreases in infant mortality and partly because of improvements in health care and preventative life-style changes.

The shifts in population that we have experienced in the past have had significant implications for public policy: for example, during the baby-boom both the elementary school system and, later, the secondary school system were forced to expand rapidly to accommodate the large numbers of children and youth. Later, in the 1970s and 1980s, a variety of problems emerged as a result of the entry of the baby-boom generation into the labour market: large numbers of

people entering the market meant that youth unemployment rates increased, youth wages declined, and traditional upward career paths were blocked.

The population changes now under way will affect both the size of the labour force and the types of goods and services, both public and private, that are demanded.[4] In other words, they will affect both 'demand' and 'supply'.

On the supply side there is, in the first place, a close linkage between population growth (or decline) and the labour force. People enter the labour force approximately 20 years after birth. As the population rises and then begins to decline, as it is expected to do after the year 2026, the size of the labour force will also rise and begin to fall, with a 20-year lag. This in turn affects the nation's ability to produce the goods and services desired.

Moreover, as the population ages, so too will the labour force, with additional consequences. Young labour force entrants not only increase the size of the labour force, they also affect its quality. They bring new skills and training, and generally have higher levels of education and training than previous generations of entrants. However, young people also have less experience, and hence may be less productive. Young workers are also more mobile, in geographic and career terms, and thus add flexibility to the labour force.

A declining population of youth also means fewer young people available for the youth labour market. Industries that rely heavily on youth labour (retail trade, babysitting, seasonal recreation, fast food, newspaper delivery) will experience difficulty attracting employees. They may respond to this constraint in one or more ways: by increasing wages in these service industries; by using automation; or by drawing on other people at the margins of the labour market, such as the growing population of seniors. In fact, all of these are visible trends in the labour market of the 1990s.

On the other hand, a decline in numbers of young people implies falling youth unemployment. Historically, youth unemployment rates have been 5% to 10% higher than the average, but this ratio has declined steadily throughout the 1980s (Yalnizyan, 1988).

While the population largely determines the size and shape of the labour force, the wealth generated by the economy in turn provides the basis for both private and public consumption. But the forms that consumption and capital investment take are also determined by the rate of growth and the age distribution of the population. During the baby boom the large and growing child population necessitated a heavy investment in the educational system. The shift to a dependent population made up increasingly of elderly people will require greater investments in health care, income security, and human services. Moreover, the per capita cost of supporting an elderly dependent population may be greater than the costs of supporting one made up of children and youth.

The declining population of children and youth also implies declining demand for child care, among other services. However, since child care services currently do not meet current demand, and female labour force participation rates are projected to continue increasing, continued pressure for improvements to child care services is expected.

Similarly, although fewer children would mean (other things held constant) that capital expenditures for education would fall, the fact that the population is shifting geographically means that schools will still be needed to cope with population growth in some areas, while new schools in other areas stand idle or are converted to other uses.

Finally, as Figure 1.4 indicated, the dependency ratio will remain *low* by historical standards until around 2026, when increases in the elderly population will begin to offset declines in the population of children and youth. This strongly suggests that in the near term the problem may not be one of inadequate national resources to support the dependent population, but rather one of the proper allocation

of those resources. The challenge may be to ensure that the future labour force is sufficiently educated and productive to support a growing elderly population, and to compete in an increasingly competitive global economy.

II Population Change: Fertility and Migration

Fertility

Three factors determine the size of the population: fertility, mortality, and migration. Of the three the single most important is the rate of fertility. In Canada, as in all Western industrialized nations, fertility has declined rapidly since the peak of the baby boom in 1961. In Ontario the Gross Reproduction Rate has declined from 1.8 in 1961 to 0.8 in 1986.[5] In the early 1970s the level of fertility in Ontario fell below the replacement rate of 2.1 births per woman (Table 1.2).

In fact, this decline started in the nineteenth century, was only briefly interrupted by the bulge of the 'baby boom' from 1946 to 1966, and is related to the shifts from an agricultural to an industrial economy and from a rural to an urban population.

It has been hypothesized that these shifts resulted, in part,

---

Table 1.2
Age-specific fertility rates, Ontario, 1961–1986[a]

	15–19	20–24	25–29	30–34	35–39	40–44	45–49	Total fertility rate[b]	Gross reproduction rate[c]	General fertility rate[d]
1961	69.5	239.8	211.6	134.2	69.8	21.9	1.6	3,742	1.824	108.3
1966	57.4	171.3	160.2	98.8	52.8	16.2	1.3	2,790	1.361	80.3
1971	44.2	137.2	145.9	77.4	31.2	7.8	0.4	2,221	1.078	68.4
1976	33.4	105.6	124.6	64.6	20.6	4.3	0.3	1,767	0.865	57.3
1981	23.1	89.1	121.9	68.6	20.4	3.4	0.1	1,633	0.799	53.1
1986	20.5	78.5	126.0	82.7	25.5	3.7	0.1	1,685	0.821	54.5

[a]Age specific fertility: birth rate per 1,000 women in the age group.
[b]Total fertility: sum of female age-specific fertility rates multiplied by five.
[c]General fertility: birth rate per 1,000 women aged 15–49.
[d]Gross reproduction: average number of live daughters that would be born to a hypothetical female cohort if subjected to age-specific fertility rates, and assuming mortality before fifty is zero.

Source: Statistics Canada, *Vital Statistics*, Cat. no. 84-204, various years.

from changes in the simple costs and benefits of having children. In the agricultural era children represented another set of hands on the farm, as well as insurance against destitution in old age. The shift to an industrial age removed at least the first incentive to produce large families (Rauch, 1989).

Similarly, improved public and private pension plans may have removed some of the individual incentive for having large families. Other factors associated with lower fertility include availability of contraception; increasing female education and labour force participation; higher age at first marriage and first birth; more liberal pregnancy termination laws; and better education in sexuality and family planning (Hamilton, 1989).

The increasing participation of women in the labour force is associated with significant changes not only in the level of fertility, but also in its age structure. While overall fertility has fallen, declines have been more rapid among women aged 15 to 24. The birth rate among women aged 15 to 19 has fallen from 69.5 births per thousand women in 1961 to 20.5 in 1986. Among 20- to 24-year-olds the rate has fallen

from 239.8 in 1961 to 78.5 in 1986 (Table 1.2).

Since the mid-1970s decline in fertility among women 25 to 34 has levelled off and, in fact, reversed. Among women aged 25 to 29 the birth rate fell from 211.6 per thousand in 1961 to 121.9 in 1981, and increased to 126.0 in 1986. Similarly, among women 30 to 34 the rate declined from 134.2 in 1961 to 64.6 in 1976, and increased again to 82.7 in 1986. The rate of fertility among women 35 to 39 has followed a similar pattern, falling from 69.8 in 1961 to 20.4 in 1981, and increasing to 25.5 in 1986. What may be emerging is a more concentrated pattern of child-bearing, in which women delay the beginning of child-bearing and space their children closer together, resulting in fewer interruptions in employment patterns.

Across Ontario fertility declines have been the largest in the north and lowest in urban areas, although fertility in the north is still higher than that in urban areas or the Ontario average. Fertility among women aged 15 to 24 has fallen across the whole province, although it has declined most in urban areas. Increasing fertility among women over 30 appears to be exclusively an urban phenomenon.[6]

Figure 1.6: Immigration to Canada, selected years, 1901-1986

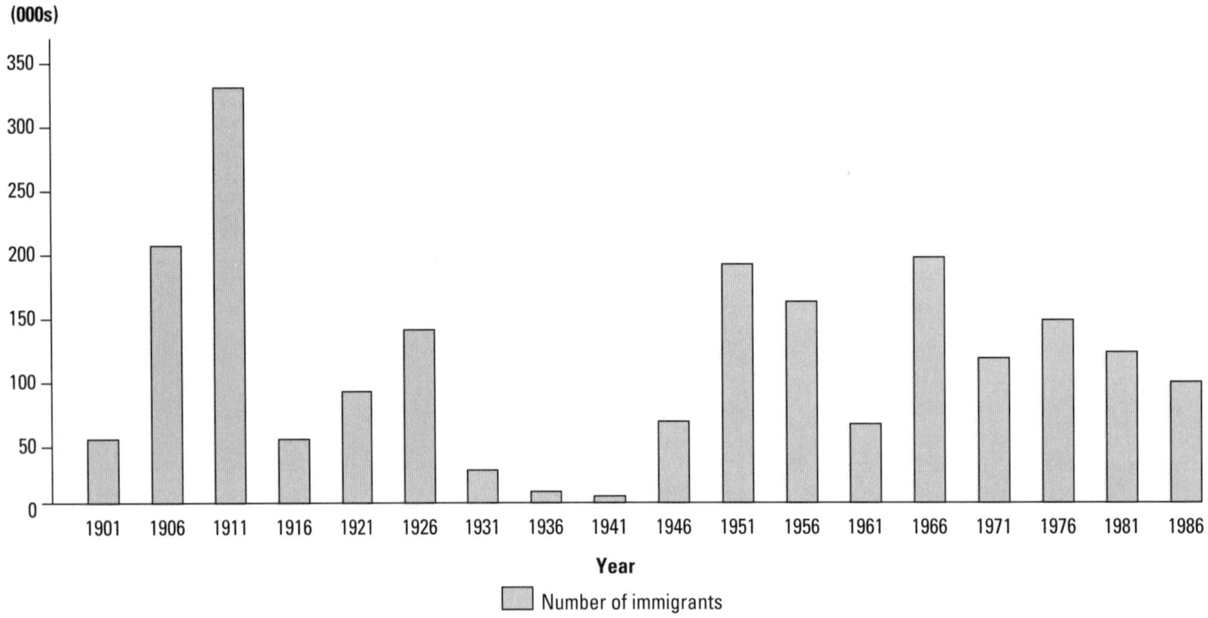

Source: Immigration statistics.

With a demographic shift away from a young population, whose fertility is declining, and towards women aged 30 to 39, whose fertility has increased slightly, overall fertility may stabilize in the 1990s.

Immigration

Immigration has always played a critical role in Canada's and Ontario's development. Figure 1.6 shows the waves of immigration to Canada in this century, beginning in the first decade and a half, then interrupted by the First World War, and resuming until the Depression and the Second World War. In the post-war period (1940–1950) the rate of immigration rose again. In the 1950s the immigration rate averaged around 155,000 per year, but it dropped during the 1960s to around 137,000 per year, mostly because of the high unemployment in 1961-62. Immigration dropped again in the early 1980s, when unemployment in Canada was high again.

Ontario received slightly more than half of the 3.8 million immigrants to Canada in the period 1946 to 1973, and in 1986 still received about half. Immigrants tend to gravitate towards urban areas, and approximately half of these Ontario immigrants settled in the Metropolitan Toronto region, having a disproportionate impact on population and labour force growth. (Similarly, the major migration flows within Ontario were from the north and the rural south to urban centres such as Ottawa-Carleton and the fringe area of Toronto Census Metropolitan Area [CMA].)

In 1986 approximately 40% of new immigrants were under 25 years of age.[7] This age distribution differed slightly from that of the general population in that immigrants were more concentrated in the young adult age group (20 to 34 years), with fewer very young children under 5 years of age or people over 40.

Whereas Great Britain was the principal source of immigration in the nineteenth and early twentieth centuries, in the post-war period the base of immigration broadened to include all of Europe (see Table 1.3). In the immediate post-war period, 1946-1955, Europe provided approximately 88% of immigrants to Canada.[8] Between 1956 and 1969 this fraction declined somewhat as Asia, North and Central America, and the Caribbean increased in significance. By 1986 Asia was the largest source of immigrants to Canada, in numbers as well as percentages.

Ontario also followed this pattern and greatly diversified its sources of immigration. Figure 1.7 shows that whereas from 1970 through 1979 almost 40% of Ontario's new immigrants came from Europe, in the 1980s this proportion fell to 28%, and Asia became the largest source at 41%.

Although without immigration Canada's below-replacement fertility rates would eventually result in the disappear-

Figure 1.7: Sources of immigration, Ontario, 1970s and 1980s

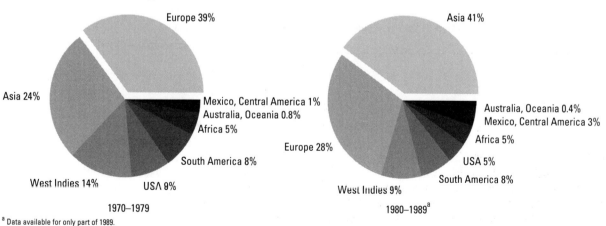

1970–1979

Europe 39%
Asia 24%
Mexico, Central America 1%
Australia, Oceania 0.8%
Africa 5%
South America 8%
West Indies 14%
USA 9%

1980–1989[a]

Asia 41%
Europe 28%
Australia, Oceania 0.4%
Mexico, Central America 3%
Africa 5%
USA 5%
South America 8%
West Indies 9%

[a] Data available for only part of 1989.

Source: Employment and Immigration Canada, Special Tabulations, October 1989.

Table 1.3
Continent of birth, immigrants to Canada, 1946-1986

Continent of origin	1946-55	1956-69	1986
Europe			
Number	1,074,657	1,564,705	22,518
%	87.9%	76.5%	22.9%
Africa			
Number	4,375	49,247	5,189
%	0.4%	2.4%	5.3%
Asia			
Number	24,985	136,817	41,417
%	2.0%	6.7%	42.2%
Australasia			
Number	8,734	35,586	449
%	0.7%	1.7%	0.5%
North & Central America			
Number	80,469	173,636	12,412
%	6.6%	8.5%	12.6%
Caribbean			
Number	5,169	58,555	8,948
%	0.4%	2.9%	9.1%
South America			
Number	3,418	21,009	6,546
%	0.3%	1.0%	6.7%
Other			
Number	20,512	5,270	740
%	1.7%	0.3%	0.8%
Total			
Number	1,222,319	2,044,825	98,219
%	100.0%	100.0%	100.0%

Source: Employment and Immigration Canada, Immigration Statistics, 1986.

III   Families

In 1986 there were 2.4 million families in Ontario, an increase of almost 1.3 million since 1951.[9] Of these 1.6 million, or 67%, had children.[10] Between 60% and 70% of all families from 1951 to 1986 had children, although this proportion began declining in the 1980s as childless families and 'empty nest' couples became more common.

Although the number of families in Ontario with children increased by approximately 12%, from 1.5 to 1.6 million, between 1976 and 1986, at the same time the number of children under 25 years of age *fell* by almost 5%, or 138,000 children. The reason for this was the decline in the average number of children per family (Table 1.4), from 2.2 in 1976 to 1.9 in 1986, among those families with children.

In 1976, 30% of all Ontario families with children had three or more children: in 1986 only 20% of families had this many children. The most dramatic decline was among very large families: those with four or more children. The number of such families fell 53% between 1976 and 1986, from 172,000 to approximately 80,000.

Smaller families have become the norm. Between 1976 and 1986 the proportion of Ontario families with only one or two children increased from 70% to 80% of all families with children. In addition, there was a modest increase of 176,000 families with no children to over 1.6 million in 1986, increasing the proportion of childless families from 31% to 33%.

Table 1.5 shows that in 1986 in Ontario 18% of children in husband-wife families had no siblings, 45% had only one sibling, and 37% had two or more siblings. Lone parent families tend to be smaller still; 36% of children in lone parent families had no siblings, and only 26% had two or more brothers or sisters. Overall, in 1986, 21%, or one in five children in Ontario, had only one sibling.

While the number of children in Ontario of all ages fell between 1976 and 1986, the number of children at home over the age of 24 *increased* by 47%, from 113,000 to over 200,000. This may be due, in part, to deteriorating job opportunities for young adults, extended education, and the increasing tendency of young adults undergoing divorce or separation to move back with their parents before re-establishing another household.

Like the province as a whole, Metropolitan Toronto experienced a decline in the number of children of all ages, from over 730,000 to 681,000, between 1976 and 1986, and an

ance of the Canadian population, it is important to note that there are some limitations on the ability of immigration to alter demographic trends. If the age structure of immigrants does not change, the level of immigration will affect the population age structure in the medium term (50 to 100 years), lowering the proportion of the population over the age of 65. In the very long term, however, the rate of fertility again becomes the dominant influence, and the trend towards an aging society reasserts itself (Health and Welfare Canada, 1989).

Table 1.4
Census families by number of children,
Ontario and Canada, 1976 and 1986

Census families with:	1976			1986			% change 1976–86 Canada	% change 1976–86 Ontario	% change 1976–86 Metro Toronto
	Canada	Ontario	Metropolitan Toronto	Canada	Ontario	Metropolitan Toronto			
0 children at home	1,726,405	650,990	176,340	2,201,545	816,530	197,960	27.5%	25.4%	12.3%
Children at home	4,001,490	1,453,550	364,355	4,533,430	1,629,215	372,370	13.3%	12.1%	2.2%
with 1 child	1,355,180	499,430	139,910	1,769,635	630,795	159,640	30.6%	26.3%	14.1%
with 2 children	1,368,375	515,540	130,080	1,820,785	666,165	141,400	33.1%	29.2%	8.7%
with 3 children	724,490	266,195	61,310	699,280	251,755	53,225	−3.5	−5.4%	−13.2%
with 4 children	329,215	111,285	22,655	182,985	62,475	13,815	−44.4%	−43.9%	−39.0%
with 5 + children	224,245	61,110	10,400	60,750	18,015	4,310	−72.9%	−70.5%	−58.6%
Total children at home less than 24 years of age	8,520,720	3,005,320	697,300	8,019,535	2,867,080	612,005	−5.9%	−4.6%	−12.2%
Total children at home less than 24 years of age	8,886,745	3,118,005	732,275	8,578,340	3,067,275	680,665	−3.5%	−1.6%	−7.0%
Average number of children per family[a]	2.22	2.15	2.01	1.89	1.88	1.83	−14.8%	−12.2%	−9.0%
Average number of children per family[b]	1.55	1.48	1.35	1.27	1.25	1.19	−17.9%	−15.4%	−11.9%

[a]among only those families with children.
[b]among all Census families.

increase in the number of children at home over the age of 24. However, in Metropolitan Toronto the latter group increased at a higher rate: 53% versus 45% for the rest of the province (exclusive of Metro). In Metropolitan Toronto these trends have been exaggerated by the high cost and limited availability of housing.

Implications

While the number of families has continued to increase as the last of the baby boomers form families, the trend towards smaller families has meant declining numbers of children. This trend will have a number of implications for families.

For parents, fewer children may mean fewer absences from the labour market. This will be particularly important for women, as they most often bear the burden of being absent from the labour market to care for children, with the consequent career interruptions. The pattern of marrying and bearing children at a later age allows women to establish themselves in the labour market before starting families.

For children themselves, the trend towards smaller families means fewer siblings, and may mean fewer friends and playmates in their neighbourhood.

The marked trend towards young adults remaining at home longer (the so-called 'boomerang' kids) has numerous implications in terms of delayed adulthood and independence. For their parents it may mean increased pressure to continue supporting their children at a time when they had expected greater freedom from family and financial responsibilities.

IV   The Changing Family

For many people, the term 'family' implies the traditional nuclear unit; a husband, a wife, and their biological children.

Table 1.5
Census families by number of children in family and Census family type, Ontario, 1986

| Census family type | Number of children in family | | | |
	One child	Two children	Three or more children	Total
Husband-wife	470,975	1,162,295	976,490	2,609,760
%	18.0%	44.5%	37.4%	100.0%
Lone parent — female	136,465	146,640	97,060	380,165
%	35.9%	38.6%	25.5%	100.0%
Lone parent — male	31,135	28,810	19,450	79,395
%	39.2%	36.3%	24.5%	100.0%
Total	638,575	1,337,745	1,093,000	3,069,320
%	20.8%	43.6%	35.6%	100.0%

Source: Census of Canada 1986, Special Tabulations, February 1990.

The reality of the family has always been very different from this image; lone parenthood, childless couples, and adoption have always been features of family life. However, the traditional image of the family has rapidly become obsolete as falling family size and increasing incidence of divorce, remarriage, and single parenthood have resulted in a great diversity of family forms that do not correspond to this image.

According to the 1986 Census, 12% of all Ontario families were lone parent families and a further 33% had no children at home. Of those families with children, nearly 40% had only one child.

Of course, the examples provided above do not begin to exhaust the range of family forms that exists in society. Apart from traditional nuclear families and lone parent families, a more complete recognition of the diversity of family forms might distinguish between lone parent families where the second parent plays a child-rearing or other supportive role, and those where the second parent is genuinely absent or unavailable. Similarly, blended or reconstituted families (the product of divorce and remarriage) are likely to differ in functioning from other traditional families. Finally, a variety of issues arise out of the growth in new reproductive technologies (see p. 16 below).[11]

Although we know from indirect and anecdotal evidence that the incidence of some of these family types is increasing, in many categories there is little direct evidence on either their prevalence or their functioning. Such evidence as is available is presented below.

Lone Parent Families

The most remarkable change in family forms in recent years is rapid growth in lone-parent families. Whereas in 1976, 9.6% of all Census families in Ontario were headed by a single parent, by 1986, 11.9% of all Census families were headed by lone parents. (Historically, it is worth noting that the incidence of lone parenthood has varied greatly in correspondence with a number of social and economic phenomena. Indeed, Census data reveal that the incidence of lone parenthood in Canada in 1931 was 13.6%, and in 1941, 12.2% — comparable to the rates prevailing in the 1980s [Statistics Canada, 1984].) Moreover, in 1986 460,000, or 15% of all children at home in Ontario lived with a lone parent. Of these 83% lived with a single mother (Table 1.6).

The formation of a lone parent family can occur for a number of reasons: widowhood, divorce or separation, or non-marital birth. The different paths into lone parenthood have assumed varying importance over time. In 1931 and 1941 approximately three-quarters of lone parents in Canada were widowed. Increasing life expectancy improved the chances of both parents' surviving until their children were adults; by the 1980s widows accounted for less than one-third of all lone parents (Statistics Canada, 1984).

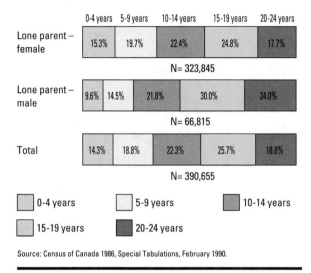

Figure 1.8: Children and youth in lone parent families by age group, Ontario, 1986

Sex of lone parent

	0-4 years	5-9 years	10-14 years	15-19 years	20-24 years
Lone parent – female	15.3%	19.7%	22.4%	24.8%	17.7%

N= 323,845

| Lone parent – male | 9.6% | 14.5% | 21.8% | 30.0% | 24.0% |

N= 66,815

| Total | 14.3% | 18.8% | 22.3% | 25.7% | 18.8% |

N= 390,655

- 0-4 years
- 5-9 years
- 10-14 years
- 15-19 years
- 20-24 years

Source: Census of Canada 1986, Special Tabulations, February 1990.

Table 1.6
Number of children in lone parent families, by sex and marital status of parent, Ontario, 1986

	Ontario
Total children	459,755
Single female lone parent	40,755
Divorced female lone parent	108,430
Separated female lone parent	122,955
Widowed female lone parent	108,025
Total female lone parent	380,170
Single male lone parent	3,455
Divorced male lone parent	19,700
Separated male lone parent	25,280
Widowed male lone parent	30,960
Total male lone parent	79,395

erhood as a path into single parenthood has also increased. In 1951 only 1.5% of lone parents were never married; by 1981 this figure had increased to almost 10% (Statistics Canada, 1984).

In Ontario in 1986, about 10% of all children in lone parent families lived with a single parent, 60% with a separated or divorced parent, and the remaining 30% with a widowed parent (Table 1.6).

Children in lone parent families are likely to differ in age according to whether the parent is male or female. Figure 1.8 indicates that female lone parents are much more likely to have younger children; 35% of children in such families were under 10 years of age in 1986, compared with only 24% in male lone parent families. This is the result of the differing paths into lone parenthood experienced by men and women. Male lone parents were more likely than females to be widowed, and less likely to be single.

Other Family Forms

While very little direct data exist that would permit us to explore the issue of changing family forms, statistics on marriage and divorce, birth, and adoption, can give us an impression of the increasing incidence of new family types over time.

For example, it was indicated above that births to single mothers accounted for an increasing proportion of lone parent families, and birth statistics bear this out. Figure 1.9 shows that the number of live births to single mothers, as a share of all live births, has increased from 3.5% in 1961 to 12.6% in 1985. In this connection it must be noted that this increase is due to births to single women in their twenties and thirties. As Table 1.2 indicated, the rate of fertility among women under 20 years of age has fallen by over 70% since 1961, and the number of births to women under 20 has also fallen.

Women who bear children outside of marriage may or may not go on to marry later, frequently to someone other than the biological father of their children, creating blended or reconstituted families. The 1984 Family History Survey, conducted by Statistics Canada, found that at the time of the survey, 83% of the respondents who reported bearing a child out of wedlock were no longer single parents; 97% of these had entered a new union.[12]

Marriage statistics indicate that marriages are increasingly taking place among men and women who are divorced —

However, the declining importance of widowhood as a cause of lone parenthood has been compensated for by the increasing incidence of separation and divorce, especially following the Divorce Acts of 1968 and 1985. Single moth-

Figure 1.9: Births to single mothers as a percentage of all births, Canada and Ontario, 1921-1985[a]

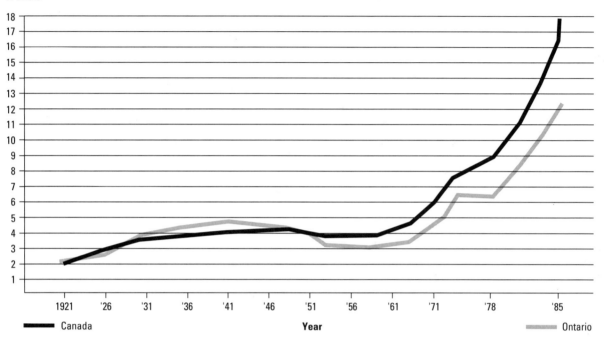

% Births

━━━ Canada   Year   ▬▬▬ Ontario

[a] Data for 1921-71 include births in which the parents were reported as not married to each other at the time of birth or registration. Data after 1971 include births to mothers who report their marital status as single, widowed, or divorced.

Source: Statistics Canada, *Births and Deaths, Vital Statistics,* vol. 1. Cat. 84-204.

especially since the liberalization of the divorce laws in 1968 — and are less likely to take place with a new partner who is a widow, because of improving life expectancy.[13] The percentage of bridegrooms who reported that they were widowed has fallen from 5.2% in 1951 to 3.6% in 1976. Among brides the percentage fell from 5.6 to 4.1. The proportion who were divorced increased from 3.3% to 14.5% among men and from 3.2% to 13.1% among women. In addition, the 1984 Family History Survey reported that approximately 10% of ever-married Canadian adults had had a legal marriage end in divorce, and approximately 5% of adult Canadians had been remarried.

Whether or not a divorce takes place between partners who have children dictates the types of families that may subsequently form. From Table 1.7 we can see the numbers of children involved in divorce in Canada (with fragmentary data for Ontario). Approximately half of all divorces involve

children: the total number of children involved in divorces in Canada climbed by 80%, from approximately 35,000 to 60,000, between 1971 and 1984.[14] In Ontario there were approximately 18,500 children involved in divorces in 1984. Over 10,000 of the 22,000 divorces in Ontario in 1984 involved children.

The issue of custody is closely related to the newer family forms. As couples divorce, either becoming lone parents, or remarrying and creating blended families, custody influences a child's place of residence, nuclear and extended family contacts, friendship ties, and school. Table 1.8 shows an interesting trend in custody awards. There is a marked trend in Ontario away from awarding custody to either the husband or the wife, and increasingly no custody award is made, suggesting that some form of out-of-court settlement was arrived at. In recent years, there has also been an increasing recognition of joint custody in the courts.

Table 1.7
Divorces by number of dependent children, Canada (1971-1984) and Ontario (1981-1984)

Year	Divorces by number of dependent children				Total divorces	Total divorces involving children	% of all divorces	Total children	Average number of children
	0	1	2	3 +					
Canada									
1971	13,241	6,189	5,430	4,812	29,672	16,431	55.4%	34,716	2.1
1976	23,996	12,272	10,523	7,416	54,207	30,211	55.7%	59,628	2.0
1981	32,559	15,423	13,973	5,716	67,671	35,112	51.9%	62,434	1.8
1984	31,156	14,756	14,174	5,086	65,172	34,016	52.2%	60,063	1.8
Ontario									
1981	11,074	4,666	4,199	1,741	21,680	10,606	48.9%	18,803	1.8
1984	11,228	4,468	4,372	1,568	21,636	10,408	48.1%	18,458	1.8

Sources: Statistics Canada, *Marriages and Divorces, Vital Statistics*, Volume II, Cat. 84-205 various years.

Table 1.8
Number of dependent children by parties to whom custody was granted, 1971–1985

Custody Award	Petitioner											
	Husband						Wife					
	1978	Per Cent	1981	Per Cent	1985	Per Cent	1978	Per Cent	1981	Per Cent	1985	Per Cent
ONTARIO												
To petitioner	2,106	34.0%	1,877	33.3%	1,469	24.0%	12,409	86.4%	10,585	82.7%	7,607	68.8%
To respondent	3,244	52.4%	3,080	51.4%	2,314	37.8%	971	6.8%	771	6.0%	648	5.9%
To other person or agency	25	0.4%	14	0.2%	8	0.1%	41	0.3%	20	0.2%	13	0.1%
No award of custody made	819	13.2%	1,027	17.1%	2,334	38.1%	937	6.5%	1,429	11.2%	2,793	25.3%
Total	6,194	100.0%	5,998	100.0%	6,125	100.0%	14,358	100.0%	12,805	100.0%	11,061	100.0%
Row %	30.1%		31.9%		35.6%		69.9%		68.1%		64.4%	

Sources: Statistics Canada, *Marriages and Divorces, Vital Statistics*, vol. II, Cat. 84-205, various years.

There is little information on adoptions in Canada, although Eichler (1988) has collected some estimates. According to these, the number of adoptions in Canada fell from 20,200 in 1970 to around 12,500 in 1980. In Ontario between 1982 and 1985 the number fell from 1,502 to 1,177.[15] In addition, the Family History Survey indicated that only about 2.5% of adults reported raising adopted children. It further reported that 16% of Canadian adult males with stepchildren later adopted them.

Implications

The growth in lone parenthood raises many complex issues. One of the most important is the degree of support, financial or other, that is available from the 'absent' parent. Lone parents and their children suffer from the social isolation and enormous financial and personal burden of raising children alone. Thus the role played by the second parent and other family members becomes critical.

The disadvantaged position of women in the labour market and the increasing necessity of two incomes to support a family intensify the problems of poverty for female lone parents, who experience the highest rate of poverty of any group in Canada (Ross and Shillington, 1989). The lack of child care is also an acute problem, as it is for the larger population of families with children. The lack of child care has been identified as a critical barrier to lone mothers' ability to remain in the labour market (Evans, 1988).

Custody arrangements resulting from a divorce or separation dictate where children will live, who their friends will be, what school they will attend, and the nature of family contacts. The growth of joint custody complicates these matters somewhat as children move back and forth between

parents, although such arrangements do allow both parents to share in child-rearing responsibilities.

Numerous legal and ethical issues arise out of the growth in new reproductive technologies.[16] The major legal questions revolve around the various rights and responsibilities of the people responsible for producing the child: semen and egg donors versus the social (but not biological) parents. Who are the parents legally? As it is illegal in Canada to sell blood or human organs, should an embryo be considered part of a human being, or simply legal property? Furthermore, is it ethical to pay one person to bear a child for another? Are such contracts legal or enforceable?

VI   Visible Minority and Aboriginal Children and Youth

As the sources of new immigrants to Ontario have diversified, Ontario's ethnic make-up has become increasingly diverse.

Table 1.9
Ontario children aged 0–24 years in Census families
by designated group status, 1986[a]

	Total children 0–24	Total children per cent	4 years and less	5–9 years	10–14 years	15–19 years	20–24 years	Per cent
Total	2,871,775	100.0%	615,375	598,130	617,530	623,720	417,025	100.0%
Aboriginals[b]	71,700	2.5%	18,335	17,600	16,755	13,255	5,755	2.5%
Black visible minorities	83,310	2.9%	16,745	17,010	18,310	19,345	11,900	2.9%
Indo-Pakistani[c]	60,995	2.1%	15,320	15,275	12,975	10,295	7,130	2.1%
Chinese	60,290	2.1%	13,650	13,120	12,010	11,640	9,870	2.1%
All other visible minorities[c]	91,255	3.2%	21,035	21,825	19,885	17,430	11,040	3.2%
Total visible minorities[c]	295,815	10.3%	66,755	67,225	63,180	58,715	39,940	10.3%
Multiple Aboriginal and visible minorities	2,570	0.1%	700	580	600	475	215	0.1%
All Aboriginal[d]	74,265	2.6%	19,030	18,180	17,355	13,730	5,970	2.6%
All visible minorities[e]	298,390	10.4%	67,450	67,810	63,785	59,185	40,150	10.4%
Non-Aboriginal and non-visible minorities	2.501,690	87.1%	529,585	512,720	536,990	551,280	371,115	87.1%

[a]Visible minority variable created by the Federal Employment Equity Group from Census ethnicity data, combined with language and place of birth data.
[b]Excluding multiple responses with visible minorities.
[c]Excluding multiple responses with Aboriginal people.
[d]Including multiple responses with visible minorities.
[e]Including multiple responses with Aboriginal people.

Source: Statistics Canada, Census of Canada, 1986, Special Tabulations, February 1990.

Table 1.10
Aboriginal population children and youth aged 0–24 years, in Census families, Ontario, 1986[a]

Census division	0–4	5–14	15–19	20–24	Total	%
Ontario	19,030	35,535	13,730	5,970	74,265	100.0%
NORTH						
Algoma	835	1,755	635	270	3,495	4.7%
Cochrane	535	925	440	150	2,050	2.8%
Kenora	1,345	2,440	930	445	5,160	6.9%
Manitoulin	200	485	260	115	1,060	1.4%
Nipissing	325	770	315	125	1,535	2.1%
Parry Sound	150	290	115	50	605	0.8%
Rainy River	235	655	285	125	1,300	1.8%
Sudbury District	170	380	225	95	870	1.2%
Sudbury R.M.	575	1,075	410	75	2,135	2.9%
Thunder Bay	990	2,185	825	355	4,355	5.9%
Timiskaming	140	435	95	40	710	1.0%
Total North	5,500	11,395	4,535	1,845	23,275	31.3%
SOUTH-EAST						
Frontenac	195	500	195	105	995	1.3%
Haliburton	10	70	25	0	105	0.1%
Hastings	405	790	310	160	1,665	2.2%
Lanark	140	215	50	20	425	0.6%
Leeds-Grenville	145	290	110	40	585	0.8%
Lennox-Addington	95	170	65	30	360	0.5%
Muskoka	100	215	95	15	425	0.6%
Northumberland	125	320	120	75	640	0.9%
Ottawa-Carleton	1,010	1,800	750	415	3,975	5.4%
Peterborough	245	575	250	95	1,165	1.6%
Prescott-Russell	100	85	35	0	220	0.3%
Prince Edward	60	140	45	20	265	0.4%
Renfrew	260	475	160	60	955	1.3%
Stormont, Dundas Glengarry	160	190	95	20	465	0.6%
Victoria	135	235	135	40	545	0.7%
Total South-East	3,185	6,070	2,440	1,095	12,790	17.2%

Census division	0–4	5–14	15–19	20–24	Total	%
Ontario	19,030	35,535	13,730	5,970	74,265	100.0%
GREATER TORONTO AREA (GTA)						
Durham	655	1,070	340	160	2,225	3.0%
Halton	265	525	235	100	1,125	1.5%
Peel	870	1,265	505	290	2,930	3.9%
Metro Toronto	2,050	2,990	1,265	695	7,000	9.4%
York	315	685	280	85	1,365	1.8%
Total GTA	4,155	6,535	2,625	1,330	14,645	19.7%
SOUTH-WEST						
Brant	565	1,245	480	265	2,555	3.4%
Bruce	115	260	100	15	490	0.7%
Dufferin	60	180	50	20	310	0.4%
Elgin	150	200	105	20	475	0.6%
Essex	700	1,185	565	220	2,670	3.6%
Grey	120	130	45	20	315	0.4%
Haldimand-Norfolk	240	530	270	120	1,160	1.6%
Hamilton-Wentworth	770	1,430	465	175	2,840	3.8%
Huron	60	130	20	0	210	0.3%
Kent	210	310	125	40	685	0.9%
Lambton	430	760	265	115	1,570	2.1%
Middlesex	670	1,125	365	135	2,295	3.1%
Niagara	660	1,210	430	215	2,515	3.4%
Oxford	140	260	65	45	510	0.7%
Perth	80	130	20	0	230	0.3%
Simcoe	600	1,355	375	145	2,475	3.3%
Waterloo	355	760	255	110	1,480	2.0%
Wellington	250	335	120	35	740	1.0%
Total South-West	6,175	11,535	4,120	1,695	23,525	31.7%

[a]User-defined variable 'Visible Minority' was created by the Federal Government Employment Equity Group.

Source: Census of Canada, 1986, Special Tabulations, February 1990.

While Great Britain provided the bulk of immigration to Canada in the nineteenth and early twentieth centuries, with succeeding waves of immigration the main sources have shifted, to Europe in the immediate post-war period, and to Asia in more recent years, as Figure 1.7 demonstrated.

Table 1.9 shows that as of the 1986 Census approximately 373,000, or 13%, of Ontario's 2.9 million children and youth in Census families belonged to an aboriginal or visible minority group.[17] Of these about 74,000, or less than 3% were aboriginals.[18]

Figure 1.10:   Visible minority and Aboriginal children and youth, Ontario, 1986

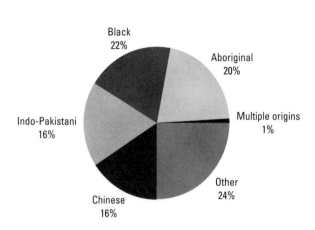

Source: Census of Canada, Special Tabulations.

Figure 1.11:   Visible minority children, provincial distribution, Ontario, 1986

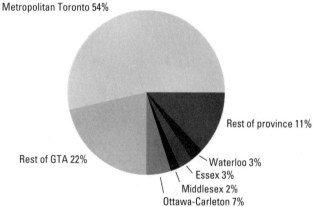

Source: Census of Canada, Special Tabulations.

Figure 1.12:   Aboriginal children and youth, Ontario, 1986

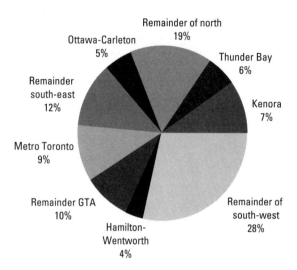

Source: Census of Canada, Special Tabulations.

Figure 1.13:   Francophone children and youth, Ontario, 1986

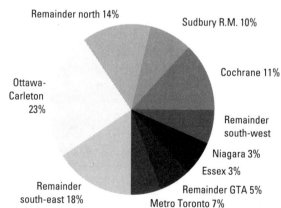

Source: Census and Ministry of Citizenship.

Table 1.11

Francophone population, children and youth, by age and Census division[a]

Census division	0–4	5–14	15–19	20–24	Total	%	Census division	0–4	5–14	15–19	20–24	Total	%
	Age group							Age group					
Ontario	28,895	65,595	37,175	48,150	179,815	100.0%	Ontario	28,895	65,595	37,175	48,150	179,815	100.0%
NORTH							**GREATER TORONTO AREA (GTA)**						
Algoma	1,045	2,140	1,035	1,180	5,400	3.0%	Durham	330	745	440	580	2,095	1.2%
Cochrane	3,570	7,660	4,195	4,415	19,840	11.0%	Halton	220	715	385	465	1,785	1.0%
Kenora	60	150	110	145	465	0.3%	Peel	570	1,600	820	1,115	4,105	2.3%
Manitoulin	5	10	5	10	30	0.0%	Metro Toronto	1,410	3,805	2,430	4,545	12,190	6.8%
Nipissing	1,495	3,280	1,905	2,065	8,745	4.9%	York	250	755	360	330	1,695	0.9%
Parry Sound	10	70	30	40	150	0.1%	Total GTA	2,780	7,620	4,435	7,035	21,870	12.2%
Rainy River	10	45	30	20	105	0.1%	**SOUTH-WEST**						
Sudbury District	550	1,450	835	735	3,570	2.0%	Brant	50	160	90	80	380	0.2%
Sudbury R.M.	2,720	7,345	4,020	4,200	18,285	10.2%	Bruce	35	105	40	45	225	0.1%
Thunder Bay	480	1,055	555	740	2,830	1.6%	Dufferin	0	45	30	25	100	0.1%
Timiskaming	800	1,700	915	930	4,345	2.4%	Elgin	25	75	40	60	200	0.1%
Total North	10,745	24,905	13,635	14,480	63,765	35.5%	Essex	540	1,935	1,120	1,335	4,930	2.7%
SOUTH-EAST							Grey	20	40	30	30	120	0.1%
Frontenac	185	300	165	415	1,065	0.6%	Haldimand-Norfolk	50	75	60	70	255	0.1%
Haliburton	5	5	0	0	10	0.0%	Hamilton-Wentworth	235	735	500	625	2,095	1.2%
Hastings	190	225	95	255	765	0.4%	Huron	15	10	10	10	45	0.0%
Lanark	70	90	45	70	275	0.2%	Kent	155	410	260	305	1,130	0.6%
Leeds-Grenville	70	150	110	115	445	0.2%	Lambton	140	350	205	215	910	0.5%
Lennox-Addington	10	35	30	25	100	0.1%	Middlesex	175	380	220	425	1,200	0.7%
Muskoka	20	40	25	40	125	0.1%	Niagara	605	1,580	1,085	1,280	4,550	2.5%
Northumberland	35	80	30	50	195	0.1%	Oxford	15	100	50	50	215	0.1%
Ottawa-Carleton	6,815	13,535	7,975	12,700	41,025	22.8%	Perth	0	35	25	30	90	0.1%
Peterborough	25	85	60	65	235	0.1%	Renfrew	435	890	555	910	2,790	1.6%
Prescott-Russell	3,250	6,440	3,390	3,780	16,860	9.4%	Waterloo	185	520	345	550	1,600	0.9%
Prince Edward	5	15	10	15	45	0.0%	Wellington	75	180	85	165	505	0.3%
Renfrew	265	450	275	580	1,570	0.9%	Total South-West	2,755	7,625	4,750	6,210	21,340	11.9%
Stormont, Dundas Glengarry	1,665	4,010	2,095	2,295	10,065	5.6%							
Victoria	10	50	25	25	110	0.1%							
Total South-East	12,620	25,510	14,330	20,430	72,890	40.5%							

[a]User-defined variable 'Francophone' includes single and multiple responses for Mother Tongue French.

Source: Census of Canada, 1986; Special tabulations courtesy of the Ontario Ministry of Citizenship.

Of Ontario's visible minority and aboriginal population, Figure 1.10 shows that approximately 22% are black, 16% are Indo-Pakistani, 16% are Chinese, and 25% are one of a number of smaller groups or of multiple origins.

Figure 1.11 shows the population of visible minority children and youth in Census families, according to the Census division in which they lived for the 1986 Census. Over three-quarters of Ontario's nearly 300,000 visible minority population lived in the Greater Toronto Area, and over half in Metropolitan Toronto. Smaller concentrations of visible minority children and youth were found in smaller urban centres in southern Ontario such as Ottawa-Carleton, London

(in Middlesex County), Windsor (in Essex County), and Waterloo. This is as expected, as new immigrants to Canada have always gravitated towards the Toronto region and other major urban areas, where the majority of job opportunities are located, and because of the opportunity for social support networks that a large urban community provides.

In 1986 the population of aboriginal children and youth in Ontario was approximately 75,000. This population was concentrated in the north and south-west areas of the province, although there were significant numbers in the Toronto area and in the south-eastern region of the province (see Table 1.10 and Figure 1.12).

VII Francophone Children and Youth

The most recent Census showed that in 1986 there were approximately 180,000 francophone children and youth between the ages of 0 and 24 years in Ontario (see Table 1.11).[19] This represented slightly over 5% of the Ontario population aged 0 to 24.

This population is concentrated heavily in the north and south-eastern part of the province, as Figure 1.13 demonstrates. In the north there are significant concentrations in Cochrane and Sudbury Regional municipalities. In the southeast the Regional Municipality of Ottawa-Carleton has a significant concentration of francophone children and youth. Smaller populations of francophone children and youth live in the Toronto region, Essex, Hamilton-Wentworth and Niagara Regional Municipality.

Glossary

Children and youth — Generally, this chapter defines children and youth as the population aged 0 to 24 years. However, in the context of a discussion of Census families, the Census defines a child as unmarried, any age, and still residing with his/her parent(s).

Family — The definition of family used herein is a *Census* family. That is, a husband and wife (with or without never-married children regardless of age), or a lone parent, with one or more never-married children, regardless of age, living in the same dwelling. For Census purposes, common-law relationships are now considered as marriages. Other definitions are useful for different purposes. For example, the definition of an *economic* family is appropriate when discussing the economic circumstances of families. An economic family is defined as a group of individuals sharing a common dwelling unit and related by blood marriage or adoption.

Crude birth rate — Number of births per 1,000 population.

Age specific fertility — Birth rate per 1,000 women in the age group.

Total fertility — Sum of female age-specific fertility rates multiplied by five.

General fertility — Birth rate per 1,000 women 15 to 49 years.

Gross reproduction rate — The average number of live daughters that would be born to a hypothetical female cohort if subjected to current age-specific fertility rates, and assuming that mortality before age 50 is zero.

Notes

[1] These projections, made by the Ontario Ministry of Treasury and Economics, make use of 'medium' assumptions about future fertility, life expectancy, and migration. Fertility is projected to remain constant at 1.68 births per woman; male life expectancy will increase from 73.5 years in 1986 to 78.3 years in 2011: female life expectancy will increase from 79.1 years in 1986 to 84.5 years in 2011: and net migration to Ontario will remain high until the early 1990s and then stabilize at 48,000 per year.

[2] The dependency ratio used here is the 'dependent' population, aged 0 to 19 and 65+ years, divided by the population aged 20 to 64, or the 'productive population'. It shows, therefore, the number of members of the 'dependent' population that each potential member of the labour force supports. Similarly, the youth dependency ratio is the population of children and youth aged 0 to 19 divided by the population aged 20 to 64.

[3] Census of Canada, 1981, 1986.

[4] The material on the relationship between the population and the economy relies heavily upon Denton and Spencer (1987).

[5] See notes and definitions at the end of the chapter.

[6] See Ministry of Treasury and Economics (1988).

[7] Employment and Immigration Canada, Immigration Statistics, 1986.

[8] Ibid.

[9] Census of Canada. The term 'family' as used in this chapter means a Census Family which refers to a husband and wife (with or without never-married children, regardless of age), or a lone-parent, with one or more never-married children, regardless of age, living in the same dwelling. For Census purposes, persons living in a common-law relationship are considered married.

[10] Census of Canada. Prior to the 1976 Census the 'children' referred only to never-married children at home under 25 years of age. With the 1976 Census 'children' included only never-married children, regardless of age, living at home.

[11] See Eichler (1988).

[12] See Moore (1988). According to the Family History Survey (1984), women who bore children out of wedlock also tended to be younger and spent the shortest average periods of time as lone parents, 4.4 years at the time of the survey.

[13] Statistics Canada, *Marriage and Divorces, Vital Statistics*, vol. 2, Cat. 84-205.

[14] Ibid.

[15]See Eichler (1988), Tables 7.8 and 7.9.

[16]See Eichler (1988).

[17]The Canadian Census does not ask questions that permit the direct identification of visible minorities. Therefore the Employment Equity Group of the Federal Government created a user-defined variable with the 1986 Census data which categorized people according to their reported ethnicity, supplemented by place of birth and mother tongue responses.

[18]Note that there was some under-reporting of the aboriginal population in the 1986 Census. These figures have not been adjusted for this under-reporting.

[19]To obtain a simple count of the number of francophones, the Ontario Ministry of Citizenship created a special 'francophone' variable with the 1986 Census results. Respondents to the Census who indicated a French mother tongue, either singly or in combination with another mother tongue, were classified as francophone.

References

Adams, Owen
1988 'Divorce Rates in Canada'. *Canadian Social Trends*, 11 (Winter). Cat. 11-008E. Ottawa: Statistics Canada.

Burch, Thomas K.
1985 'Family History Survey, Preliminary Findings'. Ottawa: Statistics Canada (November).

Burch, Thomas K., and Ashok K. Madan
1986 'Union Formation and Dissolution: Results from the 1984 Family History Survey'. Ottawa: Statistics Canada (November).

Denton, Frank T., and Byron G. Spencer
1987 'Population Change and the Canadian Economy: A Survey of the Issues'. Discussion Paper on the Demographic Review. Institute for Research on Public Policy. Ottawa (January).

Doyle, Robert, and Andrew Mitchell
1988 'Lone Parent Families in Transition'. Social Planning Council of Metropolitan Toronto, Social Infopac, vol. 7, no. 4 (November).

Eichler, Margrit
1988 *Families in Canada Today: Recent Changes and Their Policy Consequences*. 2nd ed. Toronto: Gage.

Evans, Patricia
1988 'Work Incentives and the Single Mother: Dilemmas of Reform'. *Canadian Public Policy*, 14 (2).

Foot, David K.
1986 'Population Aging and Immigration Policy in Canada: Impli-

cations and Prescriptions'. University of Toronto Department of Economics and Institute for Policy Analysis, Working Paper Series no. 8606 (March).

Hamilton, S.C.
1989 'Research Study on Demography, Causes and Consequences', for Senator Paul David (February).

Health and Welfare Canada
1989 *Charting Canada's Future: A Report of the Demographic Review*.

McKie, D.C., B Prentice, and P. Reed
1983 'Divorce: Law and the Family in Canada'. Cat. 89-502E(F). Ottawa: Statistics Canada (February).

Ministry of Treasury and Economics
1988 'Demographic change and its Implications for Ontario'. Toronto.

Moore, Maureen
1988 'Female Lone Parenthood: The Duration of Episodes'. *Canadian Social Trends*, Autumn. Ottawa: Statistics Canada.

Myles, J., G. Picot, and T. Wannell
1988 'Wages and Jobs in the 1980s: Changing Youth Wages and the Declining Middle'. Statistics Canada, Analytical Studies Branch, Research Paper Series no. 17 (July).

1986 *Lone Parenthood: Characteristics and Determinants, Results from the 1984 Family History Survey*. Ottawa: Statistics Canada (November).

Ross, David P., and Richard Shillington
1989 *The Canadian Fact Book on Poverty—1989*. Ottawa: Canadian Council on Social Development.

Rauch, Jonathon
1989 'Kids As Capital'. *The Atlantic Monthly*, August: 56-61.

Seward, Shirley B.
1987 'The Relationship Between Immigration and the Canadian Economy'. Discussion Paper on the Demographic Review. Institute for Research on Public Policy. Ottawa: January.

Statistics Canada
1984 'Canada's Lone-Parent Families'. Cat. 99-933. Ottawa: Ministry of Supply and Services (May).

Vlassoff, Carol
1987 'Fertility and the Labour force in Canada: Critical Issues'. Discussion Paper on the Demographic Review, Institute for Research on Public Policy. Ottawa (January).

Yalnizyan, Armine
1988 'A Statistical Profile of Toronto's Labour Market, 1976-1987'. Social Planning Council of Metropolitan Toronto (May).

CHAPTER TWO

The Economic Circumstances of Ontario's Families and Children

Highlights

- Average income among families with children in Ontario was $48,799 in 1987; an increase in real terms of 11% over 1979, and 20% since 1973.

- Since 1973, increases in the median incomes of the upper half of the income distribution were above 20%, in real terms. In the bottom half of the distribution, increases averaged approximately 14%.

- In 1973, the median income in the top decile was 7.3 times the median in the bottom decile. By 1987 this ratio had increased to 7.9.

- Families received approximately 83% of their income in 1987 from employment, a decrease from over 88% in 1973. Couples with children received almost 92% of their family income in 1987 from employment, a decrease from over 94% in 1973.

- Ontario female-led lone-parent families' share of income from earnings increased over the period from 64% in 1973 to 70% in 1987.

- The proportion of families with children in Ontario officially classified as 'poor' grew from 10.8% of the total in 1973 to 11.5% in 1987. The proportion in the 'Mainstream' fell from 70.8% in 1973 to 66.7% in 1987. The number of 'Advantaged' and 'Affluent' increased from 18.4% to 21.9% of the total.

- Although 11.5% of families with children were poor, another 4.9% who fell between the poverty line and a line 25% above it were considered 'Vulnerable.'

- Nearly 53% of poor families with children in Ontario were couple families. Nearly 39% were female-led lone parent families. Nearly 57% of poor children were in couple families. Approximately 37% were in female-led lone parent families.

- The incidence, or risk, of poverty among families where the head was between 15 and 24 years of age increased from 20.7% in 1973 to 39.3% in 1987. Among families with children headed by a person aged 25 to 34, the incidence increased from 12.4% to 15.3%.

- The incidence of child poverty among female-led lone parent families in 1987 was 43%, down from nearly 57% in 1973.

- The incidence of child poverty in families headed by a person aged 15 to 24 increased from 23.6% in 1973 to 41.3% in 1987. Among families headed by a person aged 24 to 34, the incidence increased from 14.7% to 16.9%.

- Despite an increase in labour force effort on the part of families with children, the overall rate of family and child poverty remained fundamentally unchanged. Without that increase, child and family poverty would have increased dramatically.

- The average poverty gap (the gap between a family's income and the poverty line) among poor families in Ontario with children was $6,910 in 1987.

- The real value (after inflation) of family allowance payments has declined by over 40% since the mid-1970s. The 'clawback' of family allowance benefits introduced in the Federal Budget of April 1989 suggests that benefits will continue to increase at less than the rate of inflation and become increasingly narrowly targeted, thus destroying its universality.

- The Child Tax Credit provides, on average, less than 1% of family income in Ontario. Among families in the lowest income decile it constitutes nearly 7% of family income. Although the real value of the credit has increased since its introduction, the income level above which the credit is reduced has fallen by approximately 36% since 1979.

This chapter was prepared by Andrew Mitchell.

Introduction

The purpose of this chapter is to examine the economic circumstances of Ontario's families and children, the level of family income, trends in the incidence of poverty, and the changing roles both of the labour market and of state income security programs.

Such an examination is critical to understanding Ontario's families and children, the opportunities they are provided, and the constraints they face. Children's health, educational achievement, and life outcomes are all closely related to the economic circumstances of the families in which they reside. Wealth and poverty are closely related to all dimensions of a child's life: health, hunger, neighbourhoods, education, and life opportunities. As the following quotations illustrate, poverty is associated with low birth-weight, higher infant mortality, generally poorer health, hunger and inattentiveness at school, and lower educational achievement:[1]

> poverty . . . brings in its wake all the obstacles to health . . . . It is the poor above all others, who live in dangerous environments, who lack the necessities and amenities, whose work, if they have any, is stressful and unfulfilling, and who are isolated from sources of information and encouragement. On top of all this, poverty is intrinsically debasing and alienating (Buck, 1985).

> The health risks associated with poverty are even more critical for poor children. They are more likely to be born prematurely, have low birth weight and suffer from malnutrition. These risks are associated with impaired physical and intellectual development and increased susceptibility to infectious diseases . . . compared to their non-welfare peers, welfare children are more likely to experience psychiatric disorders, poor school performance, chronic health problems and low participation in extra curricular activities (Harding, 1987).

In general, children have no resources of their own. Their economic status is determined entirely by that of the households in which they live, and the direct and indirect supports offered to families by the state; direct income support to families with children in the form of income security programs such as the Family Allowance and the Child Tax Credit, and indirect supports through state subsidized health care and public education.

An examination of family economic circumstances invar-iably focuses on income; invariably, also, categorization of some families as 'poor' or 'affluent' involves inferences about family well-being. Such judgements ought to be made with caution; it is sometimes difficult to form conclusions about need solely on the basis of income.[2] Moreover, focusing on income ignores the resources that may be available to families through wealth holdings. There is a lack of appropriate data for investigating this issue, and no agreement on either the significance of this omission or an appropriate method of correcting for it.

Data for this chapter, unless otherwise noted, come from special tabulations from Statistics Canada's Survey of Consumer Finances, which is an annual survey of approximately 40,000 Canadian households on the amount and sources of income in Canada.[3] For Ontario in 1987 this sample size provided approximately 8,000 households. Although for most of the analysis this is a sufficient number of cases to allow reliable estimates and conclusions, for certain small categories — for example, lone parent males — the sample is too small to allow reliable conclusions to be drawn, and so they have not been analysed. Where such data have been presented, this is largely for the purpose of completeness.

In this chapter a child is defined as under 18 years of age and living in an *economic* family: that is, a group of individuals sharing a common dwelling unit and related by blood, marriage, or adoption. This category is further subdivided into Husband-Wife Families, Lone Parent Families, and 'Other'. The category 'Other' includes extended families with relatives beyond the standard Census or nuclear family.

The years chosen for comparison are 1973, 1979, and 1987: 1973, because it was the first year Statistics Canada presented low-income data based on its revised low-income measure; 1979, because of the apparent significance of economic developments between the 1970s and 1980s, and 1987 because it was the most recent year for which data were available.

I Incomes

Average Incomes of Families with Children

The average income among families with children in Ontario in 1987 was $48,799: an increase of 20%, in real terms, since 1973 (Table 2.1). Among couples with children the average income increased 21%, from $43,080 to $52,110.

Table 2.1
Average income by family type, Ontario and Canada, 1973 and 1987

Family type	Average income 1973 (1987 $)		Average income 1979 (1987 $)		Average income 1987 (1987 $)		% increase 1973–79		% increase 1979–87	
	Ontario	Canada	Ontario	Canada	Ontario	Canada	Ontario	Canada	Ontario	Canada
All families with children	$40,792	$37,532	$43,971	$42,152	$48,799	$44,618	7.8%	12.3%	11.0%	5.9%
Couples with children	$43,080	$39,494	$47,070	$45,060	$52,110	$48,082	9.3%	14.1%	10.7%	6.7%
Female lone parent	$16,959	$16,575	$17,019	$17,916	$22,400	$18,945	0.4%	8.1%	31.6%	5.7%
Male lone parent	$35,180	$32,651	$40,116	$36,102	$39,971	$38,891	14.0%	10.6%	−0.4%	7.7%
Couples without children	$39,608	$36,205	$43,810	$42,094	$48,643	$43,346	10.6%	16.3%	11.0%	3.0%
Sample size	4,371	15,997	4,202	21.567	4,152	23,155				

Source: Statistics Canada, Survey of Consumer Finances, Special Tabulations.

The average income among female-led lone parent families increased from $16,959 to $22,400, or 32%.

However, this period was not characterized by a steady upward rise in incomes. The high rates of growth in family incomes from the 1950s to the mid-1970s were followed in the late 1970s and the 1980s by a stagnation attributable to a slowdown in the increase of female labour force participation, the recession of 1981-82, and the stagnation of individual incomes generally. Growth in both family and per capita income declined markedly after the mid-1970s (Statistics Canada, 1989). From 1951 to 1961 family incomes grew, in real terms, at an average rate of 3.3% per year, and from 1961 to 1971 they grew even faster, at an average annual rate of 4.6%. In the 1970s, however, the rate of growth slowed considerably, to an average 2.6% per year, and from 1981 to 1988 family incomes grew at an average annual rate of only 0.5%, with several years of real declines in incomes.

If we return to Table 2.1, we can examine this general trend among different family types. Among all families with children in Canada, average family income grew by 12.3% between 1973 and 1979, an average annual rate of 2.1%, and only 5.9% from 1979 to 1987, or 0.7% per year. Couples with children had their rate of growth in real income fall from 2.4% in the first period to 0.8% in the second. In female-led lone parent families the rate of increase fell from 1.4% per year in the 1973-79 period to 0.7% in the 1979-87 period.

In Ontario the situation is somewhat different, because of the disproportionate share of Canada's economic growth that has accrued to Ontario since the recession of 1981-83. Over the periods 1973-79 and 1979-87, the average rate of income increase among couples with children fell only slightly, from 1.6 to 1.3% annually. The average increase among female lone parents went up substantially because of their increased labour force participation, while among couples without children the rate of increase fell from 1.8% per year to 1.4% per year.

The median incomes among different family types are reported in Figure 2.1[4]. The median income among couples with children in Ontario increased from $39,834 to $48,284, or 21%, again in real terms. Female-led lone parent families experienced an increase of 43%, from $13,715 to $19,640. The median income of male-led lone parent families increased from $29,205 to $36,213, or 24%.

The stagnation of family incomes during the 1970s and 1980s also appears in the statistics on median incomes. It can be seen from Figure 2.1 that the rate of growth in median incomes has deteriorated for most family types, in Canada as a whole and in Ontario. Between the periods 1973-79 and 1979-87 the annual rate of increase among couples with children in Canada fell from 2.6% to 0.6%. Among lone parent females it fell from 1.0% to 0.2%. In Ontario the annual increase among couples with children fell slightly, from 1.7% to 1.3% on average. Among lone parent females the annual increase grew from 0.2% in 1973-79 to 5.2% in 1979-87.

Figure 2.1

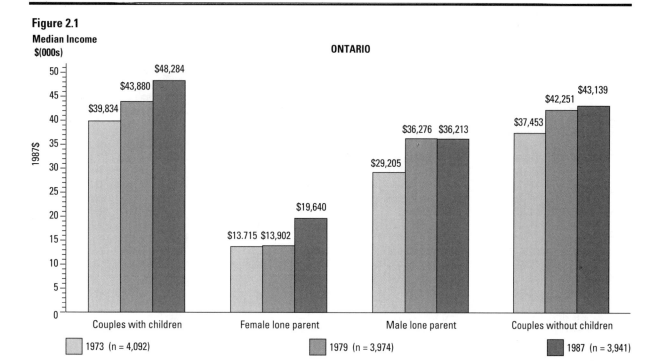

Median Income
$(000s)

ONTARIO

1987$

Legend	
1973 (n = 4,092)	1979 (n = 3,974)
	1987 (n = 3,941)

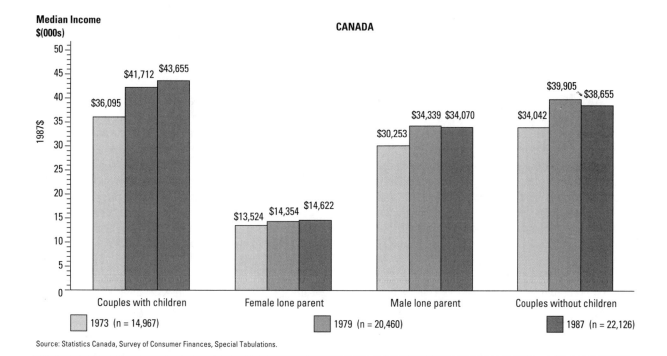

Median Income
$(000s)

CANADA

1987$

Legend	
1973 (n = 14,967)	1979 (n = 20,460)
	1987 (n = 22,126)

Source: Statistics Canada, Survey of Consumer Finances, Special Tabulations.

Table 2.2

Median income by decile (1987 $), families with children, Ontario and Canada, 1973 and 1987

Decile	1973 median		1979 median		1987 median		% increase 1973–79		% increase 1979–87		% increase 1973–87	
	Ontario	Canada	Ontario	Canada	Ontario	Canada	Ontario	Canada	Ontario	Canada	Ontario	Canada
FAMILIES WITH CHILDREN												
1	$10,748	$9,633	$ 9,328	$ 9,316	$12,347	$10,299	− 13.2%	− 3.3%	32.4%	10.6%	14.9%	6.9%
2	$21,386	$17,879	$21,189	$19,142	$23,085	$19,110	− 0.9%	7.1%	8.9%	− 0.2%	7.9%	6.9%
3	$27,448	$23,686	$29,130	$26,333	$31,390	$26,515	6.1%	11.2%	7.8%	0.7%	14.4%	11.9%
4	$31,832	$28,256	$34,475	$32,091	$37,611	$32,705	8.3%	13.6%	9.1%	1.9%	18.2%	15.7%
5	$36,124	$32,425	$39,290	$36,853	$42,326	$38,134	8.8%	13.7%	7.7%	3.5%	17.2%	17.6%
6	$40,383	$36,675	$44,054	$41,820	$48,452	$43,461	9.1%	14.0%	10.0%	3.9%	20.0%	18.5%
7	$45,005	$41,506	$48,861	$47,221	$54,222	$49,586	8.6%	13.8%	11.0%	5.0%	20.5%	19.5%
8	$51,006	$47,302	$55,059	$53,579	$61,070	$56,363	7.9%	13.3%	10.9%	5.2%	19.7%	19.2%
9	$58,961	$55,530	$64,870	$62,938	$71,273	$66,668	10.0%	13.3%	9.9%	5.9%	20.9%	20.1%
10	$78,446	$75,662	$87,403	$85,215	$97,415	$90,708	11.4%	12.6%	11.5%	6.4%	24.2%	19.9%
Sample size	3,242	12,352	3,128	16,370	2,955	16,848						

Source: Statistics Canada, Survey of Consumer Finances, Special Tabulations.

Lastly, the rate of growth in incomes among families with children was higher in the rest of Canada over the 1973-79 period — 12.3% — than in Ontario, where growth amounted to 7.8%. This pattern reversed in the 1980s as family income growth in Ontario reached 11.0% among families with children, versus 5.9% for Canada as a whole.

Median Incomes by Decile

Table 2.2 reports median incomes, in 1987 dollars, by decile[5] for families with children in Ontario and Canada in 1973, 1979, and 1987. It shows that among families with children the percentage increase in family income was greater in the upper income deciles. While in the bottom decile median income increased by almost 15% between 1973 and 1987, in the middle deciles increases ranged from 15 to 20%, and in the top decile the rate of increase was almost 25%.

The falling rate of growth in family income is also apparent in Table 2.2. It can be seen that average yearly growth rates declined in the 1979-87 period from the 1973-79 period. In the top decile the average annual rate of growth declined from 1.9% over the 1973-79 period to 1.5% over the period 1979-87. In the 5th decile the rate of growth declined from 1.5% per year to 0.3% over the same period.

The higher rates of growth in the upper income deciles

have meant increased income inequality among families with children. In 1973 in Ontario the median income in the top decile was 7.4 times the income in the bottom decile. In 1979 this ratio had worsened to 9.4 times. By 1987 it had improved somewhat, to 7.9 times the median income in the bottom decile.

Sources of Income by Family Type

Families obtain their income through a variety of sources, the single most important of which is labour market earnings. In 1987 Ontario families received, on average, 83% of their income from labour market earnings. Couples with children received 92% of their income from employment, while female-led lone parent families on average received only 70% of their income from this source (Statistics Canada, Survey of Consumer Finances, Special Tabulations).

Among families as a group there was slightly less reliance on the labour market in 1987 than in 1973. In 1973 Ontario families of all types received over 88% of their income from earnings. This had fallen to 83% by 1987. Income from investments, the Canada Pension Plan (CPP/QPP), private pensions, and 'other sources' increased from 6.8% in 1973 to 11.7%, on average, in 1987.[6]

Female-led lone parent families in Ontario, despite their

increased reliance on the labour market, received higher-than-average proportions of their income from public sources. In 1973 female lone parents received 64% of their income, on average, from employment earnings. The next most important source of income was social assistance, which provided an average 17%. Other public sources of income such as CPP, unemployment insurance, and family allowance provided another 7% of total income.

By 1987 female lone parents received approximately 70% of their income from employment earnings, on average, and 10% from social assistance. Other public sources, including CPP, unemployment insurance, the Child Tax Credit, and the Family Allowance, remained at 7% of income. In addition, 'other' sources of income increased from 6.7% to 8.5% of total income.

Sources of Income by Decile — Families with Children

It is informative to examine average family income trends in Ontario by decile. Again, it is evident that most family income comes from earnings; in 1987 Ontario families with children obtained over 90% of their income, on average, from employment. This tendency occurs in each decile. However, the proportion of income from earnings declined between 1973 and 1987. Overall it fell from 93.3% to 90.5%, while in the lowest decile it fell from 59.7% to 45.9%. At the same time CPP, the Child Tax Credit, and other income sources rose, while the proportion of income from the Family Allowance fell (Statistics Canada, Survey of Consumer Finances, Special Tabulations).

Although on average families with children derive most of their income from earnings, there is a marked difference between the first and second deciles, where the share of income from earnings jumps from 46% to 80% in 1987. Those in the bottom decile received relatively more income from unemployment insurance benefits, social assistance, the Child Tax Credit, and the Family Allowance. The benefits of these transfer programs decline in relation to total income as income rises.

II Families

Poor Families — One in Nine

In 1987 nearly 143,000 Ontario families with children — that is, one family in nine — were officially categorized as poor,

an increase of over 18,000, or 15%, since. (For the purposes of this chapter, 'poor' means below Statistics Canada's Low Income Cut-Offs [LICOs], which are popularly referred to as 'poverty lines'.)[7] As Table 2.3 indicates, this was almost twice as great as the increase in the number of families in general, whose numbers increased by approximately 8%. As a result, the incidence of poverty among families with children increased slightly, from 10.8% in 1973 to 11.5% in 1987.

Table 2.3 divides family types into five 'income classes'. The category 'Mainstream' (not shown) refers to those between the poverty line and up to 3 times the LICO, or poverty line. In the table this category is broken down into 'Vulnerable' — those who are up to 25% above the poverty line — and 'Other Mainstream', referring to those who are between 1.25 and 3 times the LICO. The 'Advantaged' are those who are between 3 and 4 times the LICO and the 'Affluent' are 4 times the LICO and above. (Table 2.4 translates these categories into family income ranges for various family sizes in different-sized urban areas in 1987 dollars.)

These categories represent an attempt to attach social significance to different points in the income distribution representing different standards of living. Thus the category 'Other Mainstream' encompasses the majority of the families with children, who do not normally experience deprivation in their day-to-day lives, while the categories 'Advantaged' and 'Affluent' reflect smaller yet well defined and recognizable parts of the income distribution.

A sub-category of the Mainstream, the category 'Vulnerable' deserves some special explanation. It is intended to encompass those who, while they are not technically poor, are 'near-poor' in the sense that their life-styles may not differ significantly from those officially categorized as poor. People in this category have little choice and flexibility in the allocation of income and very little ability to cope with unexpected contingencies or interruptions in income.

As Table 2.4 illustrates, a two-person family in the Vulnerable category could have an income at most $4,190 above the poverty line in 1987; this amounts to approximately $5.75 per day per person. A four-person family in the Vulnerable category could have an income between $24,531 and $30,663, or $4.20 per person per day above the poverty line. It is noteworthy that these levels of income are still significantly below other widely used indicators of poverty such as that of the Canadian Council on Social Development (CCSD). As the Appendix notes, there are many different possible poverty lines, such as the CCSD lines, which are utilized by

Table 2.3
Economic circumstances of families with children by family type, Ontario, 1973–1987

| Family type | Income class | Families with children | | | | | % Increase (Decrease) 1973–87 |
		1973 Number	%	1987 Number	%	
ONTARIO						
Couples	Poor	63,090	6.7%	75,303	7.6%	19.4%
with	Vulnerable	43,480	4.6%	41,567	4.2%	− 4.4%
children	Other mainstream	650,710	69.0%	629,257	63.7%	− 3.3%
	Advantaged	123,210	13.1%	156,385	15.8%	26.9%
	Affluent	62,870	6.7%	85,525	8.7%	36.0%
	Total	943,360	100.0%	988,037	100.0%	4.7%
Lone	Poor	49,170	56.7%	55,361	46.7%	12.6%
parent—	Vulnerable	9,120	10.5%	8,827	7.5%	− 3.2%
female	Other mainstream	27,200	31.4%	50,201	42.4%	84.6%
	Advantaged	890	1.0%	2,625	2.2%	194.9%
	Affluent	280	0.3%	1,428	1.2%	410.0%
	Total	86,660	100.0%	118,442	100.0%	36.7%
Lone	Poor	1,590	9.6%	2,373	14.5%	49.2%
parent—	Vulnerable	650	3.9%	962	5.9%	48.0%
male	Other mainstream	11,060	66.8%	8,558	52.2%	− 22.6%
	Advantaged	2,390	14.4%	2,487	15.2%	4.1%
	Affluent	860	5.2%	2,010	12.3%	133.7%
	Total	16,550	100.0%	16,390	100.0%	− 1.0%
Other	Poor	10,410	10.4%	9,504	8.1%	− 8.7%
	Vulnerable	8,350	8.3%	8,982	7.6%	7.6%
	Other mainstream	60,810	60.6%	78,092	66.4%	28.4%
	Advantaged	16,070	16.0%	16,544	14.1%	2.9%
	Affluent	4,760	4.7%	4,460	3.8%	− 6.3%
	Total	100,400	100.0%	117,582	100.0%	17.1%
Total	Poor	124,260	10.8%	142,541	11.5%	14.7%
	Vulnerable	61,600	5.4%	60,338	4.9%	− 2.0%
	Other mainstream	749,780	65.4%	766,108	61.8%	2.2%
	Advantaged	142,560	12.4%	178,041	14.4%	24.9%
	Affluent	68,770	6.0%	93,423	7.5%	35.8%
	Total	1,146,970	100.0%	1,240,450	100.0%	8.2%
Sample size		3,242		2,955		

Source: Statistics Canada, Survey of Consumer Finances, Special Tabulations.

a variety of groups according to their different perspectives. Many of these poverty lines would include as 'poor' many or all of those here included in the 'Vulnerable' category.

As Table 2.3 showed, the number of poor families with children in Ontario grew nearly 15% between 1973 and 1987, compared with 8.2% among families with children as a group. The greatest amount of growth in poor families took place among couples with children (the apparent growth in

Table 2.4
Dollar income limits corresponding to income categories,
urban and rural areas, 1987, (1986–based LICO)

Income category and family size	Large urban area population 500,000 +		Urban area population 100,000–499,999		Small urban area population 30,000–99,999		Less than 30,000		Rural	
	Lower limit	Upper limit	Lower limit	Upper limit	Lower limit	Upper limit	Lower limit	Upper limit	Lower limit	Upper limit
One person — poor		$12,365		$10,860		$10,609		$9,671		$8,417
Vulnerable	$12,366	$15,457	$10,861	$13,575	$10,610	$13,262	$9,672	$12,089	$8,418	$10,522
Other mainstream	$15,458	$37,097	$13,576	$32,582	$13,263	$31,829	$12,090	$29,015	$10,523	$25,253
Advantaged	$37,098	$49,463	$32,583	$43,443	$31,830	$42,439	$29,016	$38,687	$25,254	$33,671
Affluent	$49,464		$43,444		$42,440		$38,688		$33,672	
Two person — poor		$16,761		$14,722		$14,382		$13,110		$11,411
Vulnerable	$16,762	$20,952	$14,723	$18,403	$14,383	$17,978	$13,111	$16,388	$11,412	$14,264
Other mainstream	$20,953	$50,285	$18,404	$44,168	$17,979	$43,148	$16,389	$39,332	$14,265	$34,235
Advantaged	$50,286	$67,047	$44,169	$58,891	$43,149	$57,531	$39,333	$52,443	$34,236	$45,647
Affluent	$67,048		$58,892		$57,532		$52,444		$45,648	
Three person — poor		$21,305		$18,712		$18,280		$16,664		$14,504
Vulnerable	$21,306	$26,632	$18,713	$23,390	$18,281	$22,850	$16,665	$20,830	$14,505	$18,130
Other mainstream	$26,633	$63,917	$23,391	$56,138	$22,851	$54,842	$20,831	$49,994	$18,131	$43,514
Advantaged	$63,918	$85,223	$56,139	$74,851	$54,843	$73,123	$49,995	$66,659	$43,515	$58,019
Affluent	$85,224		$74,852		$73,124		$66,660		$58,020	
Four person — poor		$24,530		$21,544		$21,046		$19,186		$16,699
Vulnerable	$24,531	$30,663	$21,545	$26,930	$21,047	$26,308	$19,187	$23,983	$16,700	$20,874
Other mainstream	$30,664	$73,592	$26,931	$64,634	$26,309	$63,140	$23,984	$57,560	$20,875	$50,099
Advantaged	$73,593	$98,123	$64,635	$86,179	$63,141	$84,187	$57,561	$76,747	$50,100	$66,799
Affluent	$98,124		$86,180		$84,188		$76,748		$66,800	
Five person — poor		$26,801		$23,539		$22,995		$20,963		$18,245
Vulnerable	$26,802	$33,502	$23,540	$29,424	$22,996	$28,744	$20,964	$26,204	$18,246	$22,807
Other mainstream	$33,503	$80,405	$29,425	$70,619	$28,745	$68,987	$26,205	$62,891	$22,808	$54,737
Advantaged	$80,406	$107,207	$70,620	$94,159	$68,988	$91,983	$62,892	$83,855	$54,738	$72,983
Affluent	$107,208		$94,160		$91,984		$83,856		$72,984	

Source: Statistics Canada, *Income Distributions by Size in Canada, 1988*, Cat. 13-207, and author's calculations.

poor male-led lone parent families is based on too small a sample to be reliable, although it is suggestive evidence[8]), whose numbers increased by over 12,000, or 19.4%, accounting for two-thirds of the total growth.

The Vulnerable category declined by 2% while the remainder of the Mainstream grew by only 2.2%. On balance, therefore, there was no growth in the Mainstream category over the period.

The Advantaged and Affluent categories (predominantly couples with children), although smaller in number than the Mainstream, have grown at rates significantly above that for families in general. The number of Advantaged families with children grew by nearly 25%, while the Affluent group grew by nearly 36%. Much of this growth can be attributed to the increase in work effort on the part of families over the period, a trend that will be analysed in more detail below.

Poor Families—Family Type

Approximately 75,000, or only 53%, of poor families with children in Ontario are husband-wife families, compared with 80% of all families (Table 2.5). Another 55,000, or 39%, are female-led lone parent families, versus 10% of all families.

Table 2.5
Distribution of poverty by family type, Ontario, 1973 and 1987

Family type	Number of families with children	Distribution of families	Number of poor families with children	Distribution of poor families
		1973		
ONTARIO				
Couple with children	943,360	82.2%	63,090	50.8%
Lone parent — female	86,660	7.6%	49,170	39.6%
Lone parent — male	16,550	1.4%	1,590	1.3%
Other[a]	100.400	8.8%	10,410	8.4%
Total	1,146,970	100.0%	124,260	100.0%
Sample size	3,242		351	
		1987		
Couple with children	988,037	79.7%	75,303	52.8%
Lone parent — female	118,442	9.5%	55,361	38.8%
Lone parent — male	16,390	1.3%	2,373	1.7%
Other[a]	117,582	9.5%	9,504	6.7%
Total	1,240,451	100.0%	142,541	100.0%
Sample size	2,955		326	

[a]'Other' includes extended families and family spending units with more than two adults.

Source: Statistics Canada, Survey of Consumer Finances, Special Tabulations.

The remainder are male-led lone parent or other family types.[9] This represents a modest shift from 1973, when just over half of poor families were husband-wife families and nearly 40% were female-led lone parent families.

It is important to distinguish between the *distribution* and the *incidence* of poverty. While 'distribution' refers to the percentage of poor families or children found in various categories (husband-wife or lone parent families, for example), 'incidence' refers to the likelihood that a family or child *within* a certain category (with a head of household aged 25 to 34 years, for example) will be poor: that is, the percentage of families or children with a head of household aged 25 to 34 who are poor. The former tells us how poverty is distributed among various groups in society, while the latter provides information about the *risk* of poverty associated with those categories.

The incidence of poverty varies greatly according to the type of family in which a child lives. In Ontario the incidence of poverty among husband-wife families with children was 7.6% in 1987, up from 6.7% in 1973 (Table 2.3). Among female-led lone parent families the incidence of poverty was 46.7%, down from 56.7% in 1973.

Poor Families—Age of Head

The nature of poverty in Ontario has changed dramatically over time. As Figure 2.2 shows, in 1973 38.8% of poor households were headed by a person aged 65 years or over, and 30.3% were headed by a person under age 35. By 1987 these positions had reversed; only 28.1% of poor households were headed by a person 65 or over, and 38.9% were headed by a person under 35.

Thus the incidence of poverty also changed considerably over the period according to the age of the head of the household. Whereas in 1973, 40.7% of households headed by a senior were poor, by 1987 this proportion had dropped to 25.4%. Whereas 28.9% of households headed by a person aged 15 to 24 were poor in 1973, by 1987 this figure had increased to 42%. Among families headed by a person aged 25 to 34, the incidence of poverty increased from 10.7% to 15.1%.

For young families with children the risk of poverty increased at a faster rate. Between 1973 and 1987 the percentage of families with children, headed by a person between the ages of 15 and 24, who were poor nearly doubled; from 20.7% to 39.3% (Table 2.6). For families with children headed by a person aged 25 to 34 the incidence of

Figure 2.2: Households and poor households by age of head, Ontario, 1973 and 1987

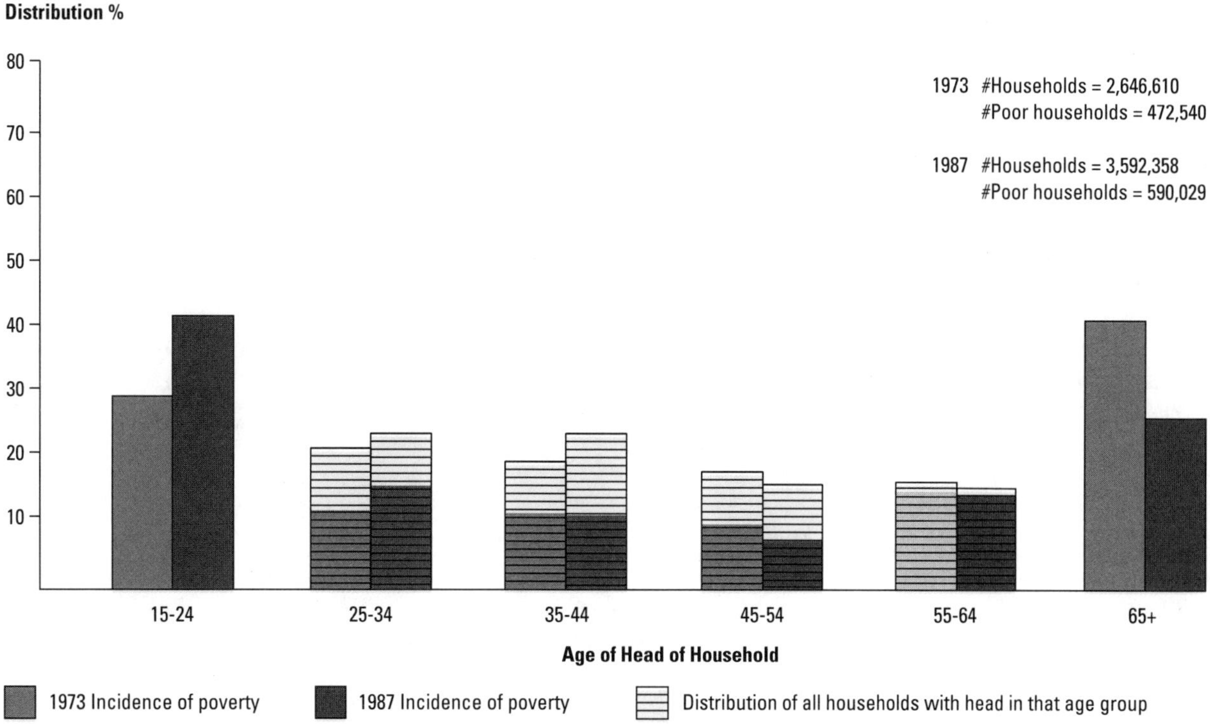

Distribution %

1973 #Households = 2,646,610
      #Poor households = 472,540

1987 #Households = 3,592,358
      #Poor households = 590,029

Age of Head of Household

■ 1973 Incidence of poverty   ■ 1987 Incidence of poverty   ▤ Distribution of all households with head in that age group

Source: Statistics Canada Survey of Consumer Finances, Special Tabulations.

poverty increased from 12.4% to 15.3%. The incidence of poverty among families with children with the head over the age of 35 declined, with the exception of families with the head over 65.

Families with Children—Labour Market Participation

One of the most significant changes for families and family life has been the tremendous increase in the participation of women in the paid labour force: from 36.3% in 1970 to 56.2% in 1987. Among Canadian women with children under the age of 16, the percentage who were participating in the paid labour force increased from 44.8% in 1977 to 65% in 1987. Of those who were employed, 72.0% were employed full-time in 1987.

It is of great interest to examine how this dramatic increase in paid labour force participation has affected the economic status of families with children. To do this we examine families with children according to the number of full-time equivalent earners (FTEs).[10] From the data in Table 2.7 it can be seen that in 1973 among Ontario couples with children it was still the norm to have only one full-time equivalent person in the labour force; approximately 47% of Ontario couples with children fit this pattern. With the increase in women's participation in the paid labour force that had already taken place by that time, another 23% had between one and two FTEs. Approximately 23% had two people working full-time, and 7% had less than one FTE or none.

This pattern of labour force effort was by and large successful in keeping couple families with children out of poverty. Table 2.7 also shows that the incidence of poverty among couples with only one full-time earner was 5% in 1973. As expected, the rate of poverty increased with fewer weeks in the labour market and decreased with increased participation; the incidence of poverty among couple families with no weeks of labour force participation was 67.3%, whereas among couples with children with two full-time earners it was only 2.8%.

By 1987 the pattern of incidence of poverty by number of FTEs had changed significantly. Among all families with children, the incidence of poverty tended to increase for those with one or fewer earners in the labour market, and decrease for those with more than one earner.

Because of the disadvantaged position of women in the labour market and the stagnation of individual wages, increased labour market participation has been a less successful strategy for avoiding poverty among female-led lone-parent families. In 1973, 39.3% of lone-parent females in Ontario were not employed at any point in the year; 40.5% were in the labour force full-time and the remainder (20.2%) were in the labour force part-time. By 1987 the proportion with no FTEs had fallen to 24.7%, while the proportion in the labour force full-time had increased to 48.5%.

However, the incidence of poverty among female lone-parent families with a full-time earner in Ontario fell from 17.6% in 1973 to 17.3% in 1987. Overall, the incidence of poverty among female-led lone-parent families fell from 56.7% to 46.7%.

Among all families with children the proportion with one FTE fell from 46.1% to 23.7%. The proportion with two FTEs increased from 21.5% to 30.5%. Those with fewer than one FTE increased slightly from 12.4% to 13.5%. Those with between one and two FTEs increased from 19.9% to 32.3%.

Table 2.6
Distribution and incidence of family poverty, by age of family head, families with children, Ontario, 1973 and 1987

Age of family head	1973				1987			
	Number of families with children	Number of poor families with children	Distribution of poor families with children	Incidence of family poverty	Number of families with children	Number of poor families with children	Distribution of poor families with children	Incidence of family poverty
ONTARIO								
15–24	58,460	12,100	9.7%	20.7%	38,226	15,021	10.5%	39.3%
25–34	356,500	44,050	35.4%	12.4%	371,662	56,807	39.9%	15.3%
35–44	401,830	42,220	34.0%	10.5%	527,094	49,467	34.7%	9.4%
45–54	248,970	16,180	13.0%	6.5%	230,816	13,481	9.5%	5.8%
55–64	66,090	7,320	5.9%	11.1%	57,061	4,457	3.1%	7.8%
65 +	15,120	2,390	1.9%	15.8%	15,632	3,308	2.3%	21.2
Total	1,146,970	124,260	100.0%	10.8%	1,240,451	142,541	100.0%	11.5%
Sample Size	3,242	351			2,955	326		

Source: Statistics Canada, Survey of Consumer Finances.

Table 2.7
Distribution of families with children
and incidence of family poverty, Ontario, 1973 and 1987

Family type	Number of FTE[a] Earners	Distribution of families with children 1973 Number	%	1987 Number	%	Distribution of poor families with children 1973 Number	%	1987 Number	%	Incidence of family poverty 1973	1987
ONTARIO											
Couples with	0	9,520	1.0%	13,155	1.3%	6,410	10.2%	11,052	14.7%	67.3%	84.0%
children	0.1–0.4	9,320	1.0%	19,191	1.9%	6,470	10.3%	14,310	19.0%	69.4%	74.6%
	0.5–0.9	49,060	5.2%	38,859	3.9%	9,840	15.6%	13,028	17.3%	20.1%	33.5%
	1.0	442,570	46.9%	198,219	20.1%	22,770	36.1%	14,458	19.2%	5.1%	7.3%
	1.1–1.4	131,690	14.0%	316,079	32.0%	7,050	11.2%	16,508	21.9%	5.4%	5.2%
	1.5–1.9	80,730	8.6%	62,446	6.3%	1,540	2.4%	1,151	1.5%	1.9%	1.8%
	2.0	220,470	23.4%	340,088	34.4%	9,010	14.3%	4,796	6.4%	4.1%	1.4%
	Total	943,360	100.0%	988,037	100.0%	63,090	100.0%	75,303	100.0%	6.7%	7.6%
Lone parent—	0	34,070	39.3%	29,255	24.7%	29,640	60.3%	26,324	47.5%	87.0%	90.0%
female	0.1–0.4	10,340	11.9%	14,141	11.9%	9,490	19.3%	10,163	18.4%	91.8%	71.9%
	0.5–0.9	7,150	8.3%	17,560	14.8%	3,850	7.8%	8,935	16.1%	53.8%	50.9%
	1.0	35,100	40.5%	57,486	48.5%	6,190	12.6$	9,939	18.0%	17.6%	17.3%
	Total	86,660	100.0%	118,442	100.0%	49,170	100.0%	55,361	100.0%	56.7%	46.7%
Lone parent—	0	630	3.8%	186	1.1%	630	39.6%	186	7.8%	100.0%	100.0%
male	0.1–0.4	680	4.1%	2,004	12.2%	680	42.8%	1,169	49.3%	100.0%	58.3%
	0.5–0.9	1,170	7.1%	282	1.7%	0	0.0%	282	11.9%	0.0%	100.0%
	1.0	14,070	85.0%	13,918	84.9%	280	17.6%	736	31.0%	2.0%	5.3%
	Total	16,550	100.0%	16,390	100.0%	1,590	100.0%	2,373	100.0%	9.6%	14.5%
Other	0	12,490	12.4%	17,255	14.7%	3,580	34.4%	5,593	34.4%	28.7%	32.4%
	0.1–0.4	1,090	1.1%	1,288	1.1%	860	8.3%	1,288	8.3%	78.9%	100.0%
	0.5–0.9	7,010	7.0%	14,268	12.1%	1,310	12.6%	1,149	12.6%	18.7%	8.1%
	1.0	36,780	36.6%	24,163	20.5%	2,460	23.6%	1,474	23.6%	6.7%	6.1%
	1.1–1.4	10,840	10.8%	18,788	16.0%	280	2.7%	0	2.7%	2.6%	0.0%
	1.5–1.9	5,840	5.8%	3,085	2.6%	0	0.0%	0	0.0%	0.0%	0.0%
	2.0	26,350	26.2%	38,735	32.9%	1,920	18.4%	0	18.4%	7.3%	0.0%
	Total	100,400	100.0%	117,582	100.0%	10,410	100.0%	9,504	100.0%	10.4%	8.1%
All families	0	56,710	4.9%	59,851	4.8%	40,260	32.4%	43,155	30.3%	71.0%	72.1%
with children	0.1–0.4	21,430	1.9%	36,624	3.0%	17,500	14.1%	26,930	18.9%	81.7%	73.5%
	0.5–0.9	64,390	5.6%	70,969	5.7%	15,000	12.1%	23,394	16.4%	23.3%	33.0%
	1.0	528,520	46.1%	293,786	23.7%	31,700	25.5%	26,607	18.7%	6.0%	9.1%
	1.1–1.4	142,530	12.4%	334,867	27.0%	7,330	5.9%	16,508	11.6%	5.1%	4.9%
	1.5–1.9	86,570	7.5%	65,531	5.3%	1,540	1.2%	1,151	0.8%	1.8%	1.8%
	2.0	246,820	21.5%	378,823	30.5%	10,930	8.8%	4,796	3.4%	4.4%	1.3%
	Total	1,146,970	100.0%	1,240,451	100.0%	124,260	100.0%	142,541	100.0%	10.8%	11.5%
Sample size		3,242		2,955		351		319			

Source: Statistics Canada, Survey of Consumer Finances, Special Tabulations.

[a] Full-Time Equivalent

Table 2.8
Number of families and impact of increased full-time equivalent
labour force participation, by family type, Ontario, 1973 and 1987

Province and family type	Distribution of families 1973	1987 families based on 1973 distribution	Incidence of family poverty 1987	Hypothetical poor families 1987	Actual number of poor families 1987
ONTARIO					
Couples with children					
0	1.0%	9,971	84.0%	8,377	11,052
0.1–0.4	1.0%	9,761	74.6%	7,279	14,310
0.5–0.9	5.2%	51,383	33.5%	17,227	13,028
1.0	46.9%	463,530	7.3%	33,810	14,458
1.1–1.4	14.0%	137,927	5.2%	7,204	16,508
1.5–1.9	8.6%	84,553	1.8%	1,558	1,151
2.0	23.4%	230,911	1.4%	3,256	4,796
Total	100.0%	988,037	8.0%	78,710	75,303
Lone parent — female					
0	39.3%	46,565	90.0%	41,900	26,324
0.1–0.4	11.9%	14,132	71.9%	10,157	10,163
0.5–0.9	8.3%	9,772	50.9%	4,972	8,935
1.0	40.5%	47,973	17.3%	8,294	9,939
Total	100.0%	118,442	55.2%	65,323	55,361
Lone parent — male					
0	3.8%	624	100.0%	624	186
0.1–0.4	4.1%	673	58.3%	393	1,169
0.5–0.9	7.1%	1,159	100.0%	1,159	282
1.0	85.0%	13,934	5.3%	737	736
Total	100.0%	16,390	17.8%	2,912	2,373
Other families with children					
0	12.4%	14,627	32.4%	4,741	5,593
0.1–0.4	1.1%	1,277	100.0%	1,277	1,288
0.5–0.9	7.0%	8,210	8.1%	661	1,149
1.0	36.6	43,074	6.1%	2,628	1,474
1.1–1.4	10.8%	12,695	0.0%	0	0
1.5–1.9	5.8%	6,839	0.0%	0	0
2.0	26.2%	30,859	0.0%	0	0
Total	100.0%	117,582	7.9%	9,307	9,504

Source: Statistics Canada, Survey of Consumer Finances, Special Tabulations.

Although lone parents do not have the option of increasing their commitment to the labour force beyond one full-time equivalent, female-led lone-parent families also significantly increased their participation in the paid labour force. The proportion with no FTE weeks in the labour force dropped from 39.3% to 24.7%. The fraction with one FTE increased from 40.5% to 48.5%.

Nevertheless, this massive increase in labour force effort by families has failed to reduce the incidence of family poverty. In 1973 the incidence of poverty among Ontario couples with children was 6.7%; in 1987 it had increased to 7.6%. Overall, the incidence of family poverty increased from 10.8% to 11.5%. In part this is because of a type of polarization in the labour market: although the amount of labour force effort is increasing on average, the proportion of families with children with less than one full-time earner has remained relatively constant, while the share of families with only one earner has declined remarkably and the proportion with more than one earner has increased. At the same time, the rate of poverty among those with one earner or less has increased: among families with only one earner the rate of poverty increased from 6% in 1973 to 9.1% in 1987. Similar or larger increases in the rate of poverty occurred among families with children with less than a full-time earner (Table 2.7).

Among female-led lone parent families the incidence of poverty nationally increased from 58.0 to 59.0%, because in Canada as a whole female lone parents tended to remain concentrated in the lower FTE groups, whose incidence of poverty actually increased. In Ontario, where female lone parents were much more successful in entering or remaining in the labour force, the incidence of poverty fell from 56.7% to 46.7%.

There are distinct limitations to the strategy of adding additional earners to the labour market to sustain family income. Couple families have only two potential earners and, as Table 2.7 suggests, are already near their maximum capacity; the average Canadian family now has 1.8 income earners (Statistics Canada, 1989: 28). Lone parent families have only one potential earner to begin with, and as was stated above, the disadvantaged position of women in the labour market means that working full-time is less successful at lifting such families out of poverty: the rate of poverty among female-led lone parent families with one FTE was, at 17.3%, more than double the rate of poverty among couple families with children with one FTE, whose rate of poverty was 7.3%.

The importance of the labour market is again illustrated by the changing patterns of labour force activity among families with children in different income categories.[11] Among the Advantaged and Affluent families with children in Canada, 50% had two full-time earners in 1987 — higher than any other income category — while only 15% had a single earner. Among the Vulnerable less than 10% had two full-time earners, and 34% had only one. In the remainder of the Mainstream category 28.7% had only one earner, and

almost 25% had two full-time earners (Statistics Canada, Survey of Consumer Finances, Special Tabulations).

The extent to which increasing labour force effort was successful in keeping families out of poverty is suggested by Table 2.8. This table estimates the number of families and children who would have been poor in 1987 if the number of FTEs in a family had remained at 1973 levels, and the incidence of poverty, for each level of FTE, had assumed the 1987 rate.[12]

Table 2.8 suggests that under 1973 patterns of labour force activity, the number of poor couples with children would have been approximately 78,710, an increase of approximately 3,407 families over the actual number of 75,303 (shown in the last column). The incidence of poverty in this group would have increased from 7.6% (1987 actual) to 8.7%.

Similarly, the number of poor female-led lone parent families would have been approximately 65,323, an increase of 9,962 over the actual 55,361. The incidence of poverty would have been 55.2% instead of 46.7%.

The total number of poor families with children in Ontario would have increased by 13,711, from its actual level of 142,541 to 156,252. The incidence of poverty among families with children would have been 13.4% instead of the actual 11.5%.

As stated earlier, there are limitations on increasing labour force participation as a strategy to avoid family and child poverty. The data document the existence of poverty even for families with two full-time people in the labour market. If family poverty is to be eliminated, a full employment strategy, with high-quality jobs, a complementary income security program, and additional family supports such as child care are necessary adjuncts to an increase in labour force effort.

III Children

Poor Children—One in Eight

While the previous section focused on the families in which children live, this section will supplement this material by focusing on the children themselves. Figure 2.3 shows that the number of children in families fell by nearly 10% between 1973 and 1987, from 2,520,450 to 2,274,241.

In 1987 there were approximately 269,913 Ontario children, or 11.9%, in poor families. This was a decrease of

Table 2.9
Incidence of child poverty by family type,
Ontario, 1973 and 1987

Family type	1973				1987			
	Number of children	Number of poor children	Distribution of poor children	Incidence of child poverty	Number of children	Number of poor children	Distribution of poor children	Incidence of child poverty
ONTARIO								
Couples with children	2,078,830	161,940	51.9%	7.8%	1,866,012	152,807	56.6%	8.2%
Lone parent — female	190,460	126,800	40.6%	66.6%	187,639	99,365	36.8%	53.0%
Lone parent — male	27,930	2,050	0.7%	7.3%	22,432	4,561	1.7%	20.3%
Other	223,230	21,370	6.8%	9.6%	198,158	13,180	4.9%	6.7%
All families with children	2,520,450	312,160	100.0%	12.4%	2,274,241	269,913	100.0%	11.9%
Sample size (households)	3,242	351			2,955	326		

Source: Statistics Canada, Survey of Consumer Finances, Special Tabulations.

Figure 2.3:   Percent of children by family income class, Ontario, 1973 and 1987

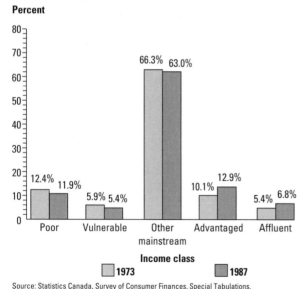

Source: Statistics Canada, Survey of Consumer Finances, Special Tabulations.

13.5% since 1973. The proportion of children in the Mainstream category fell from 72.2% to 68.4%, while the subcategory Vulnerable fell slightly from 5.9% to 5.4%. The Advantaged and the Affluent categories increased from 10.1% and 5.4% to 12.9% and 6.8%, respectively.

For Canada as a whole, the number of children in the Mainstream fell from 71% of the total in 1973 to 67.2% in 1987. The share in the Vulnerable category fell 8.6% to 6.3%, while Other Mainstream also declined, from 62.4% to 60.9%. The number of Advantaged children grew from 8.3% of the total to 10.6%. The proportion of children who were Affluent increased, from 4.2% to 5.7%.

The decrease in the number of Poor and Vulnerable children relative to the numbers of Advantaged and Affluent, especially in the context of the increased incidence of poverty among families with children, can be attributed to the increase in labour force effort expended by those families, an issue that was explored above. In addition, there have been changes in the composition of the poor population; as the family head is likely to be younger, the family may not have completed family formation, possibly accounting for increasing incidence of poverty among families with children at the same time as child poverty is falling.

Family Type

The types of families in which poor children live have changed since 1973. In 1973, 51.9% of poor children in

Table 2.10
Distribution of children and poor children and incidence of child poverty
by number of full-time equivalent earners (FTEs)
Ontario, 1973 and 1987

Family type	Number of FTE earners	Distribution of children				Distribution of poor chilren				Incidence of child poverty	
		1973		1987		1973		1987		1973	1987
		Number	%	Number	%	Number	%	Number	%		
ONTARIO											
Couples with	0	21,430	1.0%	25,255	1.4%	16,590	10.2%	20,731	13.6%	77.4%	82.1%
children	0.1–0.4	27,280	1.3%	37,772	2.0%	19,200	11.9%	29,173	19.1%	70.4%	77.2%
	0.5–0.9	123,680	5.9%	72,992	3.9%	23,900	14.8%	28,157	18.4%	19.3%	38.6%
	1.0	1,018,070	49.0%	419,459	22.5%	60,270	37.2%	27,955	18.3%	5.9%	6.7%
	1.1–1.4	263,910	12.7%	603,932	32.4%	16,960	10.5%	32,978	21.6%	6.4%	5.5%
	1.5–1.9	160,450	7.7%	109,672	5.9%	3,820	2.4%	3,478	2.3%	2.4%	3.2%
	2.0	464,010	22.3%	596,930	32.0%	21,200	13.1%	10,335	6.8%	4.6%	1.7%
	Total	2,078,830	100.0%	1,866,012	100.0%	161,940	100.0%	152,807	100.0%	7.8%	8.2%
Lone parent —	0	88,330	46.4%	53,956	28.8%	79,610	62.8%	49,207	49.5%	90.1%	91.2%
female	0.1–0.4	24,840	13.0%	24,233	12.9%	23,170	18.3%	17,579	17.7%	93.3%	72.5%
	0.5–0.9	14,410	7.6%	30,639	16.3%	8,860	7.0%	17,816	17.9%	61.5%	58.1%
	1.0	62,880	33.0%	78,811	42.0%	15,160	12.0%	14,763	14.9%	24.1%	18.7%
	Total	190,460	100.0%	187,639	100.0%	126,800	100.0%	99,365	100.0%	66.6%	53.0%
Lone parent —	0	1,090	3.9%	186	0.8%	1,090	53.2%	186	4.1%	100.0%	100.0%
male	0.1–0.4	680	2.4%	3,640	16.2%	680	33.2%	2,431	53.3%	100.0%	66.8%
	0.5–0.9	1,950	7.0%	282	1.3%	0	0.0%	282	6.2%	0.0%	100.0%
	1.0	24,210	86.7%	18,324	81.7%	280	13.7%	1,662	36.4%	1.2%	9.1%
	Total	27,930	100.0%	22,432	100.0%	2,050	100.0%	4,561	100.0%	7.3%	20.3%
Other families	0	22,810	10.2%	22,287	11.2%	6,370	29.8%	7,627	57.9%	27.9%	34.2%
with children	0.1–0.4	2,360	1.1%	1,288	0.6%	2,130	10.0%	1,288	9.8%	90.3%	100.0%
	0.5–0.9	18,350	8.2%	21,440	10.8%	2,970	13.9%	1,149	8.7%	16.2%	5.4%
	1.0	80,650	36.1%	32,505	16.4%	5,880	27.5%	3,116	23.6%	7.3%	9.6%
	1.1–1.4	20,900	9.4%	34,742	17.5%	280	1.3%	0	0.0%	1.3%	0.0%
	1.5–1.9	11,840	5.3%	8,346	4.2%	0	0.0%	0	0.0%	0.0%	0.0%
	2.0	66,320	29.7%	77,550	39.1%	3,740	17.5%	0	0.0%	5.6%	0.0%
	Total	223,230	100.0%	198,158	100.0%	21,370	100.0%	13,180	100.0%	9.6%	6.7%
All families	0	133,660	5.3%	101,684	4.5%	103,660	33.2%	77,751	28.8%	77.6%	76.5%
with children	0.1–0.4	55,160	2.2%	66,933	2.9%	45,180	14.5%	50,471	18.7%	81.9%	75.4%
	0.5–0.9	158,390	6.3%	125,353	5.5%	35,730	11.4%	47,404	17.6%	22.6%	37.8%
	1.0	1,185,810	47.0%	549,099	24.1%	81,590	26.1%	47,496	17.6%	6.9%	8.6%
	1.1–1.4	284,810	11.3%	638,674	28.1%	17,240	5.5%	32,978	12.2%	6.1%	5.2%
	1.5–1.9	172,290	6.8%	118,018	5.2%	3,820	1.2%	3,478	1.3%	2.2%	2.9%
	2.0	530,330	21.0%	674,480	29.7%	24,940	8.0%	10,335	3.8%	4.7%	1.5%
	Total	2,520,450	100.0%	2,274,241	100.0%	312,160	100.0%	269,913	100.0%	12.4%	11.9%
Sample size (households)		3,242		2,955		351		326			

Source: Statistics Canada, Survey of Consumer Finances, Special Tabulations.

Table 2.11
Number of children and impact of increased full-time equivalent
(FTE) labour force participation, by family type,
Ontario, 1973 and 1987

Province and family type	Distribution of children 1973	1987 children based on 1973 distribution	Incidence of child poverty 1987	Hypothetical poor children 1987	Actual number of poor children 1987
ONTARIO					
Couples with children					
0	1.0%	19,239	82.1%	15,792	20,731
0.1–0.4	1.3%	24,487	77.2%	18,912	29,173
0.5–0.9	5.9%	111,018	38.6%	42,825	28,157
1.0	49.0%	913,846	6.7%	60,908	27,955
1.1–1.4	12.7%	236,892	5.5%	12,937	32,978
1.5–1.9	7.7%	144,024	3.2%	4,567	3,478
2.0	22.3%	416,507	1.7%	7,210	10,335
Total	100.0%	1,866,012	8.7%	163,151	152,807
Lone parent — female					
0	46.4%	87,021	91.2%	79,362	49,207
0.1–0.4	13.0%	24,472	72.5%	17,753	17,579
0.5–0.9	7.6%	14,197	58.1%	8,255	17,816
1.0	33.0%	61,949	18.7%	11,604	14,763
Total	100.0%	187,639	62.3%	116,973	99,365
Lone parent — male					
0	3.9%	876	100.0%	876	186
0.1–0.4	2.4%	546	66.8%	365	2,431
0.5–0.9	7.0%	1,566	100.0%	1,566	282
1.0	86.7%	19,444	9.1%	1,764	1,662
Total	100.0%	22,432	20.4%	4,570	4,561
Other					
0	10.2%	20,248	34.2%	6,929	7,627
0.1–0.4	1.1%	2,095	100.0%	2,095	1,288
0.5–0.9	8.2%	16,289	5.4%	873	1,149
1.0	36.1%	71,592	9.6%	6,863	3,116
1.1–1.4	9.4%	18,553	0.0%	0	0
1.5–1.9	5.3%	10,510	0.0%	0	0
2.0	29.7%	58,871	0.0%	0	0
Total	100.0%	198,158	8.5%	16,760	13,180

Source: Statistics Canada, Survey of Consumer Finances, Special Tabulations.

Ontario lived in couple families; a further 40.6% lived in female-led lone parent families (Table 2.9). By 1987 the proportion of poor children in couple families had increased to 56.6%, while the share in female-led lone parent families had decreased to 36.8%.

Overall, the incidence of child poverty in Ontario fell marginally between 1973 and 1987, from 12.4% to 11.9%. But it increased slightly in couple families, from 7.8% to 8.2%, and decreased in female lone parent families, from 66.6% to 53.0% (Table 2.9). Nationally, the incidence of child poverty was unchanged at 16.5% in both 1973 and 1987, although it fell among children in couple families and female-led lone parent families and increased in other family types.

Age of Family Head

As was demonstrated above, there have been dramatic changes in the age of poor family heads. Among children in Ontario families headed by a person aged 15 to 24 years, the incidence of child poverty increased from 23.6% in 1973 to 41.3%, in 1987 (Figure 2.4). Among children in families where the head was between 25 and 34 the incidence of poverty increased from 14.7% to 16.9%. Among children in families where the head was older than 34, the incidence of poverty declined, with the exception of families with heads over the age of 65.

Labour Market Participation of Family Members

The increase in the labour force effort of families with children has already been noted. Among children in couple families, nearly half in 1973 had only one full-time equivalent earner in the labour market; 42% had more than one FTE, and 15% had two FTEs (Table 2.10). In 1987 only 23% of children were in couple families with one FTE, while 70% were in families with more than one; 32% were in two-FTE families.

Among children in female-led lone parent families, 46% were in no-FTE families in 1973 and only 33% had one FTE. In 1987 the number with no FTEs had dropped to approximately 29%, while the proportion in one FTE families had increased to 42%.

For families with less than one FTE, the rate of child poverty increased sharply between 1973 and 1987, highlighting the inadequacy of income security programs and the deterioration of labour market opportunities for those working less than full-time. This is of special significance in the labour market of the 1980s and 1990s, when many of the jobs created are part-time low-wage service jobs.

Table 2.11 replicates the calculations in Table 2.8 to estimate the number of children affected by the increase in labour market activity. The number of children in couple

Figure 2.4: Incidence of poor children by age of family head, Ontario, 1973 and 1987

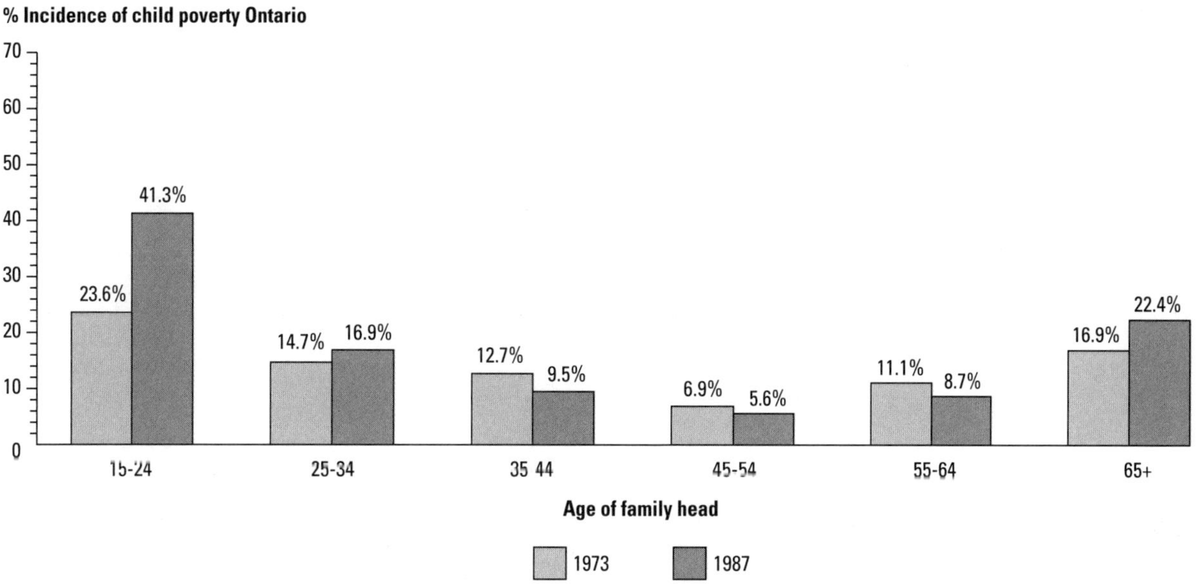

% Incidence of child poverty Ontario

Source: Statistics Canada Survey of Consumer Finances, Special Tabulations.

families who would have been poor, had labour force participation not increased dramatically, would have been approximately 163,151, an increase of 10,344 over the actual number, 152,807. On the other hand, even such a massive increase in paid labour succeeded in keeping only about 10,000 children out of poverty; without it the incidence of child poverty in couple families would have been 8.7% in 1987, not 8.2%. Similarly, among female-led lone parent families the increase in work effort kept only 17,608 children from being poor, and lowered the incidence of child poverty to 53%, from a potential 62.3%.

Overall, in Ontario, 301,454 children would have been poor in 1987, an increase of 31,541 from the actual 1987 level of 269,913. The incidence of child poverty would have been 13.3% instead of 11.9%.

IV   Poverty

The Poverty Gap

One of the defects of traditional poverty analysis is the precipitous nature of a poverty line: those who are below it are categorized as 'poor', and those who are above it, no matter by how little, are not. This discussion has attempted to avoid this problem by extending the analysis to the whole income distribution, showing the relationships among different parts of the distribution.

This section is designed to extend the analysis of poverty in another direction, by examining the *depth* of poverty: that is, how far the poor fall below the poverty line. The difference between the income of a poor household and the poverty line is termed the 'poverty gap'.

Poverty Gap by Family Type

Table 2.12 shows the approximate size of the poverty gap in Ontario for various family types, in 1987 dollars, for 1973 and 1987. The poverty gap among poor families with children narrowed between 1973 and 1987, albeit very slightly, from $7,032 to $6,910. Among couples with children the average gap grew from $6,466 to $7,002. Among female-led lone parent families the gap fell from $7,981 to $7,151.

For poor Canadian families as a whole, the average poverty gap grew from $5,714 to $6,736 for couples with children. Female-led lone parent families were the furthest below the poverty line, with a poverty gap of $7,606, almost exactly the same level as in 1973.

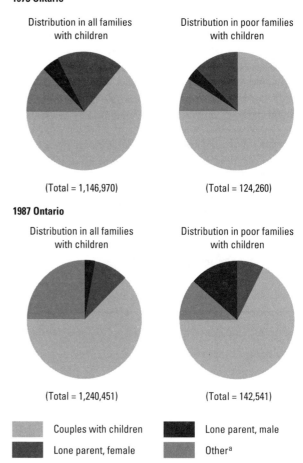

Figure 2.5:   Distribution of poverty by family type, Ontario, 1973 and 1987

1973 Ontario

Distribution in all families with children

Distribution in poor families with children

(Total = 1,146,970)

(Total = 124,260)

1987 Ontario

Distribution in all families with children

Distribution in poor families with children

(Total = 1,240,451)

(Total = 142,541)

Couples with children   Lone parent, male

Lone parent, female   Other[a]

[a] 'Other' includes extended families and family spending units with more than two adults.
Source: Statistics Canada, Survey of Consumer Finances, Special Tabulations.

Poverty Gap by Age of Family Head

Table 2.13 shows that the poverty gap for Ontario families headed by a person under the age of 35 declined between 1973 and 1987: from $7,215 to $5,740 for families with a head under the age of 25 years, and from $7,488 to $7,227 for families headed by a person between the ages of 25 and 34. For families headed by a person between the ages of 35 and 54 the gap increased. The gap declined for families headed by a person above the age of 54.

Table 2.12
Average poverty gap by family type, Ontario, 1973 and 1987

Family type	1973 (1987 $)		1987	
	Number of poor households	Average poverty gap	Number of poor households	Average poverty gap
ONTARIO				
All poor families with children	124,260	$7,032	142,541	$6,910
Poor couples with children	63,090	$6,466	75,303	$7,002
Poor female single parent	49,170	$7,981	55,361	$7,151
Poor male single parent	1,590	$8,185	2,373	$3,947
Other poor families with children	10,410	$5,821	9,504	$5,511
Poor couples without children	23,200	$5,865	27,002	$5,096
Sample size	419		390	

Source: Statistics Canada, Survey of Consumer Finances, Special Tabulations.

Table 2.13
Average poverty gap by age of head, poor families with children, Ontario, 1973 and 1987

Age of family head	1973		1987	
	Number of poor households	Average poverty gap	Number of poor households	Average poverty gap
ONTARIO				
Total	124,260	$7,032	142,541	$6,910
15–24	12,100	$7,215	15,021	$5,740
25–34	44,050	$7,488	56,807	$7,227
35–44	42,220	$6,715	49,467	$7,268
45–54	16,180	$6,463	13,481	$6,909
55–64	7,320	$7,822	4,457	$4,834
65 +	2,390	$4,799	3,308	$4,219
Sample size	349		325	

Source: Statistics Canada, Survey of Consumer Finances, Special Tabulations.

Poverty Gap by Number of Children

The poverty line increases with family size, and therefore a family with children is more likely to be categorized as poor than a family without children, given that earnings do not vary in accordance with family circumstances. Put another way, some families are poor simply by virtue of the presence of children; in the absence of children the family's income would be sufficient to keep them above the poverty line.

Table 2.14 shows the average poverty gap for families with various numbers of children. It can be seen that the poverty gap tends to increase with the number of children; in Ontario from $4,166 for a family with no children to $8,689 for poor families with four or more children. For Canada as a whole the average poverty gap increases from $4,265 among families with no children to $8,037 for families with four or more children.

Table 2.14
Average poverty gap by number of children, Ontario, 1973 and 1987

| | 1973 | | 1987 | |
Number of children	Number of poor households	Average poverty gap	Number of poor households	Average poverty gap
ONTARIO				
Zero	348,280	$4,100	447,488	$4,166
One	31,410	$6,353	59,113	$6,092
Two	42,110	$7,163	51,280	$6,707
Three	26,800	$6,187	22,887	$8,759
Four +	23,940	$8,646	9,261	$8,689
Total	472,540	$4,871	590,029	$4,829

Source: Statistics Canada, Survey of Consumer Finances, Special Tabulations.

V Income Support for Families with Children

Canada, of course, offers income security programs specifically directed to families with children. These programs serve various purposes: they transfer income to families with children, offsetting some of the costs of child-raising and thus contributing to horizontal equity and providing recognition of society's collective interest in child-raising. In addition, such programs serve a broader economic interest by increasing aggregate purchasing power. This section is intended to outline the characteristics of some of the main programs: the Family Allowance, tax deductions for child care expenses, and the Child Tax Credit. Social assistance is not addressed here because of space limitations. Its inadequacies with respect to income support for families and children are well documented elsewhere.[13]

The Family Allowance, introduced in Canada near the end of the Second World War, is paid monthly to all families with children up to the age of 18 years. It is universally available, but is part of income for tax purposes, thus providing a greater benefit to those with lower incomes. For example, in 1989 a couple with two children and an income of $10,000 would retain the full benefit of the Family Allowance, $786 per year, after taxes. At higher levels of income, however, the after-tax amount of the benefit would be reduced

Table 2.15
Family Allowance Payments

Year	Family allowance per child	Constant dollar ($ 1989)	Year	Family allowance per child	Constant dollar ($ 1989)
1963	$6.00	$27.79	1977	$23.89	$53.13
1964	$6.00	$27.79	1978	$25.68	$52.47
1965	$6.00	$26.65	1979	$20.00	$37.42
1966	$6.00	$25.74	1980	$21.80	$37.03
1967	$6.00	$24.82	1981	$23.96	$36.18
1968	$6.00	$23.84	1982	$26.91	$36.67
1969	$6.00	$22.82	1983	$28.52	$36.75
1970	$6.00	$22.10	1984	$29.95	$36.98
1971	$6.00	$21.47	1985	$31,27	$37.12
1972	$6.00	$20.50	1986	$31,58	$36.02
1973 (to Sept.)[a, b]	$6.00	$18.60	1987	$31.93	$34.89
Oct.–Dec. 1973	$12.00	$36.83	1988[b]	$32.38	$34.00
1974	$20.00	$57.20	1989	$32.24	$32.74
1975	$22.08	$56.99	1990	$33.33	$31.44
1976	$22.08	$53.01			

[a]Before October, 1973, families did not receive benefits for children 16–17.
[b]There were some minor differences in the amounts for children of different ages before October, 1973.

Source: Statistics Canada, Cat. 86-508, Social Security, National Programs, Vol. 4, Family Allowances and Related Programs, 1982.

until above $55,000 the net benefit levelled off at $433 (National Council of Welfare, 1989).

When it was first introduced, the Family Allowance provided approximately 5% of average family income. By the 1980s this had declined to approximately 1.4% (Statistics Canada, 1982). In 1987 in the lowest income decile the Family Allowance provides only about 5% of family income, or about $639 (before taxes). Although the Family Allowance is not designed as a poverty reduction tool, it is useful to note its role in that respect. Given that the average poverty gap among Ontario families with children was almost $7,000 in 1987, it is clear that the Family Allowance does not contribute very much to the reduction of family and child poverty.

In 1990 the gross monthly payment was $33.33 per child. Table 2.15 shows that although the Family Allowance has increased slightly in value, it has deteriorated significantly in real terms since the mid-1970s, when its value (in 1989 dollars) was between $50 and $60. Since 1986 the amount of the payment has increased by only the rate of inflation less 3%, causing it to erode further in real terms.

The 'clawback' of Family Allowances that was introduced by the federal government in 1989 will sharply raise the rate of taxation on this form of income for parents with a net income above $50,000. Above $55,000 the rate of taxation reaches 100%, reducing the net benefit to zero, and eliminating its universal character. In addition, the $55,000 income level will not be fully indexed, and will increase at only the rate of inflation less 3%. Over time the base population of families eligible for Family Allowance will get narrower.

The Child Tax Credit, introduced in 1979, is designed to benefit families with incomes lower than average. In 1990 the credit was $565, paid to families whose income in 1989 did not exceed $24,355.[14] The benefit is reduced 5% on net income above that level. Table 2.16 shows that, although the real value of the credit has increased since the inception of the program, the income base above which the credit is reduced has fallen drastically, from $36,779 in 1979 (1978 income) to $24,355 in 1989 (1988 income).

The net tax credit enjoyed by tax filers in different income categories illustrates the progressive nature of the benefit. Above the $23,000 net family income level the average credit is $582; below that level the average credit is $854 (Revenue Canada, Taxation Statistics, 1989 ed.). In 1987 the Child Tax

Credit provided approximately 6.8% of fam[...] lowest income decile among families with child[...] imately 1% in the middle deciles and still smaller b[...] to those in the highest deciles (Statistics Canada, Survey of Consumer Finances, Special Tabulations). Again, the dollar figures are too small to make a meaningful contribution to the goal of eliminating child poverty: in the lowest decile the Child Tax Credit yielded only about $818 in 1987.

Families with children can also deduct child care expenses from taxable income. Such expenses are deducted by the earner with the lowest income in two-adult families and must have been paid to allow the person claiming them to work or take an approved training course. In 1989 the maximum allowable claim was $4,000 for a child aged 6 or younger and $2,000 for each child aged 7 to 14.

Since tax deductions benefit those in higher tax brackets relatively more (because they have a higher marginal tax rate and thus save more in taxes from each dollar of deduction), the benefits of the child care deduction are highly unequally distributed. Table 2.17 shows the amount of allowable deduction per filer claiming child care expenses and the amount

Table 2.16
Child Tax Credit 1978–1990

Income Year	Child tax credit current dollars[1]	Child tax credit constant $ 1990	Family income base[2] current $	Family income base $ 1990
1978	$200	$391	$18,000	$38,383
1979	$218	$408	$19,620	$38,339
1980	$238	$404	$21,380	$37,924
1981	$261	$394	$23,470	$37,055
1982	$343	$467	$26,330	$37,497
1983	$343	$442	$26,330	$35,464
1984	$367	$453	$26,330	$33,967
1985	$384	$456	$26,330	$32,693
1986	$454	$518	$23,500	$28,012
1987	$489	$534	$23,760	$27,128
1988	$559	$587	$24,090	$26,441
1989	$565	$565	$24,355	$25,466

[1]Received in following year.
[2]Income above which tax credit is reduced by five cents on the dollar.

Ontario

Table 2.17
care expenses deduction by individual income class 1987

	umber claiming	(3) Allowable deductions	(4) Average deduction per filer	(5) Marginal tax rate (average)	(6) Average tax expenditure (per filer)	(7) Total tax expenditure
	110,820	$108,445	$979	16%	$157	$17,351,200
10,000	209,390	$331,923	$1,585	18%	$285	$59,746,140
20,000–30,000	165,440	$303,917	$1,837	20%	$367	$60,783,400
30,000–40,000	68,700	$135,440	$1,971	25%	$493	$33,860,000
40,000–50,000	30,440	$61,121	$2,008	25%	$502	$15,280,250
50,000–100,000	17,810	$37,846	$2,125	30%	$637	$11,353,800
100,000 +	1,740	$4,409	$2,534	34%	$862	$1,499,060
Total	604,340	983,101				$199,873,850

Source: Revenue Canada, Taxation Statistics, 1989 Edition.

of tax revenue forgone, or 'tax expenditure' created, by income category in 1987. Column 6 shows the average tax expenditure per filer in each income category and column 7 shows the total amount of tax expenditures. It is evident that the benefits of such a system are highly unequal: in the $100,000-plus income category, filers claiming child care expenses in 1987 saved approximately $867 in taxes, while those nearer the bottom saved less than $200. In total, the federal government spent an estimated $200 million dollars for child care through the mechanism of tax expenditures in 1987.[15]

Until 1988, families with children could also claim a personal exemption for wholly dependent children. Except for the fact that exemptions act as entitlements for people with certain characteristics and do not require any contribution or payment, as deductions do, the tax impact of exemptions is similar to that of deductions: that is, they benefit high-income earners more than low-income earners. With the 1988 tax year this exemption has been converted into a $67 tax credit, which will make this category of tax expenditure more equitable, similar to the Child Tax Credit.

APPENDIX

What is Poverty?
In advantaged industrialized countries such as Canada, poverty can best be understood in terms of *relative* deprivation. This belief can be traced back even to Adam Smith, who wrote that poverty was to be without 'whatever the custom of the country renders it indecent for creditable people, even of the lowest order, to be without'. That is, people are poor when they lack the resources to allow them access to the goods and services that are available to most other people and that have come to be accepted as essential to a decent standard of living.

From this perspective, people are considered to be living in poverty when their resources are insufficient to obtain the living conditions that permit their full participation in the larger community. This approach yields poverty lines that are defined *relative* to average standards of living or average incomes.

On the other hand, some would define poverty in *absolute*

terms: that is, as the minimum income necessary to purchase a basket of goods that allows for physical survival. From this perspective, a homeless person who relies on shelters, purchases his or her clothing second-hand, and uses food banks and soup kitchens could be said to have an income that permits physical survival. Obviously, however, such living conditions are hardly conducive to growth or participation in the larger community, and are considerably below what most people would prescribe as the socially sanctioned minimum.

These two opposite approaches form the conceptual boundaries within which a multitude of possible poverty lines, combining aspects of both the relative and absolute approaches, could be defined. For example, the Social Planning Council of Metropolitan Toronto, through its *Guides for Family Budgeting*, defines an income level required to provide for physical *and* social functioning in the Metropolitan Toronto area. This approach incorporates the basket-of-goods notion of the absolute approach, but constructs that basket of goods on the basis of social norms, in keeping with the relative approach.

Statistics Canada's Low Income Cut-Offs (LICOs)

In Canada the most commonly used poverty lines are the Statistics Canada Low Income Cut-Offs (LICOs). Statistics Canada emphasizes that these are not poverty lines as such, but simply 'low income' lines, or the levels below which individuals and families can be said to living in 'straitened circumstances'. However, they are widely treated as poverty lines by social policy analysts and activists, the media, and the general public. This chapter similarly uses these lines for the analysis of poverty, and the terms 'poverty line' and 'low income line' are used interchangeably.

The LICOs are derived from surveys of consumer incomes and spending patterns. Statistics Canada begins by identifying the average proportion of gross income of Canadian households that is spent on the basic necessities of food, clothing and shelter. The LICOs are set at the income level above which, on average, households spend an additional 20% on the three basic necessities.

When the LICOs were first developed they were based on the 1959 Survey of Family Expenditures (FAMEX), which showed that Canadian families spent about 50% of their income on food, clothing, and shelter. Application of the 20% parameter led to the use of 70% of the average family

income as the level below which families were deemed to be living in 'straightened circumstances'.

The fraction of income devoted to necessities should decline as living standards improve, and the next FAMEX, which examined family expenditure patterns in 1969, revealed that the proportion of income spent on the three necessities by Canadian families had declined to 42%. Therefore the cut-off level was revised downward to 62%. The next FAMEX, in 1978, showed that there had been a further drop in the proportion of income devoted to food, clothing, and shelter, to 38.5%. The 20% was again applied and the cut-off set at 58.5%. Since the next FAMEX, in 1982, indicated only negligible changes in the data (which correspond with the intuitive impression that living standards did not improve between 1978 and 1982), the LICOs were not revised at that time.

The revisions to the LICOs that are the product of the 1986 FAMEX have not yet been officially adopted by Statistics Canada and — as occurred with the 1978 revisions — have been published only in an appendix to the regular incomes report. However, they have been adopted for use by social policy analysts. This report, which analyses data from 1973, 1979, and 1987, uses poverty lines based on 1969 consumption patterns for 1973 data, 1978 consumption patterns for 1979, and 1986 consumption patterns for 1987.

Notes

I am indebted to the Child Poverty Action Group, and especially the publication *Unequal Futures: The Meaning of Child Poverty in Canada*, for the development of several of the concepts employed in this chapter, particularly the creation of the categories Poor, Vulnerable, Other Mainstream, Advantaged and Affluent, and the development of the analysis of family labour force participation.

[1] See Harding (1987).

[2] See Palmer, Smeeding, and Torrey (1988), Chap. 1.

[3] Special tabulations were carried out by Tristat Resources Ltd.

[4] The median is the value that one-half of the distribution lies below, and the other half lies above. In statistical terms, the median is a better measure of central tendencies than the 'average' when a distribution is highly skewed, as is the case with the distribution of income.

[5] A decile is 10% of the population of families or families with children, arranged in ascending order of income.

[6]'Other' includes child support payments, workers' compensation benefits, training allowances, veteran's pensions, pensions to the blind and disabled, and scholarships.

[7]Refer to Appendix (p. 44) for a brief review of the methodology of the Low Income Cut-Offs and their application for this study. For a thorough review of the methodology of the Statistics Canada Low Income Cut-Offs and various alternatives see Wolfson and Evans (1989).

[8]Readers should be warned that small sample size may jeopardize analysis of some of these categories. I have attempted to confine myself to commenting on those trends where the sample size was sufficient to generate reliable results.

[9]The family type 'other' includes extended families and family spending units with more than two adults, for example.

[10]A Full-Time Equivalent Earner (FTE) is defined as a family head and/or spouse who, between them, work full-time for 49 or more weeks in a year. Thus a husband-wife family with two FTEs would work a combined 98 to 104 weeks in a year. Similarly, the category 0.1-0.4 FTEs is equivalent to 1-24 weeks; 0.5-0.9 is equivalent to 25 to 48 weeks; 1.1-1.4 FTEs is equivalent to 53 to 78 weeks; 1.5-1.9 FTEs is equivalent to 79 to 97 weeks in the labour force.

[11]Readers are cautioned that because of the limitations of sample size, these results are suggestive only.

[12]For example, for each family type, the percentage distribution of families by FTE as it was in 1973 (column 2), is multiplied by the *total* number of families in 1987 to arrive at an estimate of the number of families that would have been in each FTE category, had patterns of labour force participation remained at the 1973 levels. The *1987* incidence of poverty by FTE category (column 4) is then applied to the hypothetical distribution of families to arrive at an estimate of the number of poor families.

[13]See, for example *Transitions*, the Report of the Social Assistance Review Committee, Ontario Ministry of Community and Social Services (1988), and National Council of Welfare (1987).

[14]Since 1988 there has also been a supplement for children under the age of six. In 1988 the maximum supplement was $100, less 25% of the allowable child care expenses. In 1989 it was $200, less 25% of allowable child care expenses.

[15]This ignores provincial income tax foregone, which averages approximately 55% of the federal tax.

References

Buck, Carol
   1985   'Beyond Lalonde — Creating Health'. *Canadian Journal of Public Health*, vol. 76, supplement 1 (May/June).

Canadian Council on Social Development
   1984   'Not Enough — The Meaning and Measurement of Poverty in Canada'. Report of the CCSD Task Force on the Definition and Measurement of Poverty in Canada. Ottawa.

Evans, P.M.
   1987   'A Decade of Change: The FBA Caseload, 1975-1986'. Background Paper for the Social Assistance Review Committee [SARC] Report (June).

Harding M.
   1987   'The Relationship Between Economic Status and Health Status and Opportunities'. Background Paper for the SARC Report (March).

Hess, M.
   1987a   'An Overview of Poverty in Ontario'. Discussion Paper for the SARC Report (June).
   1987b   'The Working Poor: Their Dilemma and Assistance Through Provincial Income Supplementation Programs'. Discussion Paper for the SARC Report (April).

Irving, A.
   1987   'From No Poor Law to the Social Assistance Review: A History of Social Assistance in Ontario, 1791-1987'. Background Paper for the SARC Report (July).

Johnson, P.
   1987   'Guaranteed Annual Income in Theory and in Practice'. Discussion Paper for the SARC Report (April).

Lightman, E.
   1987   'Work Incentives and Disincentives in Ontario'. Background Paper for the SARC Report (February).

Mitchell, Andrew
   1990   'A Look at Poverty Lines'. Social Planning Council of Metropolitan Toronto, Social Infopac, vol. 9, no. 2 (June).

National Council of Welfare
   1987   'Welfare in Canada: The Tangled Safety Net'. Ottawa (November).
   1989   'The 1989 Budget and Social Policy'. Ottawa (September).

Novick, Marvyn, and Richard Volpe
   1990   'Perspectives on Social Practice'. A review prepared for the Children at Risk Sub-Committee of the Laidlaw Foundation (February).

Palmer, John L., Timothy Smeeding, and Barbara Boyle Torrey (eds)
   1988   *The Vulnerable*, Washington, D.C.: The Urban Institute Press.

Ross, D.
   1987   'Benefit Adequacy in Ontario'. Background Paper for the SARC Report (March).

Ross, D., and R. Shillington
1989 'The Canadian Fact Book on Poverty — 1989'. Canadian Council on Social Development. Ottawa.

Social Assistance Review Committee
1988 *Transitions*. Report of the Social Assistance Review Committee, Ontario Ministry of Community and Social Services. Toronto.

1988 *Guides for Family Budgeting, 1987*. Toronto.

Statistics Canada
1982 *Family Allowances and Related Programs*. Cat. no. 86-508.

1989 *Income Distributions by Size in Canada, 1988*. Cat. no. 13-207.

Wolfson, Michael C., and J.M. Evans
1989 'Statistics Canada's Low Income Cut-Offs: Methodological Concerns and Possibilities, A Discussion Paper'. Statistics Canada, Analytical Studies Branch, Research Paper Series (December).

Yalnizyan, Armine
1988 'A Statistical Profile of Toronto's Labour Market, 1976-1987'. *Social Planning Council of Metropolitan Toronto* (May).

Child Care in Ontario

Highlights

- There were about 119,945 children in Ontario enrolled in licensed centre-based child care programs in 1989. About 58% of these children also attend school.
- In Ontario, about 9,600 children were enroled in licensed private home day care in 1988. About 51% of these children also attend school.
- Schools are increasingly being used as sites for centre-based child care programs. In 1983 18% of the licensed capacity was located in schools. By 1989 this percentage had increased to 28%.
- Between 1983 and 1989 a total of 26,380 new licensed spaces were created. Of that total, about 50% of the spaces were created in centres located in schools.
- Employer/employee supported child care had a total of

2,601 licensed child care spaces as of 1988, or about 3% of the total number of spaces currently available.
- The licensed child care system currently accommodates fewer than one in 10 Ontario children.
- Child care fees consume a substantial amount of the income that most families in Ontario earn. It costs $4,140 to $6,480 per year to care for a child in a full day licensed child care centre, depending upon the age of the child. This amounts to 8% to 13% of the income of a typical Ontario family.
- The annual turnover rate of child care staff in Ontario is about 40%.
- The salaries of full-time child care staff in Ontario averaged $16,853.

Introduction

In Ontario three of the primary institutions that care for, socialize, and educate children are the family, the educational system, and the child care system. This chapter will focus on describing the child care system in Ontario, but it will also briefly discuss the variety of child care needs of families in Ontario, the settings in which child care is offered, the cost of care, and staffing issues. In addition, the relation between the educational and child care systems will be considered.

Child care meets a variety of needs. It assists working families by providing care for their children while they work; it assists parents who are being educated or pursuing further training; and it can provide children with an opportunity for social interaction and cognitive development. Child care can also be a necessary social support for high-risk families, and

it can be used by children who are physically or developmentally handicapped.

The child care system cares for children ranging in age from very young infants and toddlers to children 10 to 12 years of age who also attend school. An important characteristic of high quality child care is that it is developmentally appropriate to the age of the child. Zigler and Ennis (1989) propose that there are three major age groupings of children in child care: infants and toddlers, pre-schoolers, and children of school age. Although child care has traditionally focused on pre-school children, it has been suggested that increasing attention needs to be given to infants and toddlers and school-aged children.

One reason for paying more attention to school-aged children is that the educational system in Ontario is expanding,

This chapter was prepared by Norman Park.

and is increasingly likely to include younger children. In the 1987 Throne Speech the Ontario government announced that in the next five years the Ministry of Education will

- ensure that all school boards offer half day junior kindergarten for four-year-olds as well as provide half-day funding for five-year-olds.
- provide funding for school boards to offer full day senior kindergarten programs where classroom space permits.

At the same time, the child care system is increasingly caring for children who also attend school. Although it is difficult to obtain precise figures (partly because the child care and educational systems function independently), estimates from data to be presented later in this chapter suggest that over half of the children enroled in licensed child care — that is, child care regulated by the province of Ontario — also attend school.

Background

Although child care has only recently become a high-profile public issue, out-of-home child care has been in existence for some time. The first day care centres in Canada were founded in the 1800s. (This section relies heavily on material presented in Schulz, 1978.) At that time, the primary function of day care was to provide care for children whose parents were forced to leave home in order to earn a living. In addition, the Salles d'Asile in Montreal and nursery schools in Ontario aimed to provide an environment that could foster the social, emotional, and educational development of the child.

Government support at this time was very limited, though provincial and municipal governments occasionally provided small grants or per diem subsidies. This changed during the Second World War, when in 1942 the federal government authorized the Ministry of Labour to enter into a cost-sharing agreement with any provincial government wanting to establish child care facilities. The federal government stipulated that at least 75% of the nursery spaces had to be occupied by children whose mothers were working in essential war-time industries.

As the war ended, the federal government informed the Ontario government that child care was a provincial responsibility in peace-time and that it would end its funding. Although the Ontario government had initially intended to

terminate its funding as well, public protests led it to reconsider its decision. In 1946 the Day Nurseries Act was passed in Ontario. It contained funding provisions and minimum standards for licensing a day nursery.

The number of children needing some form of out-of-home child care increased dramatically when more and more women joined the work force. The increase in the female employment rate is a relatively recent phenomenon. In 1951 the female labour force participation rate in Ontario was 24%; today it is about 60%. As shown in Figure 3.1, between 1976 and 1988 the employment rate of mothers with children under 16 years of age in Ontario increased from about 45%

Figure 3.1: Maternal Labour Force Employment Rate, Ontario, 1976-1988

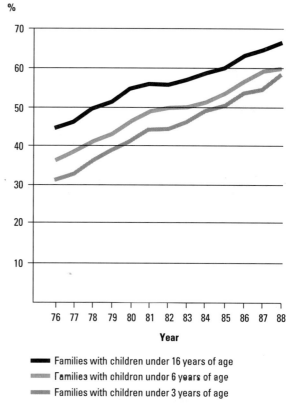

Source: Statistics Canada, Labour Force Survey. Cat. 71-001.

to 67%; that of mothers with children under 6 years increased from 36% to 59%; and that of mothers with children under 3 years increased from 32% to 56%.

As Figure 3.2 shows, similar increases are found when the employment rates of single mothers are examined, although the increases are attenuated, particularly for mothers with younger children. For single mothers with children under 16, the employment rate has increased between 1976 and 1986 from 51% to 61%; for those with children under 6, from 41% to 46%. and for those with children under 3, from 30% to 35%. One factor that may be responsible for the smaller increases in the employment rates of single mothers is that they have more difficulty finding accessible, affordable care for their children: for this reason they are

unable to find and keep jobs. According to a recent Statistics Canada (1988a) report, a March 1988 Survey of Job Opportunities for Canadian women revealed that of 88,000 mothers with children under 16 years of age who indicated that they wanted a job but had not taken active steps to seek work recently, 21,000, or 24%, had not sought work because of child care demands.

As shown in Table 3.1, the general pattern of results described above for Ontario as a whole is also found when trends in maternal employment rates are examined separately for Greater Toronto Area (GTA; Durham, Halton, Metro Toronto, Peel, York Regions) and the rest of the province, with maternal employment rates about 3% higher in the GTA than in the rest of Ontario.

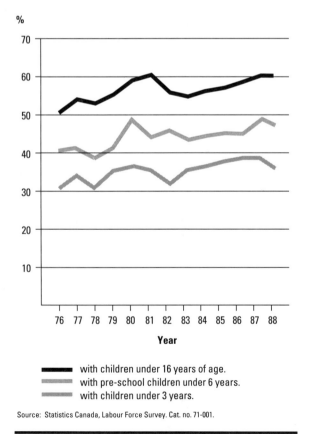

Figure 3.2:   Maternal labour force rate, no husband present, Ontario, 1976-1988

with children under 16 years of age.
with pre-school children under 6 years.
with children under 3 years.

Source: Statistics Canada, Labour Force Survey. Cat. no. 71-001.

Table 3.1
Maternal labour force employment rate
Greater Toronto Area (GTA) and rest of province

		with children < 16 years	with children < 6 years	with children < 3 years
1985	GTA	61.0	54.0	50.8
	Rest	58.9	52.6	50.2
1986	GTA	66.7	60.5	58.4
	Rest	60.6	54.0	50.4
1987	GTA	65.8	58.7	55.5
	Rest	63.2	56.7	54.1
1988	GTA	69.1	61.0	57.1
	Rest	65.4	57.6	55.1
1989	GTA	69.7	61.4	58.7
	Rest	66.9	58.8	55.9

Source: Statistics Canada, Labour Force Survey, Special Tabulations.

I   Supply of Child Care

In Ontario, the child care system operates in a variety of settings. In the educational system, by contrast, 97% of children use the publicly funded part of that system (either public or separate school), with only 3% attending privately funded schools. (Educational Statistics, 1987). The following list of possible child care arrangements is not intended to be exhaustive (for a more detailed discussion of different child care arrangements, see Lero, Brockman, Pence, and Charlesworth, 1985; Biemiller, Regan, and Lero, 1987), but it does describe some of the more common sorts of arrangements and illustrates the diversity in types of child care:

- children are cared for in their own home by their parents;
- children are cared for in their own homes by someone other than their parents (e.g., nanny, relative, sibling);
- children are cared for in another person's unlicensed home through an arrangement between the caregiver and the family;
- children are cared for in another person's home, which has been approved and is affiliated with a licensed private home day care agency;
- children are cared for in a licensed child care centre;
- children between 2 and 5 years of age are cared for in a nursery school for part of the day.

Biemiller, Regan, and Lero (1987) report that, according to a national 1981 survey performed by Statistics Canada (1982), the kind of child care arrangement depends upon the age of the child. When children are under 3 years of age they are most likely to be cared for either in their home, by their parents or some other caregiver, or in another home, by a relative or non-relative. When children reach 4 and 5 and attend kindergarten, they are more likely to use a form of non-home child care, and many are cared for in two or more non-parental settings.

The above list of child care arrangements can be classified into those that are unlicensed (the first three arrangements) and the remainder, which are licensed under the Day Nurseries Act (DNA) of Ontario.

By far the most frequently used form of child care is an unlicensed arrangement. Although accurate estimates are difficult to obtain, it has been estimated that over 80% of the children receiving non-parental care are in unlicensed child care (Report on the Task Force on Child Care, 1986). Responsibility for the supervision and monitoring of this sort of arrangement rests with the parent. No minimum training is required of the caregiver, and there are no safety requirements. For this reason it can be assumed that the quality of care received in informal arrangements is more varied than that offered in licensed centres. A powerful attraction of the unlicensed child care system for parents is that it costs considerably less than licensed care. The Ontario Municipal Social Services Association (OMSSA) (1987) cites evidence suggesting that the informal system costs 40% less than centre-based care.

The DNA provides the authority for the Ministry of Community and Social Services to establish conditions or standards that programs must satisfy in order to obtain and keep a license. These requirements cover a variety of areas including characteristics of the physical environment, nutrition, safety standards, and management, and are designed to prevent harm to the child. In addition, there are other standards that most experts agree promote high quality child care; these include staff-child ratios and staff qualifications.

In Ontario, two primary forms of licensed child care are available: group or centre-based child care and supervised private home day care. Centre-based programs provide temporary care for more than five children of 12 years and under. In the case of handicapped children, care may be provided up to 18 years of age. Group care facilities include day care centres, nursery schools, and before- and after-school programs.

Private home day care is the temporary care in a private home of five or fewer children of 12 years and under. The maximum number that can be cared for in a private home depends upon the ages of the children being looked after by the caregiver (including her own). Caregivers are not permitted to care for more than five children and if the children are young or handicapped, the number allowed is reduced: for example, no more than two children under 2 years of age, or three children under 3 can be cared for at any one time. Licensed private home day care agencies are responsible for recruiting, supervising, and supporting the individual providers, who are responsible for the care of children under their supervision in their homes. Providers themselves, however, are not licensed.

Figure 3.3 shows the enrolment of children in centre-based licensed child care programs from 1984 to 1989, by age of child, for the GTA and the rest of the province. The data were supplied by the Day Nurseries Information System (DNIS), a computerized database system of the Ministry of Community and Social Services, that keeps track of a variety of aspects of centre-based child care. According to that system, children are considered to be *enrolled* if they attend the program for either part of a day or a full day. Such enrolment has increased substantially. In 1984, a total of 84,114 children were enrolled in centre-based programs. By 1989, this total had increased by 40% to 119,045. In presenting the data, the age breakdown of children and the labels used to describe them are taken from the DNIS system, which was developed several years ago. One difficulty with the age breakdown is

Figure 3.3:   Child care enrolment in centre-based programs by age grouping, GTA [a] and rest of province

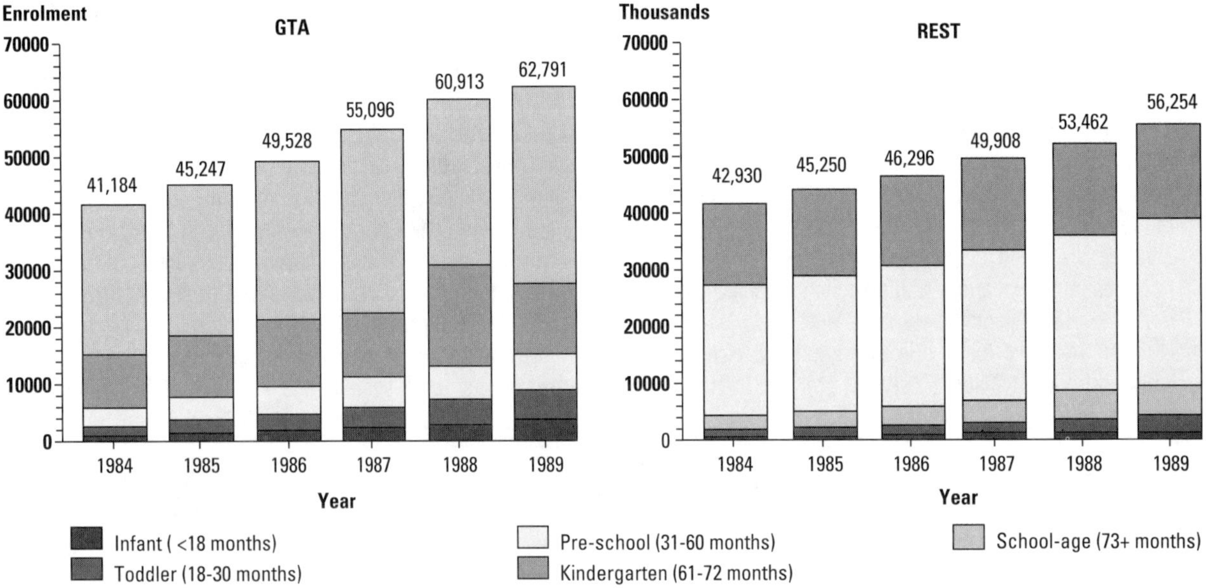

Source: Ministry of Community and Social Services, Day Nurseries Information System.
a) GTA – Greater Toronto Area (Durham, Halton, Metro Toronto, Peel, York regions).

Table 3.2
Child care enrolment by age grouping, GTA and rest of province

		Infant	Toddler	Pre-school	Kindergarten	School age	Total[a]
1984	GTA	.9	2.2	29.2	10.9	5.7	100
	Rest	.7	2.6	28.1	17.6	2.0	
1985	GTA	1.0	3.0	28.7	11.4	5.9	100
	Rest	.8	3.0	27.0	17.2	1.9	
1986	GTA	1.0	3.6	28.1	11.6	7.4	100
	Rest	.8	2.9	26.6	16.1	2.0	
1987	GTA	1.1	4.0	28.8	10.2	8.5	100
	Rest	.9	3.4	25.7	15.1	2.4	
1988	GTA	1.4	4.3	27.9	10.3	9.4	100
	Rest	.8	3.5	25.3	14.1	3.0	
1989	GTA	1.4	4.2	28.0	10.2	8.9	100
	Rest	.9	3.7	25.2	13.6	3.9	

[a]Some totals may not add up to 100 because of rounding.

Source: Ministry of Community and Social Services, Day Nurseries Information System.

Table 3.3
Number of children of different ages enrolled in PHDC by region, 1988

Region	Infant	Toddler	Pre-school	Kindergarten	School age	Total
Central	960	750	1,317	577	916	4,520
Rest of province	757	716	1,419	670	1,455	5,017
Total	1,717	1,466	2,736	1,247	2,371	9,537
%	18	15	29	13	25	100

Source: Norpark (1989), *Report on the PHDC in Ontario*. Toronto: Ministry of Community and Social Services.

that the 'pre-school' category now actually represents a mixture of pre-schoolers and children in the school system.

Table 3.2 indicates the percentage of children, by age group, enrolled in centre-based programs between 1984 and 1989. As it shows, the age distribution has changed in that today programs are more likely to have younger children (infants and toddlers) and school-age children than they were in 1984.

A second point to note is that with the government announcement in the 1987 Throne Speech that all school boards throughout the province will offer junior kindergarten programs, it is probable that the majority of the children in centre-based care will also attend school. Indeed, it can be estimated that when this announcement is implemented, as many as 58% of the children who attend centre-based programs in Ontario will be attending school.

Data about changes in the enrolment of children in family day care or licensed private home day care (PHDC) programs are more difficult to obtain because this information is not systematically collected and stored in a database. Nonetheless, on the basis of data collected and reviewed by Norpark (1989), the following points can be made. First, as shown in Table 3.3, about 9,600 children were enrolled in private home day care programs in 1988; that is, about one-tenth as many as in centre-based programs. Second, the age distribution of children attending PHDC programs is dramatically different. Infants, toddlers, and school-age children are much more likely to be found in PHDC than in centre-based programs, while pre-schoolers and kindergarten-aged children are more likely to be found in centre-based programs. This result can in part be attributed to the choices of parents (Lero, Brockman, Pence, and Charlesworth, 1985; Norpark, 1989; Pence and Goelman, 1987), who prefer to have their

children in a more home-like or family atmosphere when they are younger, and want them to have more opportunities for social interaction with similarly aged children when they are older.

It can be estimated from data collected by Norpark (1989) that about 51% of the children enrolled in PHDC also attend school. The same study shows that numbers in private home day care are growing rapidly. Between 1981 and 1988, enrolment in the Ministry of Community and Social Services Central Region (which roughly corresponds to the GTA) has more than doubled, from 2,063 to 4,386 children, while in the rest of the province it has risen from 2,899 to 5,888. In all, the number of children enrolled in PHDC grew from 4,962 to 10,274.

Table 3.4 summarizes enrolment in centre-based and PHDC programs in 1988 and compares the enrolment of children of different ages to the number of children of that age as determined from the 1986 Census. The result of this comparison is shown in the last column, showing the percentage of children in licensed child care (either centre-based or PHDC). Although some error has been introduced by virtue of the fact that 1988 enrolment data are being compared with 1986 Census data, this error is small and should not affect the conclusions drawn here.

The first point to note is that, overall, about 9% of the children 10 and under living in Ontario are enrolled on either a part-or full-day basis in some form of licensed child care. Second, the percentage of children enrolled in licensed care varies greatly with age. Only about 2% of all infants are cared for in the licensed child care system. This increases to about 8% when children are toddlers (18 to 30 months), and to over 20% at 30 to 72 months. Finally, at ages over 6 but under 11, the percentage drops dramatically, to about

Table 3.4
Enrolment in licensed child care programs by age of child,
compared with number of children in Ontario of that age

Age of child	Centre-based[a]	PHDC[b]	Total enrolment in licensed care	Census[c]	% of children in licensed care
Infant (< 18 mos.)	2,509	1,717	4,226	188,652	2
Toddler (18–30 mos.)	8,922	1,466	10,388	122,895	8
Pre-school (30–60 mos.)	60,926	2,736	63,662	303,709	21
Kindergarten (61–72 mos.)	27,871	1,247	29,118	120,420	24
School-age (73–132 mos.)	14,147	2,371	16,518	599,525	3
Total	114,275	9,537	123,912	1,335,200	9

[a]See Figure 3.3.
[b]See Table 3.3.
[c]Number of children by age group in Census families in private occupied households, Province of Ontario, 1986.

3%.

A number of factors are responsible for the variation in the percentage of children enrolled in day care. Very young children are less likely to be enrolled in licensed care programs because, given maternity policies and voluntary leaves of absence, fewer mothers with very young children work full-time outside the home. In addition, licensed infant/toddler care is expensive and in short supply.

The increase in the percentage of children aged 30 to 72 months enrolled in licensed programs can probably be attributed to several factors, including a higher maternal employment rate; parental preferences for child care situations that provide an opportunity for social interaction and educational stimulation; somewhat lower child care fees; and increased availability of space.

A number of factors are probably responsible for the low enrolment of children over 6 in the licensed child care system. One reason may be that parents believe that licensed care is less critical for such children because they are older and also because the number of hours of care needed to cover the gap between school and the parents' return from work is small. In addition, parents are probably more likely to permit these older children to be cared for by a brother or sister. It is also possible that the licensed child care system has not been designed with this age group in mind. The training that staff receive and the activities and environment of child care programs may be less appropriate for this age group, in which case children may 'vote with their feet' and leave the program. All of this raises the possibility that a number of older children spend time on their own after school before their parents return home. These have been called 'latchkey' children. It is difficult to estimate how frequently children are left alone, though a 1981 nationally conducted survey of Statistics Canada and reported by Biemiller, Regan, and Lero (1987) found that as children become older they are increasingly likely to be left either on their own or in the care of a sibling. Parents reported leaving about 5% of children aged 6 to 9 on their own, about 13% of children aged 10 to 11, and 26% of children aged 12 to 13.

Operator Type

There is considerable discussion (e.g., Report of the Task Force on Child Care, 1986) in the child care community about whether there should be commercial child care in Ontario. Those who support commercial care argue that it increases competition among agencies, which may result in higher quality at lower cost. Opponents of commercial care argue that there is little incentive for commercial agencies to compete by improving the quality of care offered, since there are too few spaces currently available to meet demand. Furthermore, in order to maintain profitability, commercial agencies may cut corners, lowering the quality of care. A recent large and well-designed study conducted in the United States has found that non-profit agencies tend to offer higher quality care than commercial agencies (Whitebook, Howes, and Phillips, 1990). Results consistent with this finding have also been obtained in Ontario (Norpark, unpublished data).

Although many different types of operators of centre-based programs are found in Ontario, the three most common are non-profit agencies, agencies operated by municipalities, and commercial or for-profit agencies. Commercial programs make up about 36% of the licensed capacity of centre-based programs in the Province (from Direct Operating Grant [DOG] database, 1988). As illustrated in Table 3.5, commercial programs tend to have a higher percentage of their licensed capacity in the younger age categories (infant, toddler, and pre-schooler), while non-profit agencies tend to have a higher percentage of their capacity occupied by school-age and handicapped children.

Operators of PHDC programs fall into the same three broad categories as centre-based programs: municipal, non-profit, and commercial. However, as Figure 3.4 demonstrates, the commercial PHDC sector is smaller than the commercial centre-based sector, with only about 8% of total enrolment in PHDC programs. Table 3.6, which shows the same data as Figure 3.4 but in percentage terms, shows that commercial PHDC agencies tend to have a higher percentage of infants and a lower percentage of pre-schoolers than do non-profit agencies.

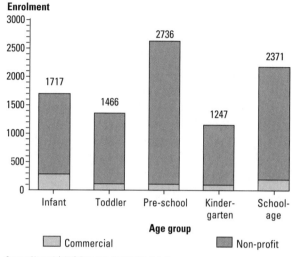

Figure 3.4: Number of children of different ages enrolled in PHDC, commercial and non-profit agencies, Ontario, 1988

Source: Norpark (1989), Report on the PHDC in Ontario. Toronto: Ministry of Community and Social Services.

Table 3.5
Licensed capacity of commercial and non-profit centre-based child care programs, Ontario, 1988

Type of child	Commercial[a]	Non-profit	Total
Infant	3.4	2.8	3.0
Toddler	11.6	8.3	9.5
Pre-school	74.2	63.3	67.2
Kindergarten	3.9	3.6	3.7
School-age	6.5	19.3	14.8
Handicapped	0.3	2.8	1.9
Total[b]	100.0	100.0	100.0

[a]Social Services, the DOG Data Base does not include the capacity of new or expanded commercial programs after December 1987; it does include closures of commercial programs during 1988. As a consequence, the total capacity of commercially operated programs is slightly underestimated.
[b]Some totals may not add up to 100 because of rounding.

Source: Child Care Branch, Ministry of Community and Social Services, Direct Operating Grant Data Base, 13 January, 1989.

Table 3.6
Number and percent of children of different ages enrolled in PHDC, commercial and non-profit agencies, Ontario, 1988[a]

Age group	Commercial		Non-Profit		TOTAL	
Infant	279	35.7%	1438	16.5%	1717	18.0%
Toddler	110	14.1%	1356	15.5%	1466	15.4%
Pre-school	107	13.7%	2629	30.0%	2736	28.7%
Kindergarten	95	12.2%	1152	13.2%	1247	13.1%
School-age	191	24.4%	2180	24.9%	2371	24.9%
TOTAL[a]	782	100%	8755	100%	9537	100%

[a]Some totals may not add up to 100 because of rounding.

Source: Norpark (1989), *Report on the PHDC in Ontario*. Toronto: Ministry of Community and Social Services.

Building Type

Table 3.7 shows the percentage of capacity for licensed centre-based programs in Ontario by type of building from 1983 to 1989. Perhaps the most striking general impression to be taken from this table is the diversity of buildings that are used for child care. Many of them were not originally designed for this purpose, and so the suitability of the physical environment for child care can be questioned. Examination of the total licensed capacity (the right-most column) shows that there has been a systematic, substantial increase in the licensed capacity of centre-based programs, from 69,766 in 1983 to 96,146 in 1989. (Careful readers may have noted that the enrolment figures in Figure 3.3 are higher than the capacity figures in Table 3.7. The differences arise because capacity counts only spaces, which can be occupied by more than one child enrolled at different times during the day.)

Has this increase in licensed capacity been concentrated in certain types of buildings? Judging by the percentages shown in Table 3.7, the growth is occurring primarily in the schools, particularly those located in the GTA. In 1983, 18% of the licensed capacity was in schools; by 1989 this percentage had increased to 28%, with most of the growth occurring in GTA, where the figure increased from 10% to 18%. The growth in the use of schools in the GTA can be attributed to the more rapid increase in the population of this region in recent years than in other parts of Ontario. More generally, the growth in the use of schools as places to locate child centres can be attributed at least in part to a policy of the Ontario government that requires new school buildings to include child care facilities and encourages school boards to retrofit all old schools with child care centres. In addition, school boards are giving priority to child care centres for the use of vacant space in schools.

One way to think of this growth in the use of schools is in terms of the absolute number of licensed spaces. Between 1983 and 1989 a total of 26,380 new licensed spaces were created. Of that total 13,203 spaces, or about 50%, were

Table 3.7
Percentage of total licensed capacity for day nurseries
by building type and location, Ontario, 1983–1989

		Apartment complex (%)	Church (%)	House (%)	Nursery bldg. (%)	Public bldg. (%)	Recreation bldg. (%)	School (%)	Other (%)	Total
1983	GTA	7	16	5	9	5	1	10	2	69,766
	Rest	1	13	5	9	4	2	8	3	
1984	GTA	7	16	5	9	4	1	11	2	70,284
	Rest	1	12	5	9	4	2	9	3	
1985	GTA	7	15	5	9	4	1	12	3	74,245
	Rest	1	11	5	9	4	2	8	3	
1986	GTA	7	14	5	8	4	2	14	3	78,884
	Rest	1	11	5	9	4	2	8	4	
1987	GTA	6	14	5	7	5	1	16	4	85,566
	Rest	1	11	5	8	4	2	8	4	
1988	GTA	6	13	5	7	4	1	17	4	92,531
	Rest	1	10	5	8	4	2	9	5	
1989	GTA	6	13	5	7	4	1	18	4	96,146
	Rest	1	10	5	7	4	2	10	5	

Source: Ministry of Community and Social Services, Day Nurseries Information System.

created in centres located in schools. Table 3.7 also indicates that the percentage of licensed programs located in churches decreased from 29% in 1983 to 23% in 1989. This decline in licensed capacity does not represent a drop in the absolute number of spaces located in churches — that number has actually increased by about 2,000 — but it does indicate that the proportion of church space has diminished.

Employer/Employee-supported Child Care

Employer/employee-supported child care has received considerable attention as a proposed solution to child care concerns. In this form of arrangement, an employer — or a group of employees, or a partnership among interested groups — sponsors a child care centre located in or near the workplace to meet the child care needs of parents employed at the workplace. In 1988 a total of 2,601 licensed child care spaces (1,169 in the GTA and 1,257 in the rest of the province) were provided in this way, or only about 3% of the total number of spaces currently available. Most of the employer/employee spaces (2,147, or 82%) are supported by public or non-profit employers such as the Ontario public service, hospitals, and colleges with only 454 (about 18%) from the private sector (Ministry of Community and Social Services [MCSS], Child Care Branch).

A number of factors appear to restrict the general applicability of this form of child care. Many workplaces are not suited for child care. Many employers do not believe that child care should be their responsibility, and in addition are concerned about the long-term cost of workplace child care. In addition, many parents prefer child care arrangements that are close to home or, for school-aged children, located in or close to their schools. For these and other reasons, employer-supported child care is probably best thought of as an arrangement that may meet certain particular needs, but will not become widely available.

II Need for Child Care

A comprehensive child care system can serve a variety of functions or goals. This section provides estimates of the number of child care spaces required to meet the needs of working parents. It also identifies circumstances other than work that result in parents' needing child care. The wide range of these needs means that flexible, responsive services are required.

Children in Ontario have varied needs as well. There are large numbers of aboriginal children, children from a variety of ethnic backgrounds, francophone children, and children with physical and developmental handicaps. Each of these groups has special needs requiring consideration in the design and operation of child care. At the same time, the care provided must be developmentally appropriate (Zigler and Ennis, 1989; Scarr, Phillips and McCartney, 1989), accommodating children from very young infants and toddlers to those 10 or 12 years of age and attending school.

Number of Child Care Spaces Needed

It is difficult to estimate how many children need child care because it is hard to decide which children to include in a count. The *New Directions* (1987) child care policy statement of the Ontario government proposed that child care should become a 'public service' to which all families should have reasonable access. On the basis of this policy an estimate of the number of child care spaces needed can be obtained from Census (1986) data, which showed 1,335,200 children under 11 years of age living in Ontario. Since there are about 129,045 children in licensed child care (119,045 in centre-based case plus about 10,000 in private home day care), it could be estimated that the licensed child care system currently accommodates fewer than 1 in 10 Ontario children who may 'need' care. This estimate exaggerates the 'need', however, because even if child care were to become a social service available to all children in Ontario, it would not be compulsory, and a number of parents might decide not to participate. Nevertheless, the estimate is useful in that it provides an upper limit on the number of spaces required.

A second and more frequently used approach to estimating 'need' is to base estimates on the labour force participation rate of mothers. The assumption made here is that because mothers have traditionally assumed primary responsibility for child care, there is a need for child care when they are working. Table 3.8, adapted from Ram (1990), indicates that because of increases in the labour-force participation of mothers between 1971 and 1986, there has been a dramatic increase in the number of children needing care in Canada. The percentage of children under 6 years needing care increased from 23% in 1971 to 50% in 1986; for children 6 to 14 years, it rose from 30% in 1971 to 54% in 1986.

Table 3.8
Children in families and estimates of children needing care by age, Canada, 1971, 1976, 1981, 1986

	1971	1976	1981	1986
Children < 6 years				
Total in families (000)	2,196	2,045	2,075	2,109
In families with wife in labour force (000)	506	641	850	1,046
% needing care	23	31	41	50
Children 6–14 years				
Total in families (000)	4,087	3,680	3,251	3,141
In families with wife in labour force (000)	1,230	1,443	1,541	1,699
% needing care	30	39	47	54

Source: Adapted from B. Ram (1990), 'Women's employment and child care'. In Statistics Canada, *Current Demographic Analysis: New Trends in the Family.* Cat. 91-535 E. Ottawa: Ministry of Supply and Services.

When these percentages are applied to Ontario, it may be estimated that about 370,000 children under 6, and about 324,000 from 6 to 11, 'need' child care. Given that there are currently about 124,000 children enrolled in licensed child care, about 18% of the need is currently met through the licensed child care system.

This latter estimate needs to be treated with some caution (Lero, 1989), however. On the one hand, it overestimates need because some families may prefer to juggle work schedules or have older siblings or relatives provide care for their children. On the other hand, it dramatically underestimates need because it assumes that only working mothers need child care, and that those whose mothers do *not* work outside the home do *not* need it. As Table 3.8 indicates, in 1986 about 50% of the children in Canada under 6 years and 46% of those 6 to 14 have mothers who do not work. Some unknown percentage of these children also need child care.

In summary, the licensed child care system in Ontario accommodates only a small fraction of those children who 'need' child care. Although precise figures are difficult to obtain, it is estimated here that the current system is meeting more than 10% but less than 18% of the need.

Variety of Needs

A number of investigators (e.g., Report of the Task Force on Child Care, 1986; Lero, 1989) have pointed out that child care serves several purposes or functions. A partial list largely based on Report of the Task Force on Child Care (1986) illustrates the variety of these functions. Child care can be used when both parents or a single parent is working or engaged in an employment-related activity; when parents work shifts or extended hours; when parents are continuing their education or are enrolled in training programs; when children or families have special needs (e.g., parents with health problems; families with a background, or risk, of child abuse); and in specific instances: during family illness, when children are sick, or in periods of seasonal employment for parents (e.g., farmers, recreational workers, etc.).

III Costs of Child Care

Paying the costs of child care is primarily the responsibility of parents in Ontario. A subsidy is provided only if financial need is demonstrated and if a subsidy program is locally available. Figure 3.5 shows the average maximum daily fees for children of different ages receiving different levels of service. Clearly there are substantial variations in the cost of care, depending upon the service offered and the age of the child. Because more staff time is required with younger children, infant care costs more than care for toddlers, which in turn is more expensive than care for pre-schoolers. Care for school-aged children costs the least, partly because the staff-child ratios are higher, and partly because school-aged children are in care programs for only a limited part of each day, typically after school and perhaps also before school begins and during lunch.

Child care fees consume a substantial amount of the income of most families in the child-care market. For example, the median income of an Ontario family with two children under 16 years of age was $48,854 in 1988 (Statistics Canada, 1988b). If one of their children were in full-day licensed care, that would cost them between $4,140 and $6,480 per year, depending upon the age of the child: from 8% to 13% of their annual income. If the same family had two children in care, those costs could easily exceed $10,000, or about 20% of the annual income of a typical family.

Another way of thinking about child care costs is to compare the fees paid by parents with the costs of providing a child's education, which are paid by the province of Ontario. In 1986, the net expenditure per pupil in elementary schools was $4,016; the cost for 41 weeks of full-day care for a child of kindergarten age would be about $3,926. In other words,

Figure 3.5: Average maximum daily fees for children of different ages, Ontario, 1988

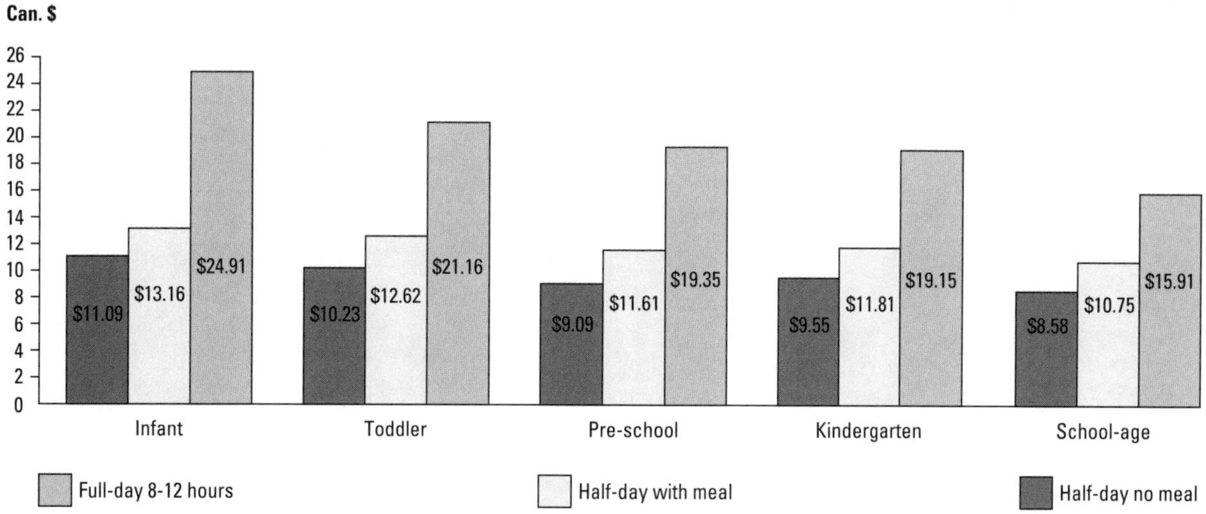

Can. $

	Infant	Toddler	Pre-school	Kindergarten	School-age
Half-day no meal	$11.09	$10.23	$9.09	$9.55	$8.58
Half-day with meal	$13.16	$12.62	$11.61	$11.81	$10.75
Full-day 8-12 hours	$24.91	$21.16	$19.35	$19.15	$15.91

◼ Full-day 8-12 hours   ◻ Half-day with meal   ◼ Half-day no meal

Source: The Levy-Coughlin Partnership (1989), *Report of Results from Phase 2 Surveys* (Toronto: Ministry of Community and Social Services).

the costs are not all that different. This similarity in costs can be attributed in part to the fact that the child care system, despite the significantly lower salaries of its staff (about half what they are in the education system) typically has many fewer children being cared for by each staff person.

Subsidies

Three levels of government are currently involved in funding subsidies for families in need. The federal government pays 50% of the cost of subsidized child care through the Canada Assistance Plan, which also provides funding for a range of other social services; the province of Ontario funds 30%; and the municipality is responsible for the remaining 20%. This funding arrangement can result in regional differences in the accessibility of subsidized care because municipalities differ in their willingness or ability to provide funding.

In Ontario, unlike most other provinces and territories (Report of the Task Force on Child Care, 1986), a needs test is used to determine whether a family is eligible for subsidy. In order to calculate how much money a family can contribute toward the cost of child care, the needs test determines the total available income (income and liquid assets) and then subtracts from it permitted expenditures (e.g., heat, telephone, rent, health costs) to arrive at the amount of money available for child care. More typically, other prov-

inces use an income test to determine eligibility; families are eligible for subsidy if the combined after-tax income of the parents is below a certain figure. In most provinces there is also a requirement that the single parent or both parents in a two-parent family are working or being trained in order to be eligible for a subsidy.

Data from the Child Care Branch of the MCSS show that the total number of subsidized spaces in Ontario increased by about 50% between 1985 and 1990, from 32,000 to 45,000 (the number remained unchanged in 1986, at 32,000, but rose to 37,000 in 1987, and to 41,000 in 1988). However, in spite of that impressive increase, the National Council of Welfare (1988) has estimated that in 1987 only about 10% of children eligible for a partial or full subsidy in Ontario actually received it. In Metropolitan Toronto in 1990, for example, 6,600 families have been approved for subsidy but are on a waiting list because there are no subsidized child care spaces available (personal communication, Ministry of Community and Social Services).

Table 3.9 shows that the child care expenditures by the province of Ontario have increased tenfold between 1977 and 1990. Some of this increase can be attributed to inflation. Even when that factor is taken into consideration, however, expenditures have increased more than four-fold over those fourteen years.

Table 3.9
Expenditure on child care
by province of Ontario,
1977–1990

Year	Child care expenditure ($)
1976–77	29,000,000
1977–78	35,000,000
1978–79	38,000,000
1979–80	42,000,000
1980–81	50,000,000
1981–82	60,000,000
1982–83	74,000,000
1983–84	81,000,000
1984–85	87,000,000
1985–86	108,000,000
1986–87	139,000,000
1987–88	179,000,000
1988–89[a]	289,000,000
1989–90[a]	343,000,000

[a] Estimate

Source: Ministry of Community and Social Services, Child Care Branch.

IV   Staffing Issues

Staffing issues are receiving increasing attention in Ontario as well as in other provinces and the United States. These issues are important because a number of studies have found that the quality of child care depends upon staff qualifications (e.g., Howes, 1983; Ruopp, Travers, Glantz and Coelen, 1979; Whitebook, Howes and Phillips, 1990).

One important staffing issue is the appropriateness of the training, education, and qualifications of staff to meet the varied needs of child care in Ontario. A second is the high turnover rate of staff. Although no systematic data have been collected in Ontario, two recent Ontario studies conducted by Norpark (unpublished data) have found annual staff turnover rates of about 40%. This estimate is very close to the result in a US national child care study, which reported an annual turnover rate of 41% (Whitebook, Howes and Phillips, 1990). These turnover rates are extremely high. By contrast, in the Ontario elementary school system the annual turnover rate for 1986-87 was only 9% (Educational Statistics, Ontario, 1987).

High turnover rates are of concern for a variety of reasons. In addition to creating serious administrative problems, there are also results indicating that children who experience a number of changes in caregivers progress less well in their social and cognitive developments than children with stable child care (e.g., Howes and Stewart, 1988).

The high turnover in child care staff is the result of a number of interrelated factors (e.g., Whitebook, Howes, and Phillips, 1990). One contributing factor is the low salaries of child care staff. In 1988 the salaries for full-time child care staff averaged $16,853, with variations depending upon the type of operator (Levy-Couglin Partnership, 1990). The average salary for full-time staff was highest in municipal centres ($23,889), followed by non-profit centres ($17,820), and then by commercial centres ($13,748). These salaries are considerably lower than those of teachers. In 1987-88 the median salary of elementary teachers was $42,663. Thus, on average, full-time child care workers received about 40% the salary of elementary teachers, or almost $26,000 less per year.

These amounts reflect the salaries received after application of the Direct Operating Grant (DOG), a major initiative of the Ministry of Community and Social Services introduced in 1988 to supplement salaries and benefits. In a recent survey the Levy-Coughlin Partnership (1990) found that the DOG increased salaries substantially, raising the salaries of full-time staff by $2,931 in non-profit agencies and $1,318 in commercial agencies.

V   Problems and Issues

In this section some underlying themes emerging from the chapter are identified and discussed. Clearly the child care system in Ontario is currently seriously underfunded. Families paying full fees must spend a considerable percentage of their annual income on child care; the number of subsidized child care spaces is far smaller than the demand for them; and child care staff are underpaid, resulting in high annual turnover.

Although notable in its diversity, the current system is not comprehensive and cannot respond to the variety of needs of parents and children in Ontario. Models of child care that can effectively meet these varied needs must be developed. The Ministry of Community and Social Services has recognized this and is currently implementing and evaluating several pilot projects that are aimed at meeting such needs as those of parents working shifts, parents needing extended hours of care for their child, parents needing emergency or short-term child care, and parents needing care for their sick children.

For high-quality child care, the curriculum, physical environment, and interactions between staff and children must be appropriate to the developmental needs of three major age groups: infants and toddlers, pre-schoolers, and school-aged children. The child care system must ensure that the training of staff, the activities in child care programs, and the physical environment are appropriate to the age group of the children being cared for.

One issue of particular concern is the care and education of school-aged children. This age group is increasingly part of the licensed child care system, and with the 1987 Throne Speech announcement that junior and senior kindergarten programs will be expanded, there is every indication that even more children will be splitting their day between school and child care.

How can the education and child care systems can be more effectively co-ordinated? Among the issues requiring consideration are (1) whether school-aged child care programs should be located on school premises; (2) how the activities of schools and child care centres can be better co-ordinated; and (3) how children should be transported between schools and child care centres.

Perhaps even more fundamental is the need to reconsider the qualifications and training that should be required of people working with children of this age. Currently there are two separate training programs culminating in different qualifications. A teacher typically has a BA or B.Ed. from university, while a child care worker has an ECE diploma from a community college. At this point, it is difficult for staff to move between the educational and child care systems because different qualifications are required by the two systems. A number of members of the child care community have indicated that it should be easier for qualified child care workers to become qualified as teachers. If this action were taken, it would increase the career options for child care staff. However, it would most probably result in an exodus from the lower-paying child care positions to the higher-paying teaching positions.

There are also differences in operating standards that need to be considered. In addition to the issues of staff training and salaries, it is important to examine the differences that exist in the set-up and organization of facilities (e.g., wash-rooms, kitchens, playgrounds) (Lero and Kyle, 1989) and in staff-child ratios. As indicated in the DNA, child care centres are required to have staff-child ratios of 1:15 for children over 6 years, 1:12 for children 5 to 6 years; and 1:8 for children 30 months to 5 years. In contrast, the educational system has a staff-child ratio of 1:20 (Educational Statistics, 1987).

A final issue requiring consideration is that of jurisdiction. Should all types of licensed child care come under the jurisdiction of education, should only school-age child care come under education, or should child care remain under the jurisdiction of social services? The jurisdiction question cannot be adequately examined in this chapter. Such a discussion should build on the work of others (e.g., Early Primary Education Project [1985]; Advisory Council on Day Care [1976]; LaPierre [1980]; Grubb and Lazerson [1982]) who have identified a number of relevant factors.

References

Advisory Council on Day Care
    1976   *Final Report.* Toronto: Ministry of Community and Social Services.

Akyeampong, E.B.
    1988   'Women Wanting Work, but Not Working Due to Child Care Demands'. *The Labour Force, Statistics Canada.*

Biemiller, A., E. Regan, and D. Lero
    1987   'Early Childhood Programs in Canada'. Pp. 32-58 in L. Katz (ed.), *Current Topics in Early Childhood Education.* New York: Plenum Press.

Borjeson, C.
    1987   *Provincial Day Care Subsidy Systems in Canada.* Background document produced for the Special Committee on Child Care.

Day Nurseries Act
    1983   (Regulation R235.) Toronto.

Early Primary Education Project
    1985   Report of the Early Primary Education Project. Toronto: Ontario Ministry of Education.

Grubb, W. Norton, and Marvin Lazerson
    1982   *Broken Promises: How Americans Fail Their Children.* New York: Basic.

Henriques, H., and F. Vaillancourt
    1988   'The Demand for Child Care Services in Canada'. *Applied Economics*, 20: 385-94.

Hernandez, J., and D.E. Myers

1988 'Family Composition, Parents' Work, and the Need for Child Care among Preschool Children: 1940-1987'. Paper presented at the annual meeting of the Population Association of America, New Orleans, La., April.

Howes, C.
1983 'Caregiver Behavior in Centre and Family Day Care'. *Journal of Applied Developmental Psychology*, 4: 99-107.

Howes, Carolee, and Phyllis Stewart
1987 'Child's Play with Adults, Toys and Peers: An Examination of Family and Child-care Influences'. *Developmental Psychology* 23: 423-30.

LaPierre, L.L.
1980 *To Herald a Child: The Report of the Commission of Inquiry into the Education of the Young Child*. Toronto: Ontario Public School Men Teachers' Federation.

Lero, D.S.
1989 *Child Care Needs and Child Care Use Patterns*. National Symposium on Social Supports, 28-29 March.

Lero, D.S., L. Brockman, A. Pence, and M. Charlesworth
1985 *Parents' Needs, Preferences, and Concerns about Child Care: Case Studies of 336 Canadian Families*. Background paper prepared for the Task Force on Child Care. Ottawa: Status of Women.

Lero, D.S. and I. Kyle
1990 'Families and Children in Ontario'. Pp. 25-72 in L. Johnson and D. Barnhorst (eds), *Children, Families and Public Policy in the 90s*. Toronto: Thompson Educational Publishing.

1988 *The National Child Care Study*. University of Guelph.

The Levy-Coughlin Partnership
1989 *Report of the Results from Phase 2 Survey*. Toronto: Ministry of Community and Social Services.

1990 *Report for Short-term Evaluation of the Direct Operating Grants*. Toronto: Ministry of Community and Social Services.

Ministry of Community and Social Services
1988 *New Directions for Child Care—Report on Year One: 1987/88*. Toronto: Author.

Ministry of Education
1985 *Report of the Early Primary Education Project*. Ontario.

1987 *Education Statistics*. Toronto: Author.

National Council of Welfare
1988 *Child Care: A Better Alternative*. Ottawa: Ministry of Supply and Services.

Norpark
1989 *Report on the PHDC in Ontario*. Toronto: Ministry of Community and Social Services.

Ontario Municipal Social Services Association
1987 *A Report on Child Care Services in Ontario*. Prepared for the Social Assistance Review Committee.

Pence, A., and H. Goelman
1987 'Silent Partners: Parents of Children in Three Types of Day Care'. *Early Childhood Research Quarterly*, 2: 103-18.

Ram, B.
1990 'Women's employment and child care'. In Statistics Canada, *Current Demographic Analysis: New Trends in the Family*. Cat. 91-535E. Ottawa: Ministry of Supply and Services.

Report of the Task Force on Child Care
1986 Ottawa: Ministry of Supply and Services.

Robins, P.K. and R.G. Spiegelman
1978 'An Economic Model of the Demand for Child Care'. *Economic Inquiry*, 16: 83-94.

Ruopp, R., J. Travers, F. Glantz, and C. Coelen
1979 *Children at the Centre: Final Results of the National Day Care Study*. Boston: Abt Associates.

Scarr, S., D. Phillips, and K. McCartney
1989 'Dilemmas of Child Care in the United States: Employed Mothers and Children at Risk'. *Canadian Psychology* 30: 126-39.

Schulz, P.V.
1978 'Day Care in Canada: 1850-1962'. Pp. 137-58 in Gallager-Ross (ed.), *Good Day Dare: Fighting for It, Getting It, Keeping It*. Toronto: Women's Educational Press.

Statistics Canada
1982 *Initial results from the 1981 survey of child care arrangements from the labour force*. Statistics Canada, Cat. 71-601, vol. 38, no. 8. Ottawa: Ministry of Supply and Services.

1988a 'Women Wanting Work but not Working due to Child Care Demands'. *The Labour Force*. Ottawa.

1988b *Income distribution by size in Canada, 1988*. Catalogue no. 13-207. Ottawa: Ministry of Supply and Services.

Status of Women
1986 *Report of the Task Force on Child Care*. Ottawa: Canada Government Publishing Centre.

Whitebook, M., C. Howes, and D. Phillips
1990 *Who Cares? Child Care Teachers and the Quality of Care in America*. Oakland, Ca: Child Care Employee Project.

Zigler, E., and P. Ennis
1989 'The Child Care Crisis in America'. *Canadian Psychology*, 30: 116-25.

CHAPTER FOUR

Child Welfare Services

Highlights

- There has been a 160% increase in the number of families served by a Children's Aid Society from 1971 to 1988. Over 74,000 families were involved with a CAS in 1988.

- In 1988, 4.4% of families in Ontario were involved with a CAS.

- Cases of suspected child physical and sexual abuse account for one-third of all families who become involved with a CAS. There is no documentation on a provincial level to account for the reasons for providing services to the remaining two-thirds of families who are involved with CASs.

- The proportion of cases being re-opened for service increased 35% from 1982 to 1988.

- The number of child welfare court orders decreased by 30% from 1980 to 1988. A family that becomes involved with a CAS has approximately a 10% chance of becoming involved with child welfare court.

- The number of children in CAS care fell 45% from 1971 to 1988.

- There were over 9,700 children in CAS care on 31 December 1988; 0.37% of children in Ontario are in CAS care at any one time of the year.

- The proportion of children re-admitted to care has increased 25% from 1982 to 1988.

- From 1981 to 1987 there was a 17% reduction in the number of foster homes and a 50% reduction in the number of foster home beds.

- There were close to 5,000 children in permanent long-term CAS care (Crown Wards) in 1988.

- The number of Crown Wardship orders decreased by 43% from 1980 to 1989. A child coming into care has approximately a 5% chance of remaining permanently in CAS care.

- The number of CAS adoptions decreased by 77% from 1970 to 1982, and a further 41% from 1982 to 1988.

Introduction

The Ontario child welfare system serves a broad spectrum of children and families. These may include children who have been, or are at risk of being, physically, emotionally, or sexually abused; parents who are having difficulty controlling their children; women with unplanned pregnancies who are considering relinquishing their children for adoption; adolescent runaways; families needing assistance with children with special needs; and adult adoptees seeking information about their birth families. Some of these families request assistance; others are referred and are either persuaded to accept services, or are ordered by the courts to do

so. Services include counselling, financial assistance, advocacy, and temporary or permanent substitute care. To further complicate matters, it should also be noted that many children with family-related problems are not identified by the child welfare system. Many cases of abuse and neglect go unreported. Some families needing substitute care make private arrangements with relatives, boarding schools, or residential treatment centres. Finally, a host of other counselling services, apart from the child welfare system, are available for parents having difficulties with their children.

Data from the child welfare system are far from being

This chapter was prepared by Nico Trocmé.

clear and comprehensive measures for assessing the well-being of children, but they are among the only sources of information about problems in children's family environments. Unlike factors such as education, health, and income, the well-being of children in their families is by and large beyond public scrutiny. The present analysis of trends in the Ontario child welfare system provides a view of the public response to problems experienced by children in their families. Where possible, this chapter also considers the relationship between this public response and the true state of affairs for children in their families.

The purpose of this chapter is to provide a comprehensive picture of the child welfare system and of general service trends. The data it relies on come from a variety of sources: Ministry of Community and Social Services (MCSS) Quarterly Reports; annual reports from the Ontario Association of Children's Aid Societies (OACAS); Family Court statistics; information provided by the three Metropolitan Toronto child welfare agencies; Crown Ward Reviews; the Ontario Child Abuse Register; and the RCMP missing children registry. Secondary data from reports on child welfare services in Ontario are also used. In general the data are of limited quality, and focus almost exclusively on caseload accounting, as opposed to documenting service provision and evaluating quality of service. Because of these limitations, two points should be noted before reading this chapter. First, the data presented document quantitative trends only; they are not an indication of changes in the quality of services provided. Second, the absence of information about any given problem does not mean that that problem is not important for children and families.

This chapter is divided into three sections. The first provides the historical and policy background material necessary for understanding the functioning of the current Ontario child welfare system. The second section describes protection services: abuse investigation and reporting, services to families in their homes, and child welfare court hearings. The third section examines services to children in substitute care: foster care, residential care, Crown Wardships, and adoptions.

I   Background

Child maltreatment has been the subject of public policy only in the last hundred years, and research on it has been carried out for less than forty years. Some areas, like sexual abuse and emotional maltreatment, have been recognized as matters of serious concern only in the last fifteen years. This relatively recent recognition of the problem of maltreatment is a key factor in trying to understand the available data on its incidence and prevalence. Indeed, not only is the 'true' incidence of various forms of maltreatment an issue of perpetual debate,[1] but researchers, policy makers, and practitioners still have not reached consensus even over definitions of maltreatment.[2] Because of this lack of consensus, official child maltreatment data should be viewed primarily as a measure of child welfare agencies' reporting and intervention practices. To interpret the relationship between this information and the real state of affairs for children, it is essential to have a basic understanding of how the child welfare system operates.

Historical Background

Ontario's child welfare system has its roots in the private philanthropic tradition of providing charity and moral guidance for the disadvantaged. Charitable institutions had developed throughout the nineteenth century in the form of orphanages and training schools. While various laws existed to regulate these institutions, no legislation had been developed to allow direct intervention with maltreating families. The concept of direct intervention originated with the establishment of the Toronto Children's Aid Society in 1891,[3] a private organization formed to 'deal with all matters affecting the moral and physical welfare of children, especially those who from lack of parental care . . . are in danger of growing up to swell the criminal classes'.

The Children's Protection Act of 1893 provided Children's Aid Societies (CASs) with extensive powers to remove children from homes they considered to be unfit. Government regulation of these private charitable organizations did not come until much later. In the 1930s the provincial government started to set standards for the provision of child welfare services, but it was only with the passage of the Child Welfare Act in 1954 that standardized accountability mechanisms were established. Provincial funding followed a similar pattern. Initially CASs were funded by private donations and municipalities, provincial funding being limited to small grants. By the 1960s the province's portion had reached close to 40%, and rapidly increased to the present level of 80% (Jones and Rutman, 1981; Farina and Hoppe, 1983).

While the province has assumed greater regulatory and financial control of CASs, the private philanthropic tradition has left its mark on Ontario's child welfare system. The agencies continue to function as private non-profit corporations with their own boards of directors. This relatively autonomous and decentralized approach is also reflected in the operation of the Ministry of Community and Social Services. Since 1979, the supervision of CASs has been allocated to thirteen area offices, which in turn report to four regional offices. Furthermore, municipalities also play a role in directing individual agencies by having representatives on CAS boards. This combination of public funding and private agencies has allowed child welfare agencies to remain flexible, but it also has limited consistency in delivery of services, and, for our present purposes, has made it difficult to gather and analyse child welfare data on a provincial level.

The Child and Family Services Act

Until the 1970s, changes in Ontario's child welfare system were primarily driven by a need to develop a sound organizational structure and to professionalize a service that still had deep roots in a private philanthropic tradition. During the 1970s the child welfare system came under closer public scrutiny. Critics maintained that in spite of good intentions, child welfare services were in many instances doing more harm than good. Advocates for reform believed that too much attention had been given to families' inabilities to meet their children's 'best interests', while not enough consideration was being given to the impact of child welfare interventions, and in particular the effects of substitute care.[4]

Born out of a concern that too many children were drifting into long-term substitute care, the permanency planning movement of the 1970s had a major impact on child welfare practice and legislation.[5] The Ontario Child Welfare Act, 1978 (CWA) reflected many of these changes, but it was in the Child and Family Services Act, 1984 (CFSA) that the key principles of this reform movement were most clearly articulated. The three major thrusts of this new legislation were (1) to balance the exclusive focus on the child's perceived 'best interests' with a recognition of the fundamental importance of the family, and an acknowledgment of the intrusive effects of state intervention; (2) to define as specifically as possible the harm or risk of harm to the child that warrants state intervention, as opposed to previous legislation that focused on the parents' morals and behaviours; and (3) to ensure that parents and children are accorded due process in the courts. The key sections of the CFSA pertaining to these principles are presented below.

From 'Best Interests' To 'Least Restrictive'

Traditionally, the protection of children in North America

and England has been primarily ensured through child welfare legislation, as opposed to criminal legislation.[6] Criminal proceedings are not considered appropriate in most cases because (1) they are punitive instead of therapeutic, and (2) the strict rules of evidence used in criminal courts would make it difficult to pursue most cases of child abuse and neglect. Child welfare legislation focuses on determining what kind of interventions would promote the 'best interests of the child', the assumption being that with some families the state has a better understanding of what is best for the child. This concept came under heavy criticism in the 1970s because of the lack of a scientific basis for determining what actually is best for children, and because of growing evidence that in many situations state intervention was worse than leaving a child in a less than ideal family.[7]

Some of these criticisms were incorporated in the definition of 'best interests' in the CWA of 1978, but it was not until the CFSA that the 'least restrictive' rule was specifically introduced to balance the 'best interest' rule. The 'least restrictive' rule specifies that for all voluntary and court-ordered child welfare interventions, the intervening agency must be able to demonstrate that a less restrictive course of action was attempted, or that the child is at such imminent risk that a less restrictive action is not possible.

**Box 1: Declaration of Principles
CFSA Section 1**

The purposes of this Act are,

(a) as a paramount objective, to promote the best interests, protection and well-being of children;

(b) to recognize that while parents often need help in caring for their children, that help should give support to the autonomy and integrity of the family unit and, wherever possible, be provided on the basis of mutual consent;

(c) to recognize that the least restrictive or disruptive course of action that is available and is appropriate . . . should be followed;

(d) to recognize . . . children's need for continuity of care and stable family relationships . . . and developmental differences among children;

(e) to respect cultural, religious and regional differences; and

(f) to recognize that Indian and native people should be entitled to provide, wherever possible, their own child and family services.

'In Need of Protection'

The second important thrust of the CFSA was to attempt to define the grounds for involuntary intervention as specifically as possible. In the 1978 CWA a child could be found 'in need of protection' for reasons such as being 'found associating with an unfit or improper person' (CWA 19[1][b][v]). To move the legislation away from such broad and vague language, the CFSA set out to limit involuntary intervention to situations where specific harm to the child or risk of specific harm could be demonstrated.

Due Process

The third major thrust of the CFSA was to ensure that children, parents, and any other interested parties (e.g., native band representatives) are given adequate opportunity to have their positions represented in court. Criteria clearly specify how a case can be brought to court (Section 40). Unless it can be demonstrated that procedural delays would put the child at substantial risk, court proceedings should start with an application for a hearing while the child is left in the care of the parents. If it is necessary that a child come into care before the first hearing, a warrant to apprehend the child can be obtained, or, in emergency situations, the child can be apprehended without a warrant. Within five days of any apprehension the case must be brought to court.

Court documentation has become much more thorough under the CFSA. Affidavits specifying in detail the reasons for the agency's application must be filed and included with the notice of proceedings given to the parents. Dispensing with notice is allowed only in circumstances where the child's health or safety may be in danger. The CFSA also includes criteria for ordering legal representation of the child by an Official Guardian. Adjournments are limited to 30 days unless a consent from all other parties states otherwise, and custody during the adjournment is given to the parents, unless the agency can demonstrate that that would put the child at substantial risk of further harm. A final order can be made only once a detailed plan for the child's care has been presented by the agency. The plan must include 'a statement of the criteria by which the society will determine when wardship or supervision is no longer required' (Section 52[b]).

Once an order has been made, the assumption continues to be that the agency's plans must be monitored. All Crown Ward placements are to be reviewed yearly by the Ministry of Community and Social Services (Section 62). All placements in residential facilities containing 10 or more children must be reviewed every 9 months by an independent Residential Placement Advisory Committee (Section 34). In addition, a child who is at least 12 years old, or his/her parent, may apply for a review by the courts of the child's wardship status, unless the child is a Crown Ward who has been living with the same foster parents for over two years (Section 60).

Ontario's child welfare system has moved in less than a

Box 2: 'In Need of Protection' CFSA Section 37(2)

A child is in need of protection where,

(a) the child has suffered physical harm inflicted by the person having charge of the child or caused by that person's failure to care and provide for or supervise and protect the child adequately;

(b) there is a substantial risk that . . . [as in subsection (a) above]

(c) the child has been sexually molested or sexually exploited . . . ;

(d) there is a substantial risk of . . . [as in (c)];

(e) the child requires medical treatment . . . and the child's parent . . . does not provide or refuses or is unavailable or unable to consent to the treatment;

(f) the child has suffered emotional harm, demonstrated by severe: anxiety, depression, withdrawal, or self-destructive or aggressive behaviour, and the parent . . . does not provide, or refuses or is unavailable or unable to consent to services . . . ;

(g) there is a substantial risk of . . . [as in (f)];

(h) the child suffers from a mental, emotional or developmental condition that, if not remedied, could seriously impair the child's development, and the parent . . . [as in (f)];

(i) the child has been abandoned . . . ;

(j) the child is less than 12 years old and has killed or seriously injured another person or caused serious property damage . . . and the parent does not provide . . . [as in (f)].

(k) the child is less than 12 years old and has on more than one occasion injured another person or caused . . . damage to another person's property with the encouragement of the person having charge of the child.

(l) the parents are unable to care for the child and . . . consent (and child consents if 12 or older) to be dealt with under this part.

century from a group of concerned philanthropists to an extensive, highly professionalized child protection system. The CFSA, reflecting the mood of child welfare reform that arose in the 1970s, attempts to balance child protection and respect for family autonomy. The emphasis is on providing services in the home as opposed to removing children, and preference is given to voluntary services over court-ordered services. The rest of this chapter will examine the extent to which these principles have been translated into practice.

II Family Services

Family Services, alternatively referred to as prevention and protection services, are the point of entry into the child welfare system. Although the primary focus of concern is the safety of the child, the focus of service is the family. In order to ensure the child's protection and well-being, the child's immediate environment — i.e., his/her parents and family[8] — becomes the primary target for intervention. Most families who have contact with child welfare agencies are involved only with Family Services, and usually for a relatively short period of time. Substitute care is used only when in-home services are not successful or are not appropriate,[9] and even then, the target of intervention usually continues to be the family.[10]

This section starts by presenting overall trends in the delivery of child welfare services in the province. Regional differences and the question of unequal representation of visible minorities and natives are examined. These trends are then considered in more detail: first in terms of the service process from referral and intake to termination, and then in terms of the specific types of services provided with regards to child physical and sexual abuse, child neglect, court interventions, adolescents, and adoption information disclosures.

Trends in Numbers of Families Served

The numbers of families served are among the standard statistics that have been systematically gathered by the provincial government. They are calculated by adding all the cases opened during a given year to the number of cases carried over from the previous year.[11] By including cases opened and cases carried over, 'families served' reflects both the volume of case openings and the length of time cases are kept open. It should be noted that the definition of a case open at intake can vary from agency to agency.[12] It should

also be noted that 1987 statistics do not include services provided by the three native-run child welfare agencies (see p. 71, below, for details). As Table 4.1 shows, although the number of children in care has declined dramatically (see Row D and Figure 4.1), the number of families served by child welfare agencies has increased by over 160% during the past 17 years (Row A). This increase can be attributed to a variety of factors. A portion of it can be explained by the increase in the number of families with children (Row B). However, even the ratio of families served compared to total number of families in the province has doubled (Row C).

A second factor has been the increasing amount of stress with which families have had to cope. From 1981 to 1986 the proportion of low-income families in Ontario increased from 11.4% to 14.3%, and from 1971 to 1986 the proportion of lone parent families increased from 12% to 18%.[13] Poverty is an important risk factor for child physical abuse and child neglect (Pelton, 1978; see also Volpe, 1989). In Metro Toronto lone parent families constitute well over 50% of families involved with child welfare;[14] poverty and lack of support are major sources of stress for these families.[15] A third factor, which is discussed in more detail in the next sections, has been the expansion of child welfare services in areas like sexual abuse, teen runaways, adoption disclosures, and services to natives.

A fourth factor has been the shift in practice philosophy from bringing children into substitute care to providing prevention services in the home. Since prevention usually

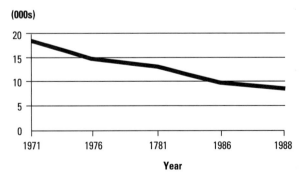

Figure 4.1: Children in Care on December 31

(000s)

Year

Source: For 1971-81, M. Farina and B. Hoppe, *Child Welfare: A Background and Issues Paper* (Toronto: Ministry of Community and Social Services, 1983); for 1986-88, MCSS, Children's Aid Society Quarterly Reports.

Table 4.1
Family services case trends, Ontario, 1971–1988

	1971	1976	1981	1986	1988
A. Family Services cases served during year	28,323	34,196	48,489	67,714	74,16
B. Ontario families with children	1,343,300	1,487,500	1,538,600	1,630,600	1,683,700
C. Families served as % of Ontario families	2.1%	2.3%	3.2%	4.2%	4.4%
D. Children in care on December 31	17,807	13,904	13,033	9,875	9,712
E. Ontario population < 19 years	2,921,900	2,881,800	2,695,800	2,564,100	2,567,000
F. Children in care as % of Ontario children (row D/row F)	0.61%	0.48%	0.48%	0.39%	0.38%
G. Ratio of children in care to families served[a] (row D/row A)	0.63	0.41	0.27	0.15	0.13

[a]This ratio does not represent the true proportion of children in care compared with children being served at home. It should be seen only as an indicator of the trend towards more in-home services. The ratio of 'admissions to openings' (Table 4.2) is a closer approximation of the proportion of children in care to children at home, although it counts each child admission but only family openings. The available statistics do not allow for more accurate accounting.

Sources: Rows A and D, for 1971–81: M. Farina and B. Hoppe, *Child Welfare: A Background and Issues Paper* (Toronto: MCSS, 1983); for 1986–88; CAS MCSS Quarterly Reports.
Rows B and E: Statistics Canada, Census and postcensal estimates.

entails providing services to a broader array of clients, it seems likely that a decrease in admissions would accompany an increase in families served. Indeed, the ratio of children in care at year end to number of families served dropped from 63% to 13% (Row G) between 1971 and 1988. Part of this drop is due to the decrease in the size of families and the number of children in the province. However, even in accounting for this change, the proportion of children in care has been almost cut in half (Row F and Figure 4.2), while the proportion of families served has doubled (Row C).

Two service variables also influence the number of families served: the length of time that cases are kept open, and the number of re-openings. There are no provincial statistics on the length of time that cases are kept open. However, by comparing openings and closings with the number of cases carried over from the previous year, one can get a sense of whether cases are being kept open longer (Figure 4.3). The ratio of re-opened to open cases serves as a good measure of the number of families returning for further service (Figure 4.4).

Until 1987, the increase in cases served was primarily driven by an increase in case openings (Figure 4.3). During that same period (1982-87) the ratio of cases carried over from the previous year to cases opened during the year had dropped steadily, suggesting that, on average, cases were being closed sooner, perhaps to compensate for the large influx of new cases (Figure 4.4: 'Carried Over'). Since 1987 a second factor has added even more cases to the system: the number of case closings dropped, which has led to an increase in the number of cases carried forward (Figure 4.3).

Figure 4.2: Children in Care as % of Ontario Children

(000s)

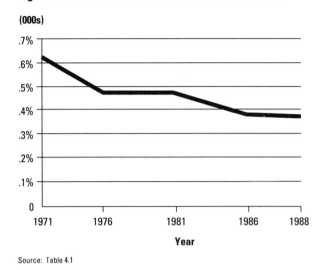

Year

Source: Table 4.1

Figure 4.3: Families served as a function of openings, closings, and cases carried over

(000s)

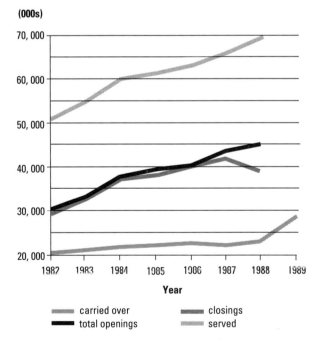

Year

carried over
total openings
closings
served

Source: Ministry of Community and Social Services, Children's Aid Society Quarterly Reports.

Figure 4.4: Re-openings vs. cases carried over as ratios to openings

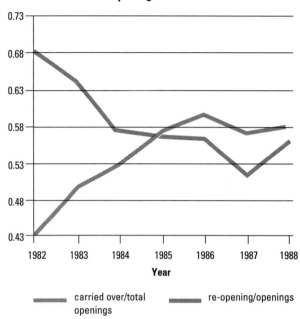

Year

carried over/total openings
re-opening/openings

Source: Ministry of Community and Social Services, Children's Aid Society Quarterly Reports.

This suggests that until 1987 agencies had managed to absorb the increasing demand for service by decreasing the length of time that cases were being kept open, but that they may have reached a saturation point and cannot process cases more quickly.

Figure 4.4 also suggests that, in the long run, closing cases sooner will result in an increase in the number of families returning for services. As the length of time cases were being kept open decreased (i.e., cases carried over total openings and re-openings), the number of families returning for services increased (i.e., re-openings/openings). Conversely, a slight decrease in re-openings occurred when cases began to be kept open longer.

In summary, from 1971 to 1988 there has been a 160% increase in the number of families served by CASs. Several factors appear to have contributed to this increase: population growth, increasing stress on families, identification of a larger number of child welfare problems, provision of more in-home services, inability to process cases more quickly, and an increase in the number of case re-openings.

Regional Comparisons

All areas in the province have been affected by increases in the numbers of families served, decreases in the numbers of children brought into care, and an overall decrease in the length of time cases are kept open (Table 4.2). However, some regional differences are noteworthy.

Northern Ontario has witnessed the most extensive changes in the province. The percentage of families involved with CASs increased 40% from 1982 to 1987; in fact, as will be seen later, this increase would be even greater if one included the families served by the three new native child welfare agencies. This dramatic increase in families served

did not lead to an increase in the number of children admitted to substitute care. In fact, the ratio of admissions to care in comparison to Family Service openings dropped 49%. In spite of these changes, Northern Ontario agencies still admit twice as many children to substitute care as do agencies in other parts of the province. Factors such as a higher rate of abuse allegations, difficulty of access to counselling services, and the difficulty of monitoring children in homes located far away from the agencies may partially explain this large number of admissions. The high proportion of native families in Northern Ontario may also contribute to the disproportionate number of children in substitute care. Native families appear to be at substantially higher risk of having children brought into care (see p. 71 below for further discussion).

The other area that has been differently affected by changes

Table 4.2
Child welfare trends by region, Ontario, 1982 and 1987

	Year	West	Central	North	East	Toronto	Ontario
A. Families served	1982	18,100	20,899	6,161	9,737	14,627	54,897
	1987	24,987	23,130	7,908	14,732	16,060	70,757
B. Families served as	1982	3.69%	3.45%	3.65%	3.00%	4.00%	3.47%
% of Ontario families	1987	4.85%	3.51%	5.12%	5.06%	4.31%	4.34%
C. Ratio of cases carried	1982	0.55	0.72	0.87	0.76	0.88	0.68
over to case openings	1987	0.44	0.59	0.49	0.52	0.72	0.51
D. Children served in	1982	6,213	7,489	4,438	4,153	5,276	22,293
substitute care	1987	5,630	6,078	3,427	3,842	4,512	18,978
E. Children served in care as	1982	0.89%	0.87%	1.79%	0.93%	1.44%	0.95%
of children under 17	1987	0.72%	0.71%	1.52%	0.87%	1.02%	0.85%
F. Ratio of admissions to	1982	0.25	0.25	0.72	0.33	0.26	0.31
care to Family Services	1987	0.16	0.17	0.37	0.19	0.19	0.19
case openings							
G. Abuse allegations[a]	1987	4,779	4,267	2,031	3,780	2,143	14,857
H. Ratio of abuse allegations	1987	0.27	0.29	0.38	0.39	0.23	0.32
to Family Services openings							

[a]The reliability of abuse allegations data is not known. Agencies may count allegations in different ways. There were no other data sources available to cross-reference these numbers.

Source: 1. Family Services and children in care data from MCSS Quarterly reports (rows A, B, C, D, E, F, and G).
2. Population data from Statistics Canada 1981 & 1986 Census, Part II, Families With Children & Children Under 17 at Home (rows B and E).
3. Abuse allegations from OACAS, Info '89: Allegations at intake in 1988. Missing data from three agencies (North and East Regions) (rows G and H).

is Metropolitan Toronto. The percentage of families served by a CAS increased by only 7% from 1982 to 1987, while it increased by about 40% in the other regions (Table 4.2). While, by 1987, Metro agencies had managed to decrease the numbers of children in care by close to 30%, Metro still had the second highest proportion of children in substitute care. Another notable difference is that cases appeared to be kept open longer in Metro Toronto (Table 4.2, Row C). These statistics may seem surprising if one considers that Toronto has the lowest rate of abuse allegations.[16] However, risk factors are higher in Toronto than in the rest of the province. In 1986, 16.5% of families in Metro Toronto were classified as low-income by Statistics Canada, compared with 14.3% in the province as a whole. In the same year, the proportion of single parent families was 22.9% in Metro Toronto, compared with 17.8% in the province.[17] In 1988, at least 30% of families involved with Metropolitan Toronto child welfare agencies lived in subsidized housing, and over 45% depended on General Welfare Assistance or Family Benefits.[18]

Services to Visible Minorities and Natives

Provincial statistics are not collected on Family Services to visible minorities and natives. The only data collected province-wide are the numbers of service hours/sessions involving Status Indians on reserves.[19] This information is used to calculate federal reimbursement for these services. While this statistic does not indicate how many Status Indian families are served, it does provide a rough estimate of changes in the amount of work done with such families. The most notable change came about with the creation in 1986-87 of three Northern Ontario native-run child welfare agencies. The intention had been to shift services from traditional agencies to native ones; instead, Family Services to Status Indians in both native and non-native Northern Ontario CASs increased overall by 40%.[20]

Service statistics for the three native-run child welfare agencies are included in neither the provincial Quarterly reports nor the yearly Ontario Association of Children's Aid Societies (OACAS) reports, and therefore they have not been included in the data presented earlier.[21] Two of these agencies reported service statistics in their 1989-90 service plans. During fiscal year 1988-89, Payukotano Family Services opened 88 Family Service cases, had 69 still open at the end of the year, and served 113 children in care.[22] During the

Figure 4.5:   Services to visible minorities and natives

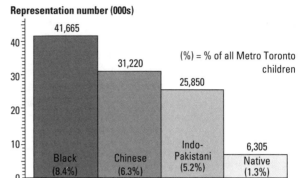

Children 0-19 in Metropolitan Toronto

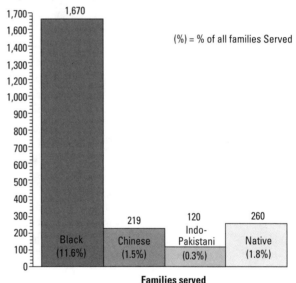

Families served

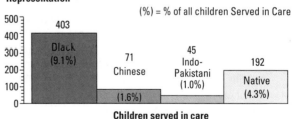

Children served in care

Source: Statistics Canada, Survey of Consumer Finances, Special Tabulations.

same period, Weechi-it-te-win Family Services served 116 children in care, and provided 'family support' services to 481 families.[23] If one included these cases in the provincial statistics reported earlier, the increase in the number of families served would be even greater. Eight more native child welfare agencies are being developed. One can therefore expect a continued expansion in the number of native families served in the province, in particular in Northern Ontario.

Data from Toronto child welfare agencies provide a rough estimate of services to visible minorities in Metropolitan Toronto.[24] As shown in Figure 4.5, natives do not appear to be significantly over-represented at the Family Service level, but they are more than twice as likely to have a child in care than are other families involved with the child welfare system. A similar over-representation was found in estimates calculated for the province in 1980: 8% of children in care were estimated to be native, whereas native children made up only 4.7% of the child population (Farina and Hoppe, 1983: 46-9). This high placement rate is an issue of concern, given the history of inappropriate placement of native children in substitute care.[25] Unfortunately, there is not sufficient data to determine the extent to which this high proportion of children in care is a function of racism or of environmental stress.[26]

Black families appear to be slightly over-represented at the Family Service level, but those families that do become involved with a child welfare agency are slightly less likely than average to have a child in care. On the other hand, Chinese and Indo-Pakistani families are significantly under-represented; they are at least five times less likely to become involved with child welfare services than are other families. While one can only speculate about the causes of this under-representation, it is significant enough to warrant further investigation.[27]

In summary, the general trend for child welfare in the province has been a continual expansion of services to families, with short-term in-home services replacing a long-term approach that often relied on bringing children into care. Part of this change can be attributed to developments with respect to the practice principles and legal framework guiding child welfare interventions. However, the key issue is to determine to what extent these service trends reflect the needs of children and their families. Since families can have contact with child welfare agencies for a variety of reasons, and sometimes for no reason other than an unsubstantiated report of maltreatment from a concerned third party,

it is essential to break down the 'families served' category into specific problems addressed by the child welfare system. To provide a problem-specific framework, the next section presents a case-flow model based on 1989 Metropolitan Toronto data. Particular child welfare issues — i.e., child abuse and neglect, courts, teen runaways and adoption information-sharing — are then discussed in more detail.

Case-Flow: From Referral to Termination

It is difficult to get an accurate picture of the service process from intake to termination. Most child welfare statistics collected in Ontario provide a restricted 'snapshot' view of services that fails to differentiate between short-term and long-term cases. For instance, at the end of 1988 there were just over 22,000 Family Service cases open and just under 10,000 children in substitute care. This 'year-end' data can give the misleading impression that there is almost a 2 to 1 ratio of families served to children in care. 'Year-end' data, and even 'cases served' data over-represent long-term cases. In order to provide a more accurate view of the service process, the cohort of families who were seen at intake in 1989 at the two largest Metropolitan Toronto child welfare agencies was tracked through the system, as shown in Figure 4.6.[28]

Referral

In Metro Toronto self-referrals accounted for 24% of the families that had contact with an intake worker in 1989. Referrals by a relative or a non-professional community source accounted for another 12%. Professional referrals account for the remainder, referrals being fairly equally distributed among the police, health services, other social service agencies, and schools. While comparable provincial data are not available, this distribution is similar to that reported in American urban settings (New York State Council, 1988; Giovannoni, 1989). Given that third-party referrals, made mostly by professionals, account for over 75% of families involved with child welfare agencies, the basis on which these decisions to report are made merits careful examination.

Section 68 of the CFSA requires that a report be made by any person who believes that a child is in need of protection. While the duty to report applies to the general public, specific provisions are made for all professionals involved with children (Section 68 [3][4][7]). Outside of the solicitor-client priv-

Figure 4.6: Case-flow Model

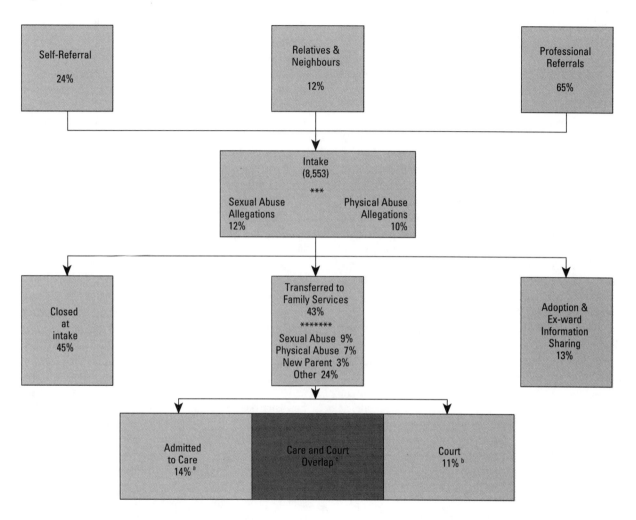

a) The proportion of families who have children placed in care is difficult to determine, since admissions are calculated per child, not per family. CASMT was able to track all admissions for Family Service cases open in 1989. The ratio of children admitted to care to the number of families with children in care was roughly 1.5 to 1. Applying this ratio to the number of admissions to care in 1989 for both agencies, one finds that admissions constituted about 14% of cases open at intake.

b) The proportion of families who end up in court is also difficult to determine. A rough estimate can be arrived at by comparing the number of openings with the number of new protection applications to court. This data was available only for CASMT. However, if was possible to estimate the number for CCAS based on the CASMT data as well as Metro Toronto data supplied by the Attorney General's office. The 11% figure is probably a slight overrepresentation, since in many cases several applications are filed for the same family.

c) Approximately 50% of children admitted to care became involved with the courts (see figure 4.10), and approximately 60% of court cases involve children in care (see Table 4.3)

Source: Children's Aid Society of Metropolitan Toronto and Catholic Children's Aid Society Information Systems, 1988 and 1989.

ilege, this duty to report has precedence over any confidentiality restrictions placed on professionals in their usual practice. As long as a report is made in good faith, no legal action can be instituted against the reporter (Section 68 [7]). The reporting criterion for making referrals is simply a reasonable belief that a child is or may be 'in need of protection', as defined in Section 37(2)(a)(e)(f)or(h) (Box 2).

While professionals involved with children have been

given a strong mandate to report suspicion of maltreatment, the guidelines for making these reports are broad enough that the decision to report is mainly left to professional discretion. Several American studies have found that between half and two-thirds of suspected maltreatment cases go unreported, and that the decision to report is influenced by extraneous factors such as class and race.[29] Studies of reporting rates have not been carried out in Ontario.

Although not addressing this issue directly, a study of child abuse and neglect deaths in Ontario produced some disturbing findings about our ability to identify high-risk situations. Sixty per cent of these children had been seen by a physician because of an earlier injury, 20% were seriously malnourished, 47% were at or below the third centile with respect to weight and/or height, and over half the cases were already receiving services from a child welfare agency (Greenland, 1986). These statistics can be seen to point either to ineffectiveness in the high-risk detection process, or to the inherent difficulty of predicting which children are at highest risk, given that the yearly incidence of child abuse deaths in Ontario is under 0.02 per thousand children 4 years old or under (Greenland, 1986).

American studies have also shown that while maltreatment reports made by professionals are more likely to be substantiated than are reports made by private individuals, the substantiation rate for professionals is only a little over 50% (Giovannoni, 1989; New York State Council, 1988). Substantiation rates are not documented in Ontario. A rough estimate of Toronto substantiation rates can be derived from the data used for the case-flow model presented above.[30] Between 70% and 80% of abuse allegations received at intake are transferred for on-going services,[31] if one includes all reports received, other than information requests, the rate drops to just under 50%.

Both the poor reporting rate and the low substantiation rate indicate that there is a gap between the professionals who are expected to identify cases of maltreatment and the child welfare agencies. Given, on the one hand, the potentially stigmatizing effects of a child welfare investigation, and, on the other hand, the risk of failing to recognize or report situations where children are at risk, this lack of reliability in the case identification process is an issue of concern.

Intake and On-Going Family Services
Considering the potential limitations of the referral process, intake services play a crucial role in determining a family's involvement in the child welfare system. Each agency has its own intake procedures. Some have specialized intake workers investigate every referral; some have all Family Service workers investigate referrals as well as provide on-going services; and some use specialized intake workers to investigate only some types of cases. Whether or not intake is carried out by specialized staff, the basic process involves a combination of investigation/assessment and negotiation with the family. Standard protocols for abuse investigations, especially sexual abuse investigations carried out with the police, are used by some agencies. Guidelines for intake assessments in non-abuse situations are not used as frequently, although these cases comprise close to 75% of Toronto referrals (excluding information-sharing cases).

The case-flow model indicates that about half of the cases opened at intake are also closed at intake. If this model approximates the service process in other parts of the province, this means that about 20,000 of the 45,000 cases opened in 1988 did not warrant on-going child welfare services.[32] This does not mean that the cases closed at intake did not receive services. Cases are closed for a variety of reasons: the allegation of maltreatment may not be substantiated; parents may refuse services, and concerns may not be strong enough to warrant court intervention; the situation may require only a brief intervention; or the family may be referred elsewhere for more appropriate services. Cases closed at intake are usually processed fairly quickly. A case-flow analysis of Children's Aid Society of Metropolitan Toronto (CASMT) indicates that 65% of cases closed at intake were closed within two months of being opened.

On-going services can take many forms, from homemaker services to in-home counselling, to foster placement, to adoption. In some instances the case is brought to court, in others a more or less explicit agreement for service is arrived at between the agency and the family. The extent of involvement and the length of time that cases are kept open can vary substantially. Case-flow data from the Toronto Catholic Children's Aid Society (CCAS) shows that close to 60% of on-going Family Service cases are closed within a year, but 20% are open for two years or more, in some instances even five years or more. On-going services can therefore be divided into relatively short-term cases, under a year, and long-term cases. The long-term cases are more likely to involve families who have children in substitute care, or families who are brought to child welfare court.

The picture that emerges is that most families are involved

with the child welfare system for a relatively short time, that few require child placement services, and that most are getting help for family problems other than abuse. However, there also is a substantial minority of families who become involved with the child welfare system on a long-term basis. Some of the specific service categories presented in this model are discussed in more detail below.

Physical and Sexual Abuse

One of the most significant recent developments in child welfare has been the expansion of services to sexually abused children. While sexual abuse is not a new problem, until the last decade it had been recognized by professionals as only a rare and unusual problem. Children were not encouraged to disclose sexual abuse, and allegations were often ignored. Professional and public recognition of the problem has led to an increase in the number of allegations, investigations, and families served for reasons of sexual abuse.

It is difficult to document precisely changes in child abuse reporting in Ontario, because there are no standard reporting methods. The following graphs present two very different measures of child abuse service activity. Figure 4.7 documents abuse allegations received by most agencies in the province, while Figure 4.8 presents substantiated abuse cases, considered serious enough to warrant registration in the provincial Child Abuse Registry. Both graphs show an overall increase in the number of abuse reports received, but the pace of this increase, current trends, and the proportions of sexual and physical abuse cases differ. These differences are due in part to changes in documentation and reporting procedures used by some agencies. Limitations with respect to Child Abuse Registry reporting procedures have been well documented.[33] Each agency has its own guidelines for deciding which cases to report, and within each agency these guidelines have changed over time. The application of more stringent guidelines after 1985 explains the recent decrease in Abuse Registry reports (Figure 4.8).

To the extent that one can rely on the Abuse Registry data, it would appear that the increase in abuse reports is primarily due to an increase in the number of sexual abuse reports received (Figure 4.8). A similar trend has also been noted in some agencies.[34] The OACAS data shows little variation in the relative proportion of physical and sexual abuse allegations received since 1985 (Figure 4.7). One possible explanation for this discrepancy is that the major increase in child

sexual abuse reports occurred between 1982 and 1985. Since OACAS did not keep separate statistics for sexual and physical abuse cases before 1985, the 1982-85 increase in the proportion of sexual abuse cases is not documented on Figure 4.8.

Increases in the number of sexual abuse reports have also been documented in the United States. Between 1983 and 1984 sexual abuse reports documented by the American Association for Protecting Children increased by 35%.[35] According to American Humane Association (1984) statistics, in 1976 3% of child maltreatment reports involved sexual abuse, by 1982 sexual abuse reports accounted for 7% of all reports received. During that same period the overall number of maltreatment reports received had more than doubled.

In spite of this increase in the number of child abuse reports, it appears that there is still a gap between reported cases and the actual incidence of abuse. The exact scope of child physical and sexual abuse remains a subject of extensive debate.[36] A conservative estimate of the number of physically abused children per year in the United States is 23 per 1,000 children (Straus and Gelles, 1988). This estimate

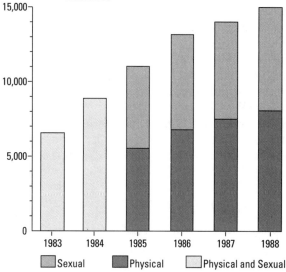

Figure 4.7: Physical and sexual abuse allegations, Ontario Association of Children's Aid Societies

Source: Ontario Association of Children's Aid Societies, *Info 1984, 1988, 1989*

Figure 4.8: Reports to Ontario Child Abuse Registry, Physical & Sexual Abuse

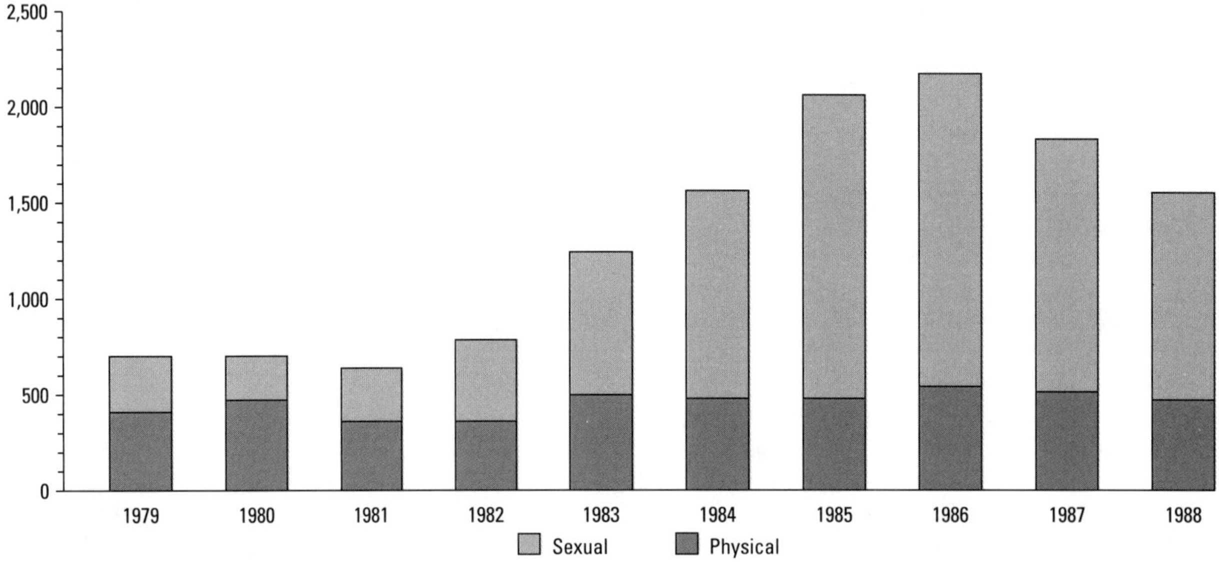

Source: Ontario Child Abuse Registry, Ministry of Community and Social Services, unpublished data.

is based on a definition of abuse that excludes 'hitting with an object'; including this latter category increases the incidence five-fold, to 110 per 1,000 children. Transposed to Ontario, these rates would mean that in 1986 between 5,000 and 25,000 children were physically abused.[37] A very conservative estimate of the prevalence of child sexual abuse in the United States is 10% for girls and 2% for boys (Finkelhor, 1984). In contrast, the Canadian Badgley Commission prevalence study found that 25% of women and 13% of men surveyed reported that by the time they were 16 they had been victims of at least one sexual offence ranging from exposure to sexual assault.[38] Using these two prevalence estimates, one can estimate that between 8,000 and 25,000 new cases of sexual abuse occurred in Ontario in 1986.[39]

On the basis of these estimates one can conclude that between 13,000 and 50,000 children were abused in Ontario in 1986. During that same year 43,464 Family Service cases were open at intake, about 15,000 of which were abuse allegations. Assuming a 75% substantiation rate,[40] this would mean that about 11,250 confirmed abuse cases were opened in 1986. Therefore it would appear that at the very least 22% of the children abused in 1986 received some form of

child welfare intervention. Using the most conservative estimate of the number of children abused, the services rate increases to 86%. A large-scale American study, using conservative yearly incidence figures, concluded that about a third of child abuse cases were identified by the American child welfare system (Daro, 1988). This clearly shows that any estimate of the service gap for abused children depends on the definition of abuse that one chooses to use.

It should be noted that psychological abuse has not been examined in this section. Data on psychological abuse are not kept. However, there is an increasing amount of evidence from the research literature that psychological abuse is an important maltreatment category (Brassard, Germain, and Hart, 1988).

Child 'Neglect'

The case-flow model presented in Figure 4.6 suggested that over half of the cases open for on-going services were open for reasons other than abuse or services to new parents. Regional comparisons (Table 4.2) revealed that abuse allegation accounted for only 32% of case openings in the province, and only 23% in Toronto. Ontario child welfare statistics do not define this 'other' category, although it appears to constitute over half of the families served in the province. American child welfare agencies refer to these cases as 'child neglect'. Cases involving child neglect alone account for between 50% and 70% of child maltreatment cases in the United States.[41]

As noted in the background section, the term 'neglect' was omitted from the CFSA as a category warranting court intervention. However, subsections 37(2)(a)(b)(e)(f)(g)(h) and (i) all include parental 'failure to provide' as a criterion for determining that a child may be in need of protection. At the time of the drafting of the Act, the concept of child neglect had come under considerable criticism because of its vagueness, because of the lack of evidence that children were actually being harmed, and because of the increasing concern that child welfare interventions, especially substitute care, could do more harm than good.[42] The concept has also been criticized because it is viewed as a convenient label used to blame parents, mostly mothers, for a problem that is primarily a result of poverty (Swift, 1988; Biller and Solomon, 1986). However, findings from several recent studies have led to a renewed emphasis on the negative long-term effects of child neglect.[43]

Although 'neglect' is indeed a poorly chosen term, its conceptual limitations do not justify avoiding very real problems.[44] The needs of the 35,000 or more families in Ontario who are receiving services because of problems not related to child abuse must be clearly defined. At first glance, these families may appear to be a heterogenous group. CASMT has 25 service categories, most of which involve situations where the child is considered to be at risk for reasons other than physical or sexual abuse. These include situations like 'lack of medical care', 'mental health of parents', 'parent's behaviour may endanger child', 'emotional neglect', 'inadequate parental supervision', 'child's disruptive behaviour', and 'environmental factors'.[45] This effort to be as specific as possible about the reason for intervention may in fact end up masking some of the common characteristics of these families: poverty, social isolation, and multiple family problems (Daro, 1988: 32).

There is not sufficient information to determine what proportion of families served by the Ontario child welfare system can be described as low-income, multi-problem families. The regional data reviewed earlier suggest that in comparison with the rest of the province, Toronto child welfare agencies are involved with a greater number of non-abuse families, and serve a higher proportion of low-income families. Similarly, a significantly higher ratio of 'neglect' cases is documented in New York City than in the rest of New York State (New York, 1988). The importance of addressing the needs of these families has also been documented by the Ontario Child Health Study, in particular with regard to the

---

Table 4.3
Child welfare court orders

	1980	1982	1984	1986	1988
A. CWA/CFSA orders made	15,927	13,452	12,754	11,533	11,059
B. Percentage of supervision orders	24.2%	26.2%	28.6%	34.7%	36.6%
C. Ratio of all orders to families served[a]	32.8	24.5	20.0	17.0	15.7
D. Criminal charges laid	224	288	809	1156	806

[a]This ratio is not the true proportion of families that end up in court. It is an overestimate, since in many instances different orders are made for each child in a family.

Source: Attorney General's Office.

finding that poverty is a major risk factor for child psychiatric disorders (Offord, 1986). Poor multi-problem families appear to be facing an ever-increasing number of stress factors; most recently, attention has been drawn to the problem of cocaine-related child neglect.[46] The needs of these families, and the appropriateness of delivering services to them through the child welfare system, warrant further investigation.

The Judicial System

The CFSA clearly stipulates that court must only be used when no less intrusive alternative is available. In fact, an agency applying for an order under the CFSA must demonstrate that efforts were made to provide services on a voluntary basis. The Toronto case-flow model indicates that a case opened at intake has only about one chance in ten of ending up in child welfare court. This rate may be slightly higher in the rest of the province, since in 1988 the ratio of court orders to cases served was 13.8 in Toronto, and 15.7 in the province.[47] Use of child welfare court (Provincial Court, Family Division) has decreased substantially over the past ten years. From 1980 to 1988 the numbers of orders made decreased by a third, while the ratio of orders made to families served in 1988 was less than half of what it was in 1980 (Table 4.3). The trend towards bringing fewer children into care is also reflected in the court data; the portion of supervision orders has increased steadily. Supervision orders are made when the child is left at home, whereas all other orders involve a child being in substitute care. In contrast, it is interesting to note that the number of criminal charges laid, as documented by the Child Abuse Registry, more than quadrupled between 1980 and 1988.[48] This could be interpreted as a move toward the criminalization of child abuse.

While fewer cases are being brought to child welfare court, there is a growing concern that more and more time is being spent in court processing cases. A major thrust of the CFSA was to formalize the court process to ensure that parents and children are given adequate opportunity to have their positions presented. A small-scale court file study, conducted before the implementation of the CFSA, indicated that court was essentially being used to ratify decisions already made by agencies.[49] In contrast, some social workers feel that court has now become too formalized, and that the interests of the child have been lost in the adversarial process (Silverman, 1989; Palmer, 1989a). Court statistics gathered by CASMT show that there are almost two adjournments for every order

made; the adjournment ratio for new protection applications is probably even higher.[50] On the other hand, the same statistics show that the ratio of trials to court applications is about 3%, suggesting that there is a surprisingly high level of dispute resolution.

The impact of the court process needs to be further investigated. While some social workers complain that the process has become too formalized and adversarial, jurists complain that child welfare court is primarily used as a diagnostic tool, and in many cases as a means to enforce the decisions of child welfare agencies (Silverman, 1989). While only a small portion of families become involved with the courts, and an even smaller portion go to trial, in practice child welfare court may influence a much broader spectrum of families. It is impossible to determine how many families agree to 'voluntary' services primarily because they believe that the courts would support the agency's position. It also is impossible to determine how many cases are closed at intake because a social worker does not think there is enough 'evidence' to warrant court intervention.[51]

Adolescent Services

As with neglect, services to adolescents have not been monitored in Ontario. However, there are two trends that indicate that adolescents may be an increasingly important group in the child welfare system. One indication that the average age of children involved with on-going Family Services is probably rising is that the ratio of re-openings to openings has increased significantly since 1982; re-opened cases are more likely to be serving older children (see Figure 4.4). A second indication of increased adolescent case activity is the growing number of runaways.[52] Month-end data from the Federal Missing Children's Registry indicates that in Ontario the number of registered runaways increased by 32% from 1987 to 1989.[53] During 1989 there were between 311 and 440 registered runaways at any one time in the province. Over 21,000 missing-children reports were registered in Ontario in 1988 (this figure includes multiple registrations) (Dalley, 1989). In 1988, 72% of Canadian missing children were runaways, and 65% were repeat or habitual runaways (Dalley, 1989).

A national study of a sample of 341 repeat runaways conducted in 1988 found that 10% were known to have been sexually abused and 26% were known to have been physically abused (Fisher, 1989).[54] The study also found that 69% were reported to use drugs (primarily alcohol, marijuana, and hashish), and that 80% were reported as having been involved in delinquent activities (primarily shoplifting and stealing money). Over 15% of these repeat runaways were reported to be involved in prostitution. Over 45% of repeat runaways were reported missing from institutions or foster homes (Fisher, 1989).

Another category of adolescent child welfare services that should be mentioned is services to young pregnant women. The case-flow model indicates that 'new parents' constitute about 3% of cases opened by child welfare agencies. A large proportion of these young pregnant women are adolescents. The number of new parents served by the two major Metropolitan Toronto child welfare agencies has been decreasing; in 1985 there were 301 new parent cases open on 31 December; in 1989 the number had dropped to 171.[55] The number of teenage pregnancies in Ontario has also decreased substantially, from 21,499 in 1975 to only 13,263 in 1986.[56] While the numbers are decreasing, it should be noted that these families are at very high risk of becoming involved with a CAS. A survey of three CASs in south-west Ontario shows that about 70% of their clients were under 20 when they had their first child.[57]

Adoption Information Sharing

A 1987 amendment to the CFSA has made it possible for adult adoptees to request disclosure of non-identifying information about their birth families.[58] Through the provincial Adoption Information Unit, adoptees can request information that must in turn be retrieved from individual agencies' own files. The work involved in searching for this information and preparing in the form of a non-identifying report has put an enormous strain on agencies. As noted in the case-flow model, 13% of all intake cases opened in Toronto in 1989 involved information-sharing with adult adoptees, and in some instance ex-wards. Provincial CASs received over 4,500 requests for identifying and non-identifying information in 1987. In 1988 they received 6,900 requests, and had a waiting list of over 5,400 requests.[59] Unfortunately, since agencies use different methods to account for these information requests it is difficult to estimate what proportion of Family Service cases are in fact information-sharing cases. However, even if one uses a conservative estimate, there is little doubt that a significant portion of the recent increase in Family Service cases served can be attributed to the surge in information-sharing cases.

III Children in Substitute Care

There are close to 10,000 children in child welfare placements at any one time in Ontario, and just under 20,000 children were in substitute care at some point during 1988.[60] Child welfare placements range from different types of foster homes to group homes, to treatment centres, and, in some instances, to young adults living on their own with some financial support from a child welfare agency. Substitute care is used for many different purposes. In some cases it can be a form of parenting relief, in others a means of protecting a child until safety can be ensured at home; some children are in care waiting for adoption, others are there permanently. What these children have in common is that they are not living at home, and that a child welfare agency has a certain amount of custodial control over them.[61]

As noted in the Background section, the value of placing children in substitute care has been the subject of extensive debate.[62] One of the difficulties with this ongoing debate is the failure to differentiate between children in short-term care and children in long-term care. Part of this confusion arises from the poor quality of information on children in care, and from the misleading way this information is usually presented. Without entering into the debate itself, this section will attempt to provide as accurate a picture as possible of the population of children in substitute care.

General Trends

The use of substitute care has changed considerably over the past two decades. As documented above in Table 4.1, the ratio of children in care at any one time to the number of families served during a year went from 0.63:1 in 1971 to 0.13:1 in 1988 — an 80% decrease. Currently, a family who becomes involved with a child welfare agency has about one chance in seven of having at least one child placed in substitute care.[63] The decrease in the absolute numbers of children in substitute care has been a little more gradual. As indicated in Table 4.4 and Figure 4.1, the actual number of children in care at any one time was cut almost in half between 1971 and 1988 (a 45% decrease; Row A). Taken as a proportion of all children in the province, the number of children in care decreased by 40% (Row D and Figure 4.2).

Statistics on the numbers of children admitted to care prior to 1982 are not available. Since 1982 the numbers of admissions remained relatively stable (Row B), and, taken as a proportion of the child population, have even increased

Table 4.4
Children in substitute care, Ontario, 1971–1988

	1971	1976	1982	1984	1986	1988
A. Children in care on 31 Dec.	17,807	13,904	11,408	10,754	9,875	9,712
B. Children admitted to care during year	n/a	n/a	10,164	10,175	8,848	10,093
C. Ontario population under 19 years	2,921,900	2,881,800	2,657,200	2,692,900	2,564,100	2,609,500
D. Year end cases as % of Ontario children	0.61%	0.48%	0.43%	0.40%	0.39%	0.37%
E. Admissions as % of Ontario children	n/a	n/a	0.38%	0.38%	0.35%	0.39%
F. Re-admissions/ admissions ratio	n/a	n/a	0.42%	0.46%	0.51%	0.52%
G. Cases open on 31 Dec./ admissions ratio	n/a	n/a	1.19	1.08	1.17	0.96

Source: 1. Population figures for 1971 & 1976 from Ontario Statistics, 1986, Ministry of Treasury & Economy (Row C).
2. Population figures for 1982 to 1988, Statistics Canada, Intercensal and
3. Postcensal Estimates (Row C).
4. Children in care data for 1971 & 1976, Farina and Hoppe (1983).
5. Children in care data from 1982 to 1988 from CAS Quarterly Reports (MCSS); missing information for 1988 supplied by Ontario Association of Children's Aid Societies, *Info '88*.

slightly from 1986 to 1988 (Row E). Because the number of children in care at any one time has decreased relative to the number of admissions, one can conclude that on average children are spending less time in care than they used to (Row G). Compared with American statistics, Ontario appears to have a larger flow of children in and out of care. The ratio of children already in care to children admitted to care during the year is about 1 to 1 in Ontario (Row G); it is about 1.4 to 1 in the United States (Maximus, Inc., 1985). In other words, there is a larger proportion of children in long-term care in the American child welfare system. It is also interesting to note that, as with Family Services (Figure 4.4), the ratio of re-admissions to admissions has increased (Row F); children are being discharged from care more quickly, but more children are returning to care. This increase in re-entry rates has also been documented in the United States (Family Impact Seminar, 1990).

Unfortunately, little is known about the factors that lead to a child's coming into care. Several American studies have had limited success in trying to determine which factors predict placement; history of abuse, poverty, geographic location, child's age and parental emotional disturbance are some of the factors that have been found to be associated with such a decision.[64] An Ontario study of children in care, mostly long-term care, found that 30% were admitted because of abuse, 28% because parents were unable or unwilling to care for the child, 12% because the child had behaviour problems, 11% because of family mental health problems, and 7% because of parent-teen conflict (Darnell Consulting, 1988: 44). It should also be noted that the decision to admit a child to substitute care is usually one that is made jointly with parents, often at the parents' request.[65] Further documentation of this decision process is essential to understand why some children/families require substitute care, while others do not.

The major trends with respect to regional and ethnic

differences were discussed earlier in sections II(ii) and II(iii). The most notable difference was that native children were significantly overrepresented in care, especially in northern Ontario. A review of Native Crown Wards indicates that the experiences of native children in permanent substitute care compare favourably with those of non-native children (James, 1988a). The only regional difference that emerges from examining rates of admission is that in northern Ontario the ratio of re-admissions to admissions is significantly higher than in the rest of the province. In 1982 the northern Ontario ratio of re-admissions to admissions was 0.64:1; in 1988 it was 0.88:1. In the province as a whole the ratio went from 0.42:1 to 0.52:1 during the same period (Row G).

Wardship Status

Care and custody of a child can be transferred to a child welfare agency in essentially two ways: either through a voluntary temporary agreement (Non-Ward), or through a court order making the child a 'ward' of the agency, either for a limited period of time (Society Ward), or permanently (Crown Ward). For both voluntary and court ordered-agreements, the agency must ensure that 'no less restrictive course of action. such as care in the child's own home, is appropriate' (CFSA, Section 29[4][b]). The terms for the transfer of care and custody from the parents to the society are clearly outlined in the CFSA (Box 3).

The distinction between voluntary care and court-ordered wardship is primarily a legal one. In practice, some parents may 'voluntarily' agree to placement because they believe that they have more to lose by going to court. The fact that some agreements are not as voluntary as they may seem is illustrated by the results of an Ontario court file study, which found that 44% of cases that came to court were breakdowns of temporary care agreements (Wildgoose, 1987). Similarly, some court orders may be the result of a truly voluntary agreement with the parents. Although in practice the voluntary/court-ordered distinction does not apply to all situations in the same way, it can nevertheless be seen as an approximate measure of the degree of intrusiveness, and of the extent to which substitute care is being used as a short-term measure aimed at fostering family change, or as a long-term approach to replacing the child's family.

The two pie charts shown in Figures 4.9 and 4.10 represent two very different methods for calculating the distribution of children in care by wardship status. Figure 4.9 illustrates the approach that has traditionally been used in Ontario: the

Box 3: Wardship Options

NON-WARD AGREEMENTS:

(1) A Temporary Care Agreement can be signed between parents and an agency for up to six months, renewable for another six months, if the parents believe that they are 'temporarily unable to care for the child adequately and have discussed with the society alternatives to residential placement' [Section 29]. If the family is requesting placement beyond the maximum 12 months, a court order for Society Wardship can be sought, for a maximum of 12 more months. A child who is 12 or older must also be a voluntary party to the agreement

(2) A Special Needs Agreement applies to situations where a child has a 'behavioural, developmental, emotional, physical or other handicap' [Section 26(d)], and the parents are unable to provide the services required by the child [Section 30]. Unlike the Temporary Care Agreement there is no time limit set.

Both types of agreements can be terminated at any time, within 5 to 21 days of written notice of termination.

WARDSHIPS:

(1) Apprehension: Any child protection worker can apprehend a child, with or without a warrant, if it is believed that the child would be at substantial risk, if left at home, during the time necessary to bring the matter to court [Section (40)(2) and (6)]. The case must then be brought to court within five days of the apprehension.

(2) Temporary Orders giving care and custody to a society can be made during an adjournment [Section (47)(2)(d)]. Unless all parties agree otherwise, adjournments are limited to thirty days. In practice, a child can remain in care under a Temporary Order for several months.

(3) Society Wardship orders place a child in the care and custody of the society for up to 12 months. These orders can be renewed, but the child cannot remain in care for more than two years, including any time spent in care under a Temporary Agreement, or a Temporary Order.

(4) Crown Wardship orders place the child in the care and custody of the society until the child turns 18, is married, or until another order, such as an adoption order, is made. Past the age of 18 an agency can continue to provide care and maintenance to the young adult [Section (67)(2)].

proportion of wards to non-wards is determined by counting all the children in care on a given day, usually 31 December. Unfortunately, this method is very misleading in that it does not account for the high turnover of children in care. Since

Figure 4.9:   Wardship status on 31 December 1986 for Ontario children in care

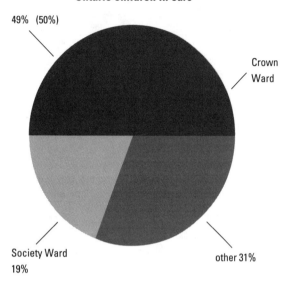

49% (50%)

Crown
Ward

Society Ward
19%

other 31%

Source: Ministry of Community and Social Services, Children's Aid Society Quarterly Reports

Figure 4.10:   Wardship outcome for children admitted to care as portion of all admissions accounted for by court orders, 1988-1989

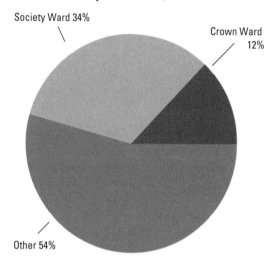

Society Ward 34%

Crown Ward
12%

Other 54%

Source: Ministry of Community and Social Services, Children's Aid Society Quarterly Reports; Office of the Attorney General.

the annual ratio of children in care to admissions to care is about 1 to 1 in Ontario (Table 4.4), the snapshot picture on 31 December fails to account for half of all children who were served in care that year. This cross-sectional approach 'exaggerates the impact of the backlog of all children who over the years have been unable to exit the foster care system' (Kadushin, 1978).

In contrast, Figure 4.10 presents a modified longitudinal view of children's wardship status. Like the case-flow model presented earlier, this chart estimates what proportion of children coming into care eventually become Crown Wards, Society Wards, or Non-Wards. This is not a true longitudinal view since it is not based on following a cohort of children through the system. The proportions were determined by comparing the number of Crown Wardship and Society Wardship court orders to the number of admissions in any given year.[66]

The longitudinal method is most suitable for evaluating the effectiveness of substitute care in terms of the CFSA principle of family reunification. In 1988-89, 12% of children who were admitted to care ended up being permanently removed from their parents. It is harder to estimate what

proportion of children end up being returned home. Some Society Wards eventually become Crown Wards; however, these are accounted for in the 12% of Crown Wards. But some Crown Wards and some Non-Wards who come into care in their mid-teens may end up going from substitute care to independent living without becoming Crown Wards. While these youths cannot be considered to have been returned home, their parents have in principle maintained custody. Thus one can conclude that 88% of parents maintain custody of their child, and in most cases have the child returned home. If one were to separate out those Crown Wards who are adopted from those who remain in care, the proportion of children who become long-term permanent Wards drops to about 5%.[67] Since fewer than 15% of families who become involved with CASs have children come into care, the risk of a family's losing a child to permanent long-term care is under 1%. While keeping permanent long-term care down to about 5% of admissions would appear to be a reasonably good outcome, it should also be remembered that this 5% of children, for whom a permanent home was not found, end up joining the ranks of the close to 5,000 Crown Wards in long-term care.

Changes in the relative proportions of Crown Wards, Society Wards, and Non-Wards over the last fifteen years show a clear trend away from using Crown and Society wardships in favour of using Non-Ward agreements. In 1971 67% of children in care on any given day were Crown Wards; by 1986 the proportion of Crown Wards had dropped to 49%. During that same period the number of Crown Wards dropped from 11,968 to 4,881.[68] Figure 4.11 shows that one can expect to continue to see a drop in the number of Crown Wards in care. The number of new Crown Wardship orders has dropped from 2,147 in 1980, to 1,231 in 1989,[69] thus fewer children are entering long-term care than are leaving. Figure 4.11 also shows that Non-Ward agreements are being used much more frequently than before. This is another indication that children who come into care are spending less time in care than they used to. These trends show that the permanency planning principles that were integrated into child welfare practice in the late 1970s have in fact been successful in keeping large numbers of children from 'drifting' into long-term substitute care. However, it should be noted that this does not necessarily mean that the children

who 'avoided' long-term care are better off than they would have been had they remained in care.[70]

Placement Type

The permanency planning movement focused primarily on keeping children out of care or, if they came into care, having them returned home or adopted as soon as possible. The attention is now shifting towards examining the most effective way of using substitute care. As stated in a recent discussion paper on children in care in Ontario, 'the real issue is providing the most effective intervention for children at the right time' (Wolfe and Jaffe, 1989). The traditional view had been that it was simply a question of providing the child with a 'better' set of parents: i.e., foster parents. Little recognition was given to the special needs of children coming into care, and even less attention was paid to the needs of the families they were leaving, and were expected to return to.

Changes in the types of placements used provide an estimate of the extent to which substitute care is expected to serve special treatment functions. Unfortunately, all the currently available data on children in care are cross-sectional, and are therefore heavily weighted on the side of long-term care. The proportion of children in foster homes on 31 December dropped from 58% in 1981 to 49% in 1987,[71] while the proportion of children in specialized foster homes, CAS group homes, and treatment centres increased. This gradual move away from using traditional foster care can be attributed to two factors: (1) a net loss in the number of available foster placements, and (2) an increasing need for specialized care, usually with a treatment component. The loss of foster homes is discussed below; the need for specialized care is examined in the following section.

From 1981 to 1987 there was a net loss of 1057 foster homes in the province, a 17% decrease. During the same time, new provincial regulations reduced the average number of placements available in any one home from 3.2 to 2, leading to an estimated 48% 'bed' reduction, from 19,632 to 10,156 (Darnell Consulting, 1988). This dramatic decrease in available foster home placements has far outpaced the decrease in the number of children in care. The ratio of children in care to the number of potential foster placements has gone from about 1:1.6 to 1:1, and the ratio of children in foster placements to the number of potential placements has gone from about 1:3.6 to 1:2 (Darnell Consulting, 1988). This drop puts pressure on agencies to place children in

Figure 4.11: **Wardship status calculated as portion of admissions accounted for by court orders**

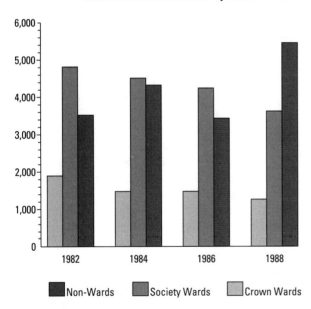

Source: Office of Attorney General and Ministry of Community and Social Services, Children's Aid Society Quarterly Reports.

other facilities, and it seriously undermines the ability of agencies to match children with appropriate homes.

A recent study of Ontario's foster care system attributes this decrease in the number of foster to homes to several factors (Darnell Consulting, 1988). Demographic changes have decreased the pool of potential foster parents. More women are working outside of the home, and the number of two-parent families is decreasing. A second factor is that while families have relied on fostering as an income supplement, the average rate paid for boarding has not kept pace with the cost of raising a child. A third factor identified by this study is that a growing number of foster parents view themselves as professionals, and are frustrated by the lack of training, responsibility, and recognition that their role deserves.

Needs of Children in Substitute Care

The needs of children in care are difficult to document. Even simple statistics, like the average age of children coming into care, are unavailable.[72] The needs of these children can be subdivided into 'basic' and 'special' needs. 'Basic needs' are those that all children share, such as having stable living conditions, and feeling part of a family. 'Special need' refers to a child who has a 'behavioural, developmental, emotional, physical, mental or other handicap' (CFSA, Section 26[d], see Box 4, p. 000, for details).

Several recent reports on children in care, especially long-term care, have found that in many cases basic needs were not being met (Silverman, 1989; Raychaba, 1988; Darnell Consulting, 1988; Kufeldt et al., 1988, 1989; James, 1988b). Stable living arrangements are not a reality for many of the children in these studies. One study found that 48% of the children had experienced more than two placement changes (Kufeldt et al., 1989), and another found that 40% had been placed in more than two different homes (Darnell Consulting, 1988). Provincial Crown Ward reviews indicate that, even once a child is made a permanent ward, placement disruptions remain the norm. Crown Wards experience *on average* three placements from the date of Crown Wardship; they also have to cope with an average of three worker changes (James, 1988b). Maintaining contact with biological families is also a problem for children in care; one study found that 38% of the children surveyed had contact less than once per month (Kufeldt et al., 1989). For those who do have regular contact, the length and quality of visiting conditions is often problematic (Kufeldt et al., 1989; Darnell Consulting,

1988). Interviews with children in long-term care reveal that many feel ill-prepared for independent living and experience a lack of financial and emotional support in making the transition to independence (Raychaba, 1988; Silverman, 1989).

Studies of Ontario children in substitute care have found that they are often at least one year behind in school, and many are described as having significant behavioural and emotional problems (Silverman, 1989; Raychaba, 1988; Darnell Consulting, 1988). One report noted in particular that there appeared to be a surprisingly high number of children in care with developmental or physical disabilities (Darnell Consulting, 1988). The study sample was primarily comprised of long-term care cases. Sixteen per cent of the children in this sample were described by their workers as having developmental or physical disabilities. In contrast, only 6% of the children in their sample had been placed through Special Needs Agreements (CFSA Section 30; see Box 4). According to CAS Quarterly Reports, 234 children, or 2% of children in care on 31 December 1986, were placed through a Special Needs Agreement. This is double the number of special-needs children in care in 1982.

The difficulty with these reports is that they lack both baseline and comparison data. There is no way of determining whether these problems are improving or getting worse. The visibility of youth in long-term care relative to younger children in long-term care has probably increased, given that fewer children are entering long-term care, but this does not mean that the problem is getting worse. In fact, as noted earlier, it seems that fewer children are drifting into long-term care. Furthermore, the lack of comparison data makes it impossible to determine to what extent the problems faced by children in care are due to their placement histories or to their own family backgrounds. A major longitudinal study, recently completed in California, compared a group of children in care with a group of children from similar circumstances at home. There was no evidence that children in care were worse off; in fact, according to some measures they were better off. However, both groups did do significantly worse than children who had not been victims of maltreatment (Wald, Carlsmith, and Lieberman, 1988).

Another limitation with the recent reports on children in care is that, by focusing primarily on children in long-term care, they do not address the needs of the children who will be returning home. As noted earlier, children in long-term permanent care account for only 5% of children admitted to care. Even those studies that have attempted to examine representative samples have failed to do so because they have relied on cross-sectional sampling.[73] The needs of the other 95% of children admitted to care (children in short-term care, as well as adopted children), and the needs of their parents, have been overlooked. An American survey of children leaving care found that compared with adoptive parents and permanent foster parents, biological parents were in the greatest need for ongoing services (Fein and Maluccio, 1984). What all these reports and studies confirm is that, as one would expect, children who are involved with child welfare agencies have more problems than average, and that continued effort needs to be put into meeting the needs of children in care,[74] as well as in meeting the needs of similarly disadvantaged children in the community.

Adoptions

The number of child welfare adoptions has decreased steadily since the early 1970s. In 1970, 5,327 child welfare adoptions were completed, by 1982 the number had dropped to 1,192, and in 1988 were only about 700 adoptions were completed.[75] The families requesting adoptions outnumber the children available for adoption, although requests have also dropped; there were 3,486 requests in 1982, and only 1,983 in 1986.[76] This decrease in the number of adoptions is due to several factors. More young women are deciding to keep their children. There has been a decrease in the birth rate for women under 20.[77] Finally, a growing number of children cannot be adopted because of outstanding access orders: i.e., court orders that give parents or other family members a right to maintain contact with the child. The CFSA does not allow for the adoption of children with access orders (CFSA, Sections 53 and 54). The Provincial Crown Ward Review conducted in 1988 found that 61% of Crown Wards had access orders, and that 51% of Crown Wards in the 0- to 9-year-old group had access orders (James, 1988b).

Given the decreasing number of infants available for adoption, it had been assumed that parents wanting to adopt would turn to older children (Westhues and Cohen, 1989). Surprisingly, from 1982 to 1988 the percentage of older-child adoptions (children over 2 years) has remained fairly constant at around 40% of all adoptions.[78] There are several possible explanations for this failure to place more older children for adoption. First, as noted previously, the number of Crown Wardship orders has been dropping; thus the need for older-child adoptions may not be as great as expected. Second,

although adoption applications far exceed the number of available children, many prospective adoptive parents may still be reluctant to adopt older children. Finally, older children are more likely to have either court ordered or informal access and therefore cannot be adopted (James, 1988b).

The numbers of Ontario native children adopted through the child welfare system have decreased. From 1982 to 1984 an average of 88 native children a year were placed for adoption; 8.3% of all adopted children were native. From 1986 to 1988 the yearly average had dropped to 38, and 5.9% of adopted children were native. During that time 90% of native children placed for adoption were placed in non-native families. The number of adoption disruptions (planned adoptions that are not completed) for native children appears to be slightly lower than for non-native children (James, 1988b). The proportion of black children being adopted has remained fairly stable. The average number of black children placed for adoption annually from 1982 to 1984 was 49 (4.6%), dropping to 33 (5.1%), for the period 1986-88. Over 55% of black children placed for adoption between 1982 and 1988 were placed in non-black homes.[79]

Conclusions

Two major conclusions can be drawn from this analysis of the state of children and families in Ontario's child welfare system: (1) the available data show that the legislative and practical reforms of the 1970s and early 1980s have had a significant impact on the numbers of families served and the numbers of children in substitute care, but (2) the poor quality and, in many cases, complete absence of service statistics make it impossible to determine how these quantitative changes have affected the quality of services.

The impact of the CFSA and the permanency planning movement is clearly reflected in the available data on Family Services and children in substitute care. Over the last fifteen years the numbers of families receiving home-based services have more than doubled, while the numbers of children in care have been cut in half. The chance that a family involved with the child welfare system will have a child placed in substitute care is now about one in ten; the chance of a family's having a child become an un-adopted Crown Ward is about one in two hundred. The mandate of Ontario's child welfare system is broad, and agencies provide services to a variety of disadvantaged children, not only those who have been physically or sexually abused. The system's ability to detect and investigate situations of child maltreatment has expanded; but if many more cases of child sexual abuse are being identified, cases of psychological maltreatment have received little attention. While more children and families are being served, it is difficult to determine how many maltreatment cases remain unidentified.

The available data present a relatively positive picture of Ontario's child welfare system, but this is partially because the data are very limited. Very few statistics are gathered province-wide; in fact, the limited data bases that had been developed over the last fifteen years are no longer being updated.[80] The quality of the data collected is limited, and different data bases produce significantly different counts of basic information like the number of children in care.[81]

Of even greater concern is the fact that in most instances the 'wrong' statistics are gathered. The case-counting method that is most commonly used is the year-end 'snapshot'. This method is used to account for expenditures by determining how many beds are being used, or how many cases workers are carrying. But financial accountability and evaluation of services from the *client's* perspective are two very different things. The 'snapshot', or cross-sectional, method is blind to the enormous volume of services that are delivered during the remaining 364 days of the year. The most dramatic example of the distorting effect of cross-sectional data is that whereas about 50% of children in care at any one time are Crown Wards, only a little over 10% of children ever become Crown Wards, and half of these are then adopted.

Not only are the 'wrong' statistics collected, but in many instances no statistics are collected. Nothing is known about the substantial number of families (70% to 80%) who are involved for reasons other than abuse, and very little is known about children who come into care on a short-term basis. Very little provincial information is collected on the actual services delivered to families, reflecting the narrow focus on finances instead of services. When service delivery data are collected, as is done for Crown Wards, the results indicate that children's needs are not being adequately met. There has been no evaluation of the effectiveness of services, nor even of the effectiveness of basic decisions, such as whether or not a case should be opened for ongoing services. CASs have 'successfully' cut back on the number of children being admitted to care, but there is no evidence that the children who have been maintained at home are actually better off.[82] Without evidence of improved services to chil-

dren, one can only wonder to what extent the decrease in admissions to foster care has been fuelled by cost-saving concerns, as opposed to child protection concerns.

Ontario has one of the oldest child welfare systems in North America. More money is spent on child and family services in Ontario than in most other North American jurisdictions (MCSS, 1988). Ontario's child welfare system offers a unique blend of government financing and a decentralized private non-profit service delivery system. But no effort has been invested in documenting and evaluating this service system. Without such accountability, it is not possible to determine whether these extensive services are accomplishing what they are intended to accomplish. Given the importance of adequately protecting children, the amount of money spent, and the intrusiveness of child welfare interventions, a comprehensive provincial child welfare data base must be developed.

Notes

[1] For a review of the American incidence and prevalence data see Daro (1988), Chap. 1.

[2] For a review of the definitional debate see (a) Giovannoni (1989); and (b) Hutchinson (1990): 60-78.

[3] The Toronto Children's Aid Society was incorporated as a charitable body in October 1891, but it received a legal mandate to intervene only with the passage of the Children's Protection Act of 1893 (Jones and Rutman, 1981, Chap. 3).

[4] E.g., Mnookin (1973); Goldstein, Freud, and Solnit (1979); for a review of this literature, see Trocmé (1989a).

[5] See Trocmé (1989a).

[6] Some physical abuse cases and a growing number of sexual cases are being taken to criminal court, but by and large the vast majority of cases are dealt with outside of the criminal system.

[7] See e.g., Mnookin (1973); Goldstein, Freud and Solnit (1979); Trocmé (1989a).

[8] While the terms 'family' and 'parent' will be used to refer to the recipients of protection services, in practice the mother is the primary target for services.

[9] The 'less restrictive' rule applies both to voluntary services (CFSA Sect. 29 [4]), and mandatory services (CFSA Sect. 47 [3] and Sect. 52 [d]).

[10] For an example of the family systems practice model used by most agencies see Maidman (1984).

[11]This is the case-volume reporting method used in Ministry of Community and Social Services (MCSS) CAS Quarterly Reports, as well as in annual reports from the Ontario Association of Children's Aid Societies.

[12]In particular, two types of cases that are counted differently from agency to agency are (1) information requests from ex-clients, usually adoption information requests, and (2) runaway youths from other jurisdictions placed overnight in CAS care before being sent home or sent to the CAS having jurisdiction in their home. Some agencies count these as intake cases, while others do not include these in their intake statistics.

[13]Statistics Canada, 1971-86 Census.

[14]In 1988 lone parents constituted 55% of families involved with the Catholic Children's Aid Society (CCAS); in 1989 they made up 58% of families involved with the Children's Aid Society of Metropolitan Toronto (CASMT).

[15]See, for example Garbarino and Sherman (1980).

[16]The reliability of abuse allegations data (Table 4.2, Row G) is not known. Agencies may count allegations in different ways. There were no other data sources available to cross-reference these numbers.

[17]Statistics Canada, Census Parts I and II.

[18]CCAS and CASMT data, 1988.

[19]This is an undefined estimate of the number of hours/sessions (it is not clear which) involving Status Indian families. Not only is the meaning of this statistic unclear, but it also appears to be influenced by extraneous factors such as an agency's decision to suddenly start reporting hours/sessions with Status Indians. For example, from 1987 to 1988 the number of hours/sessions claimed by agencies that do not have reserves in their catchment area jumped from 277 to 2,235, simply because of changes in reporting procedures. However, according to Tom Goff, Department of Indian Affairs and Northern Development, agencies with reserves have been relatively consistent in the way they report this information.

[20]Tom Goff, Department of Indian Affairs and Northern Development.

[21]Unfortunately, data from the native agencies were also excluded from the province-wide statistics presented in this report, because of differences in definitions and in reporting methods.

[22]Payukotayno Family Services, 1989-90 Service Plan.

[23]Weechi-it-te-win Family Services, 1989-90 annual report. Note that it uses a broader definition of 'family support' services that does Payukotayano. These may not all be services that fall under the provisions of the CFSA.

[24]Some of these statistics are questionable because of incomplete information on over 30% of cases served. There also are some differences in the ways both agencies report these statistics. Some of the data presented here is pro-rated to account for these differences.

[25]See, for example, McKenzie and Hudson (1985).

[26]For further discussion, see Trocmé (1989b).

[27]Ibid.

[28]This analysis of the service process was based on data provided by the Children's Aid Society of Metropolitan Toronto and the Toronto Catholic Children's Aid Society. Where appropriate, data from both agencies were combined. In some cases it was possible to use data from only one agency; in these instances the data source is marked by an asterisk, but the specific agency is not identified. Transients and adoption disclosure cases are not included in this data.

[29]For a recent review of this literature see Giovannoni (1989), as well as Daro (1988), Chap. 1.

[30]This estimate is very approximate, since a case is not necessarily kept open after intake because an allegation was confirmed. Some cases of confirmed maltreatment are closed at intake, and some cases where no maltreatment was found are kept open for preventive services.

[31]Abuse substantiations based on CCAS data for 1988 and 1989. Coding difficulties makes it difficult to make a similar comparison for CASMT.

[32]In 1988, 74,000 families were 'served' (Table 4.1); of these, 45,000 were opened in 1988, the remaining 29,000 having been carried over from the previous year.

[33]See Bala (1987); Greenland (1987).

[34]CASMT abuse statistics follow a similar trend. In 1985, 45% of abuse cases involved sexual abuse; in 1989 this proportion had increased to 64%.

[35]See Daro (1988).

[36]See, for instance: Straus and Gelles (1988); Daro (1988).

[37]The method for estimating annual incidence is borrowed from D. Finkelhor (1984). Annual incidence = prevalence/17 (0-17 being the definition of 'child' used).

[38]Badgley et al., (1984). The data presented in the report failed to specify the percentage of abused sexually children (under 17). The numbers used in the present report, 13% males and 25% females, are estimates based on the tables on pages 180-3. These estimates correspond well to the recent findings of an American survey using an equally broad definition of sexual abuse. This latter survey found that 16% of males and 27% of females disclosed a history of *child* sexual abuse. (Finkelhor et al., 1990).

[39]See note 37 above.

[40]As noted earlier (p. 74) 70% to 80% of abuse cases are transferred for ongoing services. Although this is not a true substantiation rate, it is the only estimate available.

[41]New York *State of the Child*: 58% of court petitions for reasons of neglect only; Illinois *State of the child*: 72% of maltreatment reports are for neglect; In 1982, 64% of US maltreatment reports were for reasons of neglect only (American Humane Association, 1984) (Daro, 1988).

[42]See, for instance, Wald (1975); Mnookin (1973).

[43]See, for instance, Egeland, Sroufe, and Pianta (1989); Crittenden (1985); Hoffman-Plotkin and Twentyman (1984).

[44]For a comprehensive discussion of these conceptual problems see Melton and Thompson (1987).

[45]CASMT Family Service Information System, form # EDP 304.

[46]Johnston (1989) examined 25 families with cocaine-addicted parents and found that in all cases severe neglect was the major reason for intervention.

[47]Metro Toronto and provincial court data ("charges disposed) provided by Ministry of The Attorney General; cases served from MCSS CAS Quarterlies.
Note: The court orders to cases served ratio should not be confused with the 11% rate of court applications documented in the case-flow model, since once a family becomes involved with court, several orders are likely to be made during the family's history with the child welfare system.

[48]This is probably an underestimation of the number of charges laid, because not all cases involving charges are reported to the registry, and even when reports are made, charges may not have yet been laid.

[49]Wildgoose (1987). In many instances the reason for making the application was not specified, and in only 1% of cases was a child brought before the courts with a 'order to produce': i.e., the case was brought to court before the child was actually removed from his or her home.

[50] CASMT, Court Activity Statistics, Legal Services Department. For 1988: 2,413 adjournments for 1378 applications; for 1989: 2,557 adjournments for 1,389 new applications.

[51]For a discussion of the impact of the court process on child welfare services see Trocmé (1989c).

[52]For a review of runaway studies see Silverman (1989).

[53]Memo from M. Dalley, Missing Children's Registry, Ottawa (1990).

[54]These figures are lower than those compiled recently in an American survey of runaway and homeless youth, which found a 12.6% rate of known sexual abuse and a 42.1% rate of known physical abuse (Powers, Eckenrode, and Jacklitsch, 1990).

[55]CASMT and CCAS Information Systems Reports.

[56]Data supplied by A. Bergman, University of Toronto, Faculty of Social Work.

[57]London Family and Children's Services, memo from L. Philips (MCSS, 1987).

[58]Amendment to the CFSA, S.O. 1987, chapter 4.

[59]OACAS *Info '88*, and *Info '89*. According to Pat O'Brien (MCSS Adoption Unit, personal communication, 1990), the backlog of information requests should start decreasing, since extra staff have been made available, and the major effect of the disclosure legislation has already been felt. A survey of 28 CASs shows that 14 agencies process requests in less than a year, 10 in one to two years, and three in over two years.

[60]Child-in-care figures for 1988 are from CAS Quarterly Reports; missing information in these reports was supplied by OACAS.

[61]Some children are not actually placed with 'strangers'; a child can be placed by a child welfare agency with relatives who act as provisional foster parents. The degree of custodial control can also vary significantly. While even a voluntary temporary care agreement transfers the child's care and custody to the agency, in practice the parents can remain actively involved in all important decisions.

[62]See, for example, Wolfe and Jaffe (1989); Trocmé (1989a), Raychaba (1988).

[63]See Figure 4.6; since the model was developed using Metropolitan Toronto Data, the 14% figure is probably a slight overestimate, since the placement rate is higher in Toronto.

[64]See, for example, Runyan et al. (1981); Seaberg (1988).

[65]Palmer (1989) found that most admissions to foster care in Ontario are made on parental request: 50% in one study of 151 placements, and 57% in another study of 139 placements; Kufeldt, Armstrong, and Dorosh (1989, 1989) found in a study of children in long-term care that 64% of the children had been admitted to care on a the basis of custody by parental agreement, and that 72% of the parents believed that substitute care was the best solution at the time.

[66]The number of admissions for any given year are compared with the number of wardship orders. Those admissions that cannot be accounted for by a wardship order are counted as Non Wards. This method leads to double counting for all children who go from being Society Wards to being Crown Wards. On the other hand, it counts as Non Wards those cases where children were made Wards on an interim basis and then sent back home; it also double-counts those Non Wards who were admitted to care twice in one year. It seems fair to assume that these errors cancel each other out. A major assumption behind this measure is that the three variables are reasonably stable. Both types of orders have decreased at a regular rate from 1982 to 1988; admissions have also been relatively stable, apart from the drop registered in 1986.

[67] In 1988 there were 1231 Crown Wardship orders made, there also were between 713 and 845 adoptions. Thus, a rough estimate of the number of permanent Crown Wards is about 500, or 5% of the 10,093 admissions to care in 1988.

[68] MCSS CAS Quarterlies.

[69] Ministry of the Attorney General, court records, 1990.

[70] Although there is a general assumption in child welfare that children are better off if they are kept out of long-term care, there is very little empirical evidence to support this position. See Trocmé (1989a).

[71] Foster home refers to 'foster homes' and 'foster group homes', as listed on MCSS Child Advocacy Information System annual reports. The total children in care used to calculate this percentage does not include 'clients in unspecified locations'.

[72] The Child Advocacy Information System (CAIS) does provide age data, but since these data are collected cross-sectionally they are vulnerable to the same problem illustrated in Figures 4.9 and 4.10. The CAIS data indicate that children in care on 31 Dec. are on average getting older. However, this is to be expected. Crown Wards are significantly overrepresented in this cross-sectional sample. Crown Wards are getting older on average because fewer new Crown Wards are coming in, therefore they are all getting older. But this does not mean that the average age of children *coming into* care is increasing.

[73] Two-thirds of the children in the Kufeldt et al. (1989) sample were Crown Wards, and 55% of the children in the Darnell (1988) sample were Crown Wards. However, Crown Wardship orders account for only 12% of children admitted to care (Figure 4.9).

[74] Some very creative programs have been developed for helping youth in care, a good example being the 'Speak Out' program run by the CASMT Pape Adolescent Resource Centre (Fay, 1989).

[75] The MCSS information system has two different and inconsistent sets of figures for the number of adoption placements from 1982 to 1988. The numbers in 1988 range from 845 to 641 adoption placements. OACAS reports that there were 713 adoptions completed in 1988; this number is most consistent with the pace in the progressive decrease in number of adoptions.

[76] CAS Quarterly reports.

[77] See note 56 above.

[78] MCSS special computer run, adoption placements by age and year, 1982-88.

[79] MCSS special run.

[80] CAS Quarterly Reports have now been replaced with Service Plan reports, but, to date, the Service Plan data are not being collected centrally.

[81] For example, CAS Quarterlies show that there were 9,874 children in care on 31 Dec. 1986; Child Advocacy Information Systems (MCSS) reports show that on the same day there were 11,632 children in the care of the child welfare system, and OACAS reports that on 30 June 1986 there were 10,700 children in care.

[82] See Trocmé (1989a).

References

American Humane Association
1984   *Trends in Child Abuse and Neglect Reporting*. Denver: Author.

Badgley, R., et al. (Committee on Sexual Offences Against Children)
1984   *Sexual Offences Against Children*. Vol. I. Ottawa: Canadian Government Publishing Centre

Bala, N.C.
1987   *Review of the Ontario Child Abuse Register*. Kingston, Ont.: Social Program Evaluation Group, Queen's University.

Biller, H.B., and R.S. Solomon
1986   *Child Maltreatment and Paternal Deprivation*. Lexington, MA: Lexington Books.

Brassard, M., R. Germain, and S. Hart
1987   *Psychological Maltreatment of Children and Youth*. Elmsford, N.Y.: Pergamon.

Cicchetti, D., and V. Carlson, eds
1989   *Child Maltreatment: Theory and Research*. Cambridge: Cambridge University Press.

Crittenden, P.
1985   'Maltreated infants: Vulnerability and Resilience'. *Journal of Child Psychology and Psychiatry*, 26 (1): 85-96.

Dalley, M.
1989   'Missing Children's Registry', *RCMP Gazette*, 51 (12): 10-19.

Darnell Consulting, Inc.
1988   *The Future of Foster Care*. Toronto: Ontario Association of Children's Aid Societies.

Daro, D.
1988   *Confronting Child Abuse: Research for Effective Program Design*. New York: The Free Press.

Egeland, B., L.A. Sroufe, and R. Pianta
1989   'Effects of Maltreatment on the Development of Young Children'. In Cicchetti and Carlson (1989).

Farina, M., and B. Hoppe
1983   *Child Welfare: A Background and Issues Paper*. Toronto: Ministry of Community and Social Services.

Fay, M.
1989   *Speak Out: An Anthology of Stories by Children in Care.* Toronto: Children's Aid Society of Metropolitan Toronto.

Fein, E., and A. Maluccio
1984   'Children Leaving Foster Care'. *Child Abuse and Neglect,* 8: 425-31.

Finkelhor, D.
1984   *Child Sexual Abuse.* New York: The Free Press.

Finkelhor, D., et al.
1990   'Sexual Abuse in a National Survey of Adult Men and Women'. *Child Abuse and Neglect,* 14: 1928.

Fisher, J.
1989   *Missing Children Research Project.* Ottawa: Solicitor General. London Family and Children's Services.

1987   *Survery of Family Formation and Marital Status.* Toronto: Ministry of Community and Social Services.

Garbarino. J., and D. Sherman
1980   'High-risk Neighbourhoods and High-risk Families'. *Child Development,* 51: 188-98.

Giovannoni, J.M.
1989   'Definitional Issues in Child Maltreatment'. In Cicchetti and Carlson, eds (1989).

Goldstein, J., A. Freud, and A. Solnit
1979   *Beyond the Best Interests of the Child.* New York: The Free Press.

Greenland, C.
1986   'Preventing Child Abuse and Neglect'. *Health Visitor,* 59 (7).

1987   *Preventing CAN Deaths.* London: Tavistock.

Hoffman-Plotkin, D., and C. Twentyman
1984   'A Multimodal Assessment of Behavioural and Cognitive Deficits in Abused and Neglected Children'. *Child Development,* 55 (3); 749-802.

Hutchinson, E.
1990   'Child Maltreatment: Can It Be Defined?' *Social Service Review,* 64 (1): 60-78.

James, B.
1988a   *Special Indian Crown Ward Review Project.* Toronto: Ministry of Community and Social Services.

1988b   *Annual Report: Crown Ward Administrative Review Unit.* Toronto: Ministry of Community and Social Services.

Johnson, C.
1996   *Children of Cocaine Addicts.* Toronto: Institute for the Prevention of Child Abuse.

Jones, A., and L. Rutman
1981   *In the Children's Aid: J.J. Kelso and Child Welfare in Ontario.* Toronto: University of Toronto Press.

Kadushin, A.
1978   'Children in Foster Families and Institutions'. In H. Maas (ed.), *Social Service Research: Review of Studies.* Washington, DC: National Association of Social Workers.

Kufeldt, K., J.D. Armstrong, and M. Dorosh
1988   'Substitute Care: A Vehicle for Development of Discontinuity?' Unpublished mimeograph, University of Calgary, Department of Social Work.

1989   'In Care, In Contact?' Unpublished mimeograph, University of Calgary, Department of Social Work.

Maidman, F.
1984   'Child Protection: Issues and Practice'. In Maidman (ed.), *Child Welfare: A Sourcebook of Knowledge and Practice.* New York: Child Welfare League of America.

Maximus, Inc.
1985   *Child Welfare Chart Book 1985.* Quoted in Family Impact Seminar, *The Crisis in Foster Care: New Directions for the 1990s.* Washington, D.C.: Author.

McKenzie, P.B., and P. Hudson
1985   'Native Children, Child Welfare, and the Colonization of Native People'. In K.L. Levitt and B. Wharf (eds), *The Challenge of Child Welfare.* Vancouver: University of British Columbia Press.

Melton, G., and R. Thompson
1987   'Legislative Approaches to Psychological Maltreatment: A Social Policy Analysis'. In Brassard, Germain, and Hart (1987).

Ministry of Community and Social Services
1988   *Investing in Children.* Toronto: Author.

Mnookin, R.H.
1973   'Foster Care: In Whose Best Interest?' *Harvard Educational Review,* 43 (4): 599-639.

New York State Council on Children and Families
1988   *The State of the Child in New York State.* Albany: Author.

Offord, D.
1986   *Ontario Child Health Study: Summary of Initial Findings.* Toronto: Ministry of Community and Social Services.

Palmer, S.
1989a   'Mediation in Child Protection Cases: An Alternative to the Adversary System'. *Child Welfare,* 68 (1): 21-31.

1989b   *Commentary on 'Children in Care of the State'.* Toronto: Child, Youth and Family Policy Research Centre.

Pelton, L.
1978 'Child Abuse and Neglect: The Myth of Classlessness'. *American Journal of Orthopsychiatry*, 48: 608-17.

Powers, J.C., J. Eckenrode, and B. Jacklitsch
1990 'Runaway and Homeless Youth', *Child Abuse and Neglect*, 14 (1): 87-98.

Raychaba, B.
1988 *A Report on the Special Needs of Youth Leaving the Care of the Child Welfare Service*. Ottawa: National Youth in Care Network.

Runyan, D.K., et al.
1981 'Determinants of Foster Care Placement'. *American Journal of Public Health*, 71 (7): 706-10.

Seaberg, J.R.
1988 'Placement in Permanency Planning'. *Social Work Research and Abstracts*, Winter: 4-7.

Sift, K.
1988 *Knowledge about Neglect: A Critical Review of the Literature*. Monograph. University of Toronto, Faculty of Social Work.

Silverman, P.
1989 *Who Speaks for the Children*? Toronto: Stoddart.

Straus, M., and R. Gelles
1988 'How Violent Are American Families?' In G. Hotaling, D. Finkelhor, et al., *Family Abuse and its Consequences*. Newbury Park, CA: Sage.

Trocmé, N.
1989a *Permanency Planning: Minimum Standard or Innovative Practice*? Toronto: Child, Youth and Family Policy Research Centre.

1989b 'Child Welfare and Children's Mental Health Services for Visible Minorities'. In *Visible Minority Youth Project*. Toronto: Child, Youth and Family Policy Research Centre.

1989c 'Mediation in Child Welfare'. Unpublished paper, Faculty of Social Work, University of Toronto.

Volpe, R.
1989 *Poverty and Child Abuse*. Toronto: Institute for the Prevention of Child Abuse.

Wald, M.
1975 'State Intervention on behalf of "Neglected" Children'. *Stanford Law Review*, 27: 985-1040.

Wald, M.S., J.M. Carlsmith, and P.H. Lieberman
1988 *Protecting Abused and Neglected Children*. Stanford, Ca.: Stanford University Press.

Westhues, A., and J. Cohen
1989 *How to Reduce the Risk: Healthy Functioning Families for Adoptive and Foster Children*. Toronto: University of Toronto Press.

Wildgoose, J.
1987 'Dispute Resolution in Child Protection Cases'. *Canadian Journal of Family Law*, 6: 61-84.

Wolfe, D., and P. Jaffe
1989 *Children in Care of the State*. Toronto: Child, Youth and Family Policy Research Centre.

CHAPTER FIVE

Child Health in Ontario

Highlights

- The past 30 years have witnessed striking reductions in mortality among children in Ontario. Infant mortality in 1985 was 7.3 deaths per 1000 live births, down from 26.0 deaths per 1000 in 1955. Although the mortality reductions among children 1 to 19 years are smaller than for infants, consistently downward trends are evident in the same time period.

- The majority of deaths during infancy occur among low birth-weight infants and those born prematurely. Injuries (motor vehicle and non-motor vehicle) are the leading cause of mortality for children and youth over the age of 1. Future mortality reductions among Ontario children will depend on our ability to resolve these problems.

- Marked economic and racial disparities exist in the health of children. Children are 2 times more likely to die if they are born into families belonging to the lowest vs. the highest quintiles of income. Depending on their age, native children are 2 to 4 times more likely to die than non-native children.

- Despite low levels of mortality in Ontario children, it appears that levels of morbidity (health problems) are high. Existing studies indicate that from 4% to 10% of children in Ontario experience some form of disability. Children with disabilities are at increased risk for experiencing a cumulation of problems in many life spheres — physical, mental, interpersonal, and educational. Some evidence suggests that the prevalence of disability in children has been going up over the past three decades.

- Student use of illicit drugs declined a great deal between 1983 and 1989, reversing the trend for use of some drugs such as stimulants, hallucinogens, and cocaine, which increased between 1977 and 1983. The smallest percentage decreases in student drug use between 1983 and 1989 were for the most frequently used drugs: alcohol and tobacco. These continue to pose important threats to the health of adolescents and young adults.

- Increasing rates of suicide and homicide among adolescents over the past few decades indicate that violence to self and others deserves special attention. Concern arises from both the increasing numbers of deaths attributable to these causes and the significance of these trends for reflecting mental disturbance in the population.

Introduction

The last few years have witnessed a number of efforts to study the health of children (e.g., United Nations Children's Fund, 1989; Avard and Hanvey, 1989; New York State Council on Children and Families, 1988; Testa and Lawlor, 1985). The most relevant of these efforts for Ontario is *The Health of Canada's Children: A Canadian Institute of Child Health Profile* (Avard and Hanvey, 1989). Arising from this document are concerns about problems that need to be solved in order to maintain or improve child health in Canada.

This chapter focuses on the health status of children from birth to age 19 in Ontario; it is intended to contribute information that can be used to identify health-related problem areas that might serve to establish priorities for policy and program development and research activity to improve the health of children. In attempting to achieve this goal, special attention will be focused on (1) identifying children at elevated risk for health problems; (2) revealing health problems that deserve special attention; and (3) evaluating health prob-

This chapter was prepared by Michael Boyle.

lem areas such as AIDS and adolescent substance use that have generated high public concern.

The chapter is divided into five sections. The first examines the concept of health, including its definition and measurement in the population. The second section reviews the mortality experience of Ontario children according to four age groupings: infant (under 1 year), early childhood (ages 1 to 4), later childhood (ages 5 to 14), and adolescence (ages 15 to 19). The third section focuses on childhood morbidity (abnormal or unhealthy states), with special attention to disability, and physical and mental health problems. The fourth section examines special issues of adolescence, including the undesirable consequences of sexual activity; use of tobacco, alcohol, and drugs; violence towards self and others; and use of motor vehicles. The fifth section summarizes and briefly discusses the central findings of the report.

I The Concept of Health

Health is an elusive concept, and no existing definition has achieved a wide consensus. Agreement does exist, however, that health is multidimensional. As early as 1948, the World Health Organization (1948) identified three dimensions of health: physical, social, and emotional. Since that time, researchers have added to and subdivided these dimensions further, depending on their theoretical orientation and the objectives they had in mind for assessing individuals (e.g., see Feinstein, 1987; McDowell and Newell, 1987).

Health Status and Health Determinants

There are two types of concepts that are useful for portraying child health: *health status*, connoting levels of health for individuals or populations, and *health determinants*, connoting opportunities for change in health status. Health status is closely aligned with the concepts of function and dysfunction. Positive health status, or normal functioning, implies that an individual is physically, emotionally, and intellectually able to carry out activities suitable to his/her age, and to pursue and attain socially desirable objectives, and is free from chronic distress and pain. Negative health status, or dysfunction, implies the presence of health conditions (trauma, disease, or injury) that interfere with functioning on a short-term (acute) or long-term (chronic) basis. Loss of function has been characterized at three levels: impairment, indicated by physiological or anatomical abnormalities that

need not have adverse consequences for the individual; disability, marked by a restriction in a person's ability to perform in a manner considered normal for a human being; and handicap, signified by social disadvantages that may arise from disability (McDowell and Newell, 1987: 25).

Health determinants are characteristics of either individuals or environments that increase the chances that a person or population will experience a change in health status. They describe opportunities for change in health status and may be either negative (in which case they are referred to as risks or hazards) or positive. There are two kinds of health determinants: (1) risk factors that are characteristics of *individuals*, which may either be inherited (e.g., haemophilia, sickle cell anaemia) or arise from trauma/injury or behaviours (e.g., smoking, alcohol abuse); and risk conditions that are characteristics of the psycho-social (including economic) *environment* of individuals and populations, such as poverty, unemployment, poor housing, and social isolation. Health determinants are revealed by establishing cause-and-effect relationships to health status or specific health conditions.

Evaluation of Health

The earliest and still most widely used means for assessing population health is frequency of death, or mortality. Identifying factors or causes that account for an excess of mortality have provided for many decades the means of setting health priorities for intervention and research. Mortality information has the advantages of being reliable, complete, available over time and collected in a form useful for comparison among different countries. As mortality decreases, however, it loses its ability to represent the health of a population. At the extreme, where no deaths occur in a segment of a population, we would know little or nothing about the health of its living members. At a practical level, this constitutes the basic problem of using mortality to portray child health beyond infancy. Mortality is insensitive to many of the types of health problems that currently afflict children aged 1 to 19 in developed countries.

Increasingly, the trend is to rely less on mortality rates and more on a broad range of health indicators observed among survivors. One set of indicators springs from the types of problems that come to the attention of the health care system. Hospital discharge diagnoses, for example, can be used to evaluate the frequency and distribution of health problems in a population. Unfortunately, such data can be misleading because the use of health care services depends not only on prevalence of ill health, but on other factors such as cost, accessibility, and the knowledge, attitude, and behaviour of caregivers and children and parents.

Another approach to evaluating health uses information from surveys. In Canada, the first comprehensive attempt to survey population health was the Canada Health Survey done in 1978-79 (Statistics Canada, 1981). This survey collected information in three broad areas: health determinants (behavioural, biomedical, and environmental factors with adverse health consequences), health status (health problems and disability, emotional health, blood pressure, and blood biochemistry) and health utilization. Subsequent national surveys, including the Canada Health and Disability Survey (Statistics Canada, 1986) and the Health and Activity Limitation Survey (Statistics Canada, 1989) paid special attention to disability in the population.

In addition to the national studies cited above, information on child health in Ontario is available from the Ontario Child Health Study done in 1983 (Cadman et al., 1986; Boyle et al., 1987; Offord et al., 1987) and the Canada Health Attitudes and Behaviours Survey done in 1984-85 (King et al., 1985). Although each of these studies provides useful information on child health, their results are difficult to compare because of differences in methodology and in the selection of health indicators. Furthermore, none of the studies provides information over time to assess trends.

The only survey in Ontario that is applicable to children and repeated at regular intervals is the Ontario Student Drug Use Survey, done by the Addiction Research Foundation every two years (Smart and Adlaf, 1989). The health-related data in these surveys focus on adolescent self-reported use of tobacco, alcohol, and psychoactive drugs. Information on physical and emotional functioning, general well-being, disease, or health perceptions is not collected.

The limiting factor in describing child health is the existing data base on health status and determinants. Extensive information on child mortality exists, but, as noted earlier, mortality tends to be an insensitive measure of child health. Information on child morbidity is also available, but morbidity information tends to be sparse, making it difficult to compare the health of children in different areas of the province or in different years. Similarly, information on child health determinants tends to be lacking. This is particularly true in the areas of child nutrition, physical activity, abuse, dental health, and mental health (Avard and Hanvey, 1989).

With these limitations in mind, the remainder of the chapter will provide a picture of child health in Ontario. The three major divisions will focus on mortality, morbidity, and special issues concerning adolescence. Special attention will be directed towards analysing differences in health by child age, year of birth (trend analysis) and place of residence (e.g., Ontario vs. other countries). The final section will highlight the central findings of the report.

II   Mortality

Among Ontario children, the highest risk for death occurs during the first year of life. Risk for death drops precipitously during early childhood and does not begin to increase until late adolescence. This pattern is evident in Figure 5.1, which shows mortality by age for Ontario children in 1985. During infancy, mortality was 7.3 per 1000 live births. Mortality for children aged 1 to 4, 5 to 14, and 15 to 19 was 0.40, 0.22 and 0.61 per 1000 respectively.

Figure 5.1:   Mortality for selected ages, Ontario, 1985

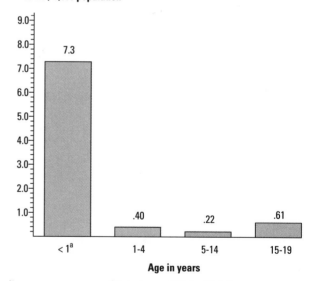

Deaths / 1,000 population

Age in years

[a] (Infants, per 1000 live births)

Source: Province of Ontario (annual), *Vital Statistics* for 1985 (Toronto: Queen's Printer).

Mortality Trends in Ontario

Mortality during infancy, childhood, and adolescence has been decreasing steadily over time. For example, infant mortality in Ontario went from 26.0 per 1000 in 1955 to 16.9 per 1000 in 1970 — a decline of 35% (Figure 5.2). Between 1970 to 1985, the decline was even more dramatic, dropping 57% from 16.9 to 7.3 per 1000.

About 70% of infant deaths occur during the neonatal period, from birth through 27 days. The ratio of deaths between the neonatal (0 to 27 days) and post-neonatal (28 to 364 days) periods remained almost constant between 1955 and 1985 (Figure 2).

Mortality during childhood and adolescence has also been decreasing over time in Ontario, as shown in Figure 5.3. Children aged 1 to 4 benefited from the largest drop in mortality, from 1.15 per 1000 in 1955 to 0.40 per 1000 in

1985 — a reduction of 65%. Mortality among adolescents aged 15 to 19 changed little between 1955 and 1970, but fell from 0.82 per 1000 in 1970 to 0.61 per 1000 in 1985.

Mortality Trends in Ontario Compared with Other Countries

Although the downward trends in child mortality evident in Ontario are comforting, comparisons with other countries suggest that room exists for improving performance. Figure 5.4 depicts changes in infant mortality for Ontario, Canada (Ontario included in the rate), the United States, Sweden, and Japan from 1955 to 1985. In 1985, infant mortality was lower in Ontario than in Canada and the United States; however, it was higher in Ontario than in Sweden and Japan.

Examining trends in infant mortality over the years reveals some interesting differences among the selected countries.

Figure 5.2: Infant and neonatal mortality, Ontario, 1955-1985

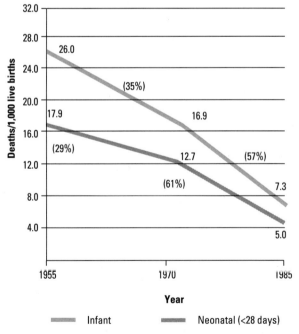

Source: Province of Ontario (annual), *Vital Statistics* for 1955, 1970, 1985 (Toronto: Queen's Printer).

Figure 5.3 Mortality for selected ages, Ontario, 1955-1985

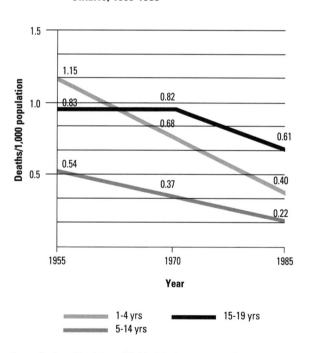

Source: Province of Ontario (annual), *Vital Statistics* for 1955, 1970, 1985 (Toronto: Queen's Printer).

Figure 5.4: Mortality in infancy for selected countries vs. Ontario, 1955-1985

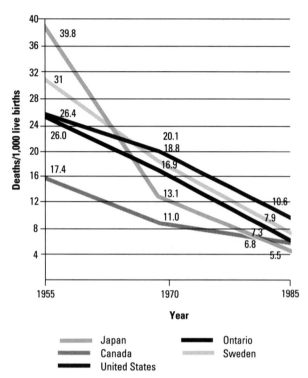

Source: Province of Ontario (annual), *Vital Statistics* for 1955, 1970, 1985 (Toronto: Queen's Printer). United Nations (annual) *Demographic Yearbook* 1975, 1972, 1987.

Figure 5.5: Mortality in infancy for selected causes, Ontario, 1955-1985

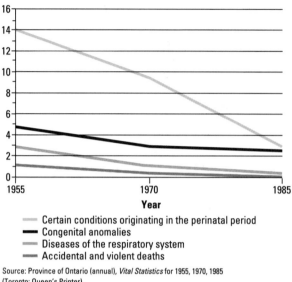

Source: Province of Ontario (annual), *Vital Statistics* for 1955, 1970, 1985
(Toronto: Queen's Printer).

Since 1955, Sweden has had comparatively low infant mortality rates. Trends in Sweden remind us that as infant mortality rates get lower and lower, the absolute gains in mortality reduction become smaller and smaller. Dramatic differences in trends between the United States and Japan indicate that the size of mortality reductions is subject to rapid change in relatively short periods of time. In the United States, for example, reduction in infant mortality was relatively modest between 1955 and 1970, going from 26.4 to 20.1 per 1000 live births (Figure 5.4). During the same period, Japan experienced extraordinary reductions in infant mortality, from 39.8 per 1000 to 13.1 per 1000. Continued reductions in infant mortality from 1970 to 1985 among the Japanese were sufficient to displace Sweden as the country with the lowest rate. This is a remarkable achievement in view of the large difference between the two countries' rates just thirty years earlier, in 1955. The reasons for Japan's large infant mortality reductions are many and complex. It has been argued that a significant proportion of these reductions is attributable to the growth in prosperity among the Japanese after the Second World War (Marmot and Smith, 1989).

Table 5.1
Mortality by age for selected countries expressed as a ratio of Ontario mortality, 1985

Country	Age in years		
	1–4	5–14	15–24
Canada	1.06	1.08	1.16
USA	1.28	1.17	1.35
Sweden	.73	.70	.77
Japan	1.21	.83	.73

Source: Province of Ontario (annual), *Vital Statistics* for 1985 (Toronto: Queen's Printer).
World Health Organization (annual), *World Health Statistics Annual* 1986, 1987, 1988 (Geneva: Author).

Among older children there are also differences in mortality between Ontario and the other countries. Table 5.1 shows age-specific death rates for Canada (Ontario included in the rate), the United States, Sweden, and Japan as a ratio of Ontario age-specific death rates in 1985. For every age group, Canada has higher death rates than Ontario. Death rates in the United States are 17% to 35% higher than in Ontario. In contrast, age-specific death rates in Sweden and Japan are considerably lower than in Ontario. The one exception to this is mortality in Japan among 1- to 4-year-olds, which is 21% higher than the corresponding rate in Ontario.

Although child mortality in Ontario is lower than in Canada and the United States, it is higher than in other industrialized countries such as Sweden and Japan. This latter comparison suggests that further mortality reductions for Ontario children are possible. In an attempt to identify a more precise focus for mortality reduction, the next two sections look separately at causes of death among infants, children, and adolescents.

There are maternal factors associated with low birth weight, including age (17 and under, 35 and over), smoking, low socio-economic and educational status, and inadequate prenatal care (Koontz, 1984; McCormick, 1985). Unfortunately, we know relatively little about the effectiveness of interventions to reduce the prevalence of low birth weight. This is attributable to a lack of research initiatives and

limitations in research methodologies available for studying these types of interventions. In contrast, various components of neonatal intensive care for low birth-weight infants have been demonstrated to be effective (e.g., see Chalmers et al., 1989). Although neonatal intensive care is effective at saving the lives of such infants, it is enormously expensive, raising questions of affordability (Joyce et al., 1988). There is also concern that mortality reductions among low birth-weight infants are accompanied by higher frequencies of health problems among survivors.

Infant Mortality — Causes

Figure 5.5 illustrates shifts in infant mortality in Ontario by cause of death from 1955 to 1985. Deaths attributable to certain conditions originating in the perinatal period have exhibited the largest absolute reduction, from 14.87 to 3.00 per 1000 live births. Deaths attributable to diseases of the respiratory system have posted the largest relative decreases, dropping from 2.67 to 0.13 per 1000 live births between 1955 and 1985 — a reduction of 95%. Although there has been a decline in infant mortality attributable to congenital anomalies, they now account for a substantial portion of deaths that occur in infancy — approximately 34.0%. Interventions for preventing congenital anomalies are complex, and their use involves larger social issues and public health policies. Prenatal diagnosis and treatment using gene replace-

Figure 5.6: Mortality in infancy for selected causes, Japan vs. Ontario, 1985

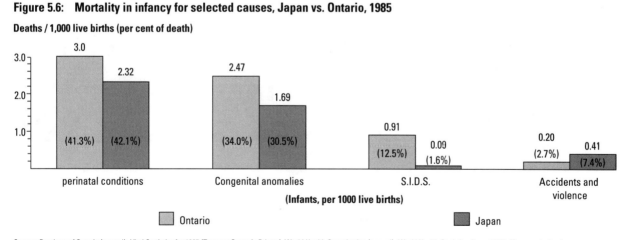

Deaths / 1,000 live births (per cent of death)

Source: Province of Ontario (annual), *Vital Statistics* for 1985 (Toronto: Queen's Printer). World Health Organization (annual), *World Health Statistics Annual* 1986. (Geneva: Author.)

ment therapy are not currently available but will undoubtedly evolve with advances in human genetics.

A comparison of selected causes of death between Ontario and Japan in 1985 reveals differences that deserve special analysis. For example, in Ontario 12.5% of infant deaths were due to sudden infant death syndrome (Figure 5.6), compared with only 1.6% in Japan. The reasons for this difference need to be studied, even given the potential controversy over the classification of sudden infant death. Figure 5.6 also suggests that the Japanese have had more success in reducing deaths attributable to congenital anomalies, and this too deserves further study.

Low Birth Weight in Infancy

To reduce infant mortality, special attention needs to be focused on low birth weight and premature birth (Silins et al., 1985; Campbell, 1989). About 67% of deaths in the neonatal period (0 to 27 days) and about 20% of deaths in the post-neonatal period (28 to 364 days) occur among infants weighing 2500 grams or less at birth (McCormick, 1985). Infants with very low birth weights (1500 grams or less) are at proportionally greater risk, and account for about half of all neonatal deaths.

There are two basic approaches for reducing the contributions made by low birth weight to infant mortality: (1) reduce birth weight specific mortality and/or (2) reduce the rate of low birth weight in the general population. Birthweight-specific mortality has been declining steadily in Onta-

rio during the past decade (Campbell, 1989), and it is generally conceded that the reason is the improved care made possible by the development of intensive hospital-based management (McCormick, 1985).

From a public health perspective, the primary objective is to reduce infant mortality by lowering the proportion of infants delivered under 2500 grams. Although Ontario has seen some success — in 1985, 5.5% of live-born infants weighed less than 2500 grams at birth, down from 7.3% in 1970 — the province lags behind other industrialized countries. For example, in 1983 the percentages of live-born infants weighing less than 2500 grams in Sweden and Japan were 4.4 and 5.4 (United Nations, 1988), compared with 5.6 in Ontario. More dramatic differences existed in the percentage of live-born infants weighing less than 1500 grams: in Sweden and Japan the percentages of infants in this category were 0.72 and 0.44 respectively, compared with 0.89 in Ontario.

Child and Adolescent Mortality — Causes

Examination of vital statistics for Ontario suggests that, with one exception, there have been no major shifts in the distribution of causes of death among children and adolescents from 1955 to 1985. The exception is deaths due to respiratory diseases such as influenza, pneumonia, bronchitis, emphysema, and asthma. In the 1-to-4 age group, for example, the percentages of deaths attributable to respiratory disease fell

Figure 5.7: Selected causes of injury mortality by age, Ontario

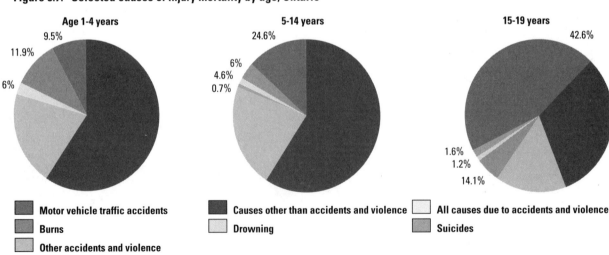

Source: Province of Ontario (annual), Vital Statistics for 1985 (Toronto: Queen's Printer).

from 14.9 in 1955, to 8.4 in 1970, to 3.5 in 1985. Similar reductions occurred in the 5-to-14 and 15-to-19 age groups over the same period.

Since 1955, injuries have been the leading cause of death in Ontario children after the first year of life. This is illustrated for 1985 in Figure 5.7, which shows that 43.8 to 72.7% of deaths in selected age groups were due to injuries. In the 1-to-4 age group, burns and motor vehicle accidents account for the largest proportion of injuries. As children grow older, motor vehicle accidents become the most frequent cause of injury mortality. During late adolescence and early adulthood, suicide is the second leading cause of death.

Comparisons with Sweden and Japan in deaths attributable to injuries indicate that Ontario rates are higher, particularly in children aged 1 to 14. For example, rates in Sweden are much lower among children aged 1 to 4 and 5 to 14 (Figure 5.8). While rates in Japan are about the same as in Ontario among 1- to 4-year-olds, they are about 35% lower in the 5-to-14 age group. Among older adolescents and young adults, differences among the countries in deaths attributable to injuries are much smaller than at younger ages.

The lower proportions for Sweden and Japan are due mainly to lower death rates stemming from motor vehicle accidents (not shown in the figure). The reasons for this are not clear and deserve careful study. When suicide is examined as a cause of death in 15- to 24-year-olds, there are only small differences among Ontario, Sweden, and Japan (0.12, 0.11 and 0.10, deaths per 1000 respectively, in 1985).

Socio-economic and Racial Disparities in Child Mortality

Native children and children living in economically disadvantaged circumstances in Ontario have higher death rates than the total population of children. In recent years, a number of articles have appeared that document the high levels of mortality among native children (Young, 1983; Mao et al., 1986; Morrison et al., 1986; Postl and Moffatt, 1988; Bobet, 1989). Table 5.2 summarizes these mortality differences for Ontario. During the first year of life, post-neonatal mortality (from 28 to 364 days) is about five times higher among native children. An analysis comparing observed and expected deaths in the post-neonatal period on native reserves between 1976 and 1983 (Morrison et al., 1986) showed that diseases of the respiratory system (89 vs. 8.96), sudden infant death (97 vs. 26.86), infective and parasitic diseases (35 vs. 2.97), and accidents/poisonings/violence (29 vs. 7.57) accounted for a substantial portion of the excess deaths. These causes have been identified closely with social factors, particularly economic disadvantage.

Beyond infancy, native children are about four times more likely to die in each age grouping (Table 5.2). A large portion

Figure 5.8: Mortality in childhood for accidents and violence, by age, Sweden and Japan vs. Ontario, 1985

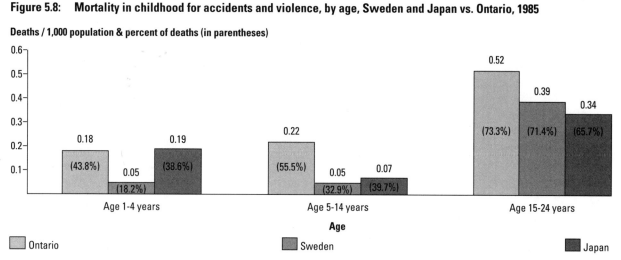

Source: Province of Ontario (annual), *Vital Statistics* for 1985 (Toronto: Queen's Printer) World Health Organization (annual), *World Health Statistics Annual* 1986, 1987. (Geneva: Author.)

Figure 5.9: Infant mortality and age-standardized mortality for children under 20 years by income quintile, urban areas, Canada, 1986, 1971

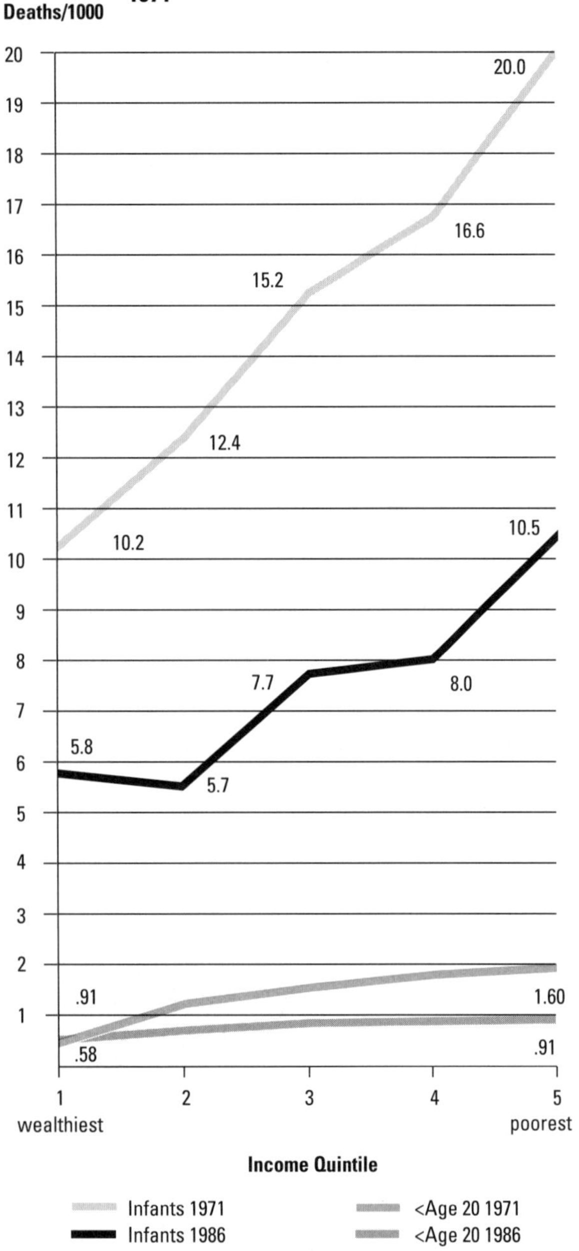

Deaths/1000

Income Quintile

- Infants 1971
- Infants 1986
- <Age 20 1971
- <Age 20 1986

Source: R. Wilkins, O. Adams, and A. Brancker, (1989), "Changes in Mortality by Income in Urban Canada" from 1971 to 1986. Health Reports. 1(2): Pg. 137-174

of excess deaths among native children aged 1 to 19 are attributable to injuries and poisonings. A recent study comparing age-standardized mortality rates due to accidents for native children and the Canadian population aged 1 to 14 (MacWilliam et al., 1987) yielded estimates of 0.67 per 1000 for native children and 0.21 per 1000 for all Canadian children. Accidental deaths caused by fire and drowning were particularly prevalent among native children. Compared with the data reported by MacWilliam et al. (1987), Table 5.2 suggests that in Ontario the differences in mortality between native children and the total Ontario population are even wider than they are across Canada for deaths due to injuries and poisonings.

Suicide is another cause of death with an extremely high prevalence in native groups. Between 1980 and 1984 the average number of suicides per 1000 in native Canadians aged 10 to 14 and 15 to 19 were 0.07 and 0.82 respectively (Avard and Hanvey, 1989). Corresponding data in 1984 for the same age groups in the Canadian population were 0.02 and 0.12 per 1000. Thus native children aged 10 to 14 and 15 to 19 have 4.9 and 6.6 times more chance of committing suicide than the total Canadian population. As indicated in Table 5.2, the differences in mortality due to suicide between native Ontario children and the total Ontario population are particularly large in the 10-to-14 age group. In the 15-to-19 group, native children in Ontario are 6.8 times more likely to commit suicide than the total Ontario population.

Economic disadvantage and ill health in children have been well established in many countries (Shah et al., 1987). Evidence exists within Canada to demonstrate that children born into economically disadvantaged families are at increased risk for death. Figure 5.9 shows infant mortality and age-standardized mortality for urban children under age 20 by income quintiles in Canada during 1971 and 1986. Currently, a child born into the poorest family is twice as likely as a child born into the wealthiest family to die during the first year. Although it is generally accepted that this relationship has social and behavioural origins, precise explanations are inconclusive. Also notable in Figure 5.9 is the uneven way in which mortality increases across the income span. There is a large increase in mortality for both the infant and under-20 groups between the 2nd and 3rd quintiles of income, and the most dramatic jump in mortality for both age groups occurs between the 4th and 5th quintiles.

An important change has taken place between 1971 and 1986 in the pattern of the relationship between family income and child mortality. In 1971, the differences in mortality

Table 5.2
Age-specific mortality rates, registered native and total Ontario population, 1983–1987 average

	All causes		Deaths/1,000 Injuries and poisonings		Suicide	
Age	Native	Total Ontario	Native	Total Ontario	Native	Total Ontario
Neonatal	6.77	4.85				
Post-neonatal	12.70	2.48				
Infant	19.47	7.32	1.52	0.21		
1–4 yrs	1.72	0.41	1.22	0.15		
5–9 yrs	.74	0.21	.53	0.10		
10–14 yrs	.90	0.22	.71	0.11	.19	.01
15–19 yrs	2.52	0.60	2.30	0.44	.61	.09

Source: Province of Ontario (annual), *Vital Statistics* for 1983–87 (Toronto: Queen's Printer).
Health and Welfare Canada (1990), *Registered Indian Mortality by Age and Cause.*
Unpublished data (Ottawa: Medical Services Branch).

between each quintile of income were about equal. In 1986, the differences in mortality between quintiles of income were particularly exaggerated between the 4th and 5th quintiles. These results suggest that health advantages throughout the broad income range are disappearing, concentrating the excess risk for mortality in the lowest income group.

III Morbidity

Disability and physical and mental health problems (morbidity) constitute a large burden for children in Ontario. The extent of morbidity in Canadian children was quantified in the Canada Health Survey (Statistics Canada, 1981). Based on interview responses from a knowledgeable household member (usually a parent), it was estimated that 34.9% of children under age 15 had experienced one or more health problems in the previous year. These included a list of chronic conditions as well as problems associated with certain behaviours that occurred prior to the survey: drug use in the previous two days, disability (restricted activity) days in the previous two weeks, and accidents leading to activity limitations in the previous year. The most frequently reported health problems were skin disorders (7.7%), hay fever and other allergies (7.1%), and acute respiratory problems (5.8%). In addition, it was estimated that 2.8% of children under age 15 had a long-term limitation in the kind or amount of play (under age 6) or school work (ages 6 to 14) they could do.

Disability

Increasing attention and concern are being focused on levels of disability among Ontario children. The Canada Health and Disability Survey (Statistics Canada, 1986) developed a measure of disability to reflect the definition given by the World Health Organization (1980): 'any restriction or lack ... of ability to perform an activity in the manner or within the range considered normal for a human being.' Children were classified as disabled if they met one or more of four criteria: if they (1) used one or more of a number of aids or prostheses excluding eye glasses, dental work, and protective devices used for sports; (2) had a long-term health condition that limited activities normal for a child of that age; (3) attended a special school or class because of a physical condition or health problem; (4) had vision or hearing trouble not corrected by an aid. The Canada Health and Disability Survey estimated that 5.7% of Canadian children aged 14 and under were disabled. The rate rose from 4.4% of those aged 0 to 4 years to 6.7% among those aged 10 to 14. The percentage of children limited in their participation in school, play, or other normal activities was 2.1%. Vision and/or hearing problems uncorrected by an aid affected 0.4% and 0.6% of children respectively. The overall estimate of disability among Ontario children was 6.0%, and rose from 5.0% at

**Table 5.3
Childhood disability in 4- to 16-year-olds, Ontario, 1983**

Category Type	%
Disability	7.2
Sensory	
Unable to see, hear and/or speak	0.3
Difficulty seeing and/or hearing uncorrected by aid	2.4
Physical	
Trouble walking, climbing stairs, bending, lifting or stooping	0.9
Limited in kind or amount of vigorous activity	1.9
Mobility	
Needs help or supervision in using transportation and/or getting around neighbourhood	0.7
Self-care	
Needs help with eating, dressing, bathing or using toilet	0.4
Role	
Limited in kind or amount of ordinary play and/or school work	3.8

Source: M.H. Boyle, (1990), 'Ontario Child Health Study: prevalence of childhood disability' (unpublished data) (Hamilton: Child Epidemiology Unit, McMaster University and Chedoke-McMaster Hospitals).

ages 0 to 4 to 8.0% for those aged 10 to 14 (Office for Disabled Persons, 1988).

The most recent effort of the federal government to estimate the prevalence of disability in the Canadian population comes from the Health and Activity Limitation Survey (HALS: Statistics Canada, 1989). Children were classified as disabled if they were reported to have one or more of the following: (1) general limitations of hearing, speech, or vision; (2) a chronic condition such as diabetes, epilepsy, or muscular dystrophy; and (3) the use of technical aids. HALS estimated that 5.2% of Canadian children aged 14 and under were disabled. The estimate for Ontario children was marginally higher at 5.3% (Office for Disabled Persons, 1990).

The Ontario Child Health Study (OCHS) done in 1983, collected extensive information on morbidity among children aged 4 to 16. Information on disability was provided by the parent (almost always the mother). Prevalence estimates for specific disabilities are given in Table 5.3. The overall prevalence of disability was 7.2%. Allowing for differences in the age structure of those sampled, this estimate is very close

to Ontario estimates from the Canada Health and Disability Survey (1983-84) for disability in the 5-to-9 (6.0%) and 10-to-14 age groups (8.0%) (Office for Disabled Persons, 1988). The most prevalent disability in the OCHS was limitation in the child's participation in play/schoolwork (3.8%). This was followed by disabilities in the sensory and physical areas.

Chronic disability leads to large reductions in life quality among children and quite rightly deserves to be a high priority for research activity and program development. Attempts to quantify the reduction in life quality associated with specific types of disability indicate that more rarely occurring limitations associated with self-care and mobility have the greatest adverse impact (Torrance et al., 1982).

Physical and Mental Health Problems

Many more children experience physical and/or mental health problems than specific disabilities. Information on the prevalence of such problems in Ontario children is available from the OCHS. Prevalence estimates for physical health problems (those reporting any of 19 conditions included on a list) and mental health problems (those reported to have enough symptoms to meet child psychiatrist criteria for disorder) are given in Table 5.4. Overall, 13.2% of children (excluding those with hay fever or some other allergy) were reported to have a physical health problem that is usually chronic or long-term. The estimated prevalence for hay fever or some other allergy was very high, at 17.4%. Unspecified health problems were the second most frequently reported, at 3.9%. These were followed by asthma (2.8%) and the experience of moderate to severe pain (2.6%).

The estimated prevalence of mental health disorders was 18.1% (Table 5.4). Although this estimate seems high, it is consistent with ones generated from recent community studies of childhood mental disorder (see reviews by Costello, 1989; Brandenburg et al., 1990). Among the individual categories, emotional disorder (characterized by anxiety and/or depression) was the most prevalent, at 9.9%, and conduct disorder (characterized by persistent antisocial behaviour) was the least prevalent, at 5.5%.

The OCHS has published numerous reports on the prevalence and distribution of physical and mental health problems and their determinants. The most notable finding, documented in Table 5.4, is the high prevalence of both physical and mental health problems in the child population. In childhood, these problems tend to be more common

Table 5.4
Childhood health problems in 4- to 16-year-olds, Ontario, 1983

Category Type	%
Physical	13.2[a]
Hay fever or some other allergy	17.4
Asthma	2.8
Moderate or severe pain	2.6
Heart problem	2.1
Developmental delay or lag	1.6
Stiffness or deformity of the foot, leg, fingers, arms or back	1.5
Epilepsy or convulsions without fever	0.7
Arthritis or rheumatism	0.7
Club foot or cleft palate	0.5
Other physical health problem specified	1.2[b]
Other physical health problem not specified	3.9
Mental	18.1
Conduct disorder	5.5
Attention deficit hyperactivity disorder	6.2
Emotional disorder	9.9
Somatization disorder	7.2[c]

[a] Excludes hay fever or some other allergies.
[b] Includes one or more of the following: kidney disease; cerebral palsy; diabetes; cancer; spina bifida; muscular dystrophy or other muscle disease; mental retardation; cystic fibrosis; missing fingers, hands, arms, toes, feet or legs; paralysis or weakness of any kind.
[c] For adolescents aged 12–16.
Source: M.H. Boyle, (1990), 'Ontario Child Health Study: prevalence of physical health problems, (unpublished data) (Hamilton: Child Epidemiology Unit, McMaster University and Chedoke-McMaster Hospitals).
D.R. Offord, M.H. Boyle, P. Szatmari, et al. (1987), 'Ontario Child Health Study: II. Six-month prevalence of disorder and rates of service utilization,' *Archives of General Psychiatry*, 44:832–36.

mental health services. The best available data suggest that mental health services are available to a minority of children with serious mental health problems. The best methods for addressing this issue (e.g., expansion of professional treatment services, development of initiatives to prevent child mental health problems, etc.) are not clear. Lack of basic knowledge about the usefulness of activities to promote mental health and to prevent and to treat child mental health problems is making it difficult to decide on a course of action for addressing the issues in the field.

Co-morbidity

Co-morbidity (overlap among different types of health problems) is extensive among children in Ontario. For example, mixed in with chronic disabilities in childhood are a host of co-existing problems that compound the life difficulties of affected children. Figure 5.10 examines the prevalence of selected problems and the utilization of services by disability status in the six-month period before the OCHS. Problems in the physical, mental and social spheres are much more common among children with disability than among those without. The prevalence of school failure is very high in the disabled group (32.9%) compared with the non-disabled group (11.0%), and almost one-quarter of these children are perceived to need professional help with emotional and behavioural problems. As indicated by the frequency of service use, many children with disabilities come into contact with some aspect of the health and social service system.

The overlap demonstrated between childhood disability and other health, social and educational problems exemplifies the way problems in different life spheres cumulate within individual children. For example, there is evidence of overlap between physical and mental health problems and between mental health problems and substance abuse (Offord et al., 1989).

Morbidity Trends

The paucity of useful information over time on the prevalence of child morbidity in Ontario makes it very difficult to analyse trends. Also, comparable information on the prevalence of child morbidity in other countries is unavailable. Although community surveys of child morbidity have been carried out elsewhere, variations in sampling, measurement, and data collection would make it difficult to make direct comparisons with existing Ontario data, including those collected in the OCHS.

among boys than girls. However, by adolescence the prevalence of these problems is almost the same between boys and girls (Cadman et al., 1986; Offord et al., 1987).

A 1990 report discusses some of the major issues of child mental health in Ontario (Boyle, 1990). Briefly, these issues include the problems of measuring child mental health, the availability and appropriate use of child mental health services, the effectiveness of mental health interventions, and structural problems in the organization and provision of child

Figure 5.10:   Associated features of childhood disability, Ontario, 1983

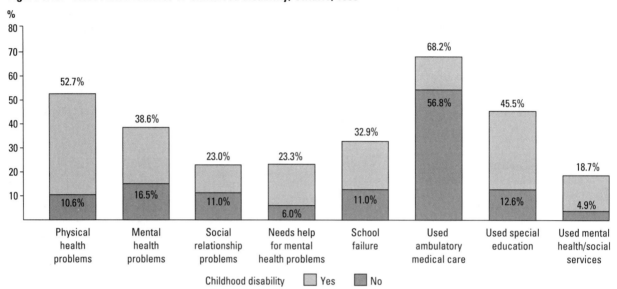

Source: M.H. Boyle (1990). Ontario Child Health Study: associated features of childhood disability (unpublished data) (Hamilton: Child Epidemiology Unit, McMaster University and Chedoke-McMaster Hospitals).

Information on hospital separations (overnight stays in hospital) is available over time for Ontario children and provides another perspective on health patterns. Whether or not this information usefully describes changes in child health is hard to say. Statistics on hospital separations per 1000 and average length of hospital stay in Canada during 1970 and 1984-85 indicate that hospital separations at all ages have decreased, particularly in the 1 to 4 age group. The trend to fewer separations was accompanied by a trend to shorter length of stay (Statistics Canada [annual], 1970, 1984-85). Unfortunately, it is difficult to know the extent to which these trends are due to changing health care policies and practices. For example, increasing concerns about health care costs may have raised thresholds for admitting and keeping children in hospital, thus decreasing separations and length of stay. Alternately, health care providers may be fostering the use of ambulatory medical services as a more appropriate intervention for the types of health problems being encountered.

Examining hospital separations by cause suggests that the downward trends apply more or less equally across the major problem areas. For example, among infants (under 1 year), separations attributable to diseases of the respiratory system declined by 37.6% from 1970 to 1984-85 (Table 5.5). Similar reductions in separations attributable to diseases of the respiratory system occurred in the other age groups. The two general problem areas that showed signs of inconsistency were separations attributable to injury and poisoning and mental disorders. In 1984-85, infant separations attributed to injury and poisoning increased by 14.1%, while decreases occurred in the other age groups (Table 5.5). Although mental disorders are infrequently given as the cause for hospitalization, it is noteworthy that there was no change in the frequency of hospitalization for this reason in the 15 to 19 age group.

Given the absence of information on trends in childhood morbidity in Ontario, it is instructive to examine findings from the United States, which suggest that the proportions of children with limitations of activity because of chronic illness have been increasing over the past three decades (Newacheck et al., 1984). In 1960-61, 1.8% of children aged 16 and under had a limitation of activity; this percentage

Table 5.5
Hospital separations for selected causes by age, Canada, 1984–85, and percentage change from 1970

Cause Age	Separations/1,000	% change from 1970
Diseases of respiratory system		
< 1	91.9	– 37.6
1–4	50.3	– 39.0
5–14	17.6	– 38.9
15–19	9.6	– 30.5
Injury and poisoning		
< 1	10.5	+ 14.1
1–4	11.3	– 28.2
5–14	9.9	– 15.4
15–19	14.8	– 17.9
Mental disorders		
< 1	0.3	– 70.0
1–4	0.4	– 56.4
5–14	1.0	– 15.0
15–19	4.2	0.0

Source: Statistics Canada (annual), *Hospital morbidity* 1970, 1984–85, Cat. 82-206 (Ottawa: Minister of Supply and Services).

increased to 2.9 in 1971 and to 3.8 in 1981. A careful analysis of this trend revealed that changes in methods used in the National Health Interview Survey, in awareness of illness, and in the age-mix of children would have contributed to the increase (Newacheck et al., 1984). Although the authors did not estimate what portion of the trend to increased activity limitation is real, they do suggest that the trend is 'cause for concern' (Newacheck et al., 1984: 235). Data from the most recent National Health Interview Survey (National Center for Health Statistics, 1989) indicate that 5.3% of children in 1988 were reported to have activity limitation. (It is noteworthy that this estimate includes children aged 17 and under — one year more than previous data.)

The findings from the United States that childhood disability has increased steadily over the past three decades are most alarming. Clearly, if we are to understand the health needs of our children, information must be collected in Ontario to evaluate trends in childhood disability. Evidence presented earlier that childhood disability is associated with a wide range of life difficulties adds to the urgency of this issue.

Socio-economic and Racial Disparities in Child Morbidity

Although large-scale survey data are not available in Ontario for comparing native and non-native children on levels of disability and physical and mental health problems, enough evidence exists to indicate that native children are at far greater risk for morbidity than any other child population in the province. Studies reviewed by Avard and Hanvey (1989) indicate that infectious diseases (e.g., intestinal and respiratory) are much more common among native children than other children in Canada. By age 7, fully 7% of Inuit children born in 1973-74 had suffered an episode of meningitis: this risk is about 200 times that expected in the general population (Postl and Moffatt, 1988). Indian infants in the first year of life have demonstrated 17 times greater rates of pneumonia requiring hospitalization than have non-Indian children (Evers and Rand, 1982). Other infectious diseases shown to have a higher prevalence among native than non-native children include otitis media (Baxter et al., 1986), gastroenteritis (Robinson and Moffatt, 1985), hepatitis A and B (Minuk et al., 1982, 1985), tuberculosis (Young, 1985), diphtheria (Shah and Farkas, 1985) and rheumatic fever (Longstaffe et al., 1982).

Children living in economically disadvantaged circumstances in Ontario exhibit higher prevalences of disability and physical and mental health problems than do children in the rest of the population. Figure 5.11 shows the prevalences of these problems by family income as determined in the OCHS. The figure shows an inverse relationship between income and child health morbidity. The highest levels of morbidity occur among families with total incomes under $10,000; once family incomes exceed the poverty line, the decrements in risk become quite small.

Some variations in child morbidity are evident for age, sex, and residence. These variations are shown in Table 5.6 for data collected in the OCHS. Whether the focus is on disability or on physical or mental health problems, prevalences are higher among adolescents than children. Boys are at greater risk than girls for physical and mental health problems, but no appreciable differences exist between boys and girls on reported disability. Children living in urban areas are reported to have higher levels of mental health problems than children living in rural areas, but no urban-rural differences are evident in levels of disability and physical health problems.

Figure 5.11: Prevalence of childhood disability, physical and mental health problems by family income levels, Ontario, 1983

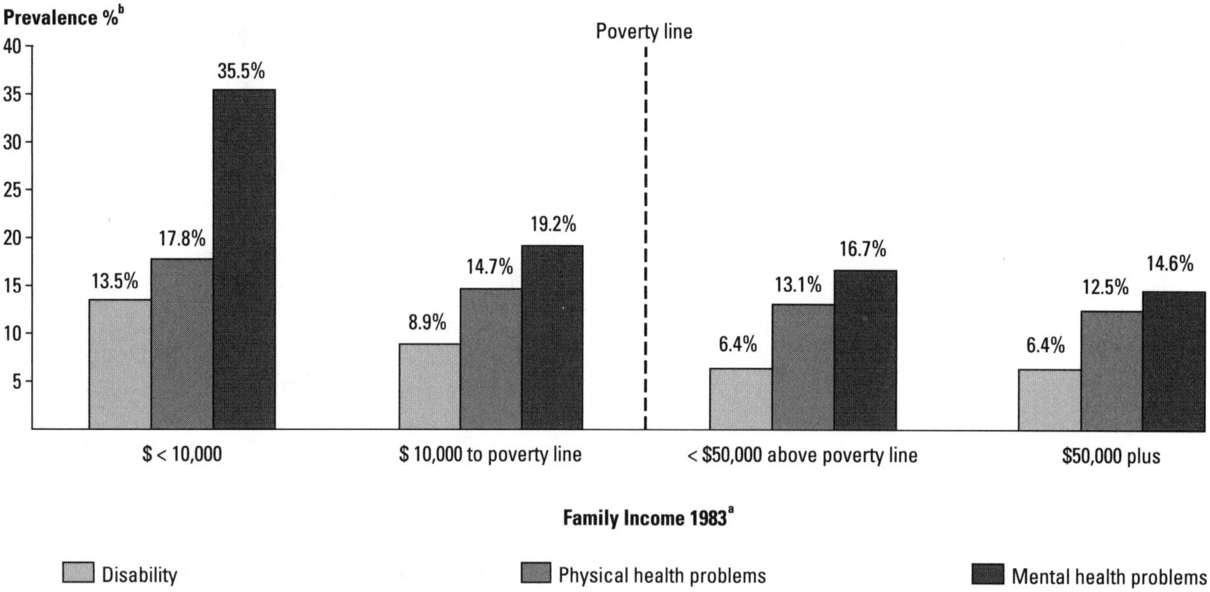

Source: M.H. Boyle (1990) Ontario Child Health Study: prevalence of childhood disability, physical and mental health problems by family income levels (unpublished data) (Hamilton: Child Epidemiology Unit,McMaster University and Chedoke-McMaster Hospitals).

Table 5.6
Prevalence of childhood disability, physical and mental health problems by child age, sex, and residence, Ontario, 1983

		% Prevalence	
Characteristics	Disability	Physical health problems	Mental health problems
Age: 12–16/4–11	10.1/5.1	16.4/11.7	20.2/16.5
Sex: boys/girls	7.2/7.1	15.1/12.2	19.2/16.9
Residence: urban/rural	7.3/6.7	13.8/13.4	19.6/14.9

Source: M.H. Boyle, (1990) 'Ontario Child Health Study: prevalence of childhood disability, physical and mental health problems by child age, sex and residence' (unpublished data) (Hamilton: Child Epidemiology Unit, McMaster University and Chedoke-McMaster Hospitals).

IV Special Issues of Adolescence

As children grow into adolescence, special concerns arise about the consequences of an evolving range of behaviours that place them at risk for a number of preventable health problems. Increased sexual activity; use of tobacco, alcohol, and drugs; aggressive-violent behaviour directed towards self and others; and use of motor and recreational vehicles are all activities that place adolescents at risk for severe and sometimes fatal health consequences.

Sexual Activity

Existing data indicate that teenagers are very active sexually. The Canada Youth and AIDS Study done in 1988 (King et al., 1988) found that by grade 9, 26% of respondents (N = 9925) reported having had sexual intercourse at least once; this estimate rose to 47% among grade 11 respondents (N = 9617) and to 75% among college/ university respondents (N

= 6911). Multiple partners are also common. In the same study, 65% of males and 47% of females who were sexually active college/university respondents reported having had three or more partners. About one-quarter of sexually active college/university respondents (22% male, 28% female) reported never using condoms to prevent AIDS and other sexually transmitted diseases (STDs).

Although longitudinal information on teenage sexual activity in Canada is not available, data from the United States suggest that sexual activity rates are continuing to increase. Between 1979 and 1982, the sexual activity rates of young women appeared to have stabilized after having risen sharply in the 1970s (Hofferth et al., 1987). However, preliminary data from the 1988 National Survey of Family Growth indicate some increase in the proportion of sexually experienced white females between 1982 and 1988, while the proportion of sexually experienced black females remained stable (London et al., 1989). The 1988 National Survey of Adolescent Males indicated that 60% of never-married young men aged 15 to 19 in the United States have had sexual intercourse (Sonenstein et al., 1989). In a comparable sample of males aged 17 to 19 and living in metropolitan areas, the rate of sexual activity reported in 1988 was 15% higher than that reported in 1979, going from 65.7% to 75.5%. At the same time, there were dramatic increases in levels of condom use among the sexually active. For example, reported condom use at last intercourse more than doubled — from 21% to 58% — between 1979 and 1988, among 17- to 19-year-old males living in metropolitan areas. The limited data available suggest that increased condom use among young men has been a relatively recent occurrence, accelerating between 1986 and 1989 (Sonenstein et al., 1989).

Although differences are bound to exist between the experiences of Canadian and American youth, it is worth noting that levels of sexual activity in 1988 were quite similar between the male college/university respondents in the Canada Youth and AIDS Study (King et al., 1988) and the 17- to 19-year-old males living in metropolitan areas in the 1988 National Survey of Adolescent Males. For example, in the Canada Youth and AIDS Study, 77% of males reported having sexual intercourse at least once; the corresponding estimate for males in the American study was 75.5%.

Sexually Transmitted Disease

Increased sexual activity places individuals at risk for a group of illnesses called sexually transmitted diseases (STDs). There are now over 20 organisms and multiple syndromes recognized as being sexually transmitted (Cates and Rauh, 1985). Women are the major sufferers of long-term complications of STDs resulting from undetected and untreated chlamydia or gonococcal infections. These consequences can include infertility, ectopic pregnancy (the fetus growing outside the womb, resulting in its death), other types of reproductive loss, neoplasia, and death.

In Canada, gonococcal infections accounted for about 94% of all STDs in 1986 (Health and Welfare Canada, 1988a). Although rates of gonococcal infections have been declining overall since 1981, they remain high in the 15-to-29 age group, which accounted for 78.3% of the reported cases, and resistant to change in the 15-to-19 group. For example, among males and females aged 15 to 19 in 1978, rates per 100,000 in Canada were 318.8 and 485.1 (Statistics Canada, 1979); in 1986, corresponding rates were 273.8 and 543.3 (Health and Welfare Canada, 1988a).

In addition to gonococcal infections, which are notifiable, there are other STDs such as chlamydia and genital herpes that are not notifiable, and appear to be increasing at alarming proportions (Health and Welfare Canada, 1988a,b). Moreover, survey estimates of the prevalence of STDs in young people suggest that they are occurring more frequently than estimates based on reports suggest. In the survey done in 1988 by King and colleagues (1988), 8% of female (N = 4044) and 7% of male (N = 2840) college/university respondents reported having had a STD. Among street youth who were surveyed as part of the same study, 30% of females (N = 299) and 16% of males (N = 357) reported having had a STD (Radford et al., 1988).

The disease that has elicited the most explicit concern in recent years is acquired immunodeficiency syndrome (AIDS). As of February 1990 13 youths in Canada aged 15 to 19 had been diagnosed with AIDS. Of these, 7 were still alive, 6 males and 1 female. In the 20-to-29 age group, 691 cases had been diagnosed in Canada, of whom 91.0% were male and 58.3% had died (Federal Centre for AIDS, 1990). Given the long incubation period, it is felt that a large number of these people contracted the virus in their teen years.

Because of reporting deficiencies, it is difficult to provide an accurate assessment over time of the health threats posed to adolescents by STDs. AIDS is a case in point. The first case of AIDS in Canada was reported in 1979. The numbers of reported cases increased steadily from that time until the period from July to September 1987, when 236 cases were reported. Since then there has been a gradual but consistent reduction in the numbers of cases reported.

Teenage Pregnancy

Pregnancy affects large numbers of girls aged 15 to 19. Figure 5.12 shows that in 1987, pregnancy (estimated by the sum of live births, stillbirths, and therapeutic abortions occurring among girls aged 19 and under) affected 38.6 per 1000 girls in Ontario. Over the past 15 years teenage pregnancy in Ontario has been decreasing steadily. The number of teenagers giving birth has been on a downward trend since 1970, going from 50.7 per 1000 in 1970 to 20.3 per 1000 in 1987. The number of therapeutic abortions among teenagers has followed a different pattern, increasing between 1975 and 1980 and then decreasing from 1980 onwards.

Although this downward trend for teenage pregnancy in Ontario is encouraging, the experience of some other countries indicates that further reductions are achievable. For example, fertility and pregnancy rates among teenagers are lower in many European countries (Westoff et al., 1983; Wallace and Vienonen, 1989). In Japan, live births to teenagers are extremely rare: in 1985, the number was only 4.1/1000 (United Nations, 1988).

Teenage parenthood constitutes a troubling problem. For some teenagers abortion is available, but the procedure is not without medical risk and represents a traumatic emotional experience for most. Carrying a pregnancy to term places both the baby and the mother at risk for a number of health problems, including low birth weight and infections. Over the longer term, teenage mothers are more likely to drop out of school and fall into a life of poverty and ongoing stress. The ill effects of these stresses combined with lack of experience make it difficult for teenagers to provide adequate parenting, in turn placing the child at risk for additional psychosocial difficulties.

Substance Use/Abuse

Cigarette smoking, alcohol consumption, and use of psychoactive drugs are risk behaviours of increasing frequency in the transition from adolescence to young adulthood (Smart and Adlaf, 1989; Johnston et al., 1988; Boyle and Offord, 1986). Early initiation into cigarette smoking places youth at risk for tobacco addiction and the health hazards associated with long-term use (O'Malley et al., 1984; Kandel and Logan, 1984). Even though problem drinking in adolescence reflects a pattern of 'maturing out' (consumption increasing with age up to the early or mid-20s, then decreasing) (Robins, 1984), it impairs judgement and behavioural control in risky circumstances (e.g., when driving a car, engaging in sexual activity, or involved in interpersonal conflict) and may lead to dependency and long-term impaired function. The use of psychoactive drugs has consequences similar to those of alcohol use (MacDonald, 1984). Use of illicit drugs also has adverse legal consequences for young offenders who are convicted of possession or trafficking.

In Ontario, alcohol is the most frequently reported drug used by students in grades 7 to 13, followed by tobacco and cannabis. Table 5.7 summarizes the results for Ontario Student Drug Use Surveys done by the Addiction Research Foundation (Smart and Adlaf, 1989). The percentage of students (N = 3915) reporting use of each drug at least once in the year prior to the 1989 survey is shown in Column 1. Column 2 gives the percentage change in use for each drug

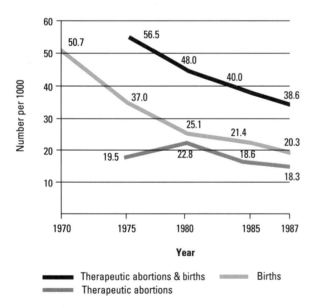

Figure 5.12: Births and therapeutic abortions per 1000, aged 15 to 19, Ontario

Source: Province of Ontario (annual),*Vital Statistics* for 1970, 1975, 1980, 1985, 1987 (Toronto: Queen's Printer).
Statistics Canada (annual),*Therapeutic abortions,* 1975, 1980, 1985, 1987, (Cat. 81-211), (Ottawa: Minister of Supply and Services).

Table 5.7
Tobacco, alcohol, and drug use among Ontario students in grades 7, 9, 11, and 13 for 1989, and percentage change since 1983 and 1977

Drug	% using at least once during the prior year (1989)	% change From 1983 to 1989	% change From 1977 to 1983
Tobacco	23.3	− 19.9	− 4.2
Alcohol	66.2	− 7.7	− 6.0
Cannabis	14.1	− 40.5	− 5.6
Glue	1.9	− 40.6	− 17.9
Other Solvents	3.1	− 24.4	− 37.9
Barbiturates (M)[a]	7.8	− 29.1	− 22.5
Barbiturates (NM)[b]	2.2	− 63.3	0.0
Heroin	1.2	− 25.0	− 20.0
Speed	2.5	− 35.9	+ 44.0
Stimulants (M)	3.3	− 36.5	− 21.2
Stimulants (NM)	6.5	− 57.8	+ 113.9
Tranquillizers (M)	3.1	− 52.3	− 24.4
Tranquillizers (NM)	2.4	− 52.0	+ 2.0
LSD	5.9	− 31.4	+ 41.0
Other Hallucinogens	4.3	− 28.3	+ 39.5
Cocaine	2.7	− 34.1	+ 7.9
PCP	1.1	− 45.0	n/a

[a](M) Medical use
[b](NM) Non-medical use
Source: R.G. Smart and E.M. Adlaf, (1989), 'The Ontario student drug use survey: trends between 1977–1989' (Toronto: Addiction Research Foundation).

from the 1983 to the 1989 surveys. Column 3 gives the percentage change in use from the 1977 to the 1983 surveys.

The majority of students (66.2%) reported use of alcohol, followed by tobacco (23.3%) and cannabis (14.1%). Use of other drugs in 1989 does not exceed 10%: examples include medical barbiturates (7.8%), non-medical stimulants (6.5%), and LSD (5.9%). Drugs showing the lowest frequency of use are PCP (1.1%) and heroin (1.2%).

The patterns of change in reported drug use from the 1977 to 1983 surveys is quite different from those observed between the 1983 and 1989 surveys. Use of many of the 'hard' drugs increased substantially between 1977 and 1983: examples include speed (44.0%), non-medical stimulants (113.9%), LSD (41.0%), and other hallucinogens (39.5%). In contrast, there was a systematic decrease in the reported medical use of drugs. Only very modest decreases were reported in the use of alcohol (6.0%) and tobacco (4.2%) between the 1977 and 1983 surveys.

As indicated in Table 5.7, there have been some dramatic downward shifts over time in student use of drugs. Between the 1983 and 1989 surveys, reported drug use decreased between 7.7% (alcohol) and 63.6% (non-medical barbiturates). The smallest percentage decreases from 1983 to 1989 occurred for the most frequently used drugs: alcohol and tobacco. It is noteworthy that the reported medical use of drugs also decreased substantially: 29.1% for barbiturates, 36.5% for stimulants, and 52.3% for tranquillizers.

Examining patterns of change in reported drug use between the survey periods suggest that alcohol and tobacco use — the two most prevalent forms of drug use — are the most resistant to change. Additional data provided by Smart and Adlaf (1989) indicate that in 1989, 5.6% of students reported using alcohol two or more times a week during the previous year and that 4.7% of students reported smoking more than 10 cigarettes daily during the previous year. In 1987, use at these levels was 5.6% (alcohol) and 4.4% (tobacco). Furthermore, the percentage of students responding 'yes' to alcohol problem items remained constant between 1981 and 1989.

Although use of drugs continues to increase with age, differences in use between male and female students have weakened over time (Smart and Adlaf, 1989). This is also true for regional estimates, where differences in use between areas of the province are no longer statistically significant.

It is important to note that the downward trends in student drug use quantified both in Ontario (Smart and Adlaf, 1989) and in the United States (Johnston et al., 1988) conflict with the popular notion that a drug epidemic exists among the young. Evidence in support of a drug epidemic comes from data on drug offences (Ontario Ministry of Treasury and Economics, 1987) and treatment admissions for cocaine use (Smart and Adlaf, in press), which have been rising steadily in the past decade. Without devaluing the importance of these indicators, it should be underlined that judicial and treatment activities are susceptible to political, social, and economic influences quite unrelated to the prevalence of a particular problem. Furthermore, the individuals involved

with the judicial and health care systems over cocaine use are rarely students, and most are over the age of 20. One might speculate that a significant portion of those now involved in the judicial and treatment processes were teenagers in the late 1970s, when use of cannabis and several 'hard' drugs reached a peak. Also fuelling the perception of a drug epidemic may be the growth in numbers and visibility of street youth, who report very high drug use. In the recent Canada Youth and AIDS Study (Radford et al., 1988), 31% of street youth (N = 712; aged 15 to 20) reported using alcohol two or more times a week. In addition 71% reported using marijuana/hashish and 31% reported using cocaine.

Violence and Related Issues

Accidents and violence account for the largest portion of death and disability in late adolescence. As shown in Figure 5.13, deaths from motor vehicle accidents increased between 1955 to 1970 and then decreased between 1970 and 1985. Countering this decline, however, was an increase in deaths attributed to suicide and homicide between 1970 and 1985. In 1955, there were no reported suicides among 15 to 19

Figure 5.13: Mortality in adolescence (aged 15-19) by selected cause, Ontario, 1955-1985

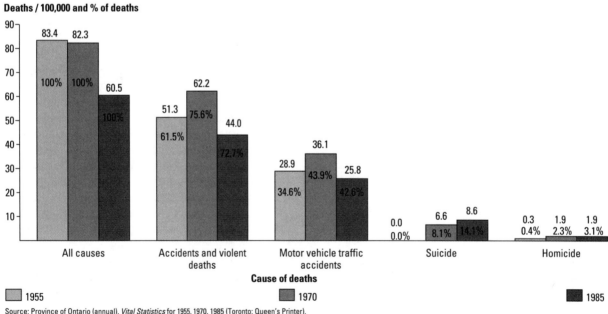

Source: Province of Ontario (annual), *Vital Statistics* for 1955, 1970, 1985 (Toronto: Queen's Printer).

year-olds in Ontario. By 1985, the rate had grown to 8.6/100,000 and accounted for 14.1% of all deaths in the age group. Inspection of suicide rates on a yearly basis reveals an unusual pattern (National Task Force on Suicide in Canada, 1987). Among males aged 15 to 19 the Ontario rate per 100,000 went from 9.3 to 14.6 between 1970 and 1971. In 1985, the rate per 100,000 was 14.7, virtually unchanged. Among females 15 to 19 the rate per 100,000 went from 1.2 to 3.0 between 1968 and 1969. In 1985, the rate per 100,000 was 2.0, down slightly from the 1969 rate. On balance, it appears that suicide rates in the 15-to-19 age group have stabilized since 1970. A significant increase in reported suicides took place in the late 1960s, some of which may have been due to changing practices in classifying this cause of death.

Although homicides occur infrequently, it is nevertheless disconcerting to observe the rates increase over time (Fig. 5.13). These increases, on a much smaller scale, parallel the experience of the United States, where homicide rates for all ages of children have increased, particularly since the mid-1950s (Christoffel, 1984).

V Discussion

This chapter has depicted the health — or more correctly, the ill health — of children aged 19 and under in Ontario. Three broad areas were covered: mortality; morbidity including disability and physical and mental health problems; and special issues of adolescence associated with risk behaviours arising in the transition from adolescence to adulthood.

Mortality
The three decades from 1955 to 1985 witnessed striking reductions in mortality among children aged 19 and under in Ontario. These trends parallel those taking place in both the developed and the developing world. As impressive as these reductions are, however, there are still countries with much better performance records. For example, the rate of mortality reduction over the past 30 years is much higher in Japan than Ontario. Furthermore, current levels of child mortality are higher in Ontario than countries such as Japan and Sweden.

The factors that distinguish Ontario from other countries with better track records need to be carefully analysed (e.g., see Marmot and Smith, 1989). Data presented in this chapter

indicate, for example, that the risk for infant death attributable to very low birth weight (under 1500g) and teenage pregnancy is lower in Sweden and Japan. Sudden infant death, which accounts for 14% of infant deaths in Ontario, is extremely rare in Japan. Deaths in childhood and adolescence attributable to injuries are substantially lower in Sweden and Japan than Ontario. The strategies available for preventing accidents are well delineated (Christophersen, 1989; Brooks and Roberts, 1990), although we need to know much more about the cost effectiveness of various alternatives.

Morbidity
Depending on age and sex, existing studies suggest that between 4% and 10% of children in Ontario experience some form of disability. As we have seen from information provided in this chapter, the life quality of children with disabilities is severely compromised. Such children are at excessive risk for experiencing a cumulation of problems in many spheres — physical, mental, interpersonal, educational, and so on. In addition to children with disabilities, there are many more reported to be suffering from physical and mental health problems. Available surveys suggest that levels of child morbidity are extremely high in Ontario.

It seems almost trite to argue that the high levels of morbidity reported to exist among Ontario children should be a priority for policy and research activity. We have relatively little knowledge about the significance of these estimates. No adequate basis exists for comparing the prevalence of child morbidity in Ontario with that in other countries. Historical information on levels of child morbidity in Ontario is simply non-existent.

Among the areas of child morbidity that deserve special attention, it appears that disability should be given first priority. It is the one area where there is reasonably strong evidence that prevalence has increased over time. To reiterate an earlier point, evidence from the United States indicates a three-fold increase in the prevalence of childhood disability, from 1.8% to 5.3% between 1961 and 1988. The precise reasons for such increases have not been identified. Some, but by no means all, of the increases have been attributed to shifts in the age distribution studied (larger proportions of the sample being older) and better recognition of children with disabilities (Newacheck et al., 1984). The portion of the increase that is 'real' (i.e., reflects actual increases in the frequency of childhood disability) could be attributed to a number of factors. For example, increasingly heroic efforts to save extremely ill or damaged children could lead to higher levels of disability over time. Whether or not this is the case deserves study.

Special Issues of Adolescence

A consensus exists that adolescence constitutes an extremely important transitional period in which an expanding array of behavioural alternatives greatly increase the risk for preventable health problems, both immediate and long-term. Many of these problems, such as AIDS, teenage pregnancy, drug abuse, and deaths from motor vehicle accidents and violence, have elicited widespread public concern. Although the current prevalence of these problems is far too high, it is worth noting that downward trends are evident. The precise mechanisms that account for these trends are unclear. It seems reasonable to assume that a clearer understanding of the factors that help to reduce the risk of such problems should be a priority for policy and research activity, the objective being to identify and support the mechanisms that might accelerate risk reductions in the future.

Despite the generally positive health trends among adolescents, there are several counter-currents that raise concern. First of all, it would appear that there are groups of adolescents in which health problems are becoming increasingly prevalent. For example, street youth, young offenders and even school dropouts are at elevated risk for a number of physical and mental health problems. In the face of improved health for the majority, it is conceivable that social forces are conspiring to concentrate health risks in identifiable groups of disadvantaged youths. Second, the downward trends in adolescent substance use are least impressive for the legal drugs — tobacco and alcohol — that happen to be the most prevalent. In the long term, use of tobacco and alcohol at current levels would seem to pose far greater health risks to youth than current levels of experimental use of illicit drugs. Without downgrading the importance of maintaining a policy and research focus on illicit drugs, we must not lose sight of tobacco and alcohol in public health attempts to reduce drug consumption in adolescence. Finally, increasing rates of suicide and homicide among adolescents over the past few decades indicate that violence to self and others deserves policy and research attention. Concern arises from both the increasing numbers of deaths attributable to these causes, and the significance of these trends for reflecting mental health levels in the population. As reported by the OCHS, the prevalence of mental health morbidity among children and adolescents is very high. Unfortunately, there is little or no context — such as trends or comparable data from other countries — that might be used to interpret available estimates from the OCHS.

Socio-economic and Racial Disparities in Health

Children from economically disadvantaged circumstances and native children, as a special subset, are at elevated risk for high levels of mortality and morbidity. Although the evidence linking poor health and economic disadvantage is incontrovertible, the mechanisms or reasons for this relationship need further clarification. This leaves much room for debate about the types of policy that might help to address the health imbalances associated with economic disadvantage. One point that is particularly important to note is that the expression of the relationship (correlation) between poor health and economic disadvantage may be changing over time. In brief, it appears that poor health and income do not relate to one another in equal steps. The concentration of high levels of childhood disability, and physical and mental health problems among families below the poverty line suggests that the effects of poverty are cumulative and expressed among the most disadvantaged. In contrast, the differences in childhood morbidity between the wealthiest families in society and families above poverty levels are not that large.

Information Requirements

Mortality data are becoming increasingly less effective for evaluating child health in Ontario, and serious problems of interpretation arise when information on the use of health services is used to describe levels of health in the population. Allowing that meaningful information on child health status and health determinants are needed to set priorities for policy and research activity, it seems inevitable that repeated surveys of child health will have to be undertaken. Information in important areas such as child nutrition and physical activity is very sparse. The data that are becoming available on childhood disability and physical and mental health problems remind us that surveys done in isolation are not necessarily the best guides in setting priorities for policy and research. Furthermore, the interconnections among disability, physical and mental health problems, and special problems of adolescence suggest that future surveys of child health need to be broadly based. Of course, the basic prerequisites for initiating repeated surveys of child health have to be in place, including clear, attainable objectives; adequate measurement; and strong survey design. The initiative and financing for such surveys must come from government, and their objectives must be closely tied to important policy questions.

Summary

In depicting child health from birth to age 19 in Ontario, this chapter has identified a number of questions that should rank as priorities for policy and research activities. For example, why is child mortality so much lower in Sweden and Japan than Ontario? What importance should we attach to the high levels of childhood morbidity prevalent in Ontario? What mechanisms explain the generally favourable health trends in adolescence? Are health problems in adolescence becoming increasingly concentrated among alienated and disadvantaged youth? What is the nature of the relationship between income and health? Are there threshold effects in the association between income and health such that the burden of ill health is focused on the economically disadvantaged?

In addition to these questions, this chapter has pointed to two fundamental concerns. First is the persistence of major health inequities that depend on the economic circumstances of children's families. While the data on changes in mortality by income in urban Canada from 1971 to 1986 show diminishing absolute differences in mortality between income quintiles, relative inequalities persist (Wilkins et al., 1990). Moreover, information from the OCHS indicates that childhood morbidity, particularly in the form of mental health problems, is far more prevalent in economically disadvantaged families than in the general population.

Second, the information available for assessing child health in the general population is woefully inadequate. For the most part, mortality statistics continue to shape our perceptions about the health needs of children. Although these statistics are reliable, available over time and collected in other countries so that cross-cultural comparisons are possible, the information they provide is relevant to only a very small fraction of the population. For instance, examination over time of mortality statistics alone indicates that dramatic gains have been made in child health, and that the room for improvement is becoming smaller and smaller. In contrast, survey information indicates that child morbidity

is growing, and that the problems arise in many different spheres: physical, emotional, interpersonal, and educational. The emergence of these problems can be expected to account for some of the increases in childhood disability documented in studies from the United States. Unfortunately, the information on child morbidity in Ontario is too sparse to permit definitive statements about trends. Furthermore, our definition and measurement of child health needs upgrading. Controversies persist about the reliability and meaningfulness of existing child health measures.

Identifying the health problems of childhood and adolescence that will need to be addressed in the upcoming decade poses important difficulties. Most of these difficulties stem from our need to rely on past information — much of which is inadequate. One thing is clear, however. Our perspectives on child health must be realigned to bring into focus those health problems that are *not* life-threatening. Childhood disability, mental health problems, educational difficulties, and violence directed towards self and others are all serving to reduce the life quality of Ontario children, if not their life expectancy. Much work needs to be done to understand the significance of these problems and the reasons for their existence. The challenge is clear, and must be taken up if the goal of 'Health for All' is to become a reality.

Note

The Ontario Child Health Study was supported by funds from the Ontario Ministry of Community and Social Services and carried out by the Child Epidemiology Unit, Department of Psychiatry, McMaster University, and the Child and Family Centre, Chedoke Division, Chedoke-McMaster Hospitals, Hamilton, Ontario. The author is supported by a faculty scholar award from the William T. Grant Foundation.

References

Avard, D. and L. Hanvey
  1989 *The Health of Canada's Children: A CICH Profile*. Ottawa: Canadian Institute for Child Health.

Baxter, J., G. Julien, T. Tewfit, H.J. Ilecki, and M.B. Craco
  1986 'Observations on the Prevalence of Ear Disease in the Inuit and Cree Indian School Population of Kuujjuaraapik'. *Journal of Otolaryngology*, 15 (1): 25-30.

Bobet, E.
  1989 'Indian mortality'. *Canadian Social Trends*, Winter: 11-14.

Boyle, M.H. and D.R. Offord
  1986 'Smoking, Drinking and Use of Illicit Drugs among Adolescents in Ontario: Prevalence, Patterns of Use and Sociodemographic Correlates'. *Canadian Medical Association Journal*, 135: 1113-21.

Boyle, M.H., D.R. Offord, H.F. Hofmann, G.P. Catlin, J.A. Byles, D.T. Cadman, J.W. Crawford, P.S. Links, and N.I. Rae-Grant
  1987 'Ontario Child Health Study: I. Methodology'. *Archives of General Psychiatry*, 44: 826-31.

Boyle, M.H.
  1990 'Children's Mental Health Issues'. In: *Children, Families and Public Policy in the 90's* (Ch. 3), L. Johnson and D. Barnhorst, eds. Toronto: Thompson Educational Publishing.

Brandenburg, N.A., R.M. Friedman, and S. Silver
  1990 'The Epidemiology of Childhood Psychiatric Disorders: Prevalence Findings from Recent Studies'. *Journal of the American Academy of Child and Adolescent Psychiatry*, 29: 76-83.

Brooks, P.H. and M.C. Roberts
  1990 'Social Science and the Prevention of Children's Injuries'. *Social Policy Report*, 4 (I): 1-11.

Cadman, D., M.H. Boyle, D.R. Offord, P. Szatmari, N.I. Rae-Grant, J. Crawford, and J. Byles
  1986 'Chronic Illness and Functional Limitation in Ontario Children: Findings of the Ontario Child Health Study'. *Canadian Medical Association Journal*, 135: 761-7.

Campbell, K.
  1989 'Perinatal Mortality in Ontario 1979-1988'. Toronto: Minister's Advisory Committee on Reproductive Care.

Cates, W. and J.L. Rauh
  1985 'Adolescents and Sexually Transmitted Diseases: An Expanding Problem'. *Journal of Adolescent Health Care*, 6: 257-61.

Chalmers, I., M. Enkin, and M.J.N.C. Keirse, (eds.)
  1989 *Effective Care in Pregnancy and Childbirth*. Volume 1. 'Pregnancy', parts I-V. Volume 2: 'Childbirth', parts VI-X. Oxford: Oxford University Press.

Christoffel, K.K.
  1984 'Homicide in Childhood: A Public Health Problem in Need of Attention'. *American Journal of Public Health*, 74: 68-70.

Christophersen, E.R.
  1989 'Injury control'. *American Psychologist*, 44: 237-41.

Costello, E.J.
  1989 'Developments in Child Psychiatric Epidemiology'. *Journal of the American Academy of Child and Adolescent Psychiatry*, 28: 836-41.

Evers, S. and C. Rand
  1982 'Morbidity in Canadian Indian and Non-Indian Children in the First Year of Life'. *Canadian Medical Association Journal*, 126: 249-52.

Federal Centre for AIDS
  1990 *Surveillance update: AIDS in Canada*. Ottawa: Health and Welfare Canada, 26 Feb. 1990.

Feinstein, A.R.
  1987 *Clinimetrics*. New Haven: Yale University Press.

Health and Welfare Canada
  1988a *Sexually Transmitted Disease in Canada 1986*. Vol. 1451E, March. Ottawa: Laboratory Centre for Disease Control, Health and Welfare Canada.

Health and Welfare Canada
  1988b *Canada Diseases Weekly Report*. Vol. 14-20, 21 May. Ottawa: Laboratory Centre for Disease Control, Health and Welfare Canada.

Hofferth, S.L., J.R. Kahn, and W. Baldwin
  1987 'Premarital Sexual Activity among U.S. Teenage Women over the Past Three Decades'. *Family Planning Perspectives*, 19: 46-53.

Johnston, L.D., P.M. O'Malley, and J.G. Bachman
  1988 *Illicit Drug Use, Smoking, and Drinking by America's High School Students, College Students and Young Adults, 1975-1987*. Rockville, M.D.: National Institute of Drug Abuse.

Joyce, T., H. Corman, and M. Grossman
  1988 'A Cost-Effectiveness Analysis of Strategies to Reduce Infant Mortality'. *Medical Care*, 26: 348-60.

Kandel, D.B. and J.A. Logan
  1984 'Patterns of Drug Use from Adolescence to Young Adulthood: I. Periods of Risk for Initiation, Continued Use, and Discontinuation'. *American Journal of Public Health*, 74: 660-4.

King, A.J.C., A.S. Robertson, and W.K. Warren
  1985 *Canada Health Attitudes and Behaviours Survey*. Kingston, Ontario: Social Program Evaluation Group, Queen's University.

King, A.J.C., R.P. Beazley, W.K. Warren, C.A. Hankins, A.S. Robertson, and J.L. Radford
  1988 *Canada Youth and AIDS Study*. Kingston, Ont.: Social Program Evaluation Group, Queen's University.

Koontz, A.
  1984 'Pregnancy and Infant Health: Progress toward the 1990 Objectives'. *Public Health Reports*, 99 (2): 184-92.

London, K.A., et al.
  1989 'Preliminary Findings from the National Survey of Family Growth, Cycle IV'. Paper presented at the Annual Meeting

of the Population Association of America, Baltimore, 31 March.

Longstaffe, S., B. Postl, H. Kao, L. Nicolle, and C.A. Ferguson
1982 'Rheumatic Fever in Native Children in Manitoba'. *Canadian Medical Association Journal*, 127: 497-8.

McCormick, M.C.
1985 'The Contribution of Low Birth Weight to Infant Mortality and Childhood Morbidity'. *New England Journal of Medicine*, 312 (2): 82-9.

MacDonald, D.I.
1984 'Drugs, Drinking, and Adolescence'. *American Journal of Diseases of Children*, 138: 117-25.

McDowell, I. and C. Newell
1987 *Measuring Health: A Guide to Rating Scales and Questionnaires*. Oxford: Oxford University Press.

MacWilliam, L., Y. Mao, E. Nicholls, and D.T. Wigle
1987 'Fatal Accidental Childhood Injuries in Canada. *Canadian Journal of Public Health*, 78: 129-35.

Mao, Y., H. Morrison, R. Semenciw, and D. Wigle
1986 'Mortality on Canadian Indian Reserves, 1977-82'. *Canadian Journal of Public Health*, 77: 263-8.

Marmot, M.G. and G.D. Smith
1989 'Why are the Japanese Living Longer'? *British Medical Journal*, 299: 1547-51.

Minuk, G.Y., J.G. Waggoner, and R. Jerrigan
1982 'Prevalence of Antibody to Hepatitis A Virus in a Canadian Inuit Community. *Canadian Medical Association Journal*, 127: 850-2.

Minuk, G.Y., H. Ling, B. Postl, J.G. Waggoner, L.E. Nicolle, and J.H. Hoofnagle
1985 'Changing Epidemiology of Hepatitis B Virus Infection in the Canadian North'. *American Journal of Epidemiology*, 121 (4): 598-604.

Morrison, H.I., R.M. Semenciw, Y. Mao, and D.T. Wigle
1986 'Infant Mortality on Canadian Indian Reserves, 1976-1983'. *Canadian Journal of Public Health*, 77: 269-72.

National Center for Health Statistics
1989 *Current Estimates from the Health Interview Survey: United States, 1988*. Vital and Health Statistics, Series 10, Number 173 (DHEW Publication No. 89-1501). Hyattsville, MD: Author.

National Task Force on Suicide in Canada
1987 *Suicide in Canada*. Cat. No. H39-107/1987E. Ottawa: Minister of National Health and Welfare.

Newacheck, P.W., P.P. Budetti, and P. McManus
1984 'Trends in Childhood Disability'. *American Journal of Public Health*, 74: 232-6.

New York State Council on Children and Families
1988 *State of the Child in New York State*. Albany, NY: Author.

Office for Disabled Persons
1988 Statistical Profile of Disabled Persons in Ontario. Toronto: Queen's Printer.

1990 Unpublished data from the health and activity limitations survey. Toronto.

Offord, D.R., M.H. Boyle, P. Szatmari, N.I. Rae-Grant, P.S. Links, D.T. Cadman, J.A. Byles, J.W. Crawford, H. Munroe Blum, C. Byrne, H. Thomas, and C.A. Woodward
1987 'Ontario Child Health Study: II. Six-month Prevalence of Disorder and Rates of Service Utilization'. *Archives of General Psychiatry*, 44: 832-6.

Offord, D.R., M.H. Boyle, J.E. Fleming, H. Munroe Blum, and N.I. Rae-Grant
1989 'Ontario Child Health Study: Summary of Selected Results'. *Canadian Journal of Psychiatry*, 34: 483-91.

O'Malley, P.M., J.G. Bachman, and L.D. Johnston
1984 'Period, Age, and Cohort Effects on Substance Use among American Youth, 1976-82'. *American Journal of Public Health*, 74: 682-8.

Ontario Ministry of Treasury and Economics
1987 *Ontario statistics 1986*. Toronto: Author.

Postl, B. and M. Moffatt
1988 'The Health of Canada's Native People: An Overview'. *Canadian Family Physician*, 34: 2413-9, 2580.

Radford, J.L., A.J.C. King, and W.K. Warren
1988 *Street Youth and AIDS*. Kingston, Ont.: Social Program Evaluation Group, Queen's University.

Robins, L.N.
1984 'The Natural History of Adolescent Drug Use'. *American Journal of Public Health*, 74: 656-7.

Robinson, E.J. and M. Moffatt
1985 'Outbreak of Rotavirus Gastroenteritis in a James Bay Cree Community'. *Canadian Journal of Public Health*, 76: 21-4.

Shah, C.P. and C.S. Farkas
1985 'The Health of Indians in Canadian Cities: A Challenge to the Health Care System'. *Canadian Medical Association Journal*, 133: 859-63.

Shah, C.P., M. Kahan, and J. Krauser
1987 'The Health of Children of Low-Income Families. *Canadian Medical Association Journal*, 137: 485-90.

Silins, J., R.M. Semenciw, H. Morrison, J. Lindsay, G.J. Sherman, Y. Mao, and D.T. Wigle
1985 'Risk Factors for Perinatal Mortality in Canada. *Canadian Medical Association Journal*, 133: 1214-9.

Smart, R.G. and E.M. Adlaf
1989 *The Ontario Student Drug Use Survey: Trends between 1977-1989*. Toronto: Addiction Research Foundation.

Smart, R.G. and E.M. Adlaf
in
press 'Trends in Treatment Admissions for Cocaine and Other Drug Abusers'. *Canadian Journal of Psychiatry*.

Sonenstein, F.L., J.H. Pleck, and L.C. Ku
1989 'Sexual Activity, Condom Use and AIDS Awareness among Adolescent Males'. *Family Planning Perspectives*, 21: 152-8.

Statistics Canada (annual)
1970,
1984-85 *Hospital Marbidity*. Cat. 82-206. Ottawa: Ministry of Supply and Services.

Statistics Canada
1979 *Annual Report of Notifiable Diseases 1978*. Cat. 82-201. Ottawa: Minister of Industry, Trade and Commerce.

1981 *The Health of Canadians: Report of the Canadian Health Survey*. Cat. 82-538E. Ottawa: Minister of Supply and Services.

1986 *Report of the Canadian Health and Disability Survey 1983-1984*. Cat. 82-555E. Ottawa: Minister of Supply and Services.

1989 *The Health and Activity Limitation Survey: Subprovincial Data for Ontario*. Cat. 82-608. Ottawa: Minister of Supply and Services.

Testa, M. and E. Lawlor
1985 *The State of the Child: 1985*. Chicago: The Chapin Hall Center for Children, the University of Chicago.

Torrance, G.W., M.H. Boyle, and S.P. Horwood
1982 'Application of Multi-attribute Utility Theory to Measure Social Preferences for Health States'. *Operations Research*, 30: 1043-69.

United Nations Children's Fund
1989 *The State of the World's Children 1989*. Oxford: Oxford University Press.

United Nations
1957-1988 *Demographic Yearbook 1955-1989*. New York: Author.

Wallace, H.M. and M. Vienonen
1989 'Teenage pregnancy in Sweden and Finland: Implications for the United States'. *Journal of Adolescent Health Care*, 10: 231-6.

Westoff, C.F., G. Calot, and A.D. Foster
1983 'Teenage Fertility in Developed Nations: 1971-1980'. *Family Planning Perspectives*, 15 (3): 105-9.

Wilkins, R., O. Adams, and A. Brancker
1990 'Highlights from a New Study of Changes in Mortality by Income in Urban Canada'. *Chronic Diseases in Canada*, 11 (3): 38-40 (Health and Welfare Canada).

World Health Organization
1948 *Basic Documents* (p.2). Geneva: Author.

1980 *International Classification of Impairments, Disabilities and Handicaps. A Manual of Classification Relating to the Consequences of Disease*. Geneva: Author.

Young, T.K.
1983 'Mortality Pattern of Isolated Indians in Northwestern Ontario: A 10-year Review'. *Public Health Reports*, 98 (5): 467-75.

1985 'BCG Vaccination among Canadian Indians and Inuit: The Epidemiological Bases for Policy Decision'. *Canadian Journal of Public Health*, 76: 124-9.

CHAPTER SIX

Education and the Child

Highlights

- Publicly supported schools in Ontario serve about 2 million children from a wide variety of social backgrounds and communities.
- Ontarians spend about one in four of their tax dollars on education.
- Pupil-teacher ratios have declined continuously over the years and vary little across the province.
- Children are placed in the Basic, General, or Advanced streams in grade 9 (soon to be grade 10).
- Ontario's school teachers are experienced, and well educated and well paid relative to other occupational groups.
- Most learning-disabled and other exceptional students attend their local schools.
- French immersion programs have grown very rapidly throughout the province.

- Heritage language programs have become quite popular, especially in central Ontario.
- Placement in the Basic, General, or Advanced streams, achievement, and dropping out depend upon a variety of social-background and school-related factors.
- In a period of about forty years, the likelihood of an Ontario child's graduating from high school has more than doubled.
- Anywhere from one-third to one-half of Ontario children leave school before graduation, although increasing numbers have been re-entering later.
- Stream placement and dropping out have major implications for a child's future social and economic prospects.
- There is little connection between home and school. Parents are a little-used resource in the Ontario school system.

Much can be done with an Ontarian, if he or she be caught young.

(Adapted from Dr Johnson)

Introduction

To school before 9:00 in the morning. Home, perhaps, for lunch. Back in class before 1:00 in the afternoon. Out between 3:30 and 4:00. That is part of the routine for about 2 million Ontario children, roughly 185 days a year. By the time most people educated in the province reach 16 years of age, they have spent about 2,000 days in school, amounting to 15,000 hours or more in the classroom. School is a big part of a child's everyday life.

Sooner or later, of course, schooldays end. But while everyone eventually leaves school, school never leaves any-

one. Formal education is an important social institution that shapes the character of those who pass through and sifts and sorts them for future social and economic roles. This chapter is about Ontario children, what happens to them in school, and what some of the consequences of schooling are for their lives.

I Who are the Children in Ontario Schools?

The children in Ontario schools are the daughters and sons of the (c. 1946-65) baby-boom generation of Canadians living in the most prosperous part of one of the world's most prosperous countries. Where there is wealth, however, there are extremes in wealth (Hunter, 1986). In Toronto, for example, the physical distance between the public housing project

This chapter was prepared by Margaret Denton and Alfred A. Hunter.

of Regent Park North and the mansions of Rosedale is a short subway ride; the economic distance is hundreds of thousands of dollars (McMillan, 1990). Moreover, Toronto and the narrow strip extending in either direction between Ottawa and Windsor constitute the affluent commercial and industrial core to an economically depressed, resource-based periphery of smaller cities, towns, and Indian reservations stretching over 1,500 kilometres north and west to Hudson Bay and the Manitoba border.

Ontario and, particularly, Toronto have long been and remain desired destinations for immigrants from around the world. Currently, one in every two immigrants to Canada gives Ontario as her or his intended place of residence. Where there is immigration, there is ethnic and linguistic diversity. Some 30% of those who live in Ontario have neither British nor French origins, the largest groups being those of Italian, German, and Dutch ancestry. Another 12% claim French or combined British and French origins. In

fact, 23% of Ontarians are foreign-born, as are fully 36% of the residents of Toronto.

Virtually all Ontario children between the ages of 5 and 15 have been enrolled in school since *The Adolescent School Attendance Act* raised the mandatory school age from 14 to 16 years in 1919. The province also funds the kindergartens, and all Ontario school boards will soon be required to offer both senior kindergarten (by 1992) and junior kindergarten (by 1994), although attendance will not be required. As a consequence, it will soon be possible for a child living anywhere in Ontario to enter the school system at 3 years, 8 months of age, and remain there until he or she either drops out after reaching 16 or eventually graduates from high school.

As Table 6.1 shows, the numbers of children enrolled in Ontario schools fell quite steadily from 1971 to 1984. More recently, they have begun to rise again in the elementary schools, although they are still low in the secondary schools.

Table 6.1
Historical trends in selected educational indicators, Ontario

Year	Schools	Enrolment	% increase or decrease	FTE[a] of all teachers
1971	4,207	1,456,840	−0.6	62,166
1972	4,126	1,445,101	−0.8	61,977
1973	4,038	1,422,885	−1.5	60,774
1974	4,005	1,404,839	−1.3	61,102
1975	4,017	1,389,478	−1.1	63,223
1976	3,995	1,360,085	−2.1	62,956
1977	3,978	1,329,396	−2.3	62,318
1978	3,969	1,290,337	−2.9	61,118
1979	3,945	1,258,761	−2.4	60,076
1980	3,925	1,240,274	−1.5	59,547
1981	3,895	1,224,880	−1.2	59,815
1982	3,874	1,217,412	−0.6	60,307
1983	3,856	1,209,567	−0.6	60,459
1984	3,815	1,204,807	−0.4	60,779
1985[b]	3,721	1,156,995	...	58,497
1986[b]	3,723	1,166,114	0.8	59,495
1987[b]	3,745	1,184,288	1.6	61,527

[a]Full-time equivalent
[b]Data are not comparable with those for the years prior to 1985 because of the extension of funding to Roman Catholic schools.
Source: Ontario Education Statistics, 1987, Table 4.141.

This reflects a number of trends. First, the baby boom of the late 1940s, the 1950s, and the early 1960s was followed by a baby bust in the late 1960s and the 1970s. In the 1980s the birth rate has stabilized and perhaps even increased somewhat in Ontario. Second, the percentage of students of secondary school age enrolled in school also fell through the 1970s, rising again in the 1980s. Finally, recent increases in immigration to Ontario have caused school enrolments to grow. The recent levelling of the birth rate should mean little dramatic change in the overall size of the province's school population in the near future.

II How do Ontarians Provide for the Children's Schooling?

In Ontario, elementary and secondary education, both public and Roman Catholic, is financed jointly by the province and local school boards (for the Roman Catholic system, financing was extended to the end of secondary school in 1987). Briefly, the government establishes a base level of funding required per pupil. To meet this level, municipalities tax at a single rate across the province, and the government makes up the difference through grants to individual school boards. Beyond this, adjustments in provincial grants are made to compensate for special local conditions, such as higher costs for goods and services in geographically remote communities. In addition, municipalities can tax at a rate higher than is required to meet the base funding level for 'unrecognized expenditures' — a possibility more readily realized in communities with large tax assessment rolls than in places with small ones.

The opportunity to tax beyond the base level is especially a problem for Roman Catholic boards. Because they have much smaller tax bases than the public boards do, they have less capacity to tax beyond the base, and they receive much higher proportions of their budgets from the province than public boards do. This problem may be exacerbated in certain municipalities by competition for Roman Catholic students, which drives educational costs up for public and Roman Catholic boards alike. Specifically, where there are large numbers of Roman Catholics, the per pupil expenditure is higher for both the public and the Roman Catholic boards (Lawton, 1989).

In 1989, approximately $10.6-billion was spent on publicly

supported elementary and secondary schooling in Ontario, $5.6-billion of which was raised through local taxes and $5-billion paid as grants from the government. This amounted to one in every four of the tax dollars Ontarians paid that year. Over time, public school expenditures in the province have been increasingly borne by local taxes. In 1970, provincial grants amounted to about 52% of the total; in 1989, they had fallen to approximately 47%. This has made it increasingly difficult for communities with small tax bases to provide the same levels of educational funding as places with large tax bases. In fact, the wealthier the board, the higher the per pupil expenditure (Michaud, 1989). (Nevertheless, inequalities in educational funding are much greater in the United States than in Canada, and greater in some provinces than in Ontario [Lawton, 1989].)

What accounts for the fact that some boards spend more on public education than others do? Approximately 60% of the differences among school board budgets are explained by teachers' salaries, average class size, and the total number of students in the board (Atherton, 1989). Specifically, the higher the teachers' salaries, the smaller the average class size, and the greater the total number of students, the higher the budget.

Over time, the cost of schooling children in Ontario has increased in real terms. In constant (1981) dollars, costs per pupil in public and Roman Catholic elementary schools rose from $1,569 in 1969 to $3,045 in 1986 (see Figure 6.1). In the secondary schools, they rose from $2,906 to $4,043. The increase in real costs per pupil has been much greater, therefore, in the elementary schools (94%) than in the secondary schools (39%).

Educational costs have risen in large part because of increases in teachers' salaries. As shown in Figure 6.2, in 1974 teachers' salaries and fringe benefits accounted for 57.1% of net day school expenditures on publicly supported schools in the province. In 1980, they accounted for 60.1%, and in 1985, 67.9%. A large increase occurred between 1981 and 1982, when the percentage jumped from 61.8 to 67.3. By contrast, supplies and other expenses as a percentage of net day school expenditures have dropped. In 1974 they stood at 9.3%, in 1980 at 8.4%, and in 1985 at 5.5%. In this case, a large decrease occurred between 1981 and 1982, when the percentage dropped from 8.4 to 5.1.

Educational policies in Canada have long been informed by the belief that schooling expenditures are investments in

Figure 6.1: Per-pupil costs (constant 1981 $), elementary and secondary schools, public and Roman Catholic, 1969-1986

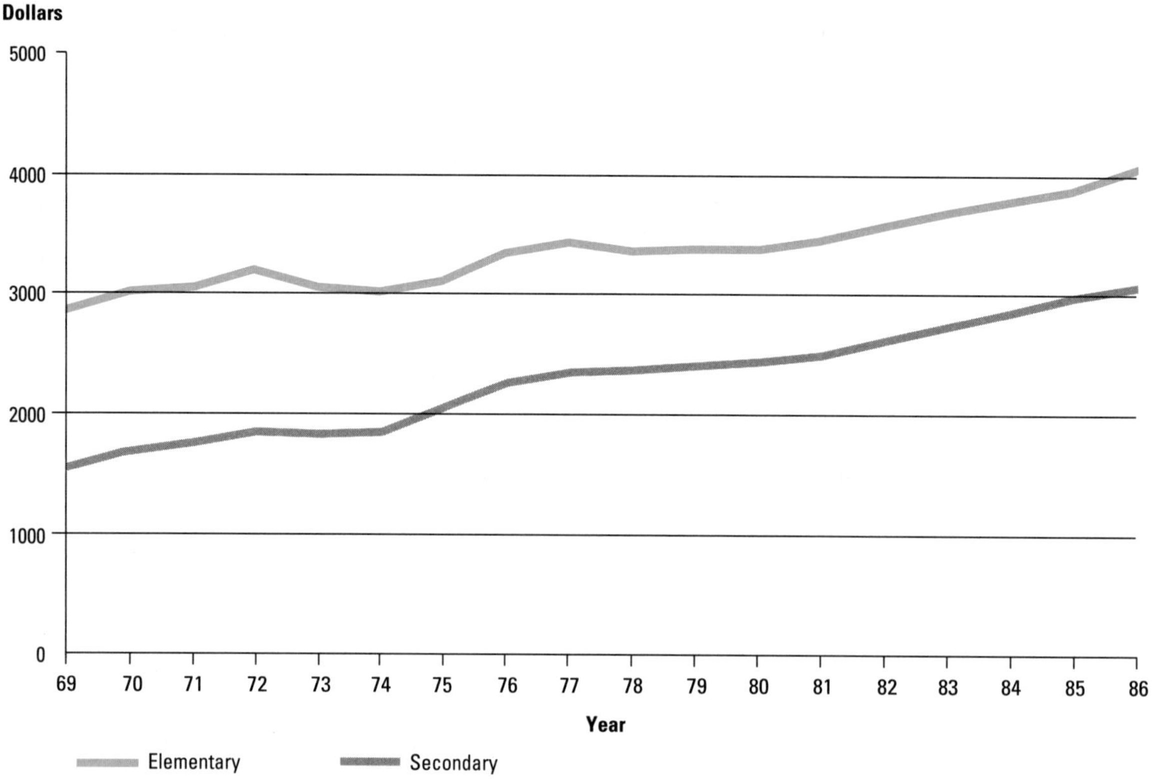

Dollars

Elementary   Secondary

Source: Ontario Education Statistics, Table 1.35, 1987.

the children required for a productive economy. At least since the revelations of Coleman and his associates (1966) in the United States, however, a continuing conundrum in educational finance has been that increases in educational expenditures appear to be only rarely or weakly reflected in conventional measurements of educational quality (also see Coleman, 1989; Hanushek, 1981, 1986). So, for example, there is no consistent evidence that raising teachers' salaries, reducing student-teacher ratios, providing better facilities, or increasing per student expenditures bring improvements in students' grades, performance on standardized tests, school attendance, or dropout rates. Still, as Livingstone (1989) points out, there are almost certainly limits below which decreases in school funding will show in such indicators.

There are, as well, other reasons for spending more on teachers, schools and students apart from raising 'educational quality' in the measurable respects described above, such as providing better working conditions for teachers and more hospitable surroundings for students.

Perhaps in partial response to the knowledge that more money has not necessarily made better schools, public confidence in the Ontario school system declined sharply in the 1980s (Moss and Rutledge, 1990), and the proportion of the Gross National Product allocated to education in Canada and other Western industrialized countries is lower now than it was a decade ago. At the same time, Ontarians remain confident that a good education is important for a person's future success (Livingstone, 1989).

Figure 6.2: Teachers' salaries and fringe benefits, supplies, and other expenses, public and Roman Catholic schools, 1974-1986

Percentage of net day school expenditure

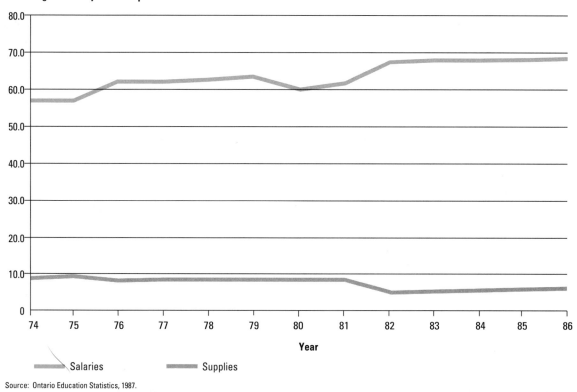

Source: Ontario Education Statistics, 1987.

III How is the Children's Schooling Organized?

The Ontario school system is the largest system of public education in Canada. In 1987, the 160 public and Roman Catholic school boards in the province operated 5,000 schools and employed 97,000 teachers full-time to teach 2 million children. Some 69% of the children enrolled in elementary or secondary schools in Ontario attend public schools (Figure 6.3). Another 28% go to Roman Catholic schools. About 3% attend private schools.

Over time, the elementary and secondary school systems in Ontario have become increasingly centralized and rationalized, especially in areas outside of major cities. In 1960,

there were 3,676 school boards in the province. This figure was reduced to 1,673 in 1965, 186 in 1970, and 161 in 1987. In 1965, the typical public or Roman Catholic school board operated fewer than 5 elementary schools, each of which had an average of 8 full-time teachers and 231 students. In 1987, the typical board operated more than 23 elementary schools, each with an average of 15 teachers and 316 students. Similar changes occurred for public and Roman Catholic secondary schools, as well.

The move to large, county-wide school boards in Ontario in the 1960s appears to have had mixed effects. It did reduce the inequalities in educational financing enormously (Lawton, 1989). At the same time, local community and school autonomy were also reduced considerably with the creation of county school board bureaucracies and a proliferation of

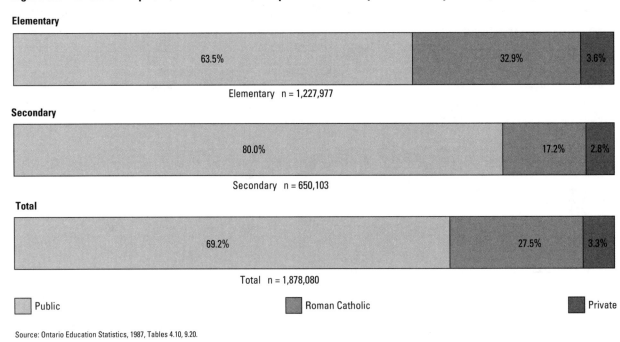

Figure 6.3:   Enrolment in public, Roman Catholic, and private elementary and secondary schools, Ontario, 1987

Elementary

| 63.5% | 32.9% | 3.6% |

Elementary   n = 1,227,977

Secondary

| 80.0% | 17.2% | 2.8% |

Secondary   n = 650,103

Total

| 69.2% | 27.5% | 3.3% |

Total   n = 1,878,080

☐ Public   ☐ Roman Catholic   ■ Private

Source: Ontario Education Statistics, 1987, Tables 4.10, 9.20.

administrative and other positions at the board level (Cameron, 1978; also see Wise, 1979).

Likewise, the move to larger schools has brought both benefits and costs. In the rural areas, school consolidation reduced the numbers of schools to be administered and properties to be maintained, while giving children greater access to expensive facilities, such as gymnasiums. It also removed many schools and the children attending them from their local communities, increased transportation costs, and lengthened the day for children travelling to and from school by bus. Larger schools require more administrators, clerical workers, and maintenance staff not directly involved in the classroom. They also permit greater teacher specialization and a more complex division of labour, both in the school and in the individual classroom. By 1975, the present social organization of the school was essentially in place. Since then, for example, there has been little change in the proportions of full-time teachers who are administrators (Principal, Vice Principal, Chair/Department Head), regular classroom teachers, and non-classroom teachers. In 1975, 7% of full-time teachers were neither administrators nor

regular classroom teachers: in 1987, the percentage was 6.5.

Physically, the schools and classrooms that contemporary urban children go to do not differ dramatically from those attended by children in cities before the First World War. In fact, many school buildings currently in use were built before 1914 and survive with additions (e.g., gymnasiums, portable classrooms), but little basic structural alteration. Likewise, as before the First World War, the children are assigned to grades and instructed in groups by a single teacher in classrooms equipped with desks, tables, chalkboards, noticeboards, and shelves of books. As before, the children also read from books and draw or write on paper. At the same time, the technology available to the modern school is considerably advanced over that in use eighty years ago. There are likely to be power tools for shop, microwave ovens for cooking, and electronic keyboards for music. There are usually television sets, video cassette recorders, and, perhaps, portable camcorders. Potentially the most revolutionary change in technology in the school, however, is the personal computer, which, unlike most of the examples cited above, is more than an extension of an earlier technology.

Despite its promise, however, the personal computer has been introduced quite slowly to Ontario schools, and it is used largely for rather conventional purposes, including arithmetic drills and language composition. There are several reasons for this. First, to provide every student with daily access to a personal computer would be expensive. Second, many teachers do not know how to use personal computers or have had no instruction in their classroom application. Third, innovative computer programs designed for educational purposes are not abundant. Finally, the province of Ontario until recently favoured computers developed to its own specifications, which were not compatible with the existing computers for which most programs have been written, such as those manufactured by IBM, Apple, Commodore, and Atari.

Pupil-teacher ratios dropped quite sharply in the 1960s, but only very slowly since the early to mid-1970s. This is true of both elementary and secondary schools. Pupil-teacher ratios have also been considerably lower in the secondary than in the elementary schools. These patterns are similar for both the public and Roman Catholic systems. In 1969, there were 25.3 pupils per teacher in the public elementary schools; in 1987, the ratio was 21.4 pupils per teacher. For Roman Catholic elementary schools, the comparable figures

are 25.5 and 22.1. In the public secondary schools, the ratio was 16.4 to 1 in both 1969 and 1987. Comparable figures are not available for Roman Catholic secondary schools, although the pupil-teacher ratio there was 16.5 in 1987 (see Figure 6.4).

Pupil-teacher ratios vary somewhat by region. In both elementary and secondary schools, they are slightly lower in mid-northern and northeastern Ontario than in the rest of the province. The range, however, is narrow—from 21.6 pupils per teacher (western) to 20.0 (northeastern) in the elementary schools, and from 16.7 (eastern) to 15.5 (mid-northern) in the elementary schools in 1987. The government of Ontario has recently announced plans to reduce the pupil-teacher ratio to 20:1 in grades 1 and 2.

Important as they may be, the physical structure of the schools that children attend, the material technology available to them, and the pupil-teacher ratio in itself are almost certainly of less moment than the teaching methodologies to which the children are exposed, along with the content and organization of the curriculum through which they must navigate. These, too, have changed considerably over time in Ontario, although in evolutionary fashion and not necessarily coherently or in any particular direction.

At all levels, corporal punishment is gone, there is less

Figure 6.4: Elementary, public and Roman Catholic school boards pupil to teacher ratio, 1971-1987

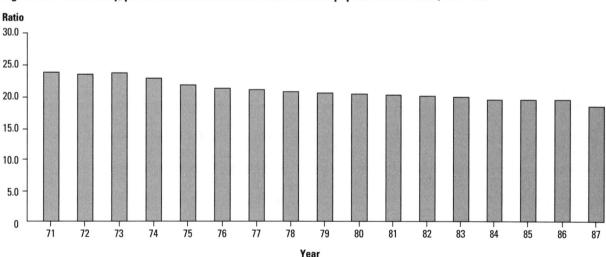

Source: Ontario Education Statistics, 1987, Table 4.141.

overt regimentation in the classroom, and discipline is more likely to be negotiated among teachers, children, and parents now than in the past. There is less rote and rule learning and more emphasis on acquiring knowledge through use, especially in language instruction. Classrooms tend to be less teacher-centred, and there is less individual work and more group learning. There is also less sex segregation in the curriculum: boys often cook and sew while girls saw and hammer, and boys and girls are likely to take instruction on such topics as sex education together.

Beginning in 1962, each course in Ontario secondary schools was allocated to one of three streams: Vocational, General, and Academic. This replaced the high school general course with core subjects in grades 9 and 10 and university preparation in grades 11 through 13. It also gave space in the secondary schools to children whose formal education had previously ended with elementary school. Failure rates under the new system remained high, however, and beginning in 1967 this system began to give way to the Credit System. In 1967, as well, provincial examinations in Grade 13 subjects were abandoned. Since 1972, all students in the secondary schools have operated with the Credit System, which, until it was subsequently revised, had few compulsory subjects and required 27 credits for high school graduation.

In 1984, the *Ontario Schools: Intermediate and Senior Divisions, Program and Diploma Requirements 1984* (OSIS) was put into place, partly in response to criticisms that the Credit System and the abolition of provincial examinations left children with too few requirements to meet. OSIS organized courses after grade 8 into three levels of difficulty: Basic, General (required for community college), and Advanced (required for university). Upon entering secondary school, students are streamed into either the Basic, General or Advanced level of education, although they can take courses at more than one level. OSIS also requires that a student accumulate 30 course credits — 16 compulsory and 14 elective — in order to graduate. To be eligible to enter university, a student must also successfully complete 6 Ontario Academic Courses, either as part of or in addition to the 30 required credits.

The implementation of OSIS has caused real changes in secondary education, although it has not immediately restored public confidence in the system. Whereas most schools, had previously offered one-credit courses, September to June, they have increasingly begun to provide one-credit courses in each half of the school year. In 1981, 57% of secondary schools were entirely on the year system and 25% on the half-year system. By 1987, the corresponding figures were 31% and 53%. For the children, new curriculum guidelines 'require the teacher to modify the domination of classroom conversation and emphasize the social nature of learning' (Moss and Rutledge, 1990, p. 5). Still, the drop-out rate seems not to have decreased.

IV   Who Teaches the Children?

Elementary school children in Ontario are taught largely by women and secondary school children by men. In 1987, 70% of elementary teachers were women; 64% of secondary teachers were men. The teachers are, on average, middle-aged and quite experienced. In 1987, the median age of the women was 39 years, with 14 years of teaching experience: the median age of the men was 42, with 18 years in the classroom.

The children's teachers are also well educated relative to the general population, with at least high school graduation and eight months of teacher training. In fact, 89% of the men and 72% of the women had at least a bachelor's degree in 1987, and 17% of the men and 7% of the women had master's degrees or doctorates. Secondary school children are more likely than elementary school children to have teachers with university degrees. In 1987, 92% of secondary teachers had degrees, versus 71% of elementary school teachers. This is true, however, largely for women teachers. Male secondary school teachers are only slightly more likely than their elementary school counterparts to have degrees.

Teachers in Ontario schools are unionized and, partly for this reason, they are well paid relative to most occupational groups. In 1987-88, full-time elementary school teachers averaged $40,697 per year; secondary school teachers averaged $48,784. Taking into account changes in the Consumer Price Index, the real earnings of full-time elementary teachers in the province increased by 22% from 1978 to 1986, while those for secondary teachers rose by 6%. This was in a period when expenditures for publicly supported schools increased by about 11% in real terms.

V What is Done for the Exceptional Child?

In most parts of Ontario, learning-disabled and other 'exceptional' children can attend special classes in regular schools. Overall, about 3% of students in the elementary schools are enrolled in such classes (see Table 6.2). The opportunity to attend special education classes varies considerably from region to region, however, and between public and Roman Catholic schools. Where fully 3.2% of elementary students are in special education classes in central Ontario, only 0.8% are in such classes in northwestern Ontario. Likewise, 3.5% of elementary school students in the public schools are enrolled in special education classes, while the corresponding figure for Roman Catholic schools is 1.7%. These figures likely reflect regional and systemic variations in policies and resources more than they do differences in the prevalence of exceptionality.

In 1987, 86,146 elementary and 42,437 secondary school students in the province were deemed exceptional by virtue of problems in communication, giftedness, or developmental delay, or physical impairment. Provision is made for such students in two ways: either in special education classes or in time spent out of class with a special education teacher, usually in a group setting. In the elementary schools, the numbers of students in self-contained classes have remained fairly stable, while the numbers periodically taken out of class to work with special education teachers ('resource with-

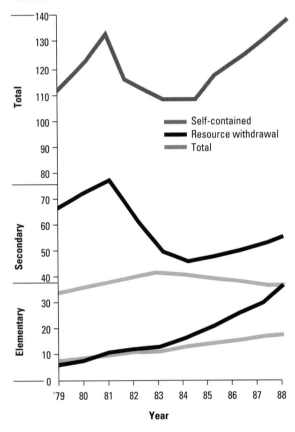

Figure 6.5:   Enrolment of Exceptional Students,[a] 1979-1988

Thousands of students

Source: Ontario Education Statistics, 1987, Table 4.80.

[a] Figures do not include students in schools for trainable retarded, provincial schools, and schools or education programs in care and treatment facilities.

[b] Dates are not comparable with those for previous years due to gradual extension of public funding to Roman Catholic schools from 1985 to 1987.

Table 6.2
Enrolment of students in special education classes in elementary schools, by region, public and Roman Catholic school boards, Ontario, 1987

Region	Public N	Public % of all students	Roman Catholic N	Roman Catholic % of all students	Total N	Total % of all students
Central Ontario	19,981	4.0	4,077	1.7	24,058	3.2
Eastern Ontario	2,550	2.9	1,363	2.3	3,913	2.6
Midnorthern Ontario	407	1.8	627	2.4	1,034	2.1
Northeastern Ontario	557	2.4	298	1.5	855	2.6
Northwestern Ontario	200	0.9	61	0.5	261	0.8
Western Ontario	3,798	3.2	560	1.0	4,358	2.5
Total	27,493	3.5	6,986	1.7	34,479	2.9

Source: Ontario Education Statistics, 1987, Table 7.21.

Table 6.3
Education for Exceptional Students by Area of Exceptionality and School Type, September 30, 1988

Area of exceptionality	Elementary schools		Secondary schools		Schools for trainable mentally retarded	Hospital, schools or provincial care and treatment centres	Total
	Self-contained classes	Resource withdrawal	Self-contained classes	Resource withdrawal			
Behavioural	2 894	5 701	716	3 400	20	2 993	15 724
Communication							
Autistic	143	152	58	52	12	86	503
Hearing impaired	549	737	131	401	9	446	2 273
Learning disabled	14 673	28 321	3 592	17 966	18	322	64 892
Speech & language impaired	2 245	4 427	95	665	139	84	7 655
Total	17 610	33 637	3 876	19 084	178	938	75 323
Intellectual							
Gifted	5 796	12 684	3 941	7 547	—	14	29 982
Educable retarded	8 203	3 671	4 431	3 715	34	35	20 089
Total	13 999	16 355	8 372	11 262	34	49	50 071
Physical							
Visual impaired	60	275	24	185	18	182	745
Orthopaedic or other	160	634	252	402	20	169	1 637
Total	220	909	276	587	38	351	2 382
Multiple	1 266	889	500	560	164	867	4 764
TOTAL	35 989	54 597	13 740	34 177	414	5 198	144 115
	89 198		47 551				

Source: Ontario Ministry of Education, Special Tabulation, 1988.

drawal' in Figure 6.5 and Table 6.3) have decreased by about a quarter in the period 1979-87. Figure 6.5 shows that in the secondary schools, the numbers in both categories have increased, by about a third for those in self-contained classes, and three and half times for those working with special education teachers.

Fully implemented in 1985, the *Education Amendment Act* (1980) gives developmentally delayed students and those with learning or physical disabilities the right to attend regular elementary or secondary schools (Wilson, 1983) (see Table 6.3). It is not obvious, however, that the schools have been provided with extra resources to accommodate such students. As noted above, the numbers of students taken out of class to work with special education teachers have actually decreased in the elementary schools. As well, expenditures for special education have not increased much in real terms between 1983 and 1988. These dollars are also largely spent for schools in central Ontario (see Figure 6.6).

Special education classes and access to learning resource teachers within or without the classroom for exceptional students in regular elementary and secondary schools are probably efficacious practices on the whole. They allow remediation, where this is required, and they enable the children to attend neighbourhood schools with their peers. Still, segregating exceptional children in their own classes or periodically removing them from regular classes to meet with learning resource teachers creates conditions whereby children can be stigmatized by their schoolmates and marginalized within the school.

VI   French Language Education

Francophones in Ontario have the right to have their children educated in French and to administer their own schools, although there are continuing problems in implementing this

Figure 6.6: Ontario School Board Special Education Costs , by region, 1983-1988

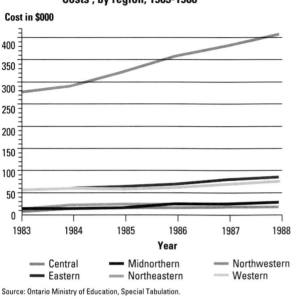

Cost in $000

Source: Ontario Ministry of Education, Special Tabulation.

policy. In 1987, about 69,000 children in the province attended schools in which the language of instruction was French. About 5,500 (8%) of these were in public schools and 64,000 (92%) in Roman Catholic schools. Between 1971 and 1987, however, there was a decrease of about 21% in the numbers of children in French-language schools.

This decrease in enrolment at French-language schools masks an increase that has occurred in the public schools. Since 1971, the numbers enrolled in French-language public schools have more than doubled — from 2,074 in 1971 to 5,489 in 1987, or a 165% increase. In the Roman Catholic schools, there was a decrease from 85,411 in 1971 to 63,398 in 1987, or 26% (see Figure 6.7).

There has been a considerable increase in the numbers of English-speaking children in Ontario schools who take French as a second language, either as a core subject or in French immersion. In 1980, about 874,000 (51.6%) took French as a second language; in 1987, just over one million (60.4%) did. This has occurred at both the elementary and the secondary levels, although elementary students are much more likely than secondary students to take French as a second language. At the elementary level 59.1% took French

Figure 6.7: Enrolment of all students enrolled in French-language public and Roman Catholic elementary instructional units, Ontario, 1971- 1987

Enrolment (in 000s)

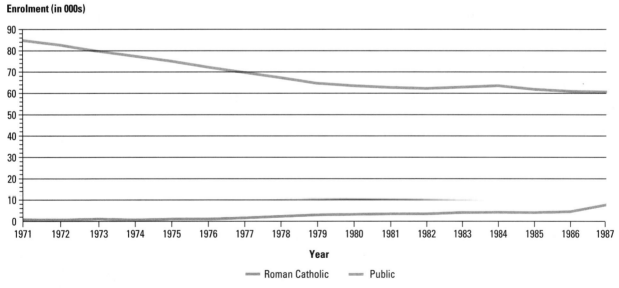

Source: Ontario Education Statistics, Table 4.50.

Figure 6.8:   English-speaking elementary and secondary school students enrolled in FSL[a], Ontario, 1974-1987

Enrolment (in 000s)

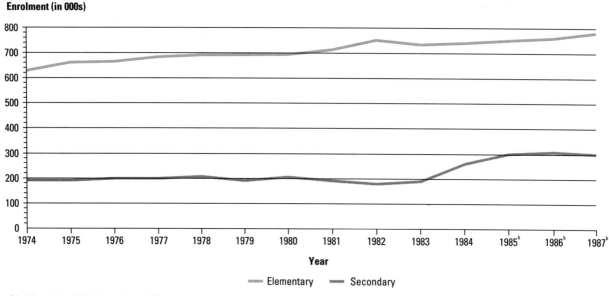

Year

— Elementary   — Secondary

a) Includes students taking 60 or more hours of French per year.
b) Data are not comparable with those from previous years because of the gradual extension of public funding to Roman Catholic schools, from 1985 to 1987.
Source: Ontario Education Statistics, Table 4.581.

as a second language in 1980; in 1987, the percentage stood at 70.4. At the secondary level 34.2% took French as a second language in 1980; in 1987 the percentage was 42.0.

A major innovation in the public school system has been the development of programs for English-speaking children in which all or part of the day is spent studying one or more subjects in French. In 1987, as Table 6.4 shows, some 2.5% of English-speaking children in grades 1 to 8 had 690 or more hours of instruction in such French immersion programs: 6.8% had 450 or more hours; and 9% had 121 or more hours. In grades 9 to 13, an average of 2.8% of the students were enrolled in French immersion (see Table 6.5).

VII   How do the Schools Recognize Ethnic Diversity?

Immigration to Ontario is a major factor behind the growth in instruction in languages other than English or French in

the province. In 1986-87, 71 school boards in Ontario offered heritage language courses in 58 different languages, in a total of 4,305 classes, to approximately 90,000 children: in 1977, the corresponding figures were 42 school boards, 30 different languages, 1,968 classes, and 53,000 children (Ontario Education Statistics, 1987, Table 4.85). School boards now must provide a heritage language program where 25 or more sign up for a language.

Heritage language programs are very unevenly distributed across the province. In fact, they are largely confined to central Ontario, especially Metropolitan Toronto. In 1986-87, 84% of the classes offered and 87% of the students were in central Ontario (Ontario Education Statistics, 1987, Table 4.85).

The most highly subscribed of the 58 heritage language programs in 1986-87 was Greek, with 29 boards offering it in 356 classes to 6,478 children. This was followed by Cantonese (19 boards, 283 classes, and 5,802 children) and Hebrew (15 boards, 185 classes and 4,101 children). Arabic was next (19 boards, 103 classes, and 1,918 children), followed by Mandarin (16 boards, 89 classes, and 1,843 chil-

Table 6.4
Elementary school enrolment in FSL, Ontario, 1987

	English-speaking students		\<60		60–120		121–449		450–689		690 +	
	N	%	N	%	N	%	N	%	N	%	N	%
JK	62,906	100.0	54,359	86.4	6,018	9.6	1,444	2.3	1,085	1.7	–	0.0
K	116,175	100.0	90,807	78.2	12,924	11.1	3,454	3.0	8,975	7.7	15	0.0
1	120,425	100.0	61,469	51.0	45,157	37.5	1,695	1.4	3,306	2.7	8,798	7.3
2	116,953	100.0	58,820	50.3	46,237	39.5	1,499	1.3	3,198	2.7	7,199	6.2
3	112,470	100.0	45,927	40.8	56,423	50.2	1,340	1.2	3,312	2.9	5,468	4.9
4	109,647	100.0	297	0.3	100,012	91.2	1,836	1.7	4,132	3.8	3,370	3.1
5	109,623	100.0	383	0.3	98,433	89.8	2,748	2.5	7,000	6.4	1,059	1.0
6	109,568	100.0	292	0.3	99,170	90.5	3,115	2.8	6,177	5.6	814	0.7
7	113,316	100.0	495	0.4	102,572	90.5	3,698	3.3	6,021	5.3	530	0.5
8	110,983	100.0	658	0.6	101,550	91.5	3,136	2.8	5,068	4.6	571	0.5
Spec. Ed.	33,304	100.0	17,022	51.0	15,747	47.3	463	1.4	52	0.0	20	0.0
Total	1,115,370	100.0	330,529	29.6	684,243	61.3	24,428	2.2	48,326	4.3	27,844	2.5
Average hours					98		242		482		831	

Source: Ontario Education Statistics, 1987, Table 4.58.

Table 6.5
Secondary school enrolment in FSL and extended/immersion French program, Ontario, 1987

Grade	English-speaking students		Enrolment in core French program		Enrolment extended/immersion program		Not enrolled in French program	
9	139,098	100.0	106,290	76.4	6,129	4.4	26,679	19.2
10	135,461	100.0	56,270	41.5	4,432	3.3	74,759	55.2
11	133,551	100.0	38,073	28.5	3,330	2.5	92,148	68.9
12	125,894	100.0	23,144	18.4	1,918	1.5	100,832	80.1
13	72,029	100.0	13,973	19.4	1,008	1.4	57,048	79.2
Total	606,731	100.0	237,761	39.2	16,817	2.8	352,153	58.0

Source: Ontario Education Statistics, Table 4.59.

dren), Portuguese (11 boards, 110 classes, and 1,826 children), German (14 boards, 91 classes and 1,463 children) and Italian (11 boards, 81 classes and 1,427 children) (Ontario Education Statistics, 1987, Table 4.82).

VIII   Streaming

Starting in grade nine (grade ten as of September 1992), Ontario children are streamed into one of three difficulty levels: Basic, General, or Advanced. Although they can take courses at more than one level, most take almost all of their courses at a single level. In 1987, as shown in Table 6.6, 57% of the courses that students took were Advanced, 36.4% were General, and 6.6% were Basic.

While data are not available on the proportions of secondary school children in the three levels across Ontario, findings from the Board of Education's *Every Student Survey* indicate that, among grade 9 children in Toronto in 1987, 64% were in the Advanced stream, 26% were in the General stream, and 10% were in the Basic stream (Cheng, Tsuji, Yau and Ziegler, 1989). While the proportion in the General stream has not changed much in recent years in Toronto, the percentage in the Advanced has increased (from 52% in 1980 to 64% in 1987), and that in the Basic has decreased (from 19% in 1980 to 10% in 1987).

Children's grades vary considerably, depending upon their stream (Cheng, Tsuji, Yau and Ziegler, 1989). Briefly, those in the Advanced stream are more likely to receive grades above 70 or 80% in English or mathematics than are children in the General stream, with children in the Basic stream in the middle.

Which stream a child is placed in is related to a number of factors (Cheng, Tsuji, Yau and Ziegler, 1989). Girls are more likely than boys to be in the Advanced stream, and boys are more likely than girls to be in the General or Basic. The Canadian-born are more likely than the foreign-born to be in the Advanced stream, and Asians and whites are more likely than blacks or native peoples. Those from high socio-economic status families are over-represented in the Advanced stream, while those from low socio-economic status families are over-represented in the General and Basic streams. And students from homes with two parents present are more likely to be in the Advanced stream than are students from homes with one parent.

There are some notable differences between public and Roman Catholic school children in the levels of courses they take. In 1987, 53.9% of the courses taken by public school children were Advanced. Among Roman Catholic school children, the percentage was 66.1 (Ministry of Education, Special Tables from the School September Report, 1987).

Streaming is important to understand for several reasons. First, remaining in General or Basic almost certainly means

Table 6.6
Enrolment[a] in guideline and non-guideline courses by level of difficulty, Ontario, 1987

	Basic		General		Advanced		Total	
	N	%	N	%	N	%	N	%
TOTAL	304,840	6.6	1,690,492	36.4	2,645,923	57.0	4,641,274	100.0
Arts	14,873	4.4	140,252	41.7	181,171	53.9	336,296	100.0
Business	16,279	3.8	251,863	59.0	158,839	37.2	426,976	100.0
Data processing/ computer studies	3,489	3.2	38,586	34.8	68,761	62.0	110,844	100.0
English	49,841	6.7	233,401	31.2	464,830	62.1	748,072	100.0
French	9,256	3.1	67,662	22.7	221,403	74.2	298,321	100.0
Geography	14,435	6.1	62,683	26.3	161,097	67.6	238,216	100.0
History	13,340	4.7	72,460	25.7	196,138	69.6	281,948	100.0
Languages	19	.1	827	2.6	31,355	97.4	32,201	100.0
Mathematics	38,439	5.9	181,284	27.5	437,133	66.5	656,856	100.0
Contemporary studies	19,058	6.2	136,698	44.5	151,720	49.3	307,476	100.0
Physical education	19,802	5.9	194,193	57.4	124,425	36.7	338,420	100.0
Science	23,235	4.0	136,607	23.8	413,943	72.2	573,785	100.0
Technological studies	82,779	28.4	173,976	59.6	35,108	12.0	291,863	100.0

Source: Ministry of Education Special Tables from the School September Report, 1987
[a]This is not a head count of students. Students may be taking more than one course within the same guidelines and courses in more than one guideline within the same subject area. Because courses can commence at any time in semestered schools, but the collection of data is as of 30 September, figures may be a combination of actual and projected.

that a child will never attend university, and remaining in the Basic stream essentially precludes a community college education. It is a decision made early. Once made, it is rarely changed. And it has major implications for a child's future economic and social prospects.

Second, in educational systems where children are streamed, those in the highest stream typically show greater gains in achievement over time than students in other streams (Natriello, Pallas and Alexander 1989). Or, to phrase it somewhat differently, students in lower streams learn at a lower rate than they would if they were in a higher stream or not streamed at all. While the reasons for this are not entirely clear, it seems that better teachers and greater resources tend to be provided for students in advanced streams. This enhances motivation among these students and fosters greater support for learning in the student subculture.

Finally, streaming tends to reinforce existing social divisions — class and race especially. The Advanced stream is disproportionately affluent and white or Asian, the General and Basic streams are poor and black or native. The distribution of advantages in the larger society is thus reproduced in the smaller society of the school and, therefore, maintained — even strengthened — in subsequent generations.

IX How do the Children Achieve?

The Ministry of Education conducts no regular, comprehensive assessments of student achievement to measure how well its programs operate to realize educational goals or to assist teachers in evaluating the problems of individual students (Moss and Rutledge, 1990). The Toronto Board, however, is in the process of implementing this kind of system. Standardized, written achievement tests in narrow ranges of competencies, usually in English and mathematics, are often administered. The results are not routinely or systematically used to inform policy or practice, however, and teachers typically lack the expertise and schools the resources to use them for diagnostic or remedial purposes.

That the achievement of Ontario school children is not closely monitored is not necessarily bad, since there is no consensus on the desired outcomes of schooling (Paquette, 1989). Should we 'go back to the basics'? We cannot agree on what the basics are. Is high performance in specific skills, measured with paper and pencil tests, preferable to holistic

capacities assessed using the intuitive judgements of experienced teachers? The question is unanswerable objectively. Or should schools strive first to eradicate those inequalities in schooling outcomes related to such accidents of birth as class, race, and sex? There is little meeting of the minds. At the same time, given the public resources devoted to schooling, some accounting of the results would seem to be in order.

Data from two major studies, one for Toronto (Cheng, Tsuji, Yau and Ziegler, 1989) and one of students from a province-wide sample of 60 secondary schools (King, 1986) show that children's achievement in Ontario schools depends upon a number of factors, including their class, race, sex, place of birth, first language, and the number of parents present in the home. Girls accumulate secondary school credits more rapidly and have higher average grades in virtually every subject than boys. Asians and whites outperform blacks in terms of these criteria. Students from high socio-economic status families tend to earn credits faster and achieve higher grades in English and mathematics than students from low socio-economic status families. Finally, students from families with two parents present in the home gain credits more rapidly and have higher grade averages than students from families with one parent.

Comparisons of the achievement of Ontario children with that of children in other provinces is made problematic because, among other things, curricula differ from place to place. In addition, because Canada has very high school participation rates relative to most other countries, our average children are often evaluated against the best children in other countries in international comparisons. Keeping this in mind, results from the Second International Science Study (Connelly, Crocker and Kass, 1989) are nevertheless instructive.

Within Canada, grade 5 and grade 9 children from Ontario scored higher on science achievement than children from the Atlantic provinces and lower than those from the western provinces. Among senior high school students, however, Ontario children ranked higher than children from the west and the east in biology and physics. No regional differences were found for chemistry. But sex differences were evident in every case. The grade 5 and grade 9 boys did better than the girls in science achievement; and the senior high school boys scored higher on biology, chemistry, and physics achievement than the girls.

Among the children of seventeen different countries, grade

5 and grade 9 Canadian children ranked sixth and fourth, respectively, in science achievement — ahead of children in England and the United States in both cases, and behind those in Japan and Hungary. Senior high school students, however, did not fare so well in relative terms, ranking eleventh in biology and physics and twelfth in chemistry among the children of thirteen different countries. In biology they scored higher, on the average, than did the students from Italy and the United States, but below those from England. In chemistry the Canadians outperformed only the children from Finland. And in physics they scored better, on average, than the students from Finland and Italy.

The concerns raised by studies such as these do not relate only to how Canadian or Ontario children perform in comparison with children elsewhere, but also to the male advantage in mathematics and science so commonly seen in the upper years in high school. Typically, the higher the school grade, the better boys perform relative to girls in mathematics and science subjects, with the possible exception of biology. Boys are also more likely than girls to take mathematics and science courses as electives, and they show a stronger preference than girls for careers in science. Since the bulk of desirable jobs in industrial societies require more than the minimal training in these subjects, this places women at a distinct disadvantage in competing with men in the labour market after they leave school.

X   How Long do Children Stay in School?

Over time, Ontario children have been receiving more and more education. In the 1940s, fewer than one in three grade 9 students received Ontario Secondary School Graduation Diplomas (SSGD) four years later (Ontario Education Statistics, 1987, Table 2.10; Stamp [1988]). This figure increased to just over one in three in the 1950s, just over one in two in the 1960s and just under two in three in the 1970s. In the 1980s, it averaged just over two in three. In a period of about forty years, therefore, the likelihood of an Ontario child's graduating from high school has more than doubled.

Of the 147,677 grade 9 students enrolled in September 1982, 68% completed their SSGDs in 1986; 49% entered grade 13 and 32% received their Ontario Secondary School Honour Graduation Diploma (SSHGD) one year later (Ontario Education Statistics, 1987, Table 2.10). (Since discontinued, this diploma was available only to those in the Advanced

stream and was required for university entrance.)

High school graduates who have met the university entrance requirements with high academic standing in approved honour graduation level or Ontario Academic Courses receive Ontario Scholar Diplomas. Over time, the percentage of university recipients awarded Ontario Scholar Diplomas has increased substantially — from 13.4% in 1970 to 31.6% in 1987 (Ontario Education Statistics, 1987, Table 6.01).

XI   Who Drops Out?

Over 70,000 young people drop out — leave school prior to graduation — every year in Ontario. Although the secondary school dropout rate has decreased over the last half-century, stabilizing in the early 1980s, it may have begun to increase again.

The available measures of dropping out are at best approximations, since there is no central statistical data base that tracks the progress of individual students through the school system. (The Student Information System presently being implemented by the Ministry of Education will provide this capacity in the future.) Two measures currently used are the *retention rate* and the *retirement rate*.

The retention rate is the proportion of students enrolled in Grade 9 who obtain the SSGD four years later. So, in 1987, 68% of the students enrolled in grade 9 in public and private schools four years earlier (1982) received the SSGD. This measure, however, has a number of weaknesses. First, it overestimates the actual number of dropouts because it does not take into account students who take longer than four years to graduate, those who leave and subsequently return, those lost through such events as death or migration, and the small minority of the mentally and physically handicapped who obtain Certificates of Training after completing grade 10. Second, it underestimates the number of dropouts because it does not include students who leave school before grade 9.

The retirement rate is the percentage of students in each year who leave the system without having graduated. In 1987, retirements without certificates were 13.3% of the total enrolment in the public secondary school system — up from 11.8% in 1981. By grade, the percentages were 8.8 for grade 9, 11.0 for grade 10, 14.3 for grade 11, and 19.9 for grade 12. Summing these figures yields an estimated dropout rate of 45.1% for those who began grade 9 in 1983 (see Table 6.7).

Table 6.7
Retirements[a] as a percentage of enrolment from secondary schools without diplomas or certificates, by grade, Ontario, 1980–1987

Year	Gr. 9		Gr. 10		Gr. 11		Gr. 12		Total	
	N	%	N	%	N	%	N	%	N	%
1980–81	10,088	7.4	15,433	11.1	18,002	13.2	19,223	16.1	62,746	11.8
1981–82	10,522	8.2	13,953	10.9	16,869	12.8	19,447	15.9	60,791	11.9
1982–83	10,727	8.6	13,573	10.9	16,334	12.9	22,204	17.9	62,838	12.6
1983–84	11,526	9.2	14,536	11.9	17,732	14.4	23,882	19.6	67,676	13.8
1984–85	12,330	8.2	15,221	10.7	17,985	15.1	23,673	20.2	69,209	13.1
1985–86	13,085	8.8	15,638	10.9	19,824	14.5	24,654	21.7	73,021	13.5
1986–87	12,803	8.8	15,783	11.0	19,404	14.3	25,830	19.9	73,820	13.3

[a]Includes students whose destination was reported as either 'Employment in Ontario' or 'Other' on the secondary school September Report. These students did not proceed to an educational institution in Ontario.
Source: Ontario Education Statistics, Table 2.9.2.

Anywhere from one-third to one-half of young people in Ontario, therefore, drop out of school before graduating from grade 12. At the same time, more and more drop-outs have been re-entering high school after leaving for a period of time, although only about one-half of all re-entrants graduate (Karp, 1988). This may account for the overall increase in the number of Secondary School Graduation Diplomas awarded.

Ontario lags behind other Western industrial countries in terms of rates of completion at the secondary level and rates of participation in post-secondary education. The Ontario rates are lower than, for example, those for the United States, Japan, and West Germany (Sloan, 1989). If a better-educated labour force is a more productive one, then increasing the level of educational attainment is important in order for the province to compete economically.

There is a substantial body of research carried out over the years both in Canada and the United States on secondary school dropouts. In 1987, the Ontario Ministry of Education formed a liaison committee for the 'Student Retention and Transition Project', in order to develop policy and support initiatives designed to reduce the secondary school dropout rate. A series of studies was commissioned, and a review of these and related literature suggests a number of possible causes of dropping out (Karp, 1988; King et al., 1988; King, 1986; Lawton et al., 1988; Radwanski, 1987; Sullivan, 1988; Wright, 1985).

Dropping out is associated with academic stream and, related to this, academic achievement. Studies show that students in the Basic and General level streams are much more likely to drop out of school than are those in the Advanced level. King and Hughes (1985) found that students who enter grade 9 taking courses at the General or Basic level are over five times as likely to drop out of school as those at the Advanced level. Radwanski (1987) reports that 12% of students dropped out from the Advanced level, 62% from the General level, and 79% from Basic level. Streaming is, of course, at least partly related to academic achievement. It is not surprising to find, therefore, that, on the average, school dropouts do less well academically than those who graduate, lagging behind their peers in accumulating the necessary credits for graduation.

A variety of family background factors have been consistently found to be related to academic achievement, academic level, and dropping out. Children with well-educated parents in professional and managerial occupations are less likely to leave school early than those with poorly educated parents in unskilled or semiskilled occupations. Studies have also shown that males, blacks and native Canadians, and children from single-parent families more likely to drop out of school than females, Asians or whites, and children from two-parent families. Research also shows that students born outside of Canada are more likely to leave school without a diploma than are the Canadian-born.

Many school leavers cite school-related reasons as important in their decision to drop out. The education system is oriented to the strong academic student involved in extra curricular activities. The student who does not fit this model often feels that leaving school is a better alternative than remaining. Lawton et al. (1988: 60) note that 'where students felt that they belonged in the school, where they perceive efforts made by the staff — sometimes just one teacher — to respond to them in a real way, to understand them as individuals and to care about how they were comprehending the work, here were students who wanted to stay. Students identified as "at risk" often reported not feeling close to a single teacher.' As well, school-related factors, such as high rates of absenteeism and strict identification and punishment of rule-breakers, also appear to be related to high dropout rates in schools. Schools with lower dropout rates tend to be those with procedures to reduce the class-skipping and without strict disciplinary policies, such as suspension, for minor infractions.

The causes of secondary school dropout, then, are multiple and cumulative. The process of dropping out is a long and complex series of events. The school system, while not in and of itself the cause of social divisions in Ontario, serves to mirror and reproduce these divisions so that dropouts are most likely to be the children of parents who themselves were not successful in their school careers.

XII Who Re-enters School?

While the number of students dropping out of secondary schools may be increasing, the number of those who have re-entered secondary school after officially withdrawing has more than tripled since 1975-76 (Ontario Education Statistics, 1987, Tables 2.95, 4.141). In 1986-87, almost 40,000 students returned to school. Interestingly, almost half of these re-entrants were over the age of 21. Males appeared to be more likely than the females to re-enter secondary school as teen-agers, whereas females were about three times as likely as males to re-enter as adults (see Table 6.8).

XIII Where do the Children Go When They Leave School?

When they leave secondary school, Ontario children typically enter the labour force or enrol at a post-secondary educational institution, either a College of Arts and Applied Technology (CAAT) or a university. Dropouts, of course, cannot enter

Table 6.8
School re-entrants,[a] 1986–1987, by age and sex

Age	Male	Female	Total
14–	74	106	180
15	297	282	579
16	1,566	1,355	2,921
17	2,839	2,249	5,088
18	3,396	2,436	5,832
19	2,810	1,849	4,659
20	1,503	1,121	2,624
21	800	787	1,587
22 +	4,047	12,385	16,432
Total	17,332	22,570	39,902

[a]Includes data on Roman Catholic schools.
Source: Ontario Education Statistics, 1987, Table 2.94.

either a CAAT or a university directly. Graduates from the General program are eligible only to register at a CAAT. And graduates from the Advanced program can attend either a CAAT or a university.

Figure 6.9 attempts to chart this course for children who were enrolled in grade 9 in 1982 (keep in mind that the data do not describe exactly the same group of children at each stage). There were 147,677 ninth graders in 1982. In 1986, 100,826 (or 68%) received a Secondary School Graduation Diploma, 18,764 (13%) entered a CAAT, and 71,890 (49%) enrolled in grade 13. In 1987, 47,107 (32%) received a Secondary School Honours Graduation Diploma, 4,244 (3%) enrolled in a CAAT and 33,685 (23%) registered at an Ontario university. An estimated two-fifths of the 1982 cohort, then, subsequently attended a CAAT or a university, most of the remaining three-fifths presumably entered the labour force, and a small proportion took longer than the minimum time to graduate. Of those who entered the labour force when they left high school, approximately one-half apparently did so without benefit of a high school diploma.

How far one goes in school, of course, has important implications for one's future social and economic prospects. In general, the better one's education, the more likely one is to move into a high-skilled, well-paying, responsible, and satisfying job (Hunter, 1986, 1988). As more and more Canadians have stayed in school longer and longer, however, the threshold for access to desirable employment — even employment itself — has risen higher and higher. Compared

Figure 6.9:   Progress of students, grade 9 to first year post-secondary (including private), 1982 - 1987

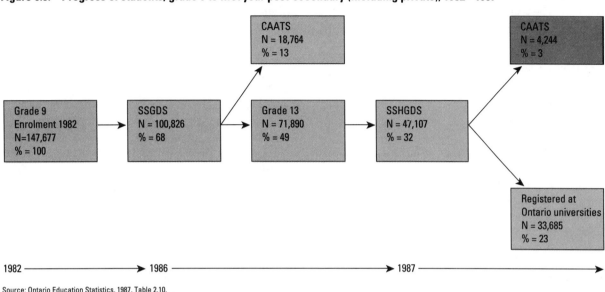

Source: Ontario Education Statistics, 1987, Table 2.10.

with those who graduate from secondary school, dropouts are more likely to be unemployed or to be employed in low-level, low-paying production and service jobs and to have lower incomes (Sullivan, 1988). Beyond this, recent research (Leiper and Hunter, 1990) suggests that the economic benefits of schooling for workers may only begin to show for those who have acquired at least some post-secondary training. High school graduates who are employed may, in fact, earn little more on the average than workers with less than high school graduation, whereas community college graduates in the labour force earn considerably more and university graduates a great deal more again. That is, high school graduation may often mean the difference between being employed and being unemployed, while some post-secondary education may mean the difference between a living wage and below the poverty line.

XIV   What Role Do Parents Play?

How well a child fares in school is determined in important part by how advantaged her/his family is and how much interest the parents take in the child's education. Otherwise, the connection between home and school is weak. Families

have little involvement in the school; and schools have little in the family. Publicly supported elementary and secondary schools in Ontario provide parents with few opportunities to participate directly in their children's education. Likewise, school representatives rarely participate in family activities related to education: for example, advising parents about how they can help their children to develop good study habits at home. At the same time, there is research showing that schools can foster parental involvement in the child's education that is so important for a child's success, and that home visits by school representatives can be successful in reducing the dropout rate (Ziegler, 1987, cited in Moss and Rutledge, 1990). When school and family meet, however, it is almost always on ritual occasions or when there are problems with the child's performance or behaviour in school.

Parents, then, have little role in the day-to-day activities of the school, in decisions involving their children directly, or in school governance generally. There are organizations, such as the Home and School Association, connected to the public school system in Ontario, although they have little presence in the school and little standing in the educational hierarchy. The most common activity of the Home and School Association is to raise money for schools (Connelly,

Crocker, and Kass, 1989). It seldom participates in important decisions, such as the hiring of principals or teachers or acquiring school resources, although it is represented on a number of provincial committees. Its membership, however, is neither comprehensive nor representative, and parents must pay a fee to belong. In fact, between them, school boards and the Ministry give local school administrators relatively little autonomy. Even school principals may or may not interview prospective teachers, but they have no authority to hire them.

In the United States in recent years there has been a strong move towards increasing the autonomy of local schools so as to make them more responsive to individual students' needs and more responsible to the local community. The school system of Chicago (often touted as the worst in the United States), for example, is in the process of radically decentralizing in this way. Already much more decentralized than Canadian school systems, those in the United States are moving toward even greater decentralization. Taken to its conclusion, however, autonomy for schools implies separate school curricula, which in a publicly supported system may be difficult to justify politically. In addition, research suggests that the economic gains associated with the growth of educational systems require a certain standardization in curriculum. At the same time, highly centralized systems, such as Ontario's, are often not well adapted to satisfy the particular requirements of the children, parents, and schools in very different communities.

Conclusions

Ontario children attend publicly supported elementary and secondary schools that are relatively well funded and staffed by well-educated, experienced, and well-paid teachers. The province's educational system is, however, highly centralized and bureaucratic, and oriented first to the academic student. It gives little recognition in its policies or practices to issues of class, race, or sex, or to children from families where both parents are employed and children from single-parent families. This makes it difficult for local schools to meet the needs of individual children from a highly differentiated population, geographically dispersed in a large number of very different communities. It may not be so surprising, then, that between one-third and one-half of all Ontario children leave school before graduation.

Although the decision on what stream a child is to be placed in is about to be moved back by a year, the practice of streaming at any time needs to be reassessed in terms of its effect on children, whose interests must be placed ahead of any other benefits that streaming might have. Disproportionately, it is those from disadvantaged backgrounds who end up in the Basic and General streams, and the advantaged who are assigned to the Advanced. Moreover, the evidence seems to be that streaming lowers the achievement levels of all but the most able students, increases the likelihood of dropping out, and therefore helps to reproduce existing social inequalities.

Dropping out has not only received a good deal of official attention, but is a genuine problem, and one that appears to have resisted recent attempted solutions. It is, moreover, likely to persist in the absence of real changes in the everyday home and school lives of children. Eliminating streaming is one promising move that could be taken. Increasing local school autonomy is another. But dropping out, among the overwhelming majority of children who have every capacity to graduate from high school, is not likely to be reduced to residual levels without substantial changes in teaching methodologies, the curriculum, and the home-school relationship. All children, not just the academically inclined from advantaged family backgrounds, have to be shown what is important in school, how it is relevant, and that they can do it.

For a long time, the large research literature showing that 'throwing money at schools' yields few measurable returns in student performance has fostered the cynical view that 'schools don't matter, families do'. Families, of course, do matter. But so can schools. What is crucial is not so much the quality of personnel and other resources that go to schools, but how these resources are actually used by teachers and children in the classroom and the school in the community.

References

Atherton, Peter J.
  1989 'Recent Developments in the Economics of Education and Their Policy Implications'. Pp. 41-50 in Lawton and Wignall (1989).

Brown, Daniel J.
  1989 'A Preliminary Inquiry into School-Based Management'. Pp. 189-209 in Lawton and Wignall (1989).

Canada
1988 *Advance Statistics of Education*. Ottawa: Statistics Canada.

Cameron, D.M.
1978 *Declining Enrolments and the Financing of Education in Ontario*. Toronto: Commission on Declining School Enrolment in Ontario. Report No. 11.

Cheng, M., G. Tsuji, M. Yau, and S. Ziegler
1989 *Every Secondary Student Survey, Fall 1987*, Toronto: Board of Education.

Coleman, James S., et al.
1966 *Equality of Educational Opportunity*. Washington, DC: US Government Printing Office.

Coleman, Peter
1989 'School Costs and Achievement: Explaining the Riddle'. Pp. 171-88 in Lawton and Wignall (1989).

Connelly, F. Michael, Robert K. Crocker, and Heidi Kass
1989 *Achievement and Its Correlates*. Science Education in Canada, Volume 2. Toronto: OISE Press.

Hanushek, E.A.
1981 'Throwing Money at Schools'. *Journal of Policy Analysis and Management*, 1: 19-41.

1986 'The Economics of Schooling, Production and Efficiency in Public Schools'. *Journal of Economic Literature*, 14: 1141-77.

Holmes, M.
1982 'Progress or Progressive Decline? A Response to Howard Russell's Review of Progress in Education by Nigel Wright'. *Curriculum Inquiry* 12: 419-32.

Hunter, Alfred A.
1986 *Class Tells*. 2nd ed. Toronto: Butterworths.

1988 'Formal Education and Initial Employment: Unravelling the Relationships between Schooling and Skills over Time'. *American Sociological Review*, 53: 753-65.

Husen, T.
1983 'Are Standards in U.S. Schools Really Lagging Behind Those in Other Countries?' *Phi Delta Kappan*, 64: 455-61.

Karp, Ellen, Goldfarb Consultants
1988 *The Drop-out Phenomenon in Ontario Secondary Schools*. A Report to the Ontario Study of the Relevance of Education and the Issue of Dropouts. Toronto: Ontario Ministry of Education.

King, A.J.C.
1986 *The Adolescent Experience*. Toronto: Ontario Secondary School Teachers' Federation.

King, A.J.C., and J. Hughes

1985 *Secondary School to Work: A Difficult Transition*. Toronto: Ontario Secondary School Teachers' Federation, Toronto.

King, A.J.C., W.K. Warren, C. Michalski, M.J. Peart
1988 *Improving Student Retention in Ontario Secondary Schools*. Report to the Ontario Study of the Relevance of Education and the Issue of Dropouts. Toronto: Ontario Ministry of Education.

Lawton, Stephen B.
1989 'Economic Models to Explain School Board Expenditures in Ontario'. Pp. 148-62 in Lawton and Wignall (1989). *Scrimping or Squandering? Financing Canadian Schools*. Toronto: OISE Press.

Lawton, Stephen B., Kenneth A. Leithwood, Elaine Batcher, E. Lisbeth Donaldson, and Rouleen Stewart
1988 *Student Retention and Transition in Ontario High Schools —Policies, Practices and Prospects*. A Report to the Ontario Study of the Relevance of Education and the Issue of Dropouts. Toronto: Ministry of Education.

Lawton, Stephen B., and Rouleen Wignall (eds)
1989 *Scrimping or Squandering? Financing Canadian Schools*. Toronto: OISE Press.

Leiper, Jean M., and Alfred A. Hunter
1990 'Academic Credentials and Earnings'. Paper read at the annual meetings of the Canadian Sociology and Anthropology Association, Victoria, BC.

Livingstone, David W.
1989 'The Intimate Relations of Education Cost and Quality: Researchers' and Public Views'. Pp. 210-14 in Lawton and Wignall (1989).

McMillan, Susan
1990 'Forty Years of Social Housing in Toronto'. Pp. 56-62 in Craig McKie and Keith Thompson (eds), *Canadian Social Trends*. Toronto: Thompson Educational Publishing.

Michaud, Pierre
1989 'Equity of Educational Finance in Eastern Ontario'. Pp. 127-39 in Lawton and Wignall (1989)

Moss, Penny, and Donald Rutledge
1990 '*Issues in Education*'. Pp. 133-52 in Laura C. Johnson and Dick Barnhorst (eds), *Children, Families and Public Policy in the 90s* (Toronto: Thompson Educational Publishing).

Natriello, Gary, Aaron M. Pallas, and Karl Alexander
1989 'On the Right Track? Curriculum and Academic Achievement'. *Sociology of Education* 62: 109-18.

Oakes, Jeannie
1985 *Keeping Track: How Schools Structure Inequality*. New Haven: Yale University Press.

Ontario
1989 *Educational Funding in Ontario*. Toronto: Ministry of Education.

1982-89 *Education Statistics*. Toronto: Ministry of Education.

Paquette, Jerry
1989 'The Quality Conundrum: Assessing What We Cannot Agree On'. Pp. 11-28 in Lawton and Wignall (1989).

The Premier's Council
1988 *Competing in the New Global Economy*. Toronto: Ministry of Education.

Radwanski, G.
1987 *Ontario Study of the Relevance of Education, and the Issue of Dropouts*. Toronto: Ministry of Education.

Sloan, Pamela J.
1990 'From School to Work'. Pp. 175-206 in Laura C. Johnson and Dick Barnhorst (eds), *Children, Families and Public Policy in the 90s*. (Toronto: Thompson Educational Publishing).

Stamp, Robert M.
1988 *Ontario Secondary School Program Innovations and Student Retention Rates, 1920s—1970s*. A Report to the Ontario Study of the Relevance of Education and Issues of Dropouts. Toronto: Ministry of Education.

Statistics Canada
1988 *Advance Statistics of Education, 1988-89*. Ottawa: Ministry of Supply and Services.

Sullivan, Michael, Decima Research
1988 *A Comparative Analysis of Drop-outs and Non Drop-outs in Ontario Secondary Schools*. A Report to the Ontario Study of the Relevance of Education and the Issue of Dropouts. Toronto: Ministry of Education.

Wilson, Anne Keeton
1983 *A Consumer's Guide to Bill 82: Special Education in Ontario*. Toronto: OISE Press.

Wise, A.
1979 *Legislated Learnings: The Bureaucratization of the American Classroom*. Berkeley: University of California Press.

Wright, E., and G.K. Tsuji
1983 *The Grade Nine Student Survey: Fall 1983*. Report no. 174. Toronto: Board of Education for the City of Toronto, Research Department.

Wright, E.
1985 *The Retention and Credit Accumulation of Students in Secondary School. A Follow-up from the 1980 Grade Nine Student Survey*, Report No. 176. Toronto Board of Education, Research Department.

CHAPTER SEVEN

Youth Employment

Highlights

- More than four out of five young adults (aged 20 to 24) in Ontario are labour force participants, along with almost two-thirds of teenagers (aged 15 to 19). Youth labour force participation has been increasing steadily over the past decade, especially among teenagers. Today, roughly half of young full-time students are also labour force participants.
- Strong economic growth and a decline in the size of the youth cohort have led to a sharp drop in youth unemployment since 1983, although youth unemployment rates remain higher than adult rates. Teenagers are more likely than young adults to be unemployed (9.9% and 6.7% in 1989). The average length of time a young person spends unemployed has also declined significantly.
- Almost 90% of Ontario youth are employed, and about one in three experience unemployment, at some time over the course of a year. Most spend large parts of the year (not just the summer) in the workforce.
- The high level of part-time work among youth is largely due to the two-thirds of teenage workers who are in part-time jobs. Most young people who work part-time do so because they are still attending school.
- Young workers, especially young women, are primarily employed in the service industries. Within this broad sector, youth, particularly teenagers, are heavily concentrated in lower level retail sales and consumer services.
- A significant number of young adults with higher educational credentials are in managerial and professional occupations, but teenage workers are largely excluded from these better jobs. Most female teenage workers are in clerical, sales and service jobs, as are over half of male teenage workers.

- High school dropouts and graduates who have no additional education appear to have considerable difficulty moving out of the 'student' labour market of low level sales and service jobs.
- Compared with the rest of the province, youth unemployment is lower in the Toronto region, the young unemployed find jobs more quickly, part-time work is less common, and young women are more likely to find clerical instead of sales and service jobs.
- The average real wages of young workers have declined in recent years. Part-time workers who are still students may not find low-paying, part-time sales and service jobs very problematic. But even full-time jobs in these areas do not pay well enough to allow youth to become independent of their parents.
- Disabled and visible minority youth encounter additional labour market barriers. Youth from lower socio-economic backgrounds are disadvantaged, in large part because fewer acquire the educational credentials needed to compete for better jobs.
- Union membership is low among youth, and only a small minority of Ontario youth enter apprenticeships. Federal and provincial youth labour market programs have been aimed primarily at disadvantaged groups. As unemployment rates and the size of the youth cohort have declined, these programs have been reduced in size.
- The high level of teenage employment, the extent of underemployment among those who have not continued in school, and the employment barriers faced by disadvantaged groups are three youth employment policy areas that require attention.

Introduction

Only a few years ago, youth unemployment was a critical public policy issue in Ontario and the rest of the country, with fears being expressed about its negative social and psychological consequences. Today, other issues appear to

---

This chapter was prepared by Harvey Krahn.

have taken centre stage. While concerns about limited employment options for high school dropouts remain high on the policy agenda (Radwanksi, 1987), young people leaving the secondary and post-secondary education systems are frequently worried not so much about finding a job as about finding one that matches their skills and aspirations. Educators and parents are often less concerned about youth unemployment than about the consequences of excessive part-time work among teenagers. Employers and labour market experts are as likely to ask whether there will be enough young workers to fill entry-level jobs as to enquire whether there are enough jobs for youth.

A number of factors have contributed to a dramatic shift in youth employment trends. Ontario's strong economic recovery following the recession of the early 1980s led to higher labour force participation and reduced rates of joblessness among youth. Youth unemployment also dropped because, by mid-decade, the youth cohort had begun to decline in size: hence fewer young people were competing for jobs. Post-secondary educational enrolments have continued to rise. This has led to delayed full-time labour force participation for a larger proportion of youth. At the same time, the shift to a service-dominated economy has continued, with both 'good' and 'bad' jobs being created (Economic Council of Canada, 1990). There is evidence that young workers are over-represented in the latter (Myles et al., 1988).

These inter-related trends require careful scrutiny if attempts to improve youth employment opportunities, and to strengthen school-labour market linkages, are to be effective. Legislation and programs based on decade-old images of the youth labour market invite failure. Consequently, this chapter begins with a detailed examination of youth employment, unemployment and underemployment patterns and trends. Several institutional features of the Ontario youth labour market (union membership, apprenticeships, and training programs) are then noted.Following some comments on legislation affecting youth employment, the chapter concludes with a discussion of several policy implications.

Today's youth are living at home with their parents for a longer time (Boyd and Pryor, 1989). Such a pattern of prolonged dependence on parents requires a rethinking of the boundaries of 'youth' and 'adult' stages in the life cycle. Hence this chapter has a broader focus than others, presenting data for both teenagers (15 to 19 years) and young adults (20 to 24). Longer educational careers and greater mixing of school and work have also led to a blurring of 'student' and 'worker' roles (Krahn and Lowe, 1991). Nev-

ertheless, students and non-students do exhibit significantly different employment patterns and motivations for working, and are compared whenever possible. And since local or regional labour markets offer different employment opportunities to youth, an attempt is made to compare youth employment patterns in the Greater Toronto Area with those in the rest of the province.

I Youth in the Ontario Labour Market

Labour Force Participation

The 1989 labour force participation rate (LFP) in Ontario was 69.8%, up 3% from a decade earlier (Table 7.1). Thus, on average throughout the year,[1] seven out of ten Ontario residents aged 15 and older were either employed or seeking work (unemployed). Men continued to have a higher LFP, but the gender difference has been slowly declining.

Teenagers exhibited a 1989 LFP (64.3%) somewhat below the provincial average (Table 7.1). Young women in this age

---

Table 7.1
Labour force participation by sex and age, Ontario, 1980–1989

	Labour force participation rate (%)[a]			
	1900	1983	1986	1989
Age 15 +				
Total	66.8	67.2	68.5	69.8
Female	54.3	56.5	58.6	61.2
Male	79.9	78.6	78.9	78.8
Age 15–19				
Total	59.1	57.0	59.8	64.3
Female	57.2	57.0	59.2	63.3
Male	61.0	57.0	60.4	65.2
Age 20–24				
Total	81.3	81.3	82.8	82.6
Female	76.5	77.0	79.1	78.9
Male	86.1	85.7	86.6	86.2

[a]Percentage of individuals who are working for pay (including the self-employed) or who are unemployed (out of work and actively seeking work).

Sources: Statistics Canada: The Labour Force, Annual Averages, Catalogue no. 71-001 (1980; 1989); Labour Force Annual Averages 1981-1988, Catalogue no. 71-529.

category were almost as likely to be in the labour force as were young men. While the overall LFP for young adults (20 to 24 years) was well above the provincial average (82.6%), the gender difference for this group was also larger. With the exception of males aged 20 to 24, youth LFP rates have increased substantially over the past decade (Table 7.1). But the increase has been most pronounced for teenagers, and particularly for young women in this age category (from 57.2% to 63.3%). A higher level of job creation (including many part-time jobs) in the service industries (Kaliski, 1986) appears to have brought more Ontario teenagers into the labour market.

Full-time students[2] are obviously less likely to be labour force participants, but a majority still are. Reversing the pattern observed for all Ontario youth, and reflecting the extensive labour force participation of high school students, we find that teenage full-time students are more likely to be in the labour force (54.5% in 1989) than are 20- to 24-year-olds (45.7%). Comparisons to the beginning of the decade (Figure 7.1) show that the increase in labour force activity of full-time students has been much more dramatic than the pattern for all youth.

Student LFP in summer, always higher than during the school term, has also been rising, particularly in the last few years. In 1980, the August LFP rate for full-time Ontario students was 68.1%. By 1983, it had risen to 70.2%, even though the high level of youth unemployment at the time might have led some students to drop out of the labour force. As the Ontario economy recovered, more full-time students were drawn into the summer time labour force, with the August 1986 LFP rate reaching 74.1%. By 1989, when separate estimates were available for teenagers and young adults, the August LFP for full-time Ontario students was 78.4% for the former and 85.5% for the latter (Statistics Canada, 1980: 75; 1984: 87; 1986: 83; 1989a: B-51).

For the total population, LFP is higher for both women and men in the Greater Toronto Area than in the rest of the province (Table 7.2), reflecting the stronger economy of the Metro Toronto area. The same pattern is observed for the 20-to-24 age group in Ontario. However, an unexpected reversal is found for teenagers, with an LFP rate (male and female combined) of 66.5% outside of Toronto, compared with only 60.7% within the Greater Toronto Area. Since, as noted below, Toronto teenagers have a lower unemployment rate,

Figure 7.1: Labour force participation of full-time Ontario students, by age and sex, 1980 and 1989

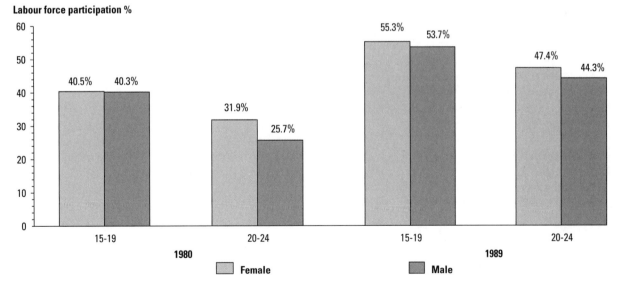

Labour force participation %

Source: Statistics Canada: The Labour Force, Annual Averages Cat. #71-001 (1980; 1989).

Table 7.2
Labour force participation by sex and age, Greater Toronto Area and other Ontario, 1984, 1986, 1989

	Labour force participation rate[a]					
	Greater Toronto Area			Other Ontario		
	1984	1986	1989	1984	1986	1989
Age 15+						
Total	70.8	71.5	72.4	65.4	66.3	67.9
Female	61.4	61.9	63.7	54.5	56.2	59.4
Male	80.8	81.7	81.7	76.9	77.0	76.8
Age 15–19						
Total	56.8	57.2	60.7	58.7	61.5	66.5
Female	58.4	56.7	59.5	57.1	60.8	65.9
Male	55.2	57.6	61.9	60.3	62.1	67.1
Age 20–24						
Total	83.7	83.1	83.3	80.1	82.7	82.0
Female	82.0	80.2	80.0	75.8	78.2	77.9
Male	85.3	86.1	86.6	84.6	87.0	85.8

[a]See Table 7.1.
Source: Special tabulations from the 1984, 1986 and 1989 Labour Force Surveys prepared by Statistics Canada.

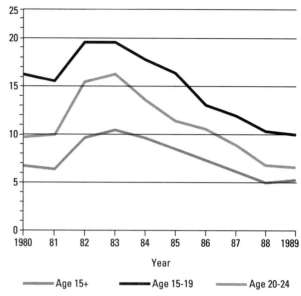

Figure 7.2:   Unemployment by age, Ontario, 1980-1989

Source: Statistics Canada: The Labour Force, Annual Averages, Cat. #71-001 (1980; 1989); Labour Force Annual Averages 1981-1988, Cat. #71-529

a restricted labour market for 15- to 19-year-olds does not appear to be the explanation for this lower LFP rate.

As for inter-provincial comparisons, Ontario youth LFP was above the national average in 1989, for young adults (82.6% compared with 81.0%) but particularly for teenagers (64.3% compared with 58.6%). Again, the stronger Ontario economy accounts for this pattern, with more job openings appearing for youth.

Unemployment
As in other provinces, unemployment rates in Ontario rose rapidly during the recession of the early 1980s, to over 10% in 1983 (Figure 7.2). Since then, they have dropped to 5.1% in 1989 (Table 7.3), well below the national annual average of 7.5%. Youth unemployment (ages 15 to 24) in Ontario increased to 17.8% in 1983, with teenagers experiencing an even higher rate of joblessness (19.6%). But these rates have also declined, to 9.9% for teenagers and 6.7% for young adults in 1989 (Table 7.3). Nevertheless, youth unemployment rates remain higher than adult rates, with teenagers facing the highest risk of being without a job. Although

precise estimates are not available, a range of studies point to the clear conclusion that high school dropouts face the highest risk of unemployment (Radwanski, 1987: 20).

Over the course of a year, full-time students report lower unemployment rates than part-time and non-students; they may stop looking for work sooner (and so withdraw from the labour force) if jobs are difficult to find. However, given the current state of the provincial economy, almost all full-time students who wish to work during the summer do manage to find jobs. In August 1989, the unemployment rate for full-time Ontario students was 6.2% for teenagers and only 2.5% for young adults (Statistics Canada, 1989b: B-51). Six years earlier (August 1983), the unemployment rate for full-time students (aged 15 to 24) was 11.3% (Statistics Canada, 1984: 87).

Across all age groups, male unemployment rates are generally lower than female rates (Table 7.3). But among youth, males have had a higher rate of unemployment every year since 1980. This pattern may reflect a greater tendency on the part of young women to leave the labour market if jobs are scarce. Table 7.3 shows that the gender difference was

Table 7.3
Unemployment by sex and age, Ontario, 1980–1989

| | Unemployment rate (%)[a] | | | |
	1980	1983	1986	1989
Age 15 +				
Total	6.9	10.3	7.0	5.1
Female	7.7	10.3	7.4	5.5
Male	6.2	10.4	6.6	4.7
Age 15–19				
Total	15.9	19.6	13.2	9.9
Female	14.6	17.3	11.9	9.0
Male	17.1	21.8	14.4	10.7
Age 20–24				
Total	9.8	16.6	10.5	6.7
Female	9.9	13.7	9.8	6.4
Male	9.7	19.3	11.1	7.0

[a]Percentage of labour force participants who are out of work and actively seeking work.
Sources: Statistics Canada: The Labour Force, Annual Averages, Catalogue no. 71-001 (1980; 1989); Labour Force Annual Averages 1981–1988, Catalogue no. 71–529.

Table 7.4
Unemployment by sex and age, Greater Toronto Area and other Ontario, 1984, 1986, 1989

| | Unemployment rate[a] | | | | | |
| | Greater Toronto area | | | Other Ontario | | |
	1984	1986	1989	1984	1986	1989
Age 15 +						
Total	7.7	5.5	4.0	10.0	8.1	5.9
Female	7.7	5.7	4.2	10.9	8.9	6.4
Male	7.6	5.3	3.7	9.4	7.5	5.5
Age 15–19						
Total	16.8	11.1	8.4	17.9	14.5	10.7
Female	13.6	11.0	7.5	16.5	12.5	9.9
Male	20.0	11.2	9.3	19.1	16.3	11.4
Age 20–24						
Total	10.9	8.3	4.6	15.0	12.1	8.6
Female	9.2	7.4	4.2	14.3	11.8	8.4
Male	12.6	9.3	5.0	15.8	12.4	8.7

[a]See Table 7.3.
Source: Statistics Canada, special tabulations from the 1984, 1986 and 1989 Labour Force Surveys.

most pronounced at the height of the recession (1983). As discussed in more detail below, male workers are more likely to be employed in construction and manufacturing, while women remain over-represented in the service industries. During the recession, job loss was more widespread in the blue-collar industries, while some job creation (particularly part-time jobs) occurred in the service sector (Kaliski, 1986; Statistics Canada, 1988a).

Some of the drop in youth unemployment since then has been due to the province's economic recovery. But evidence that young people today represent a smaller proportion of the total population points to another important factor. With fewer young people, the relative number of new labour force entrants has declined (Gower, 1988:93), particularly compared with the 'baby boom' cohort that preceded it (Foot and Li, 1986). In 1975, young people made up 25.5% of the provincial labour force. By 1986, this group represented 22.3% of the labour force, and projections to 1996 show only 17.4% of the labour force in the 15-to-24 age category. Thus demand for entry-level and 'student' jobs is not as high as it was in the early 1980s, and will continue to decline.

Finally, compared with other provinces, youth employ-

ment in Ontario is lower. In 1989, the Canadian teenage unemployment rate was 13.1% (9.9% in Ontario), with 10.1% of young adults (6.7% in Ontario) unemployed. Thus, as already suggested, the stronger economy of the province also benefits young workers. The post-recession economic recovery has been most pronounced in the Greater Toronto Area, as demonstrated by its lower overall 1989 unemployment rates (Table 7.4). Compared with teenagers outside of the Greater Toronto Area who experienced a 10.7% rate of unemployment in 1989, the rate for 15-to 19-year-olds in the Metro Toronto region was 8.4%. For young adults, in Toronto the 1989 unemployment rate was only 4.6% — much lower than the rate in the rest of the province (8.6%).

Full-time and Part-time Employment

Young workers are much more likely to be working part-time (less than 30 hours per week) than older ones. This pattern has become more pronounced in the past ten years (Figure 7.3). In 1980, 26.8% of employed youth were in part-time jobs. By 1989, well over one-third (36.3%) reported part-time work, compared with only 9.3% of those aged 25 to 44 and 12.8% of those 45 and older. The percentage of older workers in part-time jobs has changed relatively little over the course of the decade.

Part-time employed teenagers are largely responsible for the substantial difference between youth and adult part-time employment rates (Table 7.5). In 1989, 66.7% of employed teenagers in Ontario were in part-time jobs, up from 62.3% five years earlier. The percentage of employed young adults in part-time jobs in 1989 (15.5%) was little different from the percentage observed in 1984, and identical to the total (all ages) part-time employment rate in 1989.

While an increase over time in the proportion of teenagers working part-time was observed throughout the province, it is interesting to note that, both for the labour force as a whole and for young adults, part-time work is relatively less common in the Greater Toronto Area (Table 7.5). The stronger, more diversified economy appears to provide more full-time work opportunities.

For the provincial labour force as a whole, women are much more likely to be working part-time than are men (24.5% versus 8.2% in 1989). However, the gender difference is smaller for young labour force participants (Table 7.5). In fact, for young adults (20 to 24) employed in the Greater

Toronto Area in 1989, there is very little difference between the female (14.8%) and male (13.7%) part-time rates. In the rest of the province, employed women in this age category are more than twice as likely as their male counterparts to be working part-time (23.0% compared with 11.3%). Again, the more diversified Toronto economy may be offering a wider range of employment options for women.

Are young workers in Ontario generally excluded from full-time jobs, or do they prefer part-time work? Figure 7.4 shows that the latter answer is closer to the truth. In 1989, 78.4% of part-time workers aged 15 to 24 said they were working part-time because they were going to school. Only one in ten (10.6%) said they could find only part-time work, and hence would be classified as 'involuntary part-time workers'.[3]

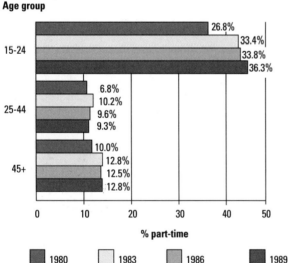

Figure 7.3: Part-time employment by age, Ontario, 1980–1989

Source: Statistics Canada: The Labour Force, Annual Averages, Cat. #71-001 (1980;1989); Labour Force Annual Averages 1981-1988, Cat. #71-529.

Table 7.5

Part-time employment by sex and age, Ontario, Greater Toronto Area, and other Ontario, 1984 and 1989

	% employed part-time[a]					
	Total Ontario		Greater Toronto area		Other Ontario	
	1984	1989	1984	1989	1984	1989
Age 15 +						
Total	15.7	15.5	12.8	13.2	17.9	17.3
Female	25.8	24.5	19.8	20.0	30.8	28.1
Male	8.0	8.2	7.1	7.6	8.6	8.7
Age 15–19						
Total	62.3	66.7	60.6	67.6	63.4	66.5
Female	65.7	72.0	62.3	71.6	68.0	72.2
Male	58.6	62.2	57.8	63.4	59.0	61.1
Age 20–24						
Total	16.3	15.5	13.7	14.2	18.4	17.0
Female	20.6	18.9	14.3	14.8	25.0	23.0
Male	12.2	12.4	12.2	13.7	12.1	11.3

[a]Full-time workers are those who usually work more than 30 hours per week and those who work less (e.g., airline pilots) but consider themselves to be full-time employed; all others are categorized as part-time workers.

Sources: Statistics Canada: The Labour Force, Annual Averages, Catalogue no. 71-001 (1989); Labour Force Annual Averages 1981–1988, Catalogue no. 71-529; Toronto area and other Ontario estimates from special tabulations prepared by Statistics Canada.

Figure 7.4: Reasons for part-time youth employment in Ontario, 1983 and 1989

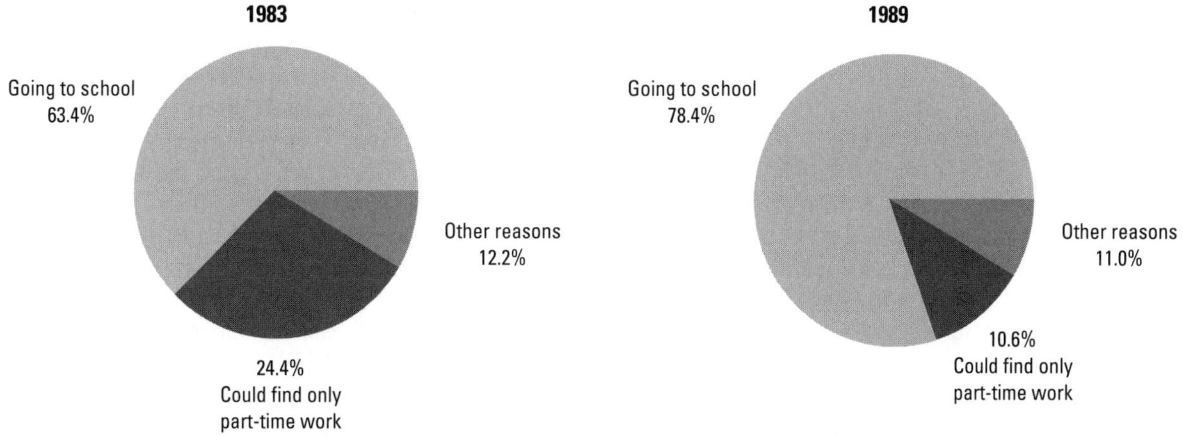

1983

Going to school
63.4%

Other reasons
12.2%

24.4%
Could find only
part-time work

1989

Going to school
78.4%

Other reasons
11.0%

10.6%
Could find only
part-time work

Source: Statistics Canada: The Labour Force, Annual Averages, no. 71-001 (1980: 1989); Labour Force Annual Averages 1981-1988, Catalogue no. 71-529.

Involuntary part-time work among Ontario youth has declined considerably since the height of the recession in 1983, when almost one in four (24.4%) young part-time workers were in this category (Figure 7.4). Such a decline might occur if more young workers found full-time jobs, or if fewer part-time workers desired full-time jobs. Since part-time youth employment has been increasing (Table 7.5), the explanation must lie in the changing preferences of young workers. The decline may be due to the larger proportions of young people mixing school and work well into their twenties. For most young students, a part-time job would best complement continued educational activity.

Nevertheless, some young part-time workers might still prefer longer hours, since they were averaging only 14.1 hours per week in Ontario in 1989 (Statistics Canada, 1989a). The 1986 Labour Market Activity Survey asked part-time workers whether they were satisfied with the number of hours they were working. Among young (aged 16 to 24) Ontario part-time workers, 76.5% said they were satisfied, 15% wanted more part-time hours, and only 8.5% said they wanted a full-time job (Statistics Canada, 1988b: Table 14). Thus, given the choice, well over half of the involuntary part-time employed youth might reject a full-time job for a part-time position with longer hours.

The annual averages displayed in the tables combine winter (school term) and summer (school break) estimates of

full-time and part-time employment. As noted earlier, youth LFP increases in the summer months, and part-time employment declines. While the 1989 annual average showed 36.3% of employed Ontario youth (aged 15 to 24) working part-time (Figure 7.3), only 20.7% (of a larger group of employed young people) were in part-time jobs in August 1989 (Statistics Canada, 1989b: B-31). Among these part-time workers, 39.1% would have preferred a full-time job (Statistics Canada, 1989b: B-32), compared with the 1989 annual average of 10.6% (Figure 7.4).

Year-round Labour Market Activity

Unemployment and LFP rates tell us, on average, how many young people would be unemployed or in the labour force at any given time. But many youth, particularly students, move in and out of the labour force during the course of the year. The 1986 Labour Market Activity Survey revealed that almost 90% of Ontario youth were employed at some point during that year (Table 7.6).[4] About one-third had been employed all year. Even among full-time students, only a small minority (11.7%) had spent less than 13 weeks in the labour force in 1986. In other words, the high labour force activity of Ontario youth does not simply reflect summertime job search and employment. The vast majority also spent large parts of the rest of the year in the labour force. Those who had been employed at some point during 1986 reported an average of about 37 weeks in which they had worked (Statistics Canada, 1988b: Table 13).

Roughly one in three Ontario youth had been unemployed at some point during 1986, compared with about one in ten Ontario adults (Table 7.6). Thus while youth unemployment rates in Ontario had declined to 11.5% by 1986 (ages 15 to 24 combined), a much larger proportion of young people had experienced unemployment during that year. For some young students, unemployment consists of a period of job-lessness before finding a summer job between school terms. However, this is clearly not the extent of youth unemployment, since 28.2% of non-student youth also reported at least one period of unemployment in 1986.

Ontario youth who were unemployed at some point during 1986 averaged 12.3 weeks of unemployment,[5] down from 17.1 weeks at the peak of the recession (Figure 7.5). By 1989, unemployed Ontario youth were reporting only 8.6 weeks without work. The same over-time pattern is observed for the adult unemployed. However, when unemployed, adult labour force participants tend to be without work for a substantially longer time (Figure 7.5). This age difference is partially explained by the extensive educational activity of

Ontario youth. Some young people may resolve their unemployment problem by returning to school. Others, unemployed while attending school, may simply quit looking for work and so, by definition, move out of unemployment.

Within the youth category, teenagers remain unemployed for a shorter period of time than do young adults (Table 7.7). Again, the 'return to school' explanation is helpful. However, teenagers may be more willing to take low-paying, part-time jobs, and hence may not spend as long looking for a job. And, as already noted several times, there is evidence that young people in the Toronto area encounter a more hospitable labour market. In both 1984 and 1989, and for both teenagers and young adults, the duration of youth unemployment spells was longer for those living outside of the Greater Toronto Area (Table 7.7).

Industry and Occupation of Employment

The service industries, broadly defined, account for over 70% of employment in Canada today, whereas in the 1950s less than half of employed Canadians were in the service sector (Lindsay, 1989: 20). While Ontario continues to be seen as the nation's industrial centre, it too has become a

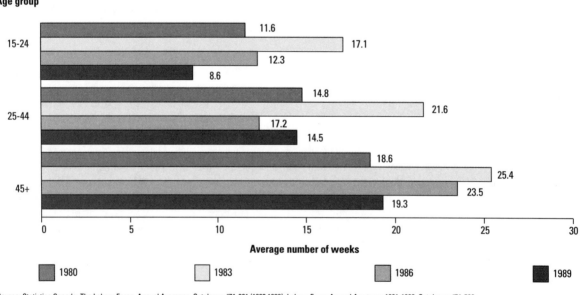

Figure 7.5: Average duration of unemployment by age, Ontario, 1980-89

Age group

Age group	1980	1983	1986	1989
15-24	11.6	17.1	12.3	8.6
25-44	14.8	21.6	17.2	14.5
45+	18.6	25.4	23.5	19.3

Average number of weeks

■ 1980   □ 1983   ▨ 1986   ■ 1989

Source: Statistics Canada: The Labour Force, Annual Averages, Catalogue #71-001 (1980;1989); Labour Force Annual Averages 1981-1988, Catalogue #71-529

Table 7.6
Labour market activity, employment, and unemployment by age, sex and student status, Ontario, 1986
(percentages)

	In labour force			Employed		Unemployed
	At some time	All of 1986	< than 13 weeks	At some time	All of 1986	At some time
Age 16–24						
Female	90.5	42.2	7.0	88.7	34.3	29.1
Male	94.3	46.4	5.6	92.7	37.0	32.2
Both Sexes						
Student[a]	90.4	25.7	11.7	88.2	21.8	32.6
Non-student	95.2	68.3	2.0	94.0	53.4	28.2
Age 25–64						
Female	73.3	55.4	2.1	71.4	49.8	11.9
Male	94.2	82.6	0.7	93.2	76.9	10.2

[a]Respondents were classified as students if they had attended an educational institution full-time at any time during the year.

Source: Statistics Canada, Labour Market Activity Survey 1986. Canada's Women/Men/Youth: A Profile of their 1986 Labour Market Experience, 1988 (Cat. nos. 71-205, 71-206, 71-207; Tables 1, 2 and 3).

service-dominated economy. More Ontario residents are employed in hospitals than in the automobile manufacturing and auto parts industry, and more work in universities and colleges than in iron and steel mills (Radwanski, 1986a: 7).

Young people in Ontario are even more likely than older workers to be employed in the service industries, a situation that is not unique to this province (Cohen, 1989:10). In turn, young workers are under-represented in the goods-producing industries (natural resource industries, construction and manufacturing), primarily because fewer are employed in manufacturing (Figure 7.6).

The service industries can be separated into an upper and a lower tier, with the latter consisting of retail sales and other consumer services (e.g. accommodation, food and beverage, amusement, and personal services) where lower-paying jobs, part-time work, and insecure employment are more common. The Census data in Figure 7.6 show that young workers, particularly young women, are much more likely to be employed in these lower-tier service industries. In 1986, 46.6% of young female workers and 36% of young male workers were employed here, compared with 29.7% and 19.2% of all Ontario female and male labour force participants. A more detailed age breakdown would reveal that teenage workers are even more concentrated in these lower level services. In turn, young workers were under-

Table 7.7
Average duration of unemployment by age, Ontario, Greater Toronto Area, and other Ontario, 1984 and 1989

	Average number of weeks[a]					
	Total Ontario		Greater Toronto area		Other Ontario	
	1984	1989	1984	1989	1984	1989
Total	18.8	13.5	19.1	11.7	18.6	14.4
Age 15–19	11.0	7.1	10.0	5.0	11.5	8.1
Age 20–24	16.3	10.1	15.4	8.0	16.7	11.1
Age 25–44	20.5	14.5	21.0	12.9	20.2	15.3
Age 45 +	24.9	19.3	27.2	16.3	23.6	21.0

[a]Calculations based on only those who had been unemployed at some point during the year.

Source: Labour Force Survey; special tabulations prepared by Statistics Canada.

represented in the upper-tier services (distributive and business services, education, health and welfare, and public administration).

The crude industrial categories in Figure 7.6 reveal some

Figure 7.6: Labour force by industry, age and sex, Ontario, 1986

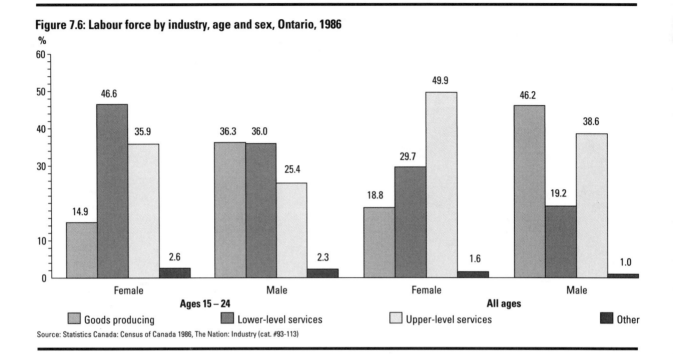

Source: Statistics Canada: Census of Canada 1986, The Nation: Industry (cat. #93-113)

Table 7.8
Labour force by occupation, age, and sex, Ontario, Greater Toronto Area, and other Ontario, 1986

	Total Ontario				Greater Toronto Area				Other Ontario			
	Age 15–19		Age 20–24		Age 15–19		Age 20–24		Age 15–19		Age 20–24	
Occupation	Female (%)	Male (%)	Female (%)	Male (%)	Female (%)	Male (%)	Female (%)	Male (%)	Female (%)	Male (%)	Female (%)	Male (%)
Managerial/Professional	6.5	4.5	20.3	13.6	6.7	4.6	20.1	14.5	6.5	4.5	20.6	12.8
Clerical	30.7	10.9	37.9	11.3	37.9	14.6	45.3	15.6	26.0	8.6	32.0	8.1
Sales	18.2	14.8	10.4	8.7	19.5	15.3	10.1	9.7	17.4	14.5	10.7	8.0
Services	30.3	25.6	17.2	12.2	23.8	26.8	12.6	11.8	34.5	24.8	20.8	12.4
Blue-collar occupations[a]	6.9	29.9	9.3	43.7	4.9	24.1	7.1	37.2	8.1	33.6	10.9	48.6
Other occupations/occupation NA[b]	7.4	14.3	4.9	10.5	7.2	14.6	4.8	11.2	7.5	14.0	5.0	10.1
Total	100.0	100.0	100.0	100.0	100.0	100.0	100.0	100.0	100.0	100.0	100.0	100.0
(N: '000)	(176)	(187)	(340)	(372)	(70)	(72)	(151)	(158)	(106)	(115)	(189)	(214)

[a]Includes primary (agriculture, fishing, forestry and mining), processing, manufacturing, construction and transportation occupations.

[b]Includes material handling and related occupations not elsewhere classified, other crafts and equipment operating occupations, occupations not elsewhere classified, and unemployed individuals who had never held a job or who had only held a job prior to 1 January 1985.

Source: Census of Canada, 1986; special tabulations prepared by the Population Research Laboratory, University of Alberta.

of the gender-based segregation within the Ontario labour market. A similar pattern is observed (in Ontario and the rest of the country) when occupational distributions are examined. For the labour force as a whole, women are much more likely to be employed in clerical, sales, and service occupations. Men are somewhat over-represented in managerial and administrative occupations and considerably more likely to be employed in blue-collar occupations (Krahn and Lowe, 1988:129-33).

Even more pronounced patterns of gender-based occupational segregation are found among young labour force participants. Table 7.8 compares occupations of female and male teenagers and young adults in Ontario. Looking first at the province as a whole, and at teenagers (aged 15 to 19), we find very few in the managerial and professional occupations. Almost four out of five (79.2%) teenage females list clerical, sales, and service occupations. Over half of male teenage workers (51.3%) report such occupations (many fewer are in clerical jobs), while most of the rest are in blue-collar occupations.

Somewhat greater diversity is observed for young adults (Table 7.8). The 1986 Census shows that a reasonable number (many of whom would have acquired higher education credentials) have managed to make their way into managerial and professional jobs. Over a third (37.9%) of young women in this age category were in clerical occupations but, compared with teenaged females, many fewer were in sales and service jobs. A small minority reported blue-collar jobs, but young men aged 20 to 24 were much more likely to be working in these traditional male occupations. Sales and service jobs were much less common among young male adults, than among teenaged males.

While a number of interesting differences between the Toronto region and the rest of the province appear in Table 7.8, one in particular is worth noting. Compared with young women outside of the Greater Toronto Area, female labour force participants within the Toronto region (both teenagers and young adults) are much more likely to be employed in clerical occupations, and less likely to be in service jobs. While clerical positions do not offer the same rewards as professional and managerial occupations, they do typically provide higher pay, more benefits, and more job security than do service jobs.

Sales and service occupations (e.g., cashiers, sales clerks, food and beverage service and janitorial jobs) make up most

Table 7.9
Occupation of high school and university graduates in Toronto and Sudbury two years after graduation (1987) by sex: non-students only[a]

Occupation	High school Female (%)	High school Male (%)	University Female (%)	University Male (%)
Managerial/professional	5.8	1.5	71.9	80.2
Clerical	46.2	6.0	15.8	6.2
Sales/service	42.2	34.3	10.8	13.6
Primary/secondary occupations[b]	5.8	58.2	1.4	—
Total	100.0	100.0	100.0	100.0

[a] Non-students were defined as those who reported no full-time education and no more than 2 months of part-time education during Year 3 of the study.

[b] Includes manufacturing, transportation, construction, and primary sector occupations such as agriculture, mining, and forestry.

Source: Study of the Transition from School to Work in Three Canadian Cities, Year 1-2-3 survey results.

of the jobs in the lower-tier service industries discussed above. Thus we find both industry and occupation data showing young workers, particularly female teenagers, heavily concentrated in lower-level jobs. The Toronto labour market, with its many large private and public sector work organizations, offers somewhat better employment opportunities for young women. In short, age and regional labour market differences accent patterns of gender-based segregation within the Ontario labour market.

Low-paying sales and service jobs with limited career potential may be less problematic for student workers, who view them as temporary. In fact, the parallel trends towards more part-time lower-level service jobs and greater post-secondary educational activity by youth may produce a relatively satisfactory match between the labour needs of employers and the work preferences of young students. But not all young people remain in school. Thus the important question is whether those who have left school, and who are attempting to become economically independent, can find more rewarding and secure employment. Since it may take some time for young labour force participants to find jobs matching their interests, skills, and financial needs, we should restrict our examination to young workers who have been out of school for some length of time.

A recent longitudinal study of high school and university seniors (graduating in 1985) in Toronto and Sudbury[6] clearly reveals the pattern of extended educational activity (Krahn and Lowe, 1991). By 1987, only 32% of the high school sample and 57% of the university sample could be classified as non-students (no more than two months of part-time education during the year). Most of these non-students were employed when surveyed in May 1987 and the types of jobs they held, two years after graduation, are shown in Table 7.9.

A university degree is clearly an important credential, since the majority of university graduates had found a managerial or professional job within two years of graduation,[7] compared with only a handful of the high school graduates (Table 7.9). But 20% of the male and over 25% of the female university graduates were still working in clerical, sales, or service positions. Some of these individuals may have preferred such jobs, but others were unable to find higher-status jobs that matched their educational credentials.

The younger high school sample reported a very different distribution of jobs (Table 7.9). A few of the young women had moved into (lower-level) managerial or professional positions, but almost none of the males were in such jobs. During their last year of high school, the majority had worked part-time in lower-level sales and service positions (Krahn and Lowe, 1991). In the two years following graduation, a number of the female graduates had moved out of sales and service jobs into clerical occupations. The proportion of young men in primary and secondary occupations had more than doubled (from the last year of high school) to 58.2% (Table 7.9). However, one-third of the male high school graduates and more than 40% of the female graduates were still in the 'student labour market', in sales and service positions.

In short, we see a continued pattern of gender-based occupational segregation as well as the inability of many high school graduates to move out of the types of jobs they held while still in school. Since such jobs tend to be part-time, low-paying, and short on skill requirements, it appears that underemployment is fairly common among recent high school graduates who have not continued their education. This conclusion is echoed by a recent Ontario study of out-of-school youth (those who had not attended school full-time at any time during the year), which concluded that 'a high school education (partial or complete) is not sufficient for

youth to compete effectively in today's labour market' (Ontario Ministry of Skills Development, 1987: 5).

More detailed analyses (results not shown) reveal that, compared with Sudbury, where sales and service jobs were more prevalent, Toronto high school graduates were somewhat more likely to have clerical and manufacturing jobs. Despite the dominance of the mining industry in this city, only one of the 130 Sudbury high school graduates who had left school two years earlier had found a job in this industry. Since the major mining employers have drastically reduced their work forces in the past few years, this may have eliminated many entry-level positions for young workers.

But the youth cohort leaving school in the early 1980s, when the Ontario economy was depressed, was very large. It may be that these two trends created the employment difficulties experienced by these high school graduates. The cohorts that have left school since then have been smaller (Ontario Ministry of Skills Development, 1987: 29-31) and have entered an expanding labour market. If so, underemployment may decline. However, job growth in the lower-level service industries continues, along with high rates of post-secondary educational activity. Young people with college diplomas and university degrees will continue to be at the head of the queue for better jobs. High school graduates and, particularly, young dropouts (Radwanski, 1987) will therefore face a high risk of underemployment even as the size of the youth cohort declines in the 1990s.

Wages

Given the occupational location of young workers, it is not surprising to find them over-represented in low-wage jobs. This pattern appears to be becoming more pronounced. Between 1981 and 1986, the average real wage of Canadian workers 16 to 24 years old dropped by 17%. The average real wage of those 25 to 34 also declined (by 5%) but older workers experienced a small increase in real wages over this five-year period (Wannell, 1989: 21-2). The decline in youth wages was observed in all parts of the country, including Ontario. It can be attributed to a number of factors, including greater part-time employment among youth, more youth jobs in the lower-level consumer services, the crowding of the labour market by a large baby-boom cohort (Wannell, 1989:23), and a pattern of job creation that saw most new jobs appearing at the upper-middle and very bottom levels of the wage distribution (Myles et al., 1988).

In 1986, when the national average minimum wage was roughly $4.00 an hour, approximately one in twelve paid employees in Canada were working at or below this level. While teenagers (16-to 19-year-olds, in this case) and young adults accounted for 9% and 16% of the 1986 paid work force, respectively, they made up 40% and 24% of those earning the minimum wage or less. Almost half of the 1986 low-wage jobs were part-time, and young workers accounted for about three in four of these part-time,low-wage jobs. And, to complete this picture of the low-wage labour market, most of the minimum wage jobs were in the service industries, particularly accommodation, food and beverage services, and retail trade (Akyeampong, 1989). While these statistics describe the national situation, the Ontario pattern is little different (Radwanski, 1986b: 14-16).

The minimum wage in Ontario has risen since 1986 (to $5.40 an hour), but the composition of the low-wage labour market remains much the same. While $5.40 an hour is itself a low wage, particularly in large urban centres where the cost of living is high, the Ontario minimum wage can be ignored if employers hire students under age 18 for less than 28 hours a week or during school holidays. In these situations, the minimum wage drops to $4.65 per hour. This option was introduced to encourage employers to hire students who, in turn, could gain work experience. No doubt it has had this effect. But it may also have contributed to the pattern of reliance on part-time student labour by lower-tier service industries.

Low-wage jobs are less problematic for teenagers mixing school and work than for young adults attempting to begin a career. But we have already noted that a considerable number of high school graduates who do not continue their education have little choice but to work in lower-level service sector jobs. In the Toronto and Sudbury longitudinal study, for example, most of the (non-student) sales and service workers were in full-time positions. Excluding the minority in part-time jobs, their average weekly take-home pay was only $211. If we add 20% to this average to estimate gross income, we calculate a weekly average of $253 and an annual average (based on 52 weeks of work) of just over $13,000.

The 1987 Statistics Canada 'low income line' for single individuals in large cities was just over $11,000 (National Council of Welfare, 1987). Thus by assuming full-time, full-year employment, we place these young sales and service workers somewhat above the poverty line. In short, sales and service jobs may be sufficient to meet the financial needs of most student workers. But even if they are full-time, such positions are unlikely to provide young adults with the income needed to become financially independent.

Subjective Evaluations of Employment

Young workers are typically less satisfied with their jobs than are older workers (Krahn and Lowe, 1988: 161). Some of this age difference may be due to different job expectations. However, young workers' generally lower position in the occupational hierarchy is also an important factor. The surveys of high school and university graduates in Toronto and Sudbury provide some insights into young Ontario workers' subjective evaluations of the jobs they were holding two years after finishing high school or an undergraduate degree.

In the high school sample (non-students and continuing students combined), 51% reported that they were satisfied with their job, 23% said they were dissatisfied, and the remainder gave a neutral answer. The university sample exhibited more job satisfaction (61% satisfied; 13% dissatisfied), as one would expect, given that most were employed in professional or managerial jobs. In both samples, gender differences and differences between continuing students and those who had left school completely were of little consequence. Instead, the type of job accounted for variation in reports of job satisfaction.

Young workers in retail sales and service jobs were generally least satisfied with their work. Specifically, they were most critical of their pay, fringe benefits, promotion opportunities, and job security. Even more pronounced were differences across occupational groups in assessments of the match between job requirements and the respondent's education. Most of those in sales and service jobs said their current job was not related to their education and training.[8]

Since a large majority of university graduates were working in managerial or professional jobs (Table 7.9), almost two-thirds (63%) agreed that their current job was related to their education and training. However, very few high school graduates had obtained such higher status positions. Thus only one in four (26%) agreed with this statement. Many of these high school graduates were continuing their education and would eventually have a chance to improve their employment situation. But young high school graduates who do not acquire additional educational credentials will find it much more difficult to move into rewarding and secure jobs (Ontario Ministry of Skills Development, 1987). The prospects for high school dropouts are, consequently, even more dismal.

Disadvantaged Groups within the Youth Labour Market

This chapter has already highlighted some of the labour market barriers encountered by young women, as well as differences between youth employment patterns in the Toronto region and the rest of the province that point to the relative disadvantage of those living outside of Toronto. In addition, several other disadvantaged groups should be noted.

A 1983-84 national survey identified 62,000 disabled youth (aged 15 to 24) in Ontario, representing 4% of the youth population in the province. While provincial estimates were not provided, the national LFP rate for disabled youth was 53.3%, well below the rate for all young Canadians. Disabled youth who were in the labour force had a higher than average unemployment rate (26.1%) in 1983-84 (Statistics Canada and Secretary of State, 1986: 70).

This unemployment rate is, no doubt, an underestimate because of the tendency to consider most of the disabled who are not labour force participants as 'unemployable', even though a considerable number could be employed if some assistance (e.g., training, transportation, access to work-sites) was provided (Rioux, 1985: 620, 628). As for the employed disabled, they tend to be found in lower-level service sector jobs (Rioux, 1985: 616-17).

The disabled encounter a variety of barriers to equal employment (Rioux, 1985: 617-26). These include less than helpful attitudes and beliefs of employers and policy-makers (e.g., all disabled are unemployable; charity is the best approach; and so on), employment policies and legislation based on such beliefs, low-level jobs that pay less than disability income schemes, inaccessible worksites, and educational institutions reluctant to admit the disabled.

In the past, the typical approach to bringing the disabled into the labour force involved training in some sheltered setting. In many cases, this training continued for years. If a placement was made, little further support was provided (Annable, 1989: 66). Today, 'supported employment' (direct hiring of the disabled with continuing support and training in the workplace) is seen as a preferred approach, but relatively few of the employable disabled have the opportunity to participate in such programs. In 1988, a total of 150 programs in Canada were assisting about 3300 workers of all ages (Annable, 1989: 29). These programs had not been in place for very long, and most were employing the disabled in low level service sector jobs, especially janitorial and food services positions. Most were paid the minimum wage, and few were earning enough to live independently (Annable, 1989: 29-54).

Visible minorities also encounter additional labour market barriers, and young people from these groups are no exception. Data from Employment and Immigration Canada show that while the 1986 LFP rate for all Canadian youth (aged 15 to 24) was 67.8%, the rate for young native Canadians was only 52.8%. Other visible minority youth reported a rate of 61.0%. The 1986 unemployment rate for other visible minority youth was only marginally higher than the overall youth unemployment rate (17.6% versus 17%), but the rate for native youth was much higher (31.6%).

Some of these young people, especially native youth, are handicapped by limited education. All of them face the same unpredictable labour market, where a (relative) lack of contacts and discriminatory employer attitudes can limit employment opportunities. A recent study of Ontario youth who had not gone beyond high school (including dropouts) revealed that visible minority youth took longer finding a job (Ontario Ministry of Skills Development, 1989: 18). An earlier (1984) study in Toronto identified one of the reasons. It revealed that many employers would tell a black or Asian applicant that a job had been filled when it had not been, and would then give consideration to a white applicant with equivalent qualifications (Henry and Ginzberg, 1985).

The demographic profile of visible minority groups in Ontario differs from that of the overall population. In 1986, 26.3% of the visible minority population were under 15 years of age, compared with 20.8% of the total provincial population. Thus in the next decade a larger proportion of the (declining) youth cohort will be composed of visible minorities. Since there is evidence now of labour market inequalities, the employment situation of visible minority youth clearly needs to be monitored.

Finally, young people from lower socio-economic backgrounds are less likely to make their way through the education system, thus obtaining the labour market advantages that higher education confers. A series of major Ontario studies have demonstrated that young people whose parents are less educated and in lower-status jobs are more likely to drop out of high school (Radwanski, 1987), are more often in non-academic high school programs, have lower educational and occupational aspirations, and are less likely to go on to higher education (Anisef et al., 1980; Porter et al., 1982). The end result of these accumulated factors is a higher probability of employment in a low-status and less rewarding job.

II Institutional Features of the Youth Labour Market

Union Membership
Young workers are much less likely than adult workers to belong to a union. Statistics Canada's 1989 General Social Survey provides (unpublished) estimates of union membership in Ontario (all employed 15- to 64-year-olds) of 17% for females and 29% for males. However, union membership was much lower for young people (15 to 24), with only 5% of employed females reporting union membership compared with 22% of employed males.[9] For both sexes combined, 13.5% of young workers (students included) were members of a union, with teenagers exhibiting a much lower level of unionization than young adults. These statistics continue a long-standing pattern of lower union membership among young workers, particularly among young women (Rose and Chaison, 1987).

A low level of union membership among young workers does not necessarily reflect widespread anti-union sentiments. In fact, the more common orientation towards unions is ambivalence (Lowe and Krahn, 1988). It is the occupational and industrial location of young workers that largely accounts for low union membership rates. In the past, manufacturing, construction, and some of the primary industries (e.g., mining) accounted for much of the labour movement's strength in Canada, and especially in Ontario. The higher level of unionization for young men in Ontario still reflects this pattern, since a reasonable number are able to find employment in traditional blue-collar 'male' jobs (Table 7.8).

But the unionization of large white-collar sectors (e.g., public administration, education, and health) over the past few decades has changed the composition of the labour movement. The typical union member today is a white-collar employee in the upper-tier service industries (Krahn and Lowe, 1988: 195). Teenagers are not employed here. They tend to work in the lower-tier (generally non-unionized) service industries. As for young adults, the majority of those

with college and university credentials will find employment in the upper tier service industries. When they do, and if a union is present, union membership will probably follow. But many 20- to 24-year-olds are still enrolled in college or university, preparing for entry into such positions. Hence membership levels for young adults are below the overall average.

Apprenticeships
While Canadian youth (and a growing number of adults) exhibit an unusually high level of post-secondary educational activity, very few participate in apprenticeship programs, especially compared with industrialized European countries (Ashton, 1988). In 1986-87, full-time post-secondary enrollment (all ages) in Canada exceeded 800,000, and almost 300,000 people were enrolled part-time in universities (Statistics Canada, 1989b: 15). An additional 240,500 Canadians were registered full-time in trade or vocational programs in community colleges and other public trade schools, a decline from over 270,000 three years earlier. But only 53,315 of those in trade or vocational programs in 1986-87 were in programs for registered apprentices, down from 68,119 in 1983-84 (Statistics Canada, 1989b: 65).

In 1987, there were just over 41,000 active apprentices in Ontario (unpublished data from the Ministry of Skills Development). Well over half were in the construction and motive power (e.g. automobile and heavy equipment mechanics) trades.[10] Fewer than 2,000 of these apprentices were women. Only 4% were teenagers, but one-half were young adults (20 to 24). Almost as many (41%) were between 25 and 34 years of age, suggesting that the decision to begin an apprenticeship may frequently be made after some years in the labour force. Fewer than one in ten (8%) of the total had more than a grade 12 education, 57% had completed grade 12, and the rest had less education.

In short, some Ontario youth (mainly young adult men without post-secondary education) continue to enter the labour force at a skilled trade level via apprenticeships. Most of these training positions are in traditional blue-collar areas of employment, areas that have been declining in terms of their relative share of the labour force. The expanding service industries provide few apprenticeship opportunities (about 3300 active apprentices in 1987). Thus while this pathway into relatively well-paying skilled jobs remains, it will not accommodate more than a minority of Ontario youth.

Other Training Programs

Training programs for young labour force participants consist of two basic types: government programs to assist the entry of youth into the labour market, and formal on-the-job training by employers. Relatively speaking, there is little of the latter, reflecting a national pattern for employees of all ages (Muszynski and Wolfe, 1989). A 1986 survey of Ontario employers showed about one-third (37%) reporting some type of formal training for their entry level employees (Environics, 1986: 16).[11] Another survey of young Ontario high school leavers (dropouts and graduates who had not continued in school) revealed that fewer than one-third had received some kind of on-the-job training since they left high school (Ontario Ministry of Skills Development, 1989: viii).

Provincial and federal youth training programs have generally been designed to assist disadvantaged youth. *Job Entry*, one part of the six-program *Canadian Jobs Strategy* (CJS) introduced in 1985, contains several component programs specifically aimed at youth. The first, *Entry*, provides funds for job training and work experience programs for unemployed youth without post-secondary credentials. *The Challenge* program contributes towards the hiring of students in career-related summer jobs. *Cooperative Education* directs funds towards educational institutions for work-study programs.[12] As youth unemployment rates and the size of the youth cohort have declined, the amount of federal money directed towards these programs has also been reduced.

The provincial government's two main youth labour market programs are the *Ontario Summer Employment Program* (OSEP), aimed at students, and *FUTURES*, which targets employment disadvantaged youth. The largest program among the five included within *FUTURES* is a work experience program (WEP) that places young people in jobs at the minimum wage for a limited period of time. *FUTURES* also includes a pre-employment program (PEP) which provides counselling and literacy training for those young people who are the most difficult to employ, and an Enhanced Training Option designed to encourage on-the-job training. Other programs provide support for youth to upgrade their education.

Currently, about 50,000 students participate in the OSEP program. Roughly 32,000 young people were involved in the *FUTURES* program in 1988-89, down from over 50,000 several years earlier. Again, declining youth unemployment has reduced both the size of this program and the amount of money put into it. A reasonable number of visible minority youth and young social assistance recipients have been among the participants in *FUTURES*, as one would expect, given that the program was designed to assist disadvantaged youth.

Youth Employment Legislation

Concerns about child labour emerged during the period of rapid industrialization in Ontario over a century ago. The efforts of trades unions, legislators, and a variety of pressure groups led to the elimination of many of the worst forms of exploitation. In some ways, current provincial legislation regarding child and youth employment still reflects these public debates. But today, with a very large majority of young workers employed in the service industries, the legislation shaped in an industrial era may be less appropriate.

The provincial Occupational Health and Safety Act specifies minimum ages for employment in different industries. Underground or hoisting work in the mining sector is restricted to those 18 years of age and older. However, the minimum age for surface work in this industry is 16, as it is in construction and logging. The Act states that children under 14 cannot work in industrial establishments or shops, but it is unclear whether the latter refers to 'workshops' or to retail 'shops' as the term is generally used today.

Younger children who deliver newspapers are presumably exempt from such legislation, since they would be considered 'independent contractors'. There does not appear to be a minimum age for employment in the agricultural sector. In short, with some exceptions, 14 appears to be the age at which Ontario teenagers can legally enter the labour market. The few restrictions on child/youth employment primarily target industries in which youth and adult employment continues to decline.

There are few effective restrictions on the hours that teenagers can work. The Child and Family Services Act states that children (under 16) cannot be in a public place between midnight and 6:00 A.M. unless their parent(s) or some other authorized adult is with them. This legislation might limit some teenage employment, although only a minority of the service jobs typically held by these youngest workers would require this kind of night shift work.[13]

The Education Act prohibits employment of those under 16 years of age during school hours, unless they have been officially excused from attending. Older high school students who could legally leave school can be employed throughout the day. This age restriction might limit the work behaviour of some younger teenagers, but presumably, if one was persistent enough, official permission to work would be forthcoming. And since it is often possible for young people to maintain high school enrolment without taking a full set of courses, the definition of 'school hours' is itself variable. Thus the few laws that might limit the extent to which teenagers work would probably be difficult to enforce.

Discussion

Less than a decade ago, unemployment was considered the most serious youth labour market problem. Today, a number of other concerns have become more prominent. Ironically, one of these concerns is that there may be *too much paid work* for youth. A part-time job can provide a young person with spending money and a chance to develop some workplace skills. But with many teenage students working excessively long hours, some educators and psychologists (and more than a few parents) have begun to worry about detrimental effects on learning, educational goals and outcomes, and psychological development (D'Amico, 1984; Greenberger and Steinberg, 1986; Mortimer and Finch, 1986; Radwanski, 1987).

Such concerns are often countered by arguments that teenagers' part-time work will have subsequent beneficial effects on career outcomes. However, the supporting evidence is limited. Most teenagers' jobs are in the retail sales and consumer services sectors. It is unlikely that many will turn these lower-status part-time jobs into rewarding careers. The reliability and punctuality that part-time jobs require could as easily be learned in volunteer work and in school. In fact, the study of high school graduates in Toronto and Sudbury showed that there was very little difference between those who had worked in their last year of high school and those who had not, in terms of employment outcomes two years after graduation (Lowe and Krahn, forthcoming).[14]

It is apparent that many service sector employers have come to rely on part-time student labour. It is also clear that many teenagers want part-time jobs. For most, extra spending money is the main motivation (Lowe and Krahn, forthcoming). Thus the current pattern appears to be mutually satisfactory. But while a reasonable amount of paid work is unlikely to be harmful,concerns about excessive part-time work should not be ignored. Given the declining size of the youth cohort, Ontario employers accustomed to hiring student workers may soon find themselves short of applicants.

One obvious response would be to encourage student employees to work extra hours. A second would be to look for younger students to fill the gap, since current legislation allows the hiring of 14-year-olds in many parts of the service sector. Thus the teenage employment trend needs to be carefully monitored.[15]

The Ministry of Labour's current review of the Employment Standards Act provides an opportunity for reconsideration of relevant legislation. Raising the minimum age for employment of students would affect teenage work patterns, as would legislation limiting hours of work. Both changes might generate opposition from employers who rely on cheap student labour, and from students wanting to work more hours. It might even be argued that limiting teenage employment could have the unintended consequence of encouraging some students to quit school in order to get a job.[16]

Elimination of the student minimum wage (which some groups consider to be discriminatory) might remove an incentive to hire younger workers, although it is an open question whether enough adult workers could be found to fill the low-paying, part-time jobs that students hold. In short, it will not be easy to find legislative solutions to these issues, especially since not all participants define them as problems. Non-legislative responses include Radwanski's (1987: 177-8) recommendations that schools should actively discourage students from working too many hours, that educators should consider co-op work programs that would provide more direct lines of communication between employers and schools, and that employers should act more responsibly when hiring young students.

A second emerging concern is that of youth underemployment. For a majority of young students, part-time work is preferable to full-time, since it fits more easily around school activities. Poorly paid, relatively menial jobs are tolerated because they can be seen as temporary and because there are few better part-time alternatives. But while such jobs may be acceptable to students, they are not the types of work needed by young adults attempting to begin a career and to become financially independent. It is becoming evident that young people who do not go on beyond high school are having difficulty finding jobs outside of this student labour market.[17]

Part of the explanation lies in the growing polarization of the labour market into 'good' and 'bad' jobs (Economic Council of Canada, 1990) and the relative decline in middle-level positions. In the past, young high school graduates and even some dropouts could move out of the student labour market and into relatively well-paying, secure positions in manufacturing, retail trade, and some of the services. But some of these jobs have disappeared and others have become part-time positions. In short, labour market opportunities for high school graduates without additional credentials, and particularly for high school dropouts, may be shrinking, even though the provincial economy has been expanding and youth unemployment is low.

These trends highlight the need for 'counselling and skill upgrading programs [for] the growing number of out-of-school youth who can only find part-time employment and who risk becoming locked into these more limited positions' (Ontario Ministry of Skills Development, 1987: 6). They also demonstrate the importance of efforts to encourage young people to stay in school, or to return to school, to obtain the diplomas and degrees needed for exit from the student labour market.

The extent of underemployment among school leavers demands more attention. However, it may be largely overlooked as concerns about the 'potential gap between the flexibility and skills of workers, and the skills our economy will demand' (Employment and Immigration Canada, 1989: 1) begin to be heard. Cognitive, problem-solving and communication skills, mathematics and science training, and general literacy are becoming increasingly important for labour market success. But currently almost a third of high school entrants fail to complete high school (Radwanski, 1987: 7). Functional illiteracy appears widespread throughout the population. At the same time, enrolments in post-secondary educational institutions have continued to rise. These trends suggest greater polarization between the educational 'haves' and 'have nots' in a future society where literacy and advanced training will increasingly come to be the prerequisites for 'good jobs' (Radwanski, 1987: 15; Economic Council of Canada, 1990).

This possibility leads to our third and final area of youth employment concerns. Labour market programs designed to reduce employment barriers for disadvantaged groups need to be maintained, reviewed, and updated, even in a period of economic expansion. For example, policy makers and program developers have been aware of the labour market problems of high school dropouts, but the difficulties faced by graduates who have not continued their education will require more attention in the future.

It is clear from the data reviewed in this chapter that gender-based occupational segregation is not disappearing.

Efforts to reduce this pattern, in the education system (encouraging higher aspirations among young women) and in the labour market (educating employers and promoting affirmative action programs), are obviously still needed.

Evidence of a more favourable youth labour market in the Toronto region points to the need for additional efforts to assist young labour market entrants in the rest of the province. Employment initiatives developed on the basis of a 'Toronto' image of the youth labour market are less likely to be effective than those that take regional differences into account.

Visible minority youth face a variety of additional barriers to equal employment. Education and skill development programs are needed, particularly for native youth. Given the shift to immigration from non-English-speaking countries, programs addressing language and communication deficiencies are needed to improve the labour market entry chances of young immigrants. And, again, affirmative action programs will probably be needed to counter the effects of discrimination in hiring practices.

Employable disabled youth face a wide range of employment barriers that must be dismantled. The need for more supported employment programs is self-evident. There are examples of employers effectively integrating disabled workers into their work organizations (Ontario Task Force, 1983), but these examples have yet to become a trend. During periods of economic growth, the demand for labour means that the marginally disabled are not as disadvantaged (Rioux, 1985: 620). While the decline in the size of the youth cohort points to a growing demand for young workers, the provincial economy is currently not as strong as it was a year or two ago. Hence, aggressive initiatives promoting the employment of disabled youth in Ontario are clearly needed.

Notes

[1] Unless otherwise mentioned, most of the data in this chapter are from the Labour Force Survey conducted monthly by Statistics Canada. Yearly estimates are 'annual averages', which take into account seasonal variations in employment patterns.

[2] Full-time students are defined by Statistics Canada as 15- to-24-year-olds who attended school full-time in March and were planning to return in autumn.

[3] Other reasons include 'personal or family responsibilities' and 'did not want full-time work'.

[4]The sample interviewed in the 1986 Labour Market Activity Survey was not as large as the samples for the monthly Labour Force Surveys. Consequently, less reliable estimates for smaller sub-groups (e.g., Ontario teenagers employed throughout 1986) are not provided. This particular survey also used 16 as its lower age boundary, whereas the Labour Force Survey includes 15-year-old respondents.

[5]This was about two weeks less than the average for the country as a whole (Statistics Canada, 1988b: Table 13), demonstrating, again, that Ontario youth face somewhat fewer labour market barriers than do young people in other provinces.

[6]The Toronto and Sudbury surveys, along with parallel surveys in Edmonton, formed the first phase of a panel study of the transition from school to work. High school graduates were selected from a mix of academic and vocational programs in a wide range of schools. University graduates were chosen from the Arts, Business, Education, Engineering, and Science faculties at the University of Toronto, Laurentian University and the University of Alberta. In Ontario, a total of 1246 high school graduates (60% from Toronto; 40% from Sudbury) and 746 university graduates (75% from Toronto; 25% from Sudbury) completed questionnaires in 1985. Attrition led to somewhat reduced sample sizes in Years 2 and 3 of the study (Krahn, 1988).

[7]A slightly smaller percentage of university graduates in managerial or professional positions was revealed by the Employment Survey of 1985 Graduates of Ontario Universities (Denton et al., 1987: 27). The difference is probably due to the inclusion of continuing students in the calculations in this larger, province-wide survey.

[8]More detailed discussion of these differences across segments of the youth labour market appear in Krahn and Lowe (1990).

[9]The 5% figure for young women may be an underestimate, since the comparable national statistic was 11%. The relatively small size of the General Social Survey sample makes estimates for small Ontario sub-samples less reliable.

[10]By 1989, the number of active Ontario apprentices had risen to approximately 48,000. An increase in apprenticeship registrations in construction trades appears to be responsible for this growth.

[11]A central finding was that employers were much less concerned about work skills when hiring youth than about personal characteristics (e.g., punctuality, maturity, good grooming). This limited emphasis on work skills (in hiring and in training) reflects the type of low-skill jobs into which many young workers are hired.

[12]Job Development, a second program in the CJS package, subsidizes employers who hire the long-term unemployed, including youth.

[13]At one point, the province had a 'taxi law' requiring employers to send women and young workers home by taxi after specified hours. Given this additional cost, some employers might have been deterred from hiring young workers for evening or night shift work. However, this law was eliminated some years ago.

[14]This particular analysis also included Edmonton high school graduates.

[15]The Labour Force Survey ignores those under 15 years of age, so alternative data collection practices may be needed. Nilsen (1984) notes that 14- and 15-year-olds are not included in US labour force statistics, even though about one in six were working or looking for work in 1983. The number of children illegally employed in hazardous industries or working too many hours has been increasing in the US. There were 10,000 violations in 1983 and 25,000 in 1989 (*Edmonton Journal*, 4 May 1990). This trend may simply reflect a tightening of enforcement practices, but it is equally probable that American employers have begun to hire more younger workers.

[16]This argument has only limited validity, since research has shown that teenagers quit school for a variety of reasons, not just because they want to work full-time (Radwanski, 1987: 86-99; Tanner, 1990: 79-82).

[17]Underemployment of university and college graduates, in terms of underutilization of skills, is a related concern that cannot be adequately addressed in this chapter.

References

Akyeampong, Ernest B.
   1989   'Working for Minimum Wage'. *Perspectives on Labour and Income* (Winter): 8-20.

Anisef, Paul J., Gottfried Paasche, and Anton H. Turrittin
   1980   *Is the Die Cast? Educational Achievements and Work Destinations of Ontario Youth*. Toronto: Ontario Ministry of Colleges and Universities.

Annable, Gary
   1989   *Supported Employment in Canada*. Winnipeg: Canadian Council on Rehabilitation and Work.

Ashton, David N.
   1988   'Sources of Variation in Youth Labour Market Segmentation: A Comparison of Youth Labour Markets in Canada and Britain'. *Work, Employment and Society*, 2: 1-24.

Boyd, Monica, and Edward T. Pryor
   1989   'The Cluttered Nest: The Living Arrangements of Young Canadian Adults'. *Canadian Journal of Sociology*, 14: 461-77.

Cohen, Gary L.
   1989   'Youth for Hire'. *Perspectives on Labour and Income* (Summer): 7-14.

D'Amico, Ronald
   1984   'Does Employment during High School Impair Academic Progress?' *Sociology of Education*, 57: 152-64.

Denton, Margaret A., C.K. Davis, L. Hayward, and A.A. Hunter
1987 *Employment Survey of 1985 Graduates of Ontario Universities.* Toronto: Ministry of Education and Ministry of Colleges and Universities.

Economic Council of Canada
1990 *Good Jobs, Bad Jobs: Employment in the Service Economy* Ottawa: Supply and Services Canada.

Employment and Immigration Canada
1989 *Success in the Works: A Profile of Canada's Emerging Workforce.* Ottawa: Author.

Environics Research Group Limited
1986 *Youth Unemployment and Entry Level Jobs: A Survey of Ontario Employers.* Report prepared for the Ontario Youth Commissioner's Office.

Foot, David K., and Jeanne C. Li
1986 'Youth Employment in Canada: A Misplaced Priority?' *Canadian Public Policy,* 12: 499-506.

Gower, David
1988 'The 1987 Labour Market Revisited'. *The Labour Force,* Statistics Canada (January): 84-111.

Greenberger, Ellen, and Laurence Steinberg
1986 *When Teenagers Work: The Psychological and Social Costs of Adolescent Employment.* New York: Basic.

Henry, Frances, and Effie Ginzberg
1985 *Who Gets the Work? A Test of Racial Discrimination in Employment.* Toronto: The Urban Alliance on Race Relations and the Social Planning Council of Metropolitan Toronto.

Kaliski, Stephen F.
1986 'Trends, Changes and Imbalances: A Survey of the Canadian Labour Market'. In W. Craig Riddell (ed.), *Work and Pay: The Canadian Labour Market.* Toronto: University of Toronto Press.

Krahn, Harvey
1988 *A Study of the Transition from School to Work in Three Canadian Cities: Research Design, Response Rates and Descriptive Results.* Edmonton: Population Research Laboratory, Dept. of Sociology, University of Alberta.

Krahn, Harvey, and Graham S. Lowe
1988 *Work, Industry and Canadian Society.* Toronto: Nelson Canada.

1990 *Young Workers in the Service Economy.* Economic Council of Canada Working Papers.

1991 'Transitions to Work: Results of a Longitudinal Study of High School and University Graduates in Three Canadian Cities'. In David Ashton and Graham Lowe (eds), *Making Their*

Way: Education, Training and the Labour Market. Milton Keynes, England: Open University Press.

Lindsay, Colin
1989 'The Service Sector in the 1980s'. *Canadian Social Trends* (Spring): 20-3.

Lowe, Graham S., and Harvey Krahn
1988 'Youth and Unions: Membership Patterns and Willingness to Join'. Proceedings of the 25th Meeting of the Canadian Industrial Relations Society, Quebec, Laval University.

forth-
coming 'Part-time Work while in School and Post-graduation Labour Market Outcomes: A Study of Three Canadian Cities'. In B. Warme and L. Lundy (eds) *Part-time Work: Opportunity or Dead-end?* New York: Praeger.

Mortimer, J., and M. Finch
1986 'The Effects of Part-time Work on Adolescent Self-concept and Achievement'. Pp. 66-89 in K. Borman and J. Reisman (eds), *Becoming a Worker.* Ablex Publishing.

Muszynski, Leon, and David A. Wolfe
1989 'New Technology and Training: Lessons from Abroad'. *Canadian Public Policy,* 15: 245-64.

Myles, John, G. Picot, and T. Wannell
1988 'The Changing Wage Distribution of Jobs, 1981-1986'. *The Labour Force,* Statistics Canada (October): 85-138.

National Council of Welfare
1987 *1987 Poverty Lines.* Ottawa: National Council of Welfare.

Nilsen, Diane M.
1984 'The Youngest Workers: 14- and 15-year-olds'. *Journal of Early Adolescence* 4 (3): 189-97.

Ontario Ministry of Skills Development
1987 *Out of School Youth in Ontario: Their Labour Market Experience.* Toronto: Ontario Manpower Commission.

1989 *Pathways: A Study of Labour Market Experiences and Transition Patterns of High School Leavers.* Toronto: Ontario Ministry of Skills Development.

Ontario Task Force on Employers and Disabled Persons
1983 *Linking for Employment.* Toronto: Ontario Ministry of Labour.

Picot, W. Garnett
1987 'The Changing Industrial Mix of Employment, 1951-1985'. *Canadian Social Trends* (Spring): 8-11.

Porter, John, Marion Porter, and Bernard R. Blishen
1982 *Stations and Callings: Making it through the School System.* Toronto: Methuen.

Radwanski, George
  1986a *Ontario Study of the Service Sector*. Toronto: Ontario Ministry of Treasury and Economics.

  1986b *Ontario Study of the Service Sector: Background Papers*. Toronto: Ontario Ministry of Treasury and Economics.

  1987 *Ontario Study of the Relevance of Education, and the Issue of Dropouts*. Toronto: Ontario Ministry of Education.

Rioux, Marcia H.
  1985 'Labelled Disabled and Wanting to Work'. Pp. 613-39 in *Research Studies of the Commission on Equality in Employment (Abella Commission)*. Ottawa: Minister of Supply and Services.

Rose, Joseph B., and Gary N. Chaison
  1987 'The State of the Unions Revisited: The United States and Canada'. In H.C. Jain (ed.), *Emerging Trends in Canadian Industrial Relations*. (Proceedings of the 24th Annual Meeting of the Canadian Industrial Relations Association).

Statistics Canada
  1980 *The Labour Force* (August). Cat. 71-001.

  1984 *The Labour Force* (August). Cat. 71-001.

  1986 *The Labour Force* (August). Cat. 71-001.

  1988a *The Daily*, 1 March 1988.

  1988b *Canada's Youth: A Profile of their 1986 Labour Market Experience*. Cat. 71-207.

  1989a *The Labour Force, Annual Averages*. Cat. 71-001.

  1989b *The Labour Force* (August). Cat. 71-001.

  1989c *Education in Canada: A Statistical Review for 1987-88* Cat. 81-229.

Statistics Canada and Secretary of State
  1986 *Report of the Canada Health and Disability Survey, 1983-84*. Cat. 82-555E. Ottawa: Ministry of Supply and Services.

Tanner, Julian
  1990 'Reluctant Rebels: A Case Study of Edmonton High School Dropouts'. *Canadian Review of Sociology and Anthropology*, 27 (1): 74-94.

Wannell, Ted
  1989 'Losing Ground: Wages of Young People, 1981-1986'. *Canadian Social Trends* (Summer):21-3.

CHAPTER EIGHT

Young Offenders

Highlights

- There are to date two young offender service systems in Ontario, one for 12- to 15-year-olds and one for 16- and 17-year-olds. Data collected on young offenders are not standardized, and in some cases not consistently reported, by the four Ontario Ministries dealing with young offenders [the Ministry of the Attorney General (court statistics), the Ministry of the Solicitor General (police statistics), the Ministry of Correctional Services, and the Ministry of Community and Social Services (service provision statistics)].

- Thus it is not easy to make comparisons between the data for the major sectors of the youth justice system in Ontario. Also, with the exception of the average number of youths in custody, it is not possible to make comparisons with other Canadian jurisdictions.

- In youth court, the number of youths charged under the YOA increased by 27% from 1985-86 to 1988-89.

- In 1988-89, the implementation of alternative measures programs may have contributed to the increase in the number of youths charged and may have extended the reach of the youth justice system to youths who would not otherwise have been involved in it.

- The youth courts ordered about 3,300 young offenders into secure custody, and about 3,550 young offenders into open custody, in 1988-89.

- Judges were increasingly likely to order a youth into either secure or open custody from 1985-86 to 1988-89. The rate of young offenders ordered into open custody (per 100 guilty findings) increased 56% and the rate for secure custody increased 15% over these years.

- Since the introduction of the *Young Offenders Acts* (YOA) in 1984, more youths have been ordered into custody than were under its predecessor, the *Juvenile Delinquents Act* (JDA). However, there is evidence that under the YOA young offenders are sent to custody for significantly shorter periods of time than they were kept in custody under the JDA. The average number of youths in secure custodial facilities on a given day decreased dramatically

- and consistently from 1970 to 1988. This 'de-institutionalization' of the youth offender population in part contradicts the contention of some commentators that the YOA is more punitive than the JDA.

- Under the YOA, most offenders are admitted to custody, secure and open, for short dispositions, about 60% for less than four months.

- There is evidence to suggest that although the new flexibility for judges to order open custody under the YOA has allowed them to send some youths to open facilities who previously would have been sent to secure ones, it has also resulted in some youths' being sent to open custody who previously would have been put on probation.

- There is evidence from police data that the courts are dealing with a higher number of offences that are defined as violent (up 7% in police data from 1986 to 1988), but this does not necessarily mean that there is a real increase in youth violence.

- The average daily number of youths in detention prior to trial has increased dramatically, by 35%, from 1986-87 to 1989-90.

- The average daily number of youths in secure and open custody tended to increase from 1986-87 to 1988-89. More striking, however, is that Ontario's rate for the average number of young offenders in custody and detention on a given day (per 10,000 youths in Ontario) was about double the rate in Quebec and British Columbia in 1989-90.

- Offenders in open residential placements pursuant to probation orders under the YOA constitute a significant, though almost hidden, segment of offenders removed from parental care.

- Aboriginal youths are in custody at four times their rate in the population.

- There is evidence many youths are in custody either for non-compliance with a previous non-custodial disposition or for the offence of break-and-enter.

This chapter was prepared by John Kenewell, Nicholas Bala and Paddy Colfer.

Introduction

Young persons who violate the law are dealt with pursuant to the federal *Young Offenders Act* (YOA),[1] legislation that replaced the *Juvenile Delinquents Act* (JDA), originally enacted in 1908. In Ontario, the YOA began to apply to youths aged 12 to 15 (at the date of the alleged offence) in April 1984, and to youths aged 16 and 17 in April 1985. The youth population in Ontario, ages 12 to 17, was 797,900 in 1986 and 788,500 in 1988, down 1%.[2]

The YOA creates a youth justice system with a philosophy, a legislative framework, and facilities separate from those of the adult criminal justice system. The youth justice system is also distinct from the child protection and mental health systems in Ontario, though there are points of overlap between them. Many, though certainly not all, young offenders have also received or will continue to receive services from child protection or mental health agencies.

The YOA is based upon principles of accountability and protection of legal rights, balanced against a recognition of the special needs of young persons and the value of minimum interference with their freedom.[3] The YOA recognizes the importance of protecting society and holding young persons responsible, but it is also premised on not holding them as accountable as adults. The principle of limited accountability is most clearly reflected in the maximum sanction under the YOA, which at present is three years in custody, although youths charged with very serious offences can be transferred into adult court where they may face the same sanctions as adults.

In Ontario, responsibility for young offenders has been divided on age lines. Those aged 12 to 15 have been dealt with by judges of the Provincial Court (Family Division), and have been the responsibility of the Ministry of Community and Social Services in regard to the provision of correctional and custodial services. Those aged 16 and 17 have been dealt with by judges of the Provincial Court (Criminal Division) and have been the responsibility of the Ministry of Correctional Services, which is also responsible for all adult offenders. Both court divisions, however, are 'youth courts' for the purposes of the YOA. Ontario's implementation of the YOA perpetuated the division of judicial and correctional jurisdictions in place prior to its enactment, and has been criticized by some observers as duplicative and submitting some youths to inappropriate treatment.[4] The Ontario government is in the process of eliminating the two levels of court, and giving sole jurisdiction to the Provincial Court (Family Division). The division of responsibility between the two ministries is being maintained.

This chapter presents the data available for Ontario young offenders. They come from four main sources: the police, the youth courts, and the two ministries providing correctional and custodial services. Statistics from the four sources are generally not comparable. In addition, the presentation of the data has had to reflect the fact that to date there are two young offender systems in Ontario, one for youths aged 12 to 15 and another for those 16 and 17. Although the data have been pieced together where possible, at other points the two youth groups have had to be discussed separately. The need for standardized and regularly reported statistics on young offenders in Ontario is obvious.

I The Youth Justice Process

Based on self-report studies, it is clear that almost all youths commit a criminal offence at some point in their adolescence, generally of a relatively minor nature. Offences become an issue for the youth justice system only if the police are involved and start the process by laying a charge.

In some cases involving young persons believed to have committed relatively minor offences, the police will not lay criminal charges. Instead, they may informally resolve the matter by warning the youth not to get in trouble again, and may speak to the youth's parents or make a referral to a social agency. If, on the other hand, the police decide to lay charges, the youth enters the formal youth justice system. This chapter deals only with youths officially reported and dealt with by the courts.

The law provides that where the case is more serious, or there is a concern that the accused may not attend court on the scheduled date, the police may seek to have the youth detained pending trial. If so, the youth must be brought before a judge within twenty-four hours for a bail hearing, where the judge may decide on either detention or release, perhaps on conditions such as restrictions on the youth's behaviour. In theory, according to the *Criminal Code*, a young person should be detained prior to trial only if this is 'necessary to ensure his attendance in court', or 'necessary in the public interest': for example, because of concern about the intimidation of potential witnesses. There are, however, indications that young persons are sometimes detained pending trial because they have no place to stay, or for other welfare-related reasons.

In less serious cases the YOA provides that a young person may be dealt with by 'alternative measures', rather than by formal court processing. Part II of this chapter discusses Ontario's implementation of alternative measures in detail.

If the case is proceeded with in court, it may go through several adjournments, and many months can pass between the initial charge and final resolution.[5] Most youths eventually plead guilty to some, or all, of the charges they face. Sometimes the guilty plea is a result of plea bargaining between the Crown prosecutor and counsel for the youth, in which case a guilty plea may result in other charges being dropped, or in a 'joint submission' by the prosecutor and the youth's lawyer as to an appropriate sentence.

If a not-guilty plea is entered, there will be a trial, which is essentially the same as a trial conducted in adult court for criminal offences, except that youth trials are always held before a judge alone and never involve a jury.

If the youth is convicted, whether after trial or as a result of a guilty plea, the case moves to the 'disposition' (sentencing) stage. At this stage the judge may use reports prepared by probation officers ('pre-disposition' reports), or medical or psychological reports. Pre-disposition reports are usually required if a custodial disposition is to be imposed: they contain information about such matters as the offender's background, family, and school record.

Section 20 of the YOA gives the court a broad range of dispositional choices:

- absolute discharge;
- fine of up to $1,000;
- compensation or restitution to victim;
- community service order of up to 240 hours;
- probation for up to 2 years;
- detention for treatment for up to 2 years;
- custody in an 'open' or 'secure' facility for up to 3 years.

An absolute discharge is in effect an 'official warning'; while a record is kept of the granting of the discharge, there are no further consequences for the youth. This disposition is generally given only for relatively minor first offences.

Probation may involve a broad range of terms, including keeping the peace, reporting regularly to a probation officer for counselling, participating in an alcohol or drug treatment program, or attending school. It is also possible for a probation order to include a 'condition to reside' clause, which can be used to require that a youth live with a particular person, or even be placed in a group home.

The YOA allows a court to order that a young offender be 'detained for treatment' in a place such as a mental health facility. Such orders can be made only with the consent of both the youth and the facility, and in practice are rarely made. It is, however, quite common for a youth to receive some form of rehabilitative services in a custody facility or on probation.

The YOA provides that a judge who is imposing a custody sentence must specify its length, as well as the level of the facility: open or secure. Open facilities are places like group homes or wilderness camps; youths in these facilities can be permitted to go into the community unescorted, and may, for example, attend school in the community. Secure facilities have a higher degree of security, which may be achieved through a combination of physical constraints (e.g., locks, bars, walls) and a higher degree of staff supervision. There is typically a closer control and supervision of youths in secure custody facilities.

Sometimes the court will impose a sentence that involves a period of time in secure custody followed by a period in open custody, or impose a custodial sentence (open or secure) followed by probation.

Young offenders are not eligible for parole or mandatory supervision release in the way that adults are, but the YOA establishes a system of judicially controlled review of original dispositions. On review the court can lessen the severity of the original sentence — for example, shortening the period in custody, or transferring the youth from secure to open custody — but it cannot increase the severity of the sentence. However, a youth who wilfully fails to comply with the terms of a disposition or escapes custody can be prosecuted for this offence and receive a further sentence for it.

The most serious eventuality for a young person facing criminal charges is transfer into the adult system under section 16 of the YOA. Such transfers are to occur only by the order of a youth court judge, after a thorough hearing; these hearings must be conducted prior to any trial in youth court. Transfer is to occur only if the judge is satisfied that this is in the 'interest of society ... having regard to the needs of the young person'. If a youth is transferred, there will be a trial in the adult court, in which case any sentencing will be under the law applicable to adults, with the sentence almost always to be served in adult correctional facilities. In theory, a youth who is over the age of 14 at the time of an

Figure 8.1: The Youth Justice Process

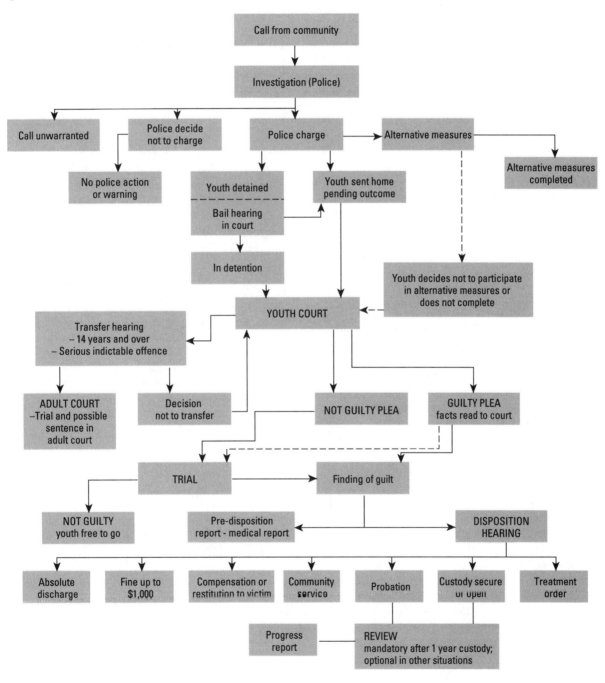

alleged offence can be transferred for a broad range of charges, but in practice the Crown generally seeks transfer only for charges of homicide or other very serious offences, and even in these cases the Ontario courts have recognized the potentially damaging effects on young persons of being placed in adult facilities; they have therefore been most reluctant to transfer.[6]

Figure 8.1 shows the various stages in and alternative routes through the youth justice process.

II The Young Offender in Court

This section contains data on the youth justice process from the time a young person first appears in court to the point of disposition (sentencing) by a judge.

The Canadian Centre for Justice Statistics (Statistics Canada) collects standardized data reported by courts for all jurisdictions except Ontario, which collects its data on a different basis. The Centre provides such information as the number of youths appearing in court, by most serious charge, and the number of youths found guilty, by length of most serious disposition. The data reported by the courts in Ontario are not comparable with those from other provinces and are significantly less detailed.

Table 8.1 reports data from both youth courts in Ontario for federal offences[7] dealt with under the YOA. Since in 1984 only youths aged 12 to 15 at the time of the alleged offence were covered by the YOA, the data in the first column pertain only to Family Division. Data from the Criminal Division (dealing with young persons aged 16 and 17) are included commencing in 1985, when the YOA began to apply to this older age group.

In both cases, the first year of the YOA produced data that must be used with caution, since charges received in one year may not be dealt with (disposed) until the next year. Since there was no such carry-over effect in the first year of the YOA for each youth court (1984-85 for Family Division, and 1985-86 for Criminal Division), the number of charges disposed and the numbers for each disposition reflect a lower level of court activity than in subsequent years.[8] The data in parentheses are thus not comparable with subsequent years, except when used as a rate or percentage: for example, the number of custodial dispositions per 100 guilty findings.[9]

Table 8.1
Youth court adjudications 1984–85 to 1988–89

	1984–85	1985–86	1986–87	1987–88	1988–89
Persons charged	(15,692)	36,356	43,431	41,828	46,109
Charges	(23,027)	56,689	67,281	65,323	73,671
Charges disposed[a]	(19,960)	(54,047)	69,056	70,214	72,686
Withdrawn	(4,636)	(14,581)	18,617	19,269	24,287
Dismissed/acquitted	(527)	(2,036)	2,437	2,737	2,704
Guilty	(13,434)	(30,752)	40,067	39,821	36,513
Dispositions:[b]					
Secure custody (persons):					
Fam. Div.	(701)	948	1,019	1,027	1,001
Crml. Div.		(1,487)	2,280	2,319	2,322
Open custody (persons):					
Fam. Div.	(775)	1,065	1,578	1,617	1,590
Crml. Div.		(854)	1,871	2,106	1,958
Probation orders:					
Fam. Div.		9,260	10,161	10,431	10,097
Crml. Div.			12,442	12,084	10,989
Community service orders:					
Fam. Div.		3,222	3,864	3,754	2,893
Crml. Div.			1,475	1,398	1,175
Restitution/compensation orders:					
Fam. Div.		1,932	1,828	1,759	1,700
Crml. Div.			1,536	1,322	991
Fines					
Fam. Div.		1,112	1,141	893	655
Crml. Div.			3,039	3,013	2,999
Absolute discharges					
Fam. Div.		2,332	2,621	2,638	1,106
Crml. Div.			1,840	1,790	1,020

[a] 'Charges disposed' include the following: (not shown in table) bench warrants ordered, charges transferred out of province, charges transferred to adult criminal court; (shown in table) charges withdrawn, charges dismissed/acquitted, and guilty.
[b] For secure and open custody, the data are for the number of youths receiving that disposition for one or more charges disposed; for non-custodial dispositions, the data are for all dispositions given on each charge disposed by the court. Multiple non-custodial dispositions are recorded for one charge when they are ordered. Data by person are not available for non-custodial dispositions.

Source: Ministry of Attorney General, Youth Court Activity Summaries (Family Division and Criminal Division), for April to March each year.

Charges and Persons Charged

From 1985-86 to 1988-89, the total number of youths charged increased by 27% and the number of charges increased by 30%. It is not possible to determine the causes of these increases: for example, whether they reflect an actual increase in the incidence of crime, or changes in police charging practices.

Alternative Measures

Under Ontario's alternative measures program, begun in April 1988, a young person charged with an offence can be referred to an alternative measures program and dealt with outside the formal court system. The youth is sent to a probation officer or a community agency for such alternative measures as providing restitution to the victim or doing community service. Generally, only youths facing relatively minor charges and without a previous record are eligible for alternative measures. Participation is voluntary, but is conditional on the youth's accepting responsibility for the offence. If the youth denies the offence, the case must be resolved in court. If the alternative measures program is completed, the charges are withdrawn and there is no record of conviction.

One of the criticisms of Ontario's method of implementing alternative measures has been the way it draws young people into the formal justice system. The youth is still charged and often must appear in court several times before the charges are withdrawn.

One concern about alternative measures programs is that they may have a tendency to 'widen the net' of the criminal law. It is possible that youths who previously would not have entered the criminal justice system, but rather would have been dealt with informally — for example, by a police warning — are now being charged and sent to an alternative measures program.

Another concern about alternative measures is that they may result in consequences more severe than those of going to court. Youths who are charged with minor offences, have no prior record, and proceed to court often receive an absolute discharge, whereas with alternative measures they may be required to do community service.

It was at least in part because of such concerns about alternative measures — in particular the possibility that they would 'widen the net' — that the Ontario government did not implement them until ordered to do so by the courts under section 15 of the *Charter of Rights*.[10]

The data for 1988-89 tend to support the concern that the net has been widened by alternative measures. In that year charges against young persons aged 12 to 15 (Family Division) increased by 20% and by 8% for youths aged 16 and 17 (Criminal Division). In 1988-89, the number of charges *withdrawn* increased by 3,425 for 12- to 15-year-olds (based on an increase of 5,422 charges) and by 1,593 for 16-and 17-year-olds.[11] In contrast, when charges against 12-to 15-year-olds increased by 2,898 in 1986-87, charges *withdrawn* increased by only 274. This suggests that some additional charges were laid in 1988-89 so that some youths could participate in alternative measures, and that these charges were subsequently withdrawn.

In 1988-89, 1,498 youths aged 16 and 17 successfully completed an alternative measures program.[12] This number nearly matches the increased number of 16- and 17-year-olds charged (1,125) in that year, suggesting that the net was widened.[13] Data for 12- to 15-year-olds are not available.

In 1988-89, there was a significant drop in the number of absolute discharges. The number of absolute discharges given to those aged 12 to 15 fell by 56% from the average of previous years, and by 44% for those aged 16 and 17. This decrease in absolute discharges at a time when the number of charges increased also seems to indicate that some young persons who previously would have been discharged absolutely are now dealt with by alternative measures.

Further research is called for to assess the impact of alternative measures. In particular, data are needed to confirm that there has been an increase in charges for the type of offences that make a youth eligible for alternative measures.

Detention Orders (pre-trial)

Specific information about the number of detention orders made by the youth courts is not available. However, data presented below (see Table 8.4) indicate that there has been a significant increase in the average number of youths in detention on a given day. This increase, particularly in those aged 12 to 15, corresponds to an increase in the number of bail hearings in both youth courts.

For youths aged 12 to 15, the number of bail hearings has increased each year, rising from 1,520 in 1985-86 to 2,601 in 1988-89 (up 71% in Family Division). For youths aged 16 and 17, bail hearings increased from 3,410 in 1986-87 to 4,718 in 1988-89 (up 38% in Criminal Division).[14]

This information, together with the data in Table 8.4, indicates that the police have presented an increasing number of youths to the courts to be considered for detention and that more youths were in detention during this period.

Charges Withdrawn and Guilty Findings
Charges withdrawn in youth court made up, on average, 27% of the charges disposed from 1985-86 to 1987-88; this figure rose to 33% in 1988-89. These data may give some indication of the extent of plea bargaining (instances in which, in return for a guilty plea to one or more charges, other charges were withdrawn by the Crown prosecutor).

After a guilty or not-guilty plea on a charge, a judge decides if a youth is guilty on that charge. Of the charges that reached this stage of the justice process, 94% resulted in a guilty finding (average, 1985-86 to 1988-89).[15] A guilty plea was entered for many of these charges. These data do not indicate the acquittal rate if the youth entered a not-guilty plea and had a trial on the charge.

Community Dispositions (probation, community service, fines, etc.)
From the data in Table 8.1, it is evident that probation is the most common non-custodial disposition, accounting for over 50% of all community dispositions. Although for Ontario it is not strictly possible to establish that the most serious disposition received by most young offenders was a community disposition,[16] it is evident that the majority of young offenders who are sentenced by the youth court are kept in the community. Data for Canada, excluding Ontario, indicate that 80% of the youths found guilty in youth court in 1988-89 received a community disposition as their most serious disposition, while 20% received a custodial disposition.[17]

Treatment Orders
There are no data for the number of treatment orders made in Ontario. It seems, however, that very few such orders have been made.

Secure and Open Custody Dispositions
In both youth courts, the numbers of youths going to custody seemed to stabilize for the three years from 1986-87 to 1988-89, after significant growth over the 1985-86 figures. The total number of youths sent to secure custody was about 3,300 per year; about 3,600 youths per year were sent to open custody.

The number of youths aged 12 to 15 sent to secure custody increased 5.6% from 1985-86 to 1988-89. The number aged 16 and 17 sent to secure custody increased 1.8% from 1986-87 to 1988-89.

The growth in the number of youths committed to open custody has been greater, especially for youths aged 12 to 15, who showed a 49% increase from 1985-86 to 1988-89. For those aged 16 and 17 the increase in open custody was about 5% from 1986-87 to 1988-89.

As the number of charges dealt with by the courts has increased, so too have the numbers of youths sent to custody. However, the rate, expressed as the number of youths sent to secure or open custody per 100 guilty findings (Figure 8.2), has also been increasing, suggesting that judges have been more likely to order custody. This increase is most evident in open custody, where the rate increased 56% from 1985-86 to 1988-89. The increase in the secure custody rate for the same period was 15%.

Further research is needed to determine the reasons for the growth both in the number of charges and in the tendency of judges to order a youth sent to custody. One factor in the increased rate for custodial dispositions may be a change in the pattern of offences dealt with by the youth courts; or perhaps there has been a change in judicial attitudes towards sentencing. Some information about the pattern of offences by youth is presented below.

Comparing Custody Dispositions Under the YOA and the JDA
There are significant differences between the YOA and its predecessor legislation, the *Juvenile Delinquents Act* (JDA), under which offenders between the ages of 7 and 15 were dealt with until March 1984. While it is not possible to isolate the impact of the new legislation from other trends in society, an examination of trends for the most serious disposition, custody, reveals some of those differences and describes one aspect of the evolution of the youth justice system in Ontario.

The JDA had a philosophy expressly stating that a child who committed an offence should be treated 'not as a criminal, but as a misguided and misdirected child ... needing aid, encouragement, help and assistance'. In practice, the JDA created a highly discretionary, paternalistic system that sometimes focused on the needs of delinquents, but at other times seemed quite harsh, and tended to ignore the legal rights of children.[18] As noted earlier, the YOA is based on principles of accountability, protection of legal rights, rec-

Figure 8.2: Number of youths (12 to 17) committed to custody per 100 guilty findings in youth courts

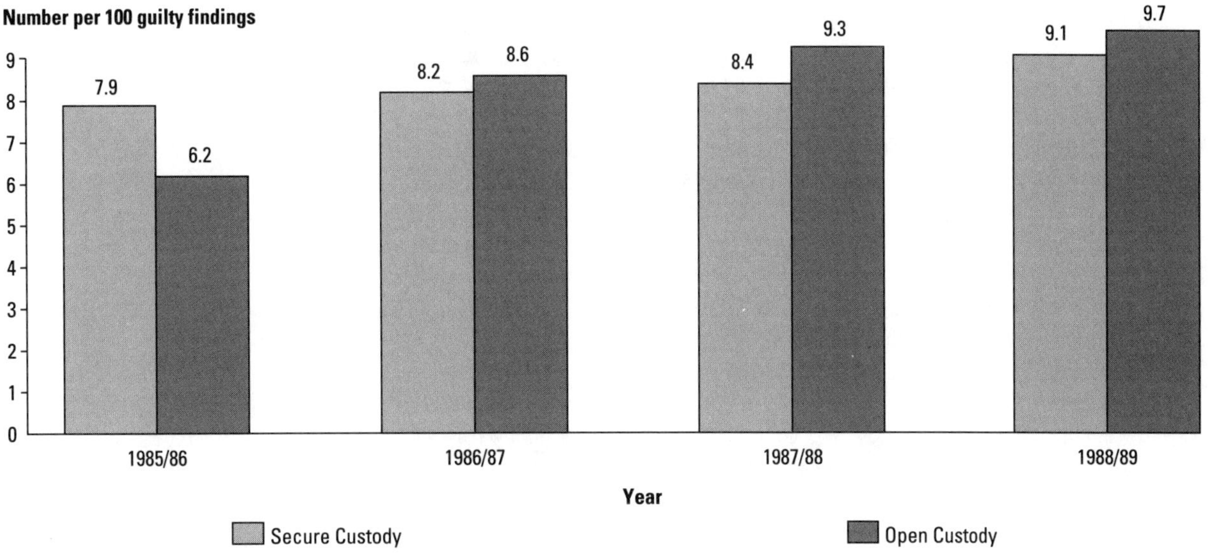

Number per 100 guilty findings

Secure Custody   Open Custody

Source: Ministry of the Attorney General, Youth Court Activity Summaries.

ognition of special needs, and minimal interference with freedom. Noting the higher number of custodial orders under the YOA, some commentators have concluded that, in practice, the YOA is more punitive than the JDA.

Comparisons between JDA and YOA data are difficult to make.[19] No data are available to compare the sentences received by 16- and 17-year-old offenders when they were treated as adults with the dispositions these youths receive under the YOA.

One possible comparison is between JDA training school (secure care) committals and YOA secure custody dispositions for 12- to 15-year-olds (Family Division). In so far as a training school committal was indeterminate in length, and imposed provincial wardship until the age of 18, it was more onerous than a secure custody disposition. Such an order could result in recommittal to an institution without a further court hearing. Correctional officials determined the length of time that a youth spent in a training school and they could direct a training school ward to a community placement (foster or group home) rather than a training school.[20] Under the YOA, by contrast, judges make secure custody orders that are for a determinate period, most often short (see Figure 8.4 below).

The average number of youths 12 to 15 sent to secure custody per year under the YOA (1,016 from 1986-8 to 1988-8) was 52% greater than the average number per year sent to training schools under the JDA (667 from 1981-82 to 1983-84).[21]

Another comparison that can be made is between youths removed from the care of their parents under the JDA (training school and Children's Aid Society committals) and under the YOA (secure and open custody dispositions, ages 12 to 15). The total number of young persons removed from 'parental' care per year has increased 154%, from 1,029 per year under the JDA to 2,611 per year under the YOA.[22]

Under the YOA the courts have dealt with a greater number of charges than under the JDA. However, this alone does not account for the increase in the number of persons sent to custody. There is also an increased rate of custodial dispositions per finding of guilt on a charge under the YOA compared with the rate per findings of delinquency on a charge under the JDA.

The rate of secure custody dispositions per 100 guilty findings (5.8) is 87% greater than the rate of training school committals per 100 delinquency findings (3.1). The rate for dispositions to secure and open custody (15.0) is 219% greater than the rate for committals to training school and Children's Aid Societies (4.7).[23]

It is not clear whether this increase is due to changing judicial attitudes or to changing underlying offence patterns, or to other factors. It is arguable that open custody is having the effect of drawing more youths more deeply into the criminal justice system — 'deepening the net'. Under the JDA judges may have been reluctant to make a training school committal as they had no control over either the level of custody (secure or open) or the duration of the committal. While the new flexibility, under the YOA, to give a secure or open custody disposition may mean that some youths who previously would have been sent to a secure facility are now being sent to an open facility, it may also be the case that some youths who would previously have received probation are now being sent to open custody. The concept of 'open' custody may obscure the severity of the sanction, or perhaps open custody is being used for child welfare reasons, as a substitute for the authority the court had under the JDA to commit a juvenile (age 7 to 15) to a Children's Aid Society.

The sentencing data for the last three years of the JDA also indicate that judges made 65% of youths removed from their homes training school wards and 35% Children's Aid Society wards.[24] From 1986-87 to 1988-89, secure custody accounted for 39% of custodial dispositions and open custody for 61% (Table 8.1, 12- to 15-year-olds). Judges seem to be using their increased ability to decide the degree of security to ensure that higher proportions of young persons go into 'open' placements.

When assessing the impact of the YOA, it is not sufficient simply to compare the number of youths receiving custodial sentences under the two statutes. The average number of youths residing in custodial care per day, the 'average daily count',[25] presents quite a different picture from the sentencing data. In particular, the number of youths under 16 in secure facilities under the YOA on a given day has *decreased* dramatically from the numbers in such facilities under the JDA.

Table 8.2 shows the average number of youths actually residing in a training school or secure custody per day. In addition, it shows the average number of young persons who, although training school wards, were residing in community placements such as group homes — an equivalent of open custody.[26]

Data for previous years indicate even higher numbers of youths residing in training school; the pattern of major

decreases in the number of young persons residing in secure facilities has been consistent since 1970. Figure 8.3 sets out the numbers of youths residing in training schools from 1969-70 to 1983-84; up to 1978-89 these numbers included some youths admitted to training schools for 'unmanageability' under provincial legislation, the now repealed *Training Schools Act*, section 8.

The number of 'beds' (capacity) of all training schools fell from 500 in 1980 to 365 in 1984, the last year of the JDA. As of June 1990, the Ministry of Community and Social Services is planning to have 282 secure beds for 12- to 15-year-old offenders by 1992.

One current issue in federal-provincial discussions is whether the level of custody (open or secure) should be determined by judges or by correctional officials.[27] Table 8.2 also shows that for the last year of the JDA 50% of training school wards were residing in secure facilities and 50% were in community (open) placements — a ratio determined by correctional officials. Under the YOA, five years of data indicate that on average 44% of offenders in custody were residing in secure and 56% in open custody.[28] As noted above, judges sentenced a greater proportion of youths to open custody under the YOA than they committed to a Children's Aid Society under the JDA.

From a policy perspective, it can be argued that the degree of limitation on an offender's liberty should be judicially determined, and not subject to administrative and resource considerations. On the other hand, it can be argued that judges put too much weight on the particular offence, while correctional officials are more experienced in determining the level of security required, based on their knowledge of and experiences with the particular youth.

From the available evidence, it would be difficult to con-

Table 8.2
Average number of youths in custody on a given day

	JDA[a]	YOA[b]	% change
Training school/secure custody	310	206	−34%
Community placement/open custody	310	265	−15%

[a] Source: Ministry of Community and Social Services, Children's Service Branch, average daily count from October 1982 to December 1983.
[b] Source: Canadian Centre for Justice Statistics, 'Young Offender Custodial Key Indicator Report', March (1990), average of average daily counts for 1985–86 to 1989–90.

Figure 8.3: **Population of training schools under JDA[a] and average daily counts in secure custody (12- to 15-year-olds) under YOA,[b] 1969-70 to 1989-90**

Population

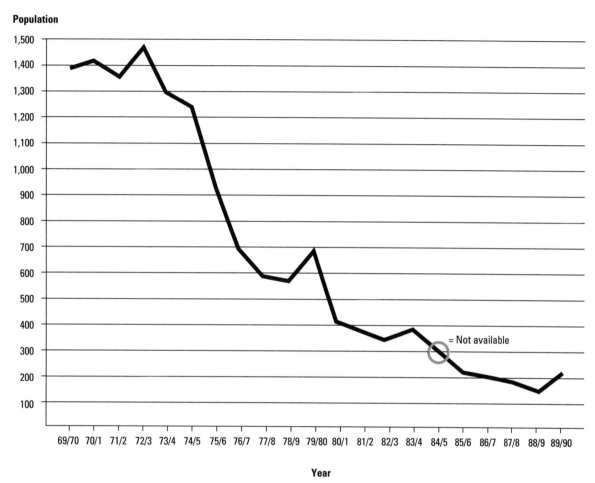

Year

[a] Data for one day, 31 March of the year. Source: Ministry of Community and Social Services, Children's Services Branch.
[b] Source: Canadian Centre for Justice Statistics, 'Young Offender Custodial Key Indicator Report', March 1990.

clude that either judges or correctional officials would more appropriately minimize the degree of restriction on offenders' liberty, keeping in mind the need to protect the public and the other principles of the YOA.

It is evident that under the YOA a greater number of youths aged 12 to 15 have been sent to custody, but the numbers in both open and secure custodial facilities at any one time have been lower than under the JDA. Table 8.2 also indicates

a shift from secure care to open care. These data indicate that under the JDA most youths were kept in custody by correctional officials for much longer periods, and that judges, able to give determinate sentence lengths under the YOA, have tended to give shorter terms in custody.

On the basis of this information, the conclusion that the YOA is, on balance, more punitive than the JDA may not be warranted.

Offences Dealt with by Youth Courts

Data on specific offence types dealt with by the youth courts in Ontario are not available, though such information is available for the rest of Canada. There are Ontario data, as reported by the police, concerning the numbers of youths charged (not the numbers of charges), by most serious offence type. These police-reported data give a general impression of the types of offences dealt with by the youth courts, but the absence of court data places significant limitations on the analysis that can be undertaken.

Neither set of data, however, can be relied upon to comment accurately on increases or decreases in the amount of crime actually committed by youth, or about changes in the proportion of offence types actually committed by youth over time. Too many other factors may account for these increases or decreases; for example, changes in the exercise of police discretion (whether to charge or not to charge), changes in reporting of offences to the police, and political pressures to deal with certain types of crimes (for example, the use of illegal drugs).

Data for Canada, excluding Ontario and the Northwest Territories, indicate that most cases in youth courts involve non-violent offences as the most serious charge. As a proportion of all cases, there was a small rise in the proportion of cases involving violent offences as the most serious charge, from 12.7% in 1986-87 to 13.5% in 1988-89. The number of such cases rose by 9.6% in the same period, from 6,619 to 7,256.[29]

The data collected by police forces in Ontario concern the number of youths charged by the most serious charge (at the time charges are laid). For several reasons, these data are of limited value. First, the nature of the charges may change during the youth justice process (for example, a sexual assault charge may be presented to the court by the Crown prosecutor as a sexual assault, but the court may find the youth guilty only of an assault). Second, some offence types are broad and reveal little about the seriousness of some of the offences within the category; this is particularly so with assault and break-and-enter offences. Third, the data are collected for a calendar year, unlike the court adjudication data (Table 8.1), which are collected for a fiscal year.

Table 8.3 indicates that in Ontario the number of youths charged with violent offences increased by 6.8% from 1986 to 1988. Within this category, varying patterns of increase and decrease in the numbers of youths charged with specific violent offences are evident; for example, sexual offences

decreased. The number of youths charged for all property offences declined by 16%, and the number of youths charged for break-and-enter offences declined by 30%. As a proportion of all persons charged, those charged for violent offences increased from 10.4% to 12.5% from 1986 to 1988. The proportion of break-and-enter offences fell from 16.8% to 13.1% in the same period.

Table 8.3
Ontario youths (12–17) charged, by most serious charge[a]

	1986	1987	1988
Total federal offences	37,227	39,370	33,234
Violent offences	3,881	4,404	4,144
Murder/manslaughter	7	6	8
Attempted murder	17	16	14
Sexual assault	370	422	344
Assault	3,010	3,501	3,253
Robbery	444	408	494
Other	33	51	31
Break and enter	6,258	6,211	4,354
Other property offences	17,247	17,966	15,277
Other criminal code and federal offences	9,841	10,789	9,459

[a]Data relate to police processing of youths; thus youths charged on more than one occasion in a year will be counted multiple times and a youth who is charged simultaneously with more than one offence will be counted only once, even if the offences occurred in more than one incident.

Source: Canadian Centre for Justice Statistics, Uniform Crime Reporting System

While many factors other than the offence are considered when a youth court imposes a custodial disposition, these data suggest that some of the increased rate of custodial dispositions during these years may in part be due to a change in the pattern of offences, in particular in the number of violent offences. In order to support this explanation of the trend in custody rates, however, it would be necessary to have data from the court system concerning the most serious disposition for the most serious charge upon which the offender was found guilty.

Transfers to Adult Court

Some politicians and members of the public, increasingly concerned about violent offences by youths, particularly murder charges, have expressed dissatisfaction with the criteria for transferring youths to adult court. There are almost no data for Ontario to assist in the debate over relaxing these criteria. Available data on the number of charges transferred are not reliable, since one youth may face many charges, and some charges are transferred at the request of youths who have reached their eighteenth birthday by the time they appear in court.

A file study of youths charged with first- or second-degree murder in Ontario from 1985 to 1988 indicated that in 37 such cases, transfer was not requested for 8, was denied for 9 and was ordered for 20. Thus 69% of these requests for transfer were granted. Of the 34 youths whose disposition in either youth or adult court is known, 15 were convicted of murder, 16 were convicted for the lesser offence of manslaughter, and 3 were convicted for other, lesser, offences.[30]

III The Young Offender in the Correctional System

This section examines what is known on a system-wide basis about young offenders and the service system they enter when they receive a custody or probation disposition. Correctional and custodial services are provided by two ministries in Ontario, the Ministry of Community and Social Services (Social Services) and the Ministry of Correctional Services (Corrections). The former provides custody and probation services to youths aged 12 to 15 at the date of the offence and the latter serves youths aged 16 and 17 at the date of the offence.

Expenditures on Young Offender Services[31]

The total expenditure by both ministries on young offender services in 1988-89 was $158.3-million: $75.3-million by Social Services and $83.0-million by Corrections. About one-third of Social Services' young offender expenditures went to provide secure custody and secure detention, and about one-third to open custody and open detention; the other third

was spent on probation and other community correctional programs. Corrections spent 42% of its portion on secure custody and detention; data are not available to break down the other 58% between open custody and non-custodial community programs.

Based on estimates of *per diem* costs from Social Services, each bed in Social Services secure custody cost the ministry about $100,000 to operate in 1988-89. The cost of each bed occupied by a young offender in Social Services open custody was about $50,000 per year in 1988-89.

There has been a trend towards the provision of correctional services by private non-profit agencies, in particular for open and secure custody. The percentage of Social Services' expenditures during these years going to such agencies rose from 40% in 1984-85 to 60% in 1988-89. Corrections has also expanded the delivery of its open custody services by contracting with private, non-profit agencies.

Probation services

Probation services in both ministries are provided by government employees. The respective ministries consider that the average caseload for each probation officer is about 40 cases in Social Services and about 55 cases in Corrections. The exact size of probation caseloads is difficult to determine, since there is no standardized definition of a probation 'case'. In the absence of exact data, it is not possible to state the average number of youths who are on probation on a given day.

Custodial facilities[32]

In 1989-90 Corrections had 868 secure custody/detention beds in 18 facilities ranging in size from 8 to 148 beds. In 1987, Social Services transferred three of its larger secure facilities to Corrections; since then it has used some Corrections beds for the young offenders admitted to Social Services secure custody. In 1990, Social Services had 204 secure beds, and planned to have 282 secure beds in 15 facilities by 1992. These Social Services facilities range in size from 8 to 42 beds. Social Services has a higher proportion of its bed capacity in small secure facilities than does Corrections.

Corrections had 477 open custody beds in 48 community facilities, generally group homes, in 1989-90. Social Services utilizes many multi-service agencies to provide open custody/detention. Since these agencies may provide care both to young offenders and to other client groups, such as

Children's Aid Society wards, it is not possible to determine the number of open custody/detention beds that are available to young offenders in the Social Services system. Both ministries are able to expand the number of beds available for open custody by contracting with community agencies.

Number of Youths in Custody and Detention

Table 8.4 suggests an upward trend in the average number of offenders (12 to 17 years) in both secure and open custody on a given day.[33] After a drop in the average number of offenders in both secure and open custody in 1988-89, the highest levels to date were reached in 1989-90.[34]

Table 8.4

Average number of young offenders (12 to 17 years) in custody or detention per day, Ontario, 1986–87 to 1989–90

	Custody		Total	Pre-trial	
---	Secure	Open	Custody	Detention	Rate[a]
1986–87	675	609	1284	294	19.8
1987–88	679	688	1366	289	20.8
1988–89	648	663	1311	324	20.7
1989–90	745	695	1440	397	23.7

[a] of custody and detention, per 10,000 Ontario youths aged 12–17

Source: Canadian Centre for Justice Statistics (Statistics Canada), 'Young Offender Custodial Key Indicator Report' (March 1990).

There has been a definite upward trend in the average number of youths in pre-trial detention, up 35% in four years. The use of detention has increased even more for 12- to 15-year-old offenders, rising 54%.[35] As noted under 'Detention Orders' (Part II above), the number of bail hearings has also increased significantly during this period. Further study is required to determine why so many youths are being detained prior to trial.

Table 8.5 provides some cross-Canada comparisons of the average number of offenders in custody and detention on a given day in other provinces. (The Canada totals include Ontario.)

What is particularly striking is that in 1989-90 Ontario had a custody and detention rate that was about twice as high as Quebec's and British Columbia's. It is not surprising that Ontario's rate is about the same as Canada's, since in real terms Ontario young offenders made up a large proportion

---

Table 8.5

Average number of young offenders in custody and detention per day — selected jurisdictions

Jurisdiction		Custody		Total	Pre-trial	
---	---	Secure	Open	Custody	detention	Rate[a]
N.B.	1986–87	90	47	137	5	19.7
	1987–88	87	66	153	7	22.4
	1988–89	70	81	152	9	22.8
	1989–90	75	107	182	8	27.4
Que.	1986–87	239	265	503	91	11.0
	1987–88	238	239	478	91	10.6
	1988–89	227	227	453	92	10.3
	1989–90	225	222	447	107	10.3
Man.	1986–87	96	127	223	78	30.4
	1987–88	88	119	208	90	30.2
	1988–89	79	112	191	90	28.8
	1989–90	85	93	178	76	26.7
Alta.	1986–87	128	240	368	106	22.2
	1987–88	132	217	349	106	21.6
	1988–89	143	211	353	121	22.7
	1989–90	144	188	331	124	21.7
B.C.	1986–87	156	135	291	47	13.8
	1987–88	142	150	292	38	13.6
	1988–89	136	141	277	41	13.3
	1989–90	125	136	261	42	12.7
Ont.	1986–87	675	609	1284	294	19.8
	1987–88	679	688	1366	289	20.8
	1988–89	648	663	1311	324	20.7
	1989–90	745	695	1440	397	23.7
Can. Total	1986–87	1609	1720	3329	685	18.0
	1987–88	1615	1803	3418	682	18.5
	1988–89	1529	1734	3263	737	18.2
	1989–90	1641	1712	3353	812	19.0

[a] of custody and detention per 10,000 young persons, age 12–17 in each jurisdiction

Source: Canadian Centre for Justice Statistics (Statistics Canada), 'Young Offender Custodial Key Indicator Report' (March 1990)

of the youths in Canada's custody and detention facilities per day: 45% of the average number of young offenders in secure custody, 41% of those in open custody, and 49% of those in detention.

Custody and detention rates (the last column in Table 8.5) show a rising trend only in Ontario and New Brunswick. Rates in Quebec, Manitoba, British Columbia, and Newfoundland have declined, while those in Nova Scotia and Alberta have fluctuated. In Saskatchewan the rate increased after the first year and then fell. In Canada as a whole, custody and detention counts have been quite stable, with 2% to 3% fluctuations up and down since 1986-87.

From 1986-87 to 1989-90, there has not been a consistent trend for custody and detention rates in the different provinces. This would seem to indicate that Ontario's experience under the YOA is more reflective of factors operating at the provincial level, such as its offence patterns and its justice system, from police charging practices to sentencing practices, than of something inherent in the YOA.

Number of Youths in Open and Secure Detention (pre-trial)

Under Ontario's *Child and Family Services Act* and *Ministry of Correctional Services Act*, a youth ordered by a judge to be detained pending trial may be placed by correctional officials in either open or secure detention. Judges have no authority to determine the level of detention; rather, correctional officials apply provincial legislation, which contains criteria for placement into secure detention. Table 8.4 shows the average number of youths (12 to 17 years) in both types of detention per day. Of 12- to 15-year-olds, about 58% were in open detention (42% in secure) from 1986-87 to 1988-89. The average number of offenders in open detention on a given day has increased by 7% (from 73 to 78) and the average number of offenders in secure detention by 31% (from 52 to 68) over these three years.[36] Very few youths aged 16 and 17 are placed by Corrections officials into open detention; the average number on a given day in 1987-88 was only one.[37]

The objective of the provincial legislation was apparently to place the detained young person in the least restrictive appropriate setting. Whether this objective is being met deserves further study.

Number of Youths in Residential Placements under Probation Orders

One possible condition of a probation order is that the young offender reside in a place determined by a correctional official (YOA, section 23 [2][f])—for example, with his or her parents, in a group home, or in a particular Children's Aid Society placement. Data are not available on how many probation orders made by judges contain this condition.

Data are available, however, for the average daily number of young offenders aged 12 to 15 (at date of offence) in those 'probation residential' placements for which Social Services must pay. (These numbers therefore exclude placements with parents and relatives and offenders who are Children's Aid Society wards.) From 1985-86 to 1987-88, an average of 155 young offenders per day were in such placements.[38]

Young offenders in 'probation residential' placements are a significant proportion (37%) of the offenders in all 'open' Social Services placements (average number of youths in open custody plus 'probation residential').[39]

The only place that Corrections officials will send a youth on probation, other than to his or her home, is to an open custody facility. There are very few offenders aged 16 and 17 (at date of offence) in Corrections' open custody facilities as a result of probation orders; an average of 6 such offenders per day in 1987-88, and 9 per day in 1988-89.[40]

The probation residential order is a serious disposition as it may result in a youth's removal from home. It therefore raises several important issues. Unlike open custody dispositions, probation residential orders are not regulated by YOA criteria, and yet under such orders young offenders may be placed by correctional officials in the same facilities used for open custody. The result is that the YOA criteria for custodial dispositions can be avoided.[41] In making such orders, therefore, judges give up their authority to decide when, for what reasons, and for precisely how long young offenders will be removed from their homes. Since the Social Services and Corrections ministries have established no objective criteria for this process, the discretion to exercise this power may be used inconsistently.

Probation residential orders may also be used by correctional officials to control 'runners' in the care of parents or Children's Aid Societies. A youth who is directed to reside with his or her parents or in a particular Children's Aid Society placement may be charged for non-compliance with the probation order if he or she runs away and, if convicted,

ve a custodial disposition. The threat of this sanc-
keep some youths from leaving.

other hand, it could be argued that this type of
order is an additional, less intrusive, sentencing option for
the court. It is also argued that such orders are less restrictive,
since they allow offenders more freedom than their counterparts in the same placement on the basis of an open custody
order. They allow correctional officials a great deal of flexibility: for example, to determine the length of time that an
offender remains in a placement.

Profiles of Young Offenders

Little is known about the characteristics of young offenders
in a systematic way. Social Services does not publish data
on the characteristics of the young offenders it serves, and
Corrections presents selective data in its Annual Reports. As
well, the data that are gathered on a systematic basis by each
Ministry do not reveal a number of important background
characteristics, such as education and disabilities.

Moreover, because of flaws in collection procedures, data
on characteristics of young offenders admitted to Social Services custody and probation under-report their numbers. While
these data are believed by Social Services officials to capture
a high proportion of all offenders admitted, because they are
incomplete they are best presented in percentage terms. It
was therefore not possible to combine the actual numbers
of offenders served by each ministry to produce an overall
profile; instead the profiles must be presented separately for
each Ministry in both Figure 8.4 (for secure custody) and
Figure 8.5 (for open custody).

Sex
In both service systems, males constituted the overwhelming
majority of offenders admitted to custody — close to 90% in
secure custody — although a somewhat lower proportion of
males was admitted to open than to secure custody.

Age
The largest group of offenders admitted to Social Services'
custody, both secure and open, were 15 years old. Those
entering Corrections' secure custody were predominantly 17
years old. The data for admitted offenders indicates a significant overlap between Social Services and Corrections in the
provision of secure custody to 16-year-olds. Offenders in
open custody tended to be somewhat younger than those in
secure custody.

While the data shown in Figures 8.4 and 8.5 reflect the
offender's age at the time of admission, other data (not shown
in the figures) on offenders discharged from custody or
residing in custody on a particular day reflect their aging
over the duration of their dispositions. Thus offenders 16
and over, rather than 15-year-olds, were the largest group
(49%) residing in Social Services' secure custody on any one
day in 1986-87; 15-year-olds constituted 38%. Similarly, in
Social Services' open custody, the proportion made up of
offenders 16 and over in 1986-87 was 35% (compared with
19% admitted) and the proportion of 15-year-olds was only
40% (compared with 46% admitted).[42]

On discharge from Corrections secure custody, 43% of
offenders were 17, and 38% were 18 years old.[43] On discharge from Corrections' open custody, 11% were 16 years
old, 50% were 17, and 38% were 18.[44]

While the young offender services provided by each ministry are divided according to the age of a youth at the time
he or she commits an offence, their facilities provide care to
youths that exceed these ages. This is worth recalling whenever the Social Services' and Corrections' systems are
described as serving youths 12 to 17 years old.

Aboriginal and other ancestry
Aboriginals admitted to both secure and open custody are
over-represented in both service systems, though it is not
known by how much, since the percentage of aboriginal
youth aged 12 to 17 is uncertain. However, one report
estimates that in 1986 aboriginal people made up 1.8% of
Ontario's population, suggesting that the proportion of aboriginal youth in custody is approximately four times greater
than their percentage in the population at large.[45]

Information on ancestry other than aboriginal is not systematically collected by either ministry.

Disposition length
Data on disposition length give an indication of court sentencing patterns. The disposition lengths shown in Figures
8.4 and 8.5 are for the total length attached to a custody
order, which may cover several offences.

A significant proportion of offenders entered *secure* custody with very short terms, less than one month. The majority
(about 60%) were sentenced to dispositions of less than four
months.

The majority of offenders admitted to Social Services' *open*
custody were sentenced to dispositions of three months or
less, and there is evidence that those entering Corrections'

Figure 8.4: Young Offenders Admitted to Secure Custody

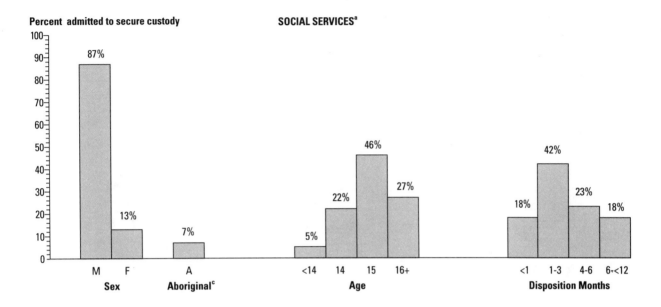

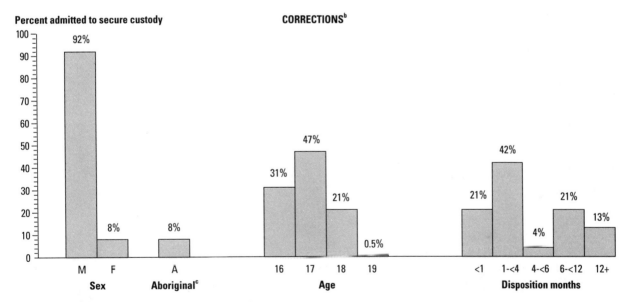

Source: a) Social Services special data run, N = 2,118 (1985/86 to 1987/88).
b) Corrections Annual Reports 1987 and 1988: for 1986/87 and 1987/88, N = 3,056 for sex, N = 2,860, with 196 unknowns excluded, for disposition length; Corrections, 'A Profile of Young Offenders Serving a Secure Custody Disposition', August 1987, N = 188 (in 1987) for aboriginals and age.
c) Includes status and non-status Indians, Inuit, and Métis.

Figure 8.5: Young Offenders Admitted to Open Custody

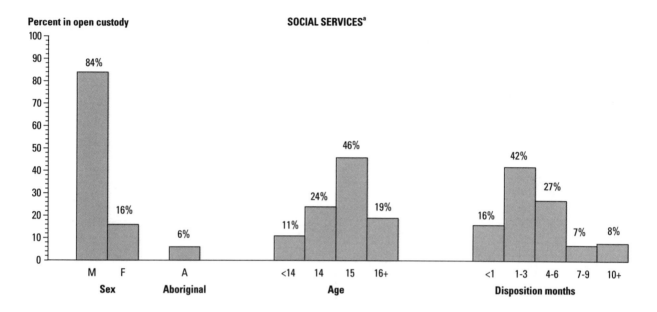

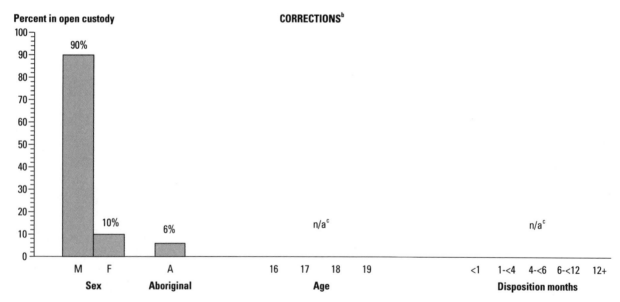

Source: a) Social Services special data run, N = 3,275 (1985/86 to 1987/88).
b) Corrections Annual Report 1988, N = 988 for sex (1987/88): Corrections, 'A Profile of Young Offenders in Open Custody ', April 1988, N = 220 (in 1986/87) for aboriginals with 6 unknown excluded.
c) See text sections 'Age', for age at *discharge* from open custody, and "Disposition length" for *average* length of disposition.

open custody also tended to receive short dispositions. The average length of disposition for male offenders admitted to Corrections' open custody was 4.8 months; for female offenders, 3.6 months.[46]

These data raise questions about the rationale for short dispositions and about programming in secure facilities. What is the custodial system to accomplish for the majority of offenders who are admitted for short periods of time? Do such dispositions reflect emphasis by the courts on the accountability principle, deterrence ('short sharp shocks'), or the least restrictive principle under the YOA?

In fact, there is some evidence of a trend towards even shorter dispositions. The proportion of offenders admitted to Social Services' open custody for three months or less rose from 49% in 1985-86 to 63% in 1987-88.[47]

Because of the rapid turnover of offenders serving short dispositions, data based on population samples of youths in custody facilities in 1986–87 show a larger proportion of youths serving longer dispositions than do the data based on all youths admitted to custody in a year. Thus, at any one time in Social Services' secure custody, 28% of offenders were serving dispositions of one year or more, 40% were serving dispositions of 6 months to less than a year, and 32% were serving dispositions of less than 6 months.[48] In other words, while the majority of offenders were admitted to Social Services' secure custody for 3 months or less, the population on a given day was made up of a majority who were serving terms of 6 months and over.

It should be remembered that young offenders may not serve their full sentences. After a court hearing or through the initiative of correctional officials, they may be released early.

Criminal records

Data on the most serious offence for which a young offender was admitted to custody constitute the only systematically available information about the past behaviour of those admitted to custody. These data are not fully satisfactory, as they do not disclose any information about prior offences or multiple offences that may have led to a custody disposition, but they may serve to raise certain issues concerning sentencing for further study.

Figures 8.6 and 8.7 suggest the types of offences that give rise to a custody disposition. The categories presented are broad and do not reveal with precision the seriousness of the conduct within the offence category. More specific data on offence types are available for offenders admitted to

Corrections' custody, but not for those admitted to Social Services'.[49] As there are some small differences between the ministries in ranking of offences as 'most serious', comparisons between the two are not made.

Offences against the person include murder, manslaughter, attempted murder, sexual assaults, assaults, robbery, criminal negligence causing death or bodily harm, and non-violent personal offences, such as sexual intercourse with a female under 14. Offences against property include 'break-and-enter' into a dwelling or non-dwelling (building), thefts, and frauds.

Non-compliance includes breach of a condition of bail or a probation order. Failure to comply with a previous court order was the most serious offence for more than one-quarter (26.1%) of youths admitted to Social Services' secure custody. This is a disturbingly high figure. To some extent, it reflects the impact of an amendment to the YOA that came into effect in September 1986: this amendment facilitated the procedure for dealing with these young offenders by creating the offence of non-compliance within the YOA to replace the previous procedure of reviewing court orders.[50] The high rate of non-compliance may also be indicative of a tendency towards deeper involvement in the correctional system once a youth has become involved with the courts.

Two additional types of information, based on population samples of offenders in Social Services secure facilities in

---

Table 8.6
Young offenders resident in Social Services' custody by most serious offence in criminal record (including admitting offence)

	Secure %	Open %
Against the person	34	26
Break and enter	46	42
Other property	11	20
(theft over $1,000)	(8)	(10)
(theft under $1,000)	(1)	(0)
Other	9	12
(escape)	(2)	(3)
(illegal drugs)	(2)	(3)
(weapons possession)	(2)	(2)

Source: Social Services special data run, N = 947 for secure custody and 1,366 for open custody (1986–87).

Figure 8.6:   Young offenders admitted to secure custody in 1987-88, by most serious admitting offence type

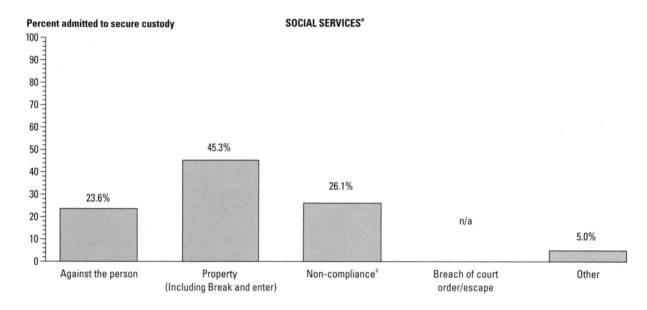

Percent admitted to secure custody   SOCIAL SERVICES[a]

Against the person — 23.6%
Property (Including Break and enter) — 45.3%
Non-compliance[c] — 26.1%
Breach of court order/escape — n/a
Other — 5.0%

CORRECTIONS[b]

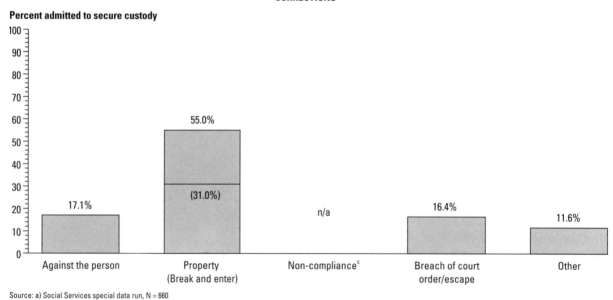

Percent admitted to secure custody

Against the person — 17.1%
Property (Break and enter) — 55.0% (31.0%)
Non-compliance[c] — n/a
Breach of court order/escape — 16.4%
Other — 11.6%

Source: a) Social Services special data run, N = 660
b) Corrections Annual Report 1988, N = 1425 (129 unknowns excluded)
c) With non-custodial YOA order.

Figure 8.7:   Young offenders admitted to open custody in 1987-88, by most serious admitting offence type

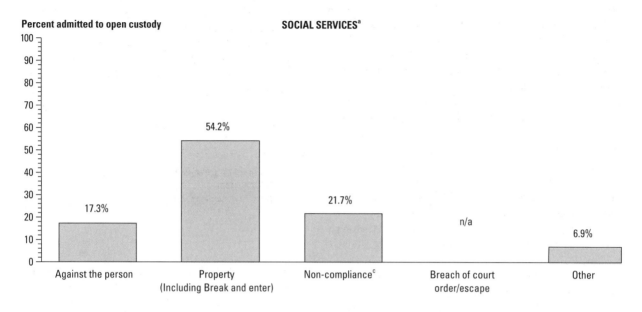

Percent admitted to open custody   SOCIAL SERVICES[a]

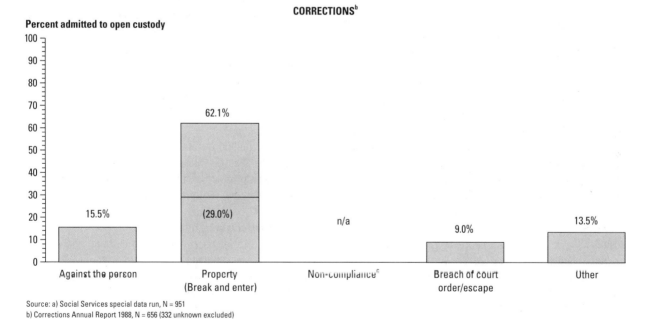

CORRECTIONS[b]

Percent admitted to open custody

Source: a) Social Services special data run, N = 951
b) Corrections Annual Report 1988, N = 656 (332 unknown excluded)
c) With non-custodial YOA order.

1986-87, have been collected.[51] One set of data shows that a high percentage of these residents had never previously been in secure custody (74%). As well, a high percentage had never previously been in open custody (65%). At a minimum, 40% of the residents had never previously been in either secure or open custody. These data suggest that many offenders are admitted to secure custody before less restrictive dispositions are imposed. It raises questions about the extent to which judges are applying the principle of 'least restrictive possible interference with the freedom' of young offenders, as articulated in the YOA, and reflected in the statutory guidelines on the use of custody.[52]

The same sample includes data for the single most serious specific offence in the resident's entire criminal history, including the admitting offence (Table 8.6).[53] This 'most serious' offence is significant because the offence for which the youth was committed to secure custody might have been a relatively minor one that followed a history of more serious offences.

Comparison of Figures 8.6 and 8.7 with Table 8.6[54] shows that a higher percentage of offenders *residing* in Social Services custody had committed an 'offence against the person' (34% in secure and 26% in open) than had those *admitted* to Social Services custody during a year (24% in secure and 17% in open). For the largest group of offenders residing in Social Services custody, break-and-enter was the most serious offence in their criminal records.

The large proportion of offenders in custody for whom break-and- enter was the most serious admitting offence (Figures 8.6 and 8.7) or the most serious offence in their history (Table 8.6) suggests the need for further study of the gravity of such offences. There is some evidence that most break-and-enters are relatively minor in nature; they do not usually involve confrontations with the owner or occupier of the property, and are usually not violent.[55]

It is also important to note that for 11% of the offenders in secure custody in 1986-87, and 20% of those in open custody, the most serious offence in their history was a property offence other than break-and-enter. Of course, the data do not reflect the total number of offences a youth may have committed.

Both the data based on admitting offences and the population sample data suggest that alternatives to custody should perhaps be examined for offenders who commit property offences.

A Profile of Young Offenders Serving Community Dispositions

Figure 8.8 shows data on community dispositions. Corrections data on community supervision refer to any supervision by a probation officer of young offenders, and include youths on probation, community service orders, and restitution and compensation orders. Since there is evidence that most community dispositions are attached to a probation order,[56] data for Social Services probation and Corrections community dispositions are presented together.

Sex
Female offenders are more heavily represented in the probation system than in the custodial system, making up about 18% of offenders admitted to probation, and only 11% of custodial admissions.

Age
As in the case of custodial dispositions, offenders admitted to Social Services' probation were predominantly 15 years old, while those admitted to Corrections' probation were predominantly 17 years old.

Offenders admitted to probation tended to be younger than offenders admitted to either secure or open custody.

Aboriginal ancestry
Aboriginal offenders were over-represented in the probation service, as they were in custodial services.

Disposition length
Offenders admitted to probation served significantly longer dispositions than did those admitted to custody. Probation dispositions for older offenders (aged 16 and 17) tended to be longer than for younger offenders (aged 12 to 15).

Most serious admitting offence
Compared with offenders admitted to custody, a lower proportion of those admitted to probation had an offence against the person as their most serious offence: 14% for Social Services and 12% for Corrections. For 62% of offenders admitted to Social Services probation, and 72% of those admitted to Corrections community service, a property offence was the most serious offence.[57] These are higher proportions than for the offenders admitted to custody.

Figure 8.8: Young offenders admitted to probation (Social Services) and community supervision (Corrections)

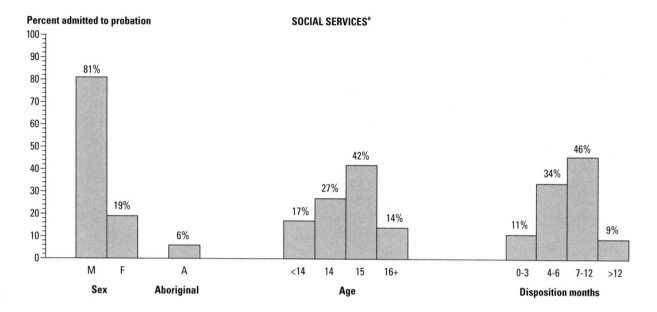

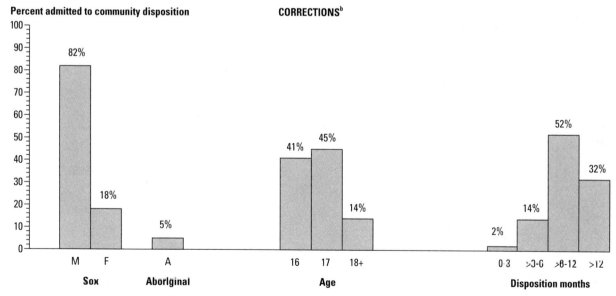

Source: a) Social Services special data run, N = 19,172 (1985/86 to 1987/88).

b) Corrections Annual Reports 1987 and 1988, N = 12,157 for sex (1986/87 to 1987/88); N = 6,059 for disposition length (1986/87); source; 'A Profile of Young Offenders Serving a Community Disposition', N = 132 (1986/87) for aboriginals and age.

Conclusion

Much more needs to be known about who young offenders are and about how they are dealt with by the youth justice system in Ontario. As a starting point in this analysis, the findings in this chapter (see Highlights) suggest some of the major questions for further study. Are more youths being involved in the youth justice system because of alternative measures? Why are the courts dealing with more youths charged under the YOA? Why are more youths in pre-trial detention? Why are judges increasingly likely to send a young offender to custody? And why are aboriginals over-represented in custodial facilities?

Several of the findings in this chapter can be placed in the larger context of a study of the purposes of a disposition. What is the rationale for imposing a probation order that may result in a correctional official's putting a young offender in a residential placement? Were such orders contemplated by the framers of the YOA and, if so, what is the intent? What is the purpose of imposing short (less than four-month) custodial dispositions? An analysis of whether dispositions are effective for their purpose could then follow.

Notes

[1] R.S.C. 1985, c. Y-1.

[2] Statistics Canada, Census and Household Statistics Branch, Demography Division, final intercensal estimates for 1986 and preliminary postcensal estimates for 1988.

[3] This chapter provides only a summary of the principles, provisions, and impacts of the YOA. For more detailed treatment, see Hudson, Hornick, and Burrows (1988).

[4] See e.g. Ontario Social Development Council (1988), pp. 72-5 and 99-109.

[5] Anecdotal evidence suggests that delays have increased significantly since the YOA came into force. This topic is not discussed in this chapter, but it merits careful study to determine the length of delays and their effects on youth.

[6] Some members of the public and politicians have been dissatisfied with the sentencing and transfer provisions of the YOA, especially as they relate to murders. In December 1989 the federal government responded to these concerns by introducing Bill C-58. This bill will increase the maximum sentence that a youth court can impose (only for murders) from three years to five years less a day, with the last two years presumptively being served on 'conditional supervision'

in the community. The test for transfer will be altered to make the protection of the public the 'paramount' consideration, and young persons convicted of murder after transfer into adult court will be eligible for parole in five to ten years. The Bill is expected to be enacted into law by the end of 1990. See Bala (1990).

[7] Provincial offences are omitted, since these are not dealt with under the YOA.

[8] These carry-over charges were disposed in 1984-85 under the JDA in the case of 12- to 15-year-olds and in 1985-86 under the Criminal Code in the case of 16- and 17-year-olds.

[9] Non-custodial dispositions for the first year in each youth court have been omitted, since these dispositions cannot even be stated as a rate. See discussion under note 16.

[10] *R. v. Sheldon S.* (1988), 16 O.A.C. 285 (C.A.) On 28 June 1990 the Supreme Court of Canada [1990] S.C.J. 66, reversed this decision and now Ontario may choose either to continue this program or to abandon it.

[11] Ministry of the Attorney General, Youth Court Activity Summaries from separate data not shown in Table 8.1.

[12] Ministry of Correctional Services Annual Report 1989, page 12.

[13] Youth Court Activity Summary 1988-9, data not shown separately in Table 8.1.

[14] Ministry of Attorney General, Youth Court Activity Summaries.

[15] Percentage is of guilty findings on a charge divided by guilty findings plus charges dismissed/acquitted. Data on the number of charges for which a not-guilty plea was entered and that resulted in an acquittal or a finding of guilt are not available. As the data for guilty findings relate to charges and not persons, the percentage of youths charged who were found guilty of some offence is not known.

[16] This is an unfortunate result of the way data are collected by the courts in Ontario. Community dispositions, as the most serious disposition, by person, are not available. The data in Table 8.1 cannot be used to calculate the percentage of charges that resulted in a community disposition because more than one disposition is recorded for some charges. Data available from Corrections and Social Services on admissions to community services cannot be used, as they include persons who were also previously admitted to custodial services.

[17] Canadian Centre for Justice Statistics (1989), Table 5.

[18] For a description of some of the problems under the JDA that prompted the enactment of the YOA, see Department of Justice (1965).

[19] JDA data include data for 7 to 15 year olds and for provincial offences (except for truancy). However, very few offenders under 12 were sent to training schools.

[20]The comparison is made between training school committals and secure custody dispositions rather than secure and open dispositions, since it is sentencing that is relevant here. Judges had no authority under the JDA over whether a delinquent committed to training school remained in such institutions or was placed in the community. Data on the total number of youths in a year that correctional officials admitted to community settings under the JDA are not available.

[21]Provincial Court (Family Division) Activity Summaries 1981-82 to 1983-84.

[22]Comparing the last three years of the JDA with the last three years of the YOA (1986-87 to 1988-89). Source for JDA: Provincial Court (Family Division) Activity Summaries 1981-82 to 1983-84.

[23]Rates compare the averages for 1986-87 to 1988-89 under the YOA with the last three years of the JDA. For the YOA the secure custody rates ranged from 5.7 to 6.1; and for secure and open from 14.6 to 15.8. For the JDA the training school rates ranged from 3.0 to 3.2; for training school and CASs from 4.7 to 4.8. (calculated from Provincial Court [Family Division] Activity Summaries).

[24]Provincial Court (Family Division) Activity Summaries. Note that judges knew that many training school wards would in reality be placed in community settings by correctional officials, some almost immediately after committal.

[25]The number of youths in custody each day divided by the number of days for the reporting period.

[26]Here the comparison is between the average numbers of youths actually in a secure or open/community placement on a given day, and not the number of youths given such sentences in a year. Even this comparison understates the number of youths residing in the community under the JDA, since an average daily count is not available for CAS wards. These youths could also be considered to have been in a form of open custody.

[27]See Department of Justice (1989).

[28]Calculated from data for 12- to 15-year-olds in Canadian Centre for Justice Statistics (1990a), for 1985-86 to 1988-89.

[29]Canadian Centre for Justice Statistics (1990b), from Table 1. A 'case' refers to one or more charges against one person adjudicated by the court on one day. If the court adjudicates other charges involving that same person on another date in the same year, two cases will be counted. Violent offences include, among others, murder, attempted murder, sexual assaults, assaults, robbery, weapons offences, kidnapping, extortion.

[30]Department of Justice (1989), from Chapter 1, Appendix, Tables 1 and 2. Data are only for files located; may under-report absolute numbers by unknown amount.

[31]Expenditure data supplied by the Ministry of Community and Social Services and the Ministry of Correctional Services.

[32]Information supplied by the Ministry of Community and Social Services and the Ministry of Correctional Services.

[33]Although these average numbers are determined by the number of offenders in custody/detention on each day, as averages they hide a considerable degree of fluctuation from day to day, and thus misrepresent the reality of service provision in facilities.

[34]Data for 1985-86 are omitted, as this was the first year of the YOA for 16- and 17-year-olds; thus Corrections began the year with a zero count in custody.

[35]Canadian Centre for Justice Statistics (1990a).

[36]Ministry of Community and Social Services, Children's Services Branch.

[37]Ministry of Correctional Services Annual Report 1988, Table 7.

[38]Ministry of Community and Social Services, Children's Services Branch.

[39]Average number of offenders in Social Services open custody per day 1985-86 to 1987-88 is 265.

[40]Ministry of Correctional Services Annual Reports for 1988 and 1989, Table 7 in each.

[41]In order to impose an open custody order a pre-disposition report is generally required and under s. 24(1) of the YOA an offender can only be given an open custody disposition if the court considers this necessary 'for the protection of society'.

[42]Social Services special data run for four days in 1986-87, secure custody N = 947 and open custody N = 1,366.

[43]Ministry of Correctional Services (1987); N = 188(1986-87).

[44]Ministry of Correctional Services (1987), N = 188; (1988a), N = 217, excluding 9 unknown.

[45]Ministry of Community and Social Services (1989). The Social Services data on aboriginal offenders are considered to under-represent aboriginals, because of flaws in the reporting of this data and difficulties in categorizing the ancestry of some non-status Indians and Métis.

[46]Ministry of Correctional Services Annual Report 1988; for males, N = 890; for females, N = 98.

[47]Social Services special data run, N = 938 for 1985/6 and N = 1,137 for 1987-88.

[48]Social Services special data run for four days in 1986-87, N = 947.

[49]Data on the number of charges, by offence type, for which an offender was admitted to custody are not presented. This information is available only for 16- and 17-year-old offenders; see Ministry of Correctional Services Annual Reports.

[50]All other offences dealt with under the YOA are created by the Criminal Code and other federal statutes.

[51]Social Services special data run, N = 947.

[52]YOA s. 3 (1)(f) with respect to this principle and s. 24(1) and s. 24.1 (3) and (4) with respect to the criteria for custodial dispositions.

[53]Residents who committed a break-and-enter offence and an offence against the person were placed in the latter group. The most serious offence was selected on the basis of the maximum sentence length in the *Criminal Code* and by 14 priorized offence categories.

[54]The authors realize that different years are being compared. If we had compared Table 8.6 with the available data for 1986-87, the differences would have been even greater for secure custody (both Social Services and Corrections) and for open custody (Social Services); 1986-87 data on most serious admitting offence for Corrections open custody were not available.

[55]See, for example, LeBlanc, and Frechette (1989) for a study of youth in Montreal; and Waller and Okihiro (1986).

[56]Ministry of Correctional Services (1988b).

[57]Social Services special data run for 1987-88, N = 5,382; Corrections Annual Report 1988, N = 6,098 (1987-88).

References

Bala, N.
1990 'Dealing with Violent Young Offenders: Transfer to Adult Court and Bill C-58'. *Canadian Journal of Family Law*, 9 (1), 11-38.

Canadian Centre for Justice Statistics
1989 'The Young Offender in Canada: A Statistical Portrait for 1989-90'. Statistics Canada (September).

1990a 'Young Offender Custodial Key Indicator Report'. Ottawa: Canadian Centre for Justice Statistics (March).

1990b 'Violent Offences by Young Offenders, 1986-87 to 1988-89'. *Juristat*, 10 (5) (April).

Department of Justice
1989 'The Young Offenders Act: Proposals for Amendment, a Consultation Document'. (July).

Department of Justice, Committee on Juvenile Justice
1965 *Juvenile Delinquency in Canada*. Ottawa: Queen's Printer.

Hudson, J., J.P. Hornick, and B.A. Burrows
1988 *Justice and the Young Offender in Canada*. Toronto: Wall and Thompson.

Leblanc, M., and M. Frechette
1989 *Male Criminal Activity from Childhood through Youth*. New York: Springer Verlag.

Ministry of Correctional Services
Annual Reports 1987, 1988, 1989

1987 'A Profile of Young Offenders Serving a Secure Custody Disposition'. (August).

1988a 'A Profile of Young Offenders in Open Custody'. (April).

1988b 'A Profile of Young Offenders Serving a Community Disposition'. (May).

Ministry of Community and Social Services
1989 *Looking Ahead: Trends and Implications in the Social Environment*. Toronto: Queen's Printer.

Ontario Social Development Council
1988 *YOA Dispositions: Challenges and Choices*. Toronto: Author.

Waller, I., and N. Okihiro
1986 'Residential Burglary in Toronto'. In R. Silverman and J. Teevan (eds), *Crime in Canadian Society*, 3rd ed. Toronto: Butterworths.

CHAPTER NINE

Children's Habitat

Highlights

- Almost 150,000 (6.0%) of children and youth in Ontario under the age of 20 live in apartment buildings of 5 or more storeys; of these, about 65% live in Metro Toronto.
- Almost 20% of renter households with children in Ontario have a total household income of less than $10,000 per year; of these, over three-quarters pay more than 50% of their income on shelter; over 40% of owner households with children with a total income of less than $10,000 pay more than 50% on housing.
- It is estimated that over 7,000 families with children in Ontario are doubling up; the majority (69.8%) of these families live in Metro Toronto.
- Over half (56%) of all persons in non-senior households living in core housing need in Ontario are children and youths 24 years or younger; about 40% of non-senior households with children in core need live in high-rise apartments, and the vast majority are renters (67.7%).
- Single-parent families, particularly those led by women, are more likely to rent, to pay at least 30% of income on shelter, and to be in core housing need than are two-parent families.
- Over 40% of aboriginal families living on reserves in Ontario

have no central heat; almost 20% live in crowded conditions.
- The number of applicants for family housing in the Metro Toronto Housing Authority who were rated in the highest need category increased by almost 100% between 1985 and 1989; for the remainder of the province the increase during the same period was 15%.
- Almost 4,000 children aged 10 to 14 with disabilities living at home in Ontario are fully housebound; over 10,000 are prevented from participating in normal activities.
- Over one-third of the children in Ontario with disabilities need but do not have special features in their homes that would allow them to enter or leave the home, and over 40% need but do not have special features to help them get around inside their homes.
- Most of the accidents that happen to pre-school children take place at home; for school-age children, most accidents occur elsewhere.
- Over 6,000 youths under the age of 25 and close to 2,000 families with children used Toronto's municipally funded shelters during 1987-88; of the families with children, almost 70% were led by single mothers.

Introduction

Children's home environment encompasses both a physical and a social dimension. The interaction between the two and their effects on a child's overall well-being have been the focus of many discussions, and although very few scientific evaluations have been conducted about the causal relationships, most experts would agree that a child's home environment affects his or her eventual life chances.

Shelter, whether a house or apartment, owned or rented, is the single largest dollar expenditure that Ontario families make over a life course. Shelter costs are the highest day-to-day living expenditures that most families incur. What an individual family can afford influences the quality both of the housing and of the surrounding neighbourhood that will be accessible to it. Simply stated, and with relatively few

This chapter was prepared by Christine Kluck Davis.

ely than others to live
od. They are also far
re likely to remain

lians by Statistics
90) revealed data
of children and
report showed
ars of life lost,
.ost all age groups), and
related to disparities in urban
income patterns. Furthermore, the research-
und that while mortality has declined since 1971 in all
income quintiles (based on Census tract incidence of low
income), the relative differences between quintiles have
remained much the same. The study leaves little doubt that
Canadian children living in 'poorer' urban areas are at a
greater health risk than those raised in middle- or upper-
class neighbourhoods.[1]

Contents of this Chapter

The main objective of this chapter is to illustrate the variations in the home environments of children and youths living
in Ontario. In doing so, it challenges the premise that living
in the wealthiest province in Canada means that all families
have equal access to a comfortable and adequate home. This
chapter presents data on family housing characteristics as
well as some indicators of the quality of home life in different
settings, including public housing. It will focus on affordability issues and other factors related to restrictions in the
physical setting such as crowding. The chapter also provides
and discusses, wherever possible, available information on
particular populations of children, including children from
single-parent and aboriginal families, children with disabilities, and homeless children.

I Types of Housing Occupied by Ontario's Children and Youth

Figure 9.1 presents recent Census data for Ontario and the
Toronto Metropolitan Municipality on the structural type of
dwelling occupied by children. As it shows, most young

people in Ontario under the age of 20 live in single detached
houses (69.0%), a proportion that increases steadily with
each age group. Thus about 64% of children aged 4 years
and under live in single detached houses; this proportion
reaches 72.5% for teens aged 15 to 19. This increase is not
surprising and corresponds to the rise in household incomes
over the course of a working life.

The proportion of young people under the age of 20 living
in single detached family houses in Metro Toronto is considerably lower than in the province as a whole (44.0% vs.
69.0%), with most living in another form of dwelling. A
sizeable proportion of the 56.0% not living in single detached
dwellings reside in such ground-oriented housing as town or
row houses, semi-detached houses, or duplexes. Almost
150,000 young people in Ontario (6.0%) live in apartment
buildings of 5 storeys or more. Of these, about 65% live in
Metro Toronto and fully 82% live in the Greater Toronto
Area, which includes the neighbouring Regions of Halton,
Peel, York, and Durham. In fact, as Figure 9.1 shows, children
and youths under the age of 20 in the Metro Toronto area
are three times as likely to live in high-rise apartment buildings as are children in the province as a whole (19.4% vs.
6%). About one-quarter (25.9%) of Metro Toronto's pre-
school children 4 years or less live in high-density settings
— more than 32,000 youngsters.

Over one-third (36.6%) of Metro Toronto's children and
youths live in low-rise buildings, row houses, and duplexes.
This proportion, which remains fairly constant across age
groups, is higher than for the province as a whole (24.1%)
and reflects the higher cost of single detached housing in
Toronto. Only a negligible number of children in Ontario
reside in portable dwellings (less than 0.5%).

The physical housing structure occupied by families with
children can play a large role in the quality of their lives. At
least one study on children's perceptions of their neighbourhood found that those living in denser urban settings were
adversely affected by traffic, lack of facilities, and the location
of play space too far from their homes (Muscovitch, 1980).
Children living in high rise-buildings will likely have less
indoor and outdoor play space available to them, and those
play areas that are available may not be safe, particularly if
the building is not well maintained. Play space is often less
accessible to children living in upper levels. For young
children, this barrier may be very isolating (Hill, 1979).

Figure 9.1: **Children and youth aged 19 and under in private households by structural type of dwelling, Ontario, Metro Toronto, 1986**

Ontario

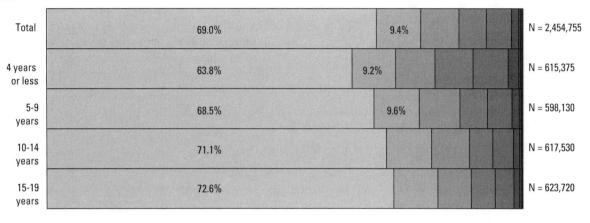

Metro Toronto

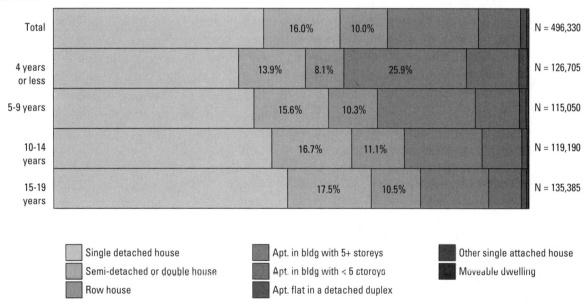

Source: Statistics Canada, 20% Sample Data, Special Tabulations, February 1990.

II   Tenure and Cost of Housing for Ontario Households with Children

Housing analysts agree that households that spend over 30% of their gross income on housing (rent or mortgage) are likely doing so at the expense of their overall quality of life. Over 235,000 households with children are in this situation in Ontario. This number represents almost one-fifth (18.2%) of all households with children. Many families pay well over this limit.

Table 9.1 compares the income levels of Ontario households with at least one child that own or rent. It also shows the proportion of these households paying more than 50% of their income on housing. The table clearly establishes that children living in renter households are disadvantaged over those in owner households with respect to both the income levels of the household and the proportion spent on housing. Over one-quarter (28.1%) of renter families report incomes of less than $15,000 — almost 100,000 families. Of these, over one-half (53.5%) or approximately 52,500 low-income renter households, can be found in the Greater Toronto Area. Only about 2% of renter families report household incomes of more than $75,000, compared with 12.2% of owner family households.

Figure 9.2 demonstrates that the families that pay the most for their housing can afford it the least. There are over 100,000 Ontario households with children paying more than 50% of their total household income on shelter. Over 90% of renter families in the low-income (less than $15,000) category fall into this group.

Substantial numbers of poor owner households with children in Ontario are also paying more than half of their limited income on housing. Of the households with children reporting total 1985 incomes of less than $15,000, 59.4% pay at least half of this amount for shelter. There is, in fact, almost an exact inverse relationship between the income level of the household and the proportion spent on housing.

Urban Variations in Housing Affordability

Statistics Canada recently reported on the high cost of living in large urban centres in Canada (Bird, 1990). The report, based on the 1986 and 1981 Censuses, presents data on the average monthly shelter costs for both tenants and owners in selected Census Metropolitan Areas. It shows that owners

generally pay about $100 more per month, on average, than tenants in most centres. What is particularly noteworthy, however, is the fact that in the ten Ontario centres covered, the percentage change in the inflation-adjusted cost of shelter for owners actually went down between 1981 and 1986 in

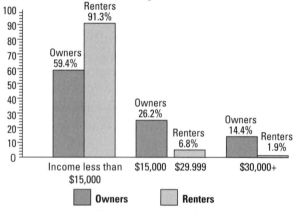

Figure 9.2:   Percentage of non-farm, non-reserve households with at least one child, by tenure, total 1985 household income, and paying more than 50% of total 1985 household income on housing, Ontario, 1986

Source: Statistics Canada, 20% Sample Data, Special Tabulations, February 1990.

Table 9.1

Non-farm, non-reserve households with at least one child by tenure, total 1985 household income, and paying more than 50% of total 1985 household income on housing, Ontario 1986

Income	Owners Total %	Owners % Paying >50% on Housing	Renters Total %	Renters % Paying >50% on Housing
<$10,000	2.5	42.3	17.9	77.5
10,000-14,999	2.1	17.1	10.2	13.8
15,000-29,999	14.4	26.2	31.7	6.8
30,000-39,999	20.1	6.9	18.9	1.2
40,000-49,999	20.6	3.7	10.8	0.4
50,000-59,999	15.4	1.9	5.3	0.1
60,000-74,999	12.7	1.3	3.3	—
75,000 +	12.2	0.5	2.0	—
Total Number	947,210	42,950	349,670	57,610

Source: Statistics Canada, 20% Sample Data, Special Tabulations, February 1990.

most cities. The exceptions were Ottawa-Hull, Oshawa, and Toronto, where increases ranged from about 2% in Oshawa and Toronto to 8% in Ottawa-Hull. For renters, on the other hand, costs rose dramatically, increasing by 7% in Thunder Bay and by 18% in London. The average increase for renters was about 12% (Bird, 1990).

Figure 9.3 shows that housing affordability for renter families with children varies across the province. The proportion of such families with a calculated rent/income ratio of more than 30% is much higher in urban centres, ranging from 23.8% in Ottawa to 34.4% in London, according to the 1987 survey. By contrast, only 18.2% of renter families living outside the major urban areas paid more than 30% of their total income on shelter.

Incidence of 'Doubling Up'

One response to the high cost of housing relative to income may be for two or more families to move in together. Evidence of this 'doubling up' can be seen in Table 9.2, which provides data on the number of two-family households with at least one child in Ontario and the Greater Toronto Area with more than one person per room[2] by their income level. The table shows that some families in Ontario are doubling up in homes likely designed for single families only.

The percentage of households 'doubling up' in all Ontario

is relatively small (0.5%). However, the majority (69.8%) of these over 7,000 family households can be found in the Greater Toronto Area. Families in doubled-up households are also more likely to have household incomes of less than $10,000 than families living in single-family households with no extra people (32.9% vs 6.3% for GTA; 29.3% vs. 3.7% for Ontario). Although in some circumstances families may 'double up' out of choice, it is likely that in many cases the families live together because the cost of housing has forced them to do so.

III Core Housing Need

The physical characteristics of the dwelling place may affect a child's health and ability to learn, play safely, and interact with others in a meaningful way. The Ontario Child Health Study (Offord, 1986), for instance, found that children living in crowded conditions were more likely to suffer from a health-related disorder. The quality of housing is very closely tied to a family's income, as the following section on core housing need shows.

A family is defined as being in 'core housing need' if its dwelling is crowded, physically inadequate, and/or costs 30% or more of family income and the cost of an uncrowded, adequate rental dwelling in the same market area would also

Table 9.2
Private Occupied Households with more than one person per room by number of Census families in the household and income group, Ontario, Greater Toronto Area (GTA), 1986

	Percentage with greater than one person per room							
	One Census family per houshold				Two or more Census families per household			
	Ontario		GTA		Ontario		GTA	
Income Group	%	N	%	N	%	N	%	N
Total	1.8	43,505	2.7	24,855	17.2	7,365	19.3	5,140
< $10,000	3.7	4,660	6.3	2,825	29.2	215	32.9	115
10,000–14,999	2.7	3,625	4.6	1,875	10.3	60	14.5	40
15,000–29,999	2.5	13,775	4.4	7,725	24.7	1,160	29.0	680
30,000–39,999	2.0	8,705	3.2	5,065	22.2	1,135	27.0	780
40,000–49,999	1.5	5,675	2.2	3,415	19.4	1,175	21.1	825
50,000–59,999	1.1	2,930	1.4	1,670	14.9	950	17.3	735
60,000 +	0.8	3,760	1.0	2,230	13.8	2,670	15.6	1,910

Source: Statistics Canada, 20% Sample Data, Special Tabulations, February 1990.

amount to 30% or more of its income. The measure is by no means perfect and is constantly being refined, but it does allow analysts to compare the housing status of Canadian families on a set of standard criteria that address both the affordability and the quality of housing.[3]

Core Housing Need and Ontario's Children and Youth

According to the most recent data, over half (56%) of all persons living in non-senior households in core housing need in Ontario (1988) are young people under the age of 24 (N = 192,000),[4] or 7% of the total number of people in this age group in the province. Almost all of the 96,000 households with children who are in core housing need live in urban areas. The following sections present some selected characteristics of households with children in core housing need compared with those not in such need.[5]

Housing Type

Figure 9.4 shows that about 40% of the households with children in core housing need live in apartments. In contrast,

under 15% of Ontario households with children not in core need live in apartments. Over two-thirds (68.1%) of the households free of core housing need live in single detached houses — double the proportion (34.4%) of households with children in core housing need.

Tenure and the Cost of Housing

There are proportionately more renter family households in core housing need (17.5%) than there are owners (3.0%). In fact, the vast majority of the 96,000 Ontario households with children in core housing need are renters (67.7%). Table 9.3 clearly shows the large discrepancy between family households in core housing need and those not in need with respect to income and amount spent on shelter.

The average income reported by households with children who are in core housing need is $15,793. This figure varies only slightly between owners and renters, but is considerably

---

Table 9.3
Private households with head aged 60 or less and children aged 24 or less by household core housing need status, tenure, average income, average shelter cost, and % spent on shelter, Ontario, 1988

	All households with children	Households with children in core need
Average income		
Owners	$58,800	$15,502
Renters	35,800	15,932
Average shelter cost		
Owners	$8,200	$7,281
Renters	6,400	6,041
% spent on shelter		
Owners	16.7	48.2
Renters	21.7	41.1

Source: Statistics Canada's Household Income, Facilities and Equipment, and Shelter Cost Survey Micro Data Tape, 1988, enhanced to facilitate calculations of core housing need made by the Research Division, Canada Mortgage and Housing Corporation.

Figure 9.3: Percentage of renter families with children whose rent/income ratio is > 30% for selected urban areas and the remainder of the province, 1987

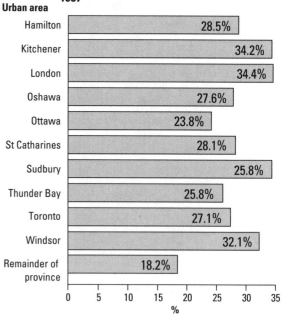

Source: Ontario Ministry of Housing, 1987 Rental Survey Preliminary Results, January 1989.

less than the averages reported by families not in core housing need, which are $58,800 for owners and $35,800 for renters.

IV Single-Parent Families

The data in this section will show that the housing characteristics of single-parent families are different from those of most two-parent families. Single-parent families that are female-led are the most disadvantaged in the housing market. These families pay the most for their housing relative to their income and are far more likely to rent than own their homes. To illustrate these disparities, Table 9.4 presents data on a selected number of housing characteristics for different family types.

Housing Type

The type of housing occupied by children in Ontario can be related to family structure. As Table 9.4 shows, two-parent family households are less likely to be living in apartment buildings with 5 or more storeys and more likely to occupy single detached houses than are single-parent families. Whereas almost three-quarters (73.6%) of all two-parent families occupy single detached houses, this is true of only about half the male-led single-parent families (54.5%), and a little over one-third (38.8) of the female-led single-parent families. About one-fifth (19.7%) of all female-led single-parent families in Ontario live in apartment buildings that are five or more storeys high.

There is evidence that for a single-parent family, whether headed by mother or father, living in a high-rise building has some added disadvantages that two-parent families may not experience to the same degree. Single parents complain of isolation, lack of interior public play areas, and laundry facilities that are too far removed (often in basements) from their private units (personal communication, Ottawa Council for Low Income Support Services, April 1990). As a result, parents without help sometimes have to leave young children sleeping unattended while short necessary errands (such as laundry) are completed.

By the very nature of their design, most multi-unit apartment buildings make it difficult for parents to casually supervise children playing outdoors. For single parents with no support this leaves few options (Klodawsky and Spector,

Table 9.4
Housing characteristics of Census families with children at home showing family structure, Ontario, 1986

	Female-led single-parent families %	Male-led single-parent families %	Two-parent families %
Housing type			
Single detached house	38.8	56.3	73.6
Apartments >5 storeys	19.7	14.1	5.4
Housing tenure			
Own	43.9	62.9	80.8
Rent	56.1	37.1	19.1
Housing costs			
% owners paying >30% on major shelter	26.9	15.8	10.8
% renters paying >30% on major shelter	54.7	29.2	20.1
Total number[a]	219,110	46,875	1,312,900

[a]Number is approximate since figures were derived from different tables.

Source: Statistics Canada, *The Nation, Families: Part II*, Cat. 93-107, Tables 1, 2, March 1989.

1988). Tenant groups have unsuccessfully tried to convince developers to provide lounge areas on every other floor for socializing with children; however, the overall economics of building high-density housing with maximum residential potential (i.e., number of units) appears to be a stumbling-block for both private and public sectors (Carss, 1985).

Housing Tenure

Single-parent families, particularly female-led, are the most disadvantaged in a rental market. Citations of landlord discrimination against single mothers are common (Wekerle, 1988), and yet for most, rental housing is the only choice. It is clear from Table 9.4 that children in single-parent families, particularly female-led, are far more likely to live in rented housing than those in either male-led single-parent families or two-parent households. In 1986, over half (56.1%) of all single-parent families in Ontario with children still at home lived in rented housing. This was true of only 19.1% of two-parent families.

Although some families rent out of choice, there is no doubt that for many families, particularly those living near the poverty line — as is the case for a significant number of single-parent families — rental accommodation is the only option. Families that rent have a much more uncertain tenure (Klodawsky and Spector, 1988). The supply of affordable housing, particularly for families, has been shrinking. Rental vacancy rates have decreased steadily over the last ten years, and have remained at far less than 1% in most urban communities across the province (5% was once considered acceptable). Rejuvenation of downtown neighbourhoods, and a resulting increase in middle-class suburban families 'rediscovering' downtown living, has further reduced the supply of affordable housing (Ontario Ministry of Housing, 1988b).

Cost of Housing and Family Structure

Table 9.4 shows that single-parent families living in rented housing are far more likely to pay at least 30% of their household income on housing than are two-parent families. Once again, female-led single-parent families are the most disadvantaged. More than half (57.4%) of all such families living in rented dwellings pay at least 30% of their income on housing. This figure can be compared with 29.2% for male-led single-parent renter families and 20.1% for two-parent renter families.

For families who own their accommodation, the percentages are lower, but the same differences occur. Over one-quarter (26.9%) of female-led single-parent families pay more than 30% of their total income for shelter, compared with 15.8% for male-led single-parent families and 10.8% for two-parent families.

Core Housing Need

Figure 9.5 illustrates the degree to which single-parent families are over-represented among the families with children in core housing need in Ontario. Nearly half (45.8%) of all families in core housing need in Ontario are led by single parents, compared with only 11.3% of all Ontario families. In fact, by this definition over one-quarter (27.7%) of all single parents in Ontario are living in unsuitable, inadequate, and unaffordable housing.

V Aboriginal Families

Canada's aboriginal families have traditionally lived in homes that fall far below the housing standards for the rest of the country. Improving the supply of adequate on-reserve housing has been cited as one of the keys to increasing life

Figure 9.4: Private households with children aged 24 or younger and head aged 60 or less by household core housing need status and housing type, 1988

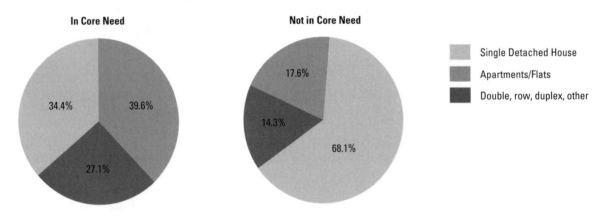

In Core Need — 34.4%, 39.6%, 27.1%

Not in Core Need — 17.6%, 14.3%, 68.1%

Single Detached House
Apartments/Flats
Double, row, duplex, other

Source: Statistics Canada's Household Income, Facilities and Equipment and Shelter Cost Survey Micro Data Tape, 1988, enhanced to facilitate calculations of core housing need made by the Research Division, Canada Mortgage and Housing Corporation.

expectancy and reducing rates of infant mortality, suicide, family violence, and alcoholism (Hagey et al., 1989). The large proportion of over-crowded households is one of the chief factors contributing to the continuing high demand for on-reserve housing.

There is evidence that conditions are improving. For instance, in 1971 the majority of on-reserve native homes in Canada were without any form of central heating. This was reduced to just under one quarter (23.1%) by 1986. Even in 1986, however, 25% of native houses still had no running water, and fully one-third (33%) were without a sewer or septic system (Indian and Northern Affairs Canada, 1988).

Table 9.5 provides some data on the state of aboriginal housing in urban and rural areas of Ontario with respect to crowding and the availability of central heating. The vast majority of this housing is occupied by families with children. The figure illustrates the disparities between the quality of housing occupied by on- and off-reserve aboriginal families and all other households.

As Table 9.5 illustrates, on-reserve households are the most crowded, with almost one-fifth (19.5%) having an average of more than one person per room. Aboriginal families living off reserves are also more likely to live in crowded

conditions than are non-aboriginal families. Of both urban and rural off-reserve aboriginal households 5.1% are crowded, compared with only 1.7% of non-aboriginal urban households and even fewer (1.3%) non-aboriginal rural households.

Table 9.5 also shows the number of aboriginal and other households without a central heating system. Once again, families living on reserves in Ontario have the lowest standard, with almost half (44.1%) of all on-reserve dwellings lacking central heating. A substantial number of off-reserve aboriginal households in rural areas are also without central heating. About one-fifth (20.2%) of these households have other forms of heat such as a heat stove or space heater, compared with 12.4% of non-aboriginal households in rural areas. Urban households are far more likely to report having central heating; however, a slightly greater proportion (3.3%) of aboriginal households are without central heating than non-aboriginal households (2.1%).

As Table 9.5 shows, there are over 50,000 aboriginal households located in urban areas in Ontario. Apart from what has been presented in this figure, very little information is available on the housing conditions of aboriginal families living in urban centres.

Figure 9.5: **Private households with children aged 24 or younger and head aged 60 or less by household core housing need status and family structure, Ontario, 1988**

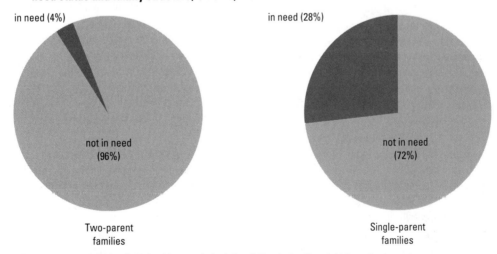

in need (4%)

not in need (96%)

Two-parent families

in need (28%)

not in need (72%)

Single-parent families

ª Estimate based on a sample count of slightly under 50, the minimum required to derive reliable estimates of households in core housing need.

Source: Statistics Canada's Household Income, Facilities and Equipment and Shelter Cost Survey Micro Data Tape, 1988, enhanced to facilitate calculations of core housing need made by the Research Division, Canada Mortgage and Housing Corporation.

Table 9.5
Occupied private dwellings by aboriginal[a] and non-aboriginal households with more than one person per room, no central heat, Ontario, 1986

	Aboriginal On Reserve	Aboriginal Off Reserve		Non-Aboriginal	
		Urban	Rural	Urban	Rural
	%	%	%	%	%
Crowded	19.5	5.1	5.1	1.7	1.3
Without central heat	44.1	3.3	20.2	2.1	12.4
Total Number	7,130	52,495	12,585	2,699,095	515,150

[a] Aboriginal households include Registered Indian private households, Inuit private households, single and multiple Aboriginal households.

Source: Indian and Northern Affairs Canada, Census Custom Tabulations, PO3184, Tables 33, 35, April 26, 1989.

VI   Affordable and Adequate Housing

Government Responses to Need

Canada was one of the last of the industrialized nations to become involved in public housing, and thus had a wealth of experience from other countries to draw upon. Considerations with respect to size (number of units in any one project), integrated versus segregated approaches, and on-site services were based on these experiences. The final decisions of the larger housing providers, however, did not always reflect this knowledge, and were affected by other factors such as cost, availability of land, and neighbourhood acceptance. As a result, the social housing experience in Ontario is seen by many housing analysts with a critical eye, and has met with mixed success.

According to the most recent figures (June 1990) available from the Ministry of Housing, there are about 145,000 rent-geared-to-income apartment units in the province, representing about 11% of all renter households in Ontario. These units include those owned by Ontario Housing Corporation as well as those provided through a variety of shared programs including co-operatives, private and municipal or regional non-profit developers such as the Metropolitan Toronto Housing Company Limited, and rent supplements. Of these, it is estimated that almost half (69,000) are occupied by families with children (units of two or more bedrooms

and those designated as family units). This number has increased by about 21% since 1986, when there were about 55,800 rent-geared-to-income family units in place. In Metro Toronto alone, there are an estimated 32,000 such units. Yet according to all indicators, particularly the lengthy waiting lists in most municipalities, the supply of affordable housing is not meeting the need.

The preceding sections have demonstrated that most low-income Ontario families with children are paying too much for housing that in many instances is far below standard. Since the federal government stopped building affordable housing directly and transferred this responsibility to the provinces, which in turn look towards the municipalities, the supply of affordable housing has been threatened. New units and projects are built on an *ad hoc* basis through a variety of funding mechanisms and partnerships.

Supply of Affordable Housing

Table 9.6 presents information on the past and future supply of affordable family housing, for the province as a whole and for the city of Toronto, categorized by sponsor. It shows that the greatest increases in the number of committed or planned family units since 1985 has come from the private non-profit sector, followed by the municipal non-profit developers. (It should be noted that not all of these commitments are realized.) In the city of Toronto, the number of family units committed by the private non-profit sector has more than

Table 9.6
Total family units committed by year, delivery agent, and type, Ontario, 1980–91

	Ontario			City of Toronto		
	< 1985	1985–91	+ %	< 1985	1985–91	+ %
Type of social housing						
Co-operative housing	13,908	8,535	+ 61	3,308	691	+ 21
Private non-profit	8,214	7,059	+ 86	678	1,051	+ 155
Municipal non-profit	10,074	8,194	+ 81	4,909	1,094	+ 22
Ontario Housing Corp.	47,832	0	+ 0	9,388	0	+ 0
Other (limited dividend, municipal assisted, rent supplement, rural)	42,440	1,663	+ 4	4,750	400	+ 8
Total rent-geared-to-income units	122,468	25,451	+ 21	23,033	3,236	+ 14

Source: Ontario Ministry of Housing, Community Housing User Management Information System, Ontario Housing Corporation, Special Tabulation, April 1990.

doubled in the last five years. The overall percentage growth in committed family units in Toronto, however, is less than for the province as a whole (14% vs. 21%). Part of the reason for this lies in the general lack of available land in the Toronto area as well as the region's housing costs, which are higher than elsewhere in the province.

Need for Affordable Housing

There is no single accurate way of assessing the need for more affordable housing. There are, however, a number of indicators suggesting that the families with the fewest resources have the least choice in the housing market. Rental vacancy rates in cities across the province for both the private and public sectors serve as one such indicator. These vacancy rates are below 1% in most Ontario municipalities (Canada Mortgage and Housing Corporation, 1989a).

Another way of assessing the need for affordable housing is to look at the active waiting lists for existing rent-geared-to-income housing units.[6] The data presented in Table 9.7 were provided by the Ontario Housing Corporation and represent its active priority list for the last five years for the Metro Toronto Housing Authority and the remainder of the province. By the summer of 1989, the Metro Toronto Housing Authority had by far the largest active waiting list for family housing, with about 7,500 applicants followed by Ottawa-Carleton (1,500), and the Peel Housing Authority (1,100).

Table 9.7 shows the total number of applicants, the number who received a home visit from staff and were rated with respect to their need for housing, and the number who received the highest rating — in other words, who had the greatest need (> 120 points).[7] As of September 1989 there were 43,563 applicants on the active waiting list across the province. Of these, 22,136 — more than half — were applicants with children.

Table 9.7 reveals a number of trends with respect to the demand for affordable family housing in Ontario. First, the number of applicants to the Metro Toronto Housing Authority (MTHA) for family housing increased at almost triple the rate in the remainder of the province (66.8% vs. 26.6%) (which, as Table 9.6 showed, is much greater than the increase in the supply of affordable housing units in the City of Toronto and the province). Second, the number of applicants who received the highest priority rating doubled between 1985 and 1989 in Metro Toronto; the other housing authorities in Ontario saw a 15.2% increase.

Fully two-thirds (67%, N = 3314) of the family applicants to MTHA in 1989 were rated in the category of greatest need ('deep core need'),[8] compared with 50% (N = 5752) for the remainder of the province. By the end of February 1990, there were 2,820 applicants on the MTHA list and 5,065 on the provincial list in the highest need category. Home visits (by MTHA staff to assess need) to applicants have remained fairly stable over the last five years and have not kept pace with the increase in the number of applicants, particularly in Metro Toronto (12%).

Table 9.8 emphasizes the fact that very little new public housing stock has entered the system. The small dent that is made annually in the waiting list for family housing in Ontario is due mainly to turnover of existing stock. Housing turnover in Metro Toronto fluctuated between 1985 and 1989,

Table 9.7
Ontario Housing Corporation priority list for family housing, 1985–89

Report for month of September	Metro Toronto			Remainder of province		
	Total number of applicants[a]	Number visited	Highest rating	Total number of applicants[a]	Number visited	Highest rating
1989	7,563	4,945	3,314	14,573	11,483	5,752
1988	10,031	4,842	2,460	15,286	11,795	4,992
1987	6,465	4,455	1,805	12,384	11,086	4,066
1986	5,065	4,973	1,879	11,881	9,658	4,952
1985	4,533	4,419	1,685	11,514	9,452	4,991
% change 1985–89	+ 66.8%	+ 11.9%	+ 96.7%	+ 26.6%	+ 21.5%	+ 15.2%

[a]Totals include housing agencies participating in a common housing priority list.

Source: Ontario Ministry of Housing, Community Housing User Management Information System, Ontario Housing Corporation, Priority List Reports for the Month of September, 1985–89, Special Tabulation, November 1989.

with a high of 247 in 1986 and a low of 146 in 1987. No trend is evident.

VII Subsidized Housing

Family Characteristics
Information on the socio-economic characteristics of families in subsidized housing in Ontario is limited, since the Ministry of Housing does not receive data from all housing authorities in the province (only about two-thirds of local housing authorities report to a centralized file). One socio-demographic profile of family tenants in public housing across the province comes from a 1985 survey of over 1000 seniors and families. The study interviewed over 500 family tenants randomly chosen from Ontario Housing Corporation's files. The data presented in the tables below have been derived from the survey's final report (Denton, Davis, and Nussey, 1987).

More than two-thirds (69.7%) of the family tenants interviewed in the study of families in assisted housing were headed by single parents — a category that makes up only 13.2% of all Ontario families. The majority of these tenants were born in Canada (68.5%), with about one-fifth (20.4%)

Table 9.8
Housing turnover and new units assigned to families on priority waiting list for housing agencies in the Metro Toronto Housing Authority participating in a common housing list, 1985–89

	Metro Toronto Housing Authority	
	Housing turnover	New units
1989	164	0
1988	161	0
1987	146	0
1986	247	0
1985	216	0

Source: Ontario Ministry of Housing, Community Housing User Management Information System, Ontario Housing Corporation, Priority List Reports for the Month of September, 1985–89, Special Tabulation, November 1989.

coming from the West Indies, Asia, and Latin American and South American countries (Denton, Davis, and Nussey, 1987). Although the exact figures are not available, this proportion is much higher in the larger urban areas such as Toronto or Ottawa.

One-third (33.5%) of families in assisted housing had more than three children, compared with only 13.8% of all Ontario families; 7.3% had pre-school children only; about one-quarter (26.7%) had children 5 to 12 years old; and about 30% had only children over 12 (Denton, Davis, and Nussey, 1987).

Tenant Attitudes towards Public Housing

Tenant groups, housing program managers, and housing analysts have been examining the quality of life in Ontario's public housing stock. Concern has been expressed about aging buildings, lack of social supports, increased vandalism and drug-related problems, and, in some areas of the province, increased racial tensions in high-density mixed buildings. One attempt to measure the extent of these concerns and their relationship to the overall management of the buildings was a province-wide series of self-administered tenant-satisfaction surveys conducted in 1987 and 1988 in all 55 local housing authorities and in 1989 in a selected number of authorities across the province. In 1988, 3,525 tenants were surveyed, with an overall response rate of 32%. The results were based on subjective ratings of over 75 separate items concerning life in public housing, as well as a number of open-ended comments about major issues (Ontario Ministry of Housing, Operations and Review Branch, 1989, 1988a). Average ratings for each housing authority were computed on a 100-point scale; the higher the rating, the more satisfied the tenant was with that particular aspect of public housing. Significantly, the items that were consistently given the lowest ratings in almost every local housing authority had to do with recreation facilities for children. These included (1) the quantity and quality of outdoor playground equipment; (2) the safety and maintenance of outdoor playground equipment; and (3) the number of indoor recreation areas.

Family tenants surveyed in 1988 were very consistent in their concern about the lack of recreational activities in their communities. This concern was repeated by those families surveyed a year later. Between 70% and 90% of all respondents identified a need for additional recreation programs in the 1989 survey. Tenants in selected sites were also asked in 1989 to state whether or not any of the following were serious problems in their housing project: (1) drugs/alcohol abuse; (2) vandalism of their home; (3) racial/ethnic tension; and (4) street youth gangs.

Well over half — and, in some housing authorities, up to three-quarters — of the family tenants surveyed reported that each of these concerns was among the most serious problems they faced as tenants. Some housing authorities are recognizing these concerns, and managers and tenants are working together to find solutions. Ongoing monitoring of their success, however, may not be possible, since the Ministry of Housing recently closed the Management, Operations and Review Section, the department responsible for conducting these surveys.

In interpreting these data, the reader is cautioned against drawing conclusions about the quality of life in public housing. Comparative data on private sector housing is almost non-existent, and what is available is survey information from a study conducted over ten years ago (Phillips and Andrews, 1982). It may very well be that conditions in low-income private-sector housing projects have worsened.

VIII   Co-operative Housing

Co-operative housing is a form of not-for-profit housing jointly owned by residents who are members of incorporated associations. Members have security of tenure at an agreed-upon price (set by the association). Residents can neither sell their units nor make capital gains. A resident wishing to leave notifies the association in writing and the unit is turned over to someone else. Co-operatives do not necessarily target low-income families, and in fact most strive for a balance. They are, however, a popular alternative for modest-income families who can afford the initial entry payment. In co-operatives built before 1985, subsidies are available to households that would otherwise have to pay more than 25% of their income on housing (Burke, 1990b). Changes in the federal program in 1985, however, stipulated that in co-operatives built since then, only households below the low-income threshold qualify for a subsidy. (In Ontario, a minimum of 25% of co-operative units must be subsidized).

The number of co-operative housing units in Ontario has increased sharply over the last decade. Since 1985, the number of committed (planned) family units in Ontario rose

61%, from 13,908 units in 1985 to 22,443 units in 1990. It is not known how many of these committed units will be realized; however, they represent about 15% of the total number of committed family units in Ontario under the various housing programs (see Table 9.6). In 1989, co-operatives made up less than 1% of all housing units (public and private) in Ontario (Burke, 1990b).

Very little is known about the characteristics of families living in co-operative housing in Ontario, since statistics are not collected in any systematic way. Recent figures based on the 1986 Census show that almost three-quarters (73%) of co-operative households in Ontario were made up of families, compared with 54% of rental and 84% of owner-occupied dwellings (Burke, 1990a). Single-parent families are over-represented in co-operative housing. In 1986, 29% of Ontario co-operative families were headed by single parents, compared with 23% of renter and just 8% of owner families.

Nearly three-quarters (72%) of Ontario husband-wife families living in co-operatives in 1986 had children living at home, compared with 51% for renter and 65% for owner two-parent families. About 14% of husband-wife families in co-operatives had three or more children in 1986, compared with 9% in rental and 15% in privately owned housing. Single parents in co-operatives, however, have smaller families than single parents living in other forms of housing in Ontario. Just 10% of co-operative single parents had three or more children, compared with 13% of renter and 14% of owner single parents (Burke, 1990a).

IX   Housing Characteristics of Children and Youth with Disabilities

A supportive home environment enhances the ability of all children to develop their potential as adults. For children with disabilities or those living in families where other members are disabled, additional supports, including physical adaptations within and around their homes, and neighbourhood supports, such as accessible playgrounds and transportation, are vital to their quality of life. Yet very little of today's housing or public space (including playgrounds) is designed for people with physical disabilities. To be poor and disabled makes the difficulties almost insurmountable.

Over half (51%) of young people and adults aged 15 and over with disabilities report total incomes of less than $10,000 (Statistics Canada, 1990). In a recent survey of a representative sample of almost 1500 disabled persons in Ontario (Environics, 1989), the respondents who were most dissatisfied with their housing situation were those who lived in rental accommodation, had family incomes of less than $20,000, were unemployed and were more severely disabled. The survey also found that fewer than one in ten (9%) of those surveyed lived in subsidized housing, and that as many as 25% of those who did not would benefit from this type of living situation (Environics, 1989).

There are systemic barriers for the families of children with disabilities. They may encounter discrimination by landlords. A low-income family with either a child or a parent who has a disability has a more difficult time finding subsidized housing. Families living in subsidized housing often do not report a recently occurring or advancing disability (on the part of a parent or a child) for fear that they may lose their housing, since the ability to live independently is one of the criteria for eligibility (see note 7).

Depending on the type of disability and the age of the child, such families may find themselves with very few options. The lack of community supports is one of the main reasons why some children with disabilities, particularly young adults (aged 19 to 24) are inappropriately institutionalized in large facilities that also house the aged. For families with disabled children who are immobile, the turning point often comes when one or the other parent can no longer lift the child. A recent report on the needs of people with physical disabilities in York Region (Community Services Council, 1989) found that there were virtually no respite care services for physically disabled children, and that waiting lists for some outreach programs like attendant care were up to a year long.

Neighbourhood Life

About half (49,145) of the children with disabilities in Ontario are limited or prevented from participating in normal activities. (Statistics Canada, 1990). Over 10,000 children aged 10 to 14 with disabilities are prevented from taking part in leisure time physical activities, largely because of the inaccessibility of most public spaces. Almost 4,000 are fully housebound. For these children, having a housing and neighbourhood environment that is safe and conducive for learning and play is no longer a luxury but a necessity. Yet the reality is that very few indoor or outdoor play spaces in Canada are designed to accommodate children who have disabilities (Melvin, 1980).

Public Transportation
The different types of transportation needed and used by children in Ontario are shown in Table 9.9. It shows that proportionately very few (3.2%) of these children use special transportation such as a mini-bus or van, and of those who need it, over 80% found it available. Just over one quarter (28.3%) of Ontario children with disabilities use the regular bus system, although about 7% report having difficulty doing so. In the absence of comparative figures for children without disabilities, it is difficult to say whether children with disabilities use the public transit less, although it has already been shown that their use of community facilities in general is restricted.

Adapted Housing
Table 9.10 clearly demonstrates the necessity for modified or adapted housing to meet the needs of children with disabilities of all ages. A significant proportion of parents stated that their homes had not been modified either inside or out. Over one-third of the children in Ontario with disabilities need but do not have special features in their homes that allow them to enter or leave, and over 40% need but do not have special features to help them get around inside the home.

Very little data exist on the number of homes in Ontario that have been retrofitted for a disabled family member. Federal and provincial programs provide some funding to assist low-income families in adapting their homes. The majority of the recipients are adults; only 6% of federal clients are under the age of 20 (Canada Mortgage and Housing Corporation, 1989b). As well, a small proportion of the social housing units in the province are retrofitted to some degree. Information provided by CMHC for 1989 show that about 8% (representing 176 homes) of the family units of two or more bedrooms funded through CMHC have been converted or designed and built for the disabled (CMHC, Special Tabulation, 1990). Looking at the overall trend since 1980, for both provincial and federal housing programs, reveals that less than 4% of all units committed during this period were

Table 9.9
Use of public transportation by children with disabilities aged 5–14, Ontario, 1986

Total number of children with disabilities aged 5–14 80,770

	% reporting	Number
Need for bus or van service for local travel	3.2%	2,575
Availability of bus or van for those who need it	80.3%	2,070
Access to local public transportation	58.6%	47,295
Use of local public transportation frequently or occasionally where available	28.3%	22,820
Trouble using public transportation	6.8%	5,515
Use of taxi frequently or occasionally where available	13.5%	10,925

Source: Statistics Canada, Health and Activity Limitation Survey, 'Highlights: Disabled Persons in Canada', Table 2, March 1990.

Table 9.10
Selected accommodation characteristics of children with disabilities aged 5–14, Ontario, 1986

	N	% who need special features
Number of children who have special features to enter/leave residence	1,135	
Number of children who need but do not have special features to enter/leave residence	715	38.6%
Number of children who have special features inside residence	790	
Number of children who need but do not have special features	625	44.2%

Source: Statistics Canada, Health and Activity Limitation Survey, 'Highlights: Disabled Persons in Canada', Table 2, March 1990.

designed to accommodate tenants with special needs (Ontario Ministry of Housing, Special Tabulations, 1990).

X Safety at Home and in the Neighbourhood

More accidents occur at home than anywhere else, particularly for very young children. Table 9.11 presents recent data on injuries compiled by the Product Safety Branch of Consumer and Corporate Affairs Canada. Although data were obtained from nine Canadian hospitals, the results presented in the following tables are those reported by the Hospital for Sick Children in Toronto, the only reporting Ontario hospital.

Table 9.11 clearly shows that children in the pre-school age range are far more likely to be injured at home than anywhere else. This trend was consistent in both years. Fully 79.3% of the reported injuries for children under the age of 2 in 1986 and 67% in 1987 occurred at home. This trend reverses for older children: after children reach school age, they are far more likely to injure themselves away from the home.

The way children injure themselves also changes with age. Very young children under the age of 2 are most likely to have accidents involving furniture (i.e., playpens, cribs), transportation (car seats, baby walkers), or playing with toys. Children in the school-age years are more prone to accidents involving sports, transportation, and playground apparatus (Consumer and Corporate Affairs, 1989).

Accidental Deaths in the Home

The data for this section come from the Canada Safety Council and are not specific to children or available for Ontario. They nevertheless give an indication of the kinds of safety-related risks faced by families with children. Of all the non-transport accidents that occurred in 1987 (N = 4472), 39.6% occurred at home. Of the almost 250 people in Canada who died in fires in their own homes, 89, or more than one-third (36.5%), were under the age of 24.

The Canada Safety Council (1987) examined the causes of death of children 0 to 14 for Canada as a whole. While provincial figures are unavailable, there is no reason to believe that the Ontario results would be significantly different. For children in this age group, the greatest risk for accidental death at home was fire (42.2% of a total of 180 deaths), followed by suffocation (23.9%), and drowning (13.9%).

XI Homeless Children and Youth

While counting the homeless is a virtually impossible task, a number of recent studies agree that the face of homeless-

---

Table 9.11

Injury counts by age group and location for children and youths treated at the Hospital for Sick Children, Toronto, 1986–87

	Place of occurrence							
	Home				Elsewhere			
	1986		1987		1986		1987	
Age range	%	N	%	N	%	N	%	N
0–<2	79.3	438	67.0	282	20.7	114	33.0	139
2–4	49.8	268	42.0	235	50.2	270	58.0	325
5–14	17.1	206	14.5	263	82.9	996	85.5	1545
15–24	11.1	18	6.5	19	88.9	144	93.5	273
Total	37.9	930	28.3	899	62.1	1524	71.1	2282

Source: Consumer and Corporate Affairs Canada, Product Safety Branch, 'Canadian Accident Injury Reporting and Evaluation (CAIRE)', Special Tabulations, 1989.

ness is changing, and that dramatic increases have occurred in the number of young people without a stable home. These include children whose mothers have sought refuge in shelters to escape family violence, as well as youths who are alienated from their families (McLaughlin, 1988, 1989; Ontario Ministry of Housing, 1986, 1988b; Mihaly, L., 1989). Children in these situations are in desperate need of intervention and are very likely to be suffering from poor physical and mental health (Goldman, 1988; Daly, 1988).

Ontario's Addiction Research Foundation recently released figures from a survey of youths under the age of 24 living on Toronto's streets. The study found that 90% of these youths had a drug problem, 95% drank alcohol (35% in the morning); and 42% had attempted to commit suicide at least once (Appleby, 1990).

The Canadian Council on Social Development (McLaughlin, 1989) estimated that over 10,000 people in Ontario were homeless on the day of their 1987 survey of a sample of shelters across the country. Of these, 11.5% were calculated to be children under 15 and another 16.4% were battered women and children. The Social Planning Council

in Ottawa recently (1989) found 169 youths 24 years of age and under seeking shelter at existing transient hostels in Ottawa during a one week period. Table 9.12 gives some figures for the use of Metro Toronto's shelter system by families and youth, collected by the Community Services Department for the Municipality of Metropolitan Toronto. They show that young men and women accounted for most of the users in this group (N = 6,210) (second only to older males aged 25 +), followed by single female parents (N = 1,304) and two-parent families with children (N = 538). There are indications that the use of Metro's shelter system by young people has increased dramatically over the last several years. In 1984, youths accounted for approximately 6.4% of the total hostel beds. In the 1987-88 survey, of the total 20,837 users (including older men and women and childless couples), almost one-third (29.8%) were youth (Metropolitan Community Services and Housing Committee, 1985).

Notes

The author wishes to thank Satya Brink, John Engeland, Sylvia Goldblatt, and Polly Hill for their helpful contributions.

[1]The researchers used street address information shown on death certificates to code Census tract of usual place of residence for deaths occurring to residents of Canada's Census Metropolitan areas (CMAs) in 1971 and 1986. After exclusion of residents of health care institutions, 73,995 deaths were included for 1971, and 88,129 for 1986. These deaths were analysed by income quintile (based on Census tract incidence of low income), age, sex, and cause of death.

[2]The National Occupancy Standard contains the common elements of all the provincial occupancy standards and was developed over several years in the latter 1980s. According to the Standard, a dwelling is suitable if it provides enough bedrooms to accommodate a household in which (a) there are no more than two persons per bedroom; (b) parents have a bedroom separate from their children; (c) household members aged 18 + have separate bedrooms unless married or otherwise living as spouses; and (d) dependents aged 5 or more of different genders do not share a bedroom (definition provided by the Housing Needs Analysis Section of the Research Division of Canada Mortgage and Housing).

[3]'Core housing need' as defined by the Housing Needs Analysis Section of the Research Division of Canada Housing and Mortgage Corporation identifies households living in dwelling units which fall below norm housing standards for suitable, adequate, and affordable housing — and then: identifies from all these households those 'for whom basic

---

Table 9.12
Use of municipally funded emergency shelters by youths and families in Metro Toronto, 1 July, 1987–30 June 1988

Families and youth	Total
Males alone < 25	4,626
Females alone < 25	1,584
Single parents — female	1,304
Single parents — male	43
Two-parent families	538
Other users	
Males alone > 25	10,568
Females alone > 25	2,064
Couples, no children	110
Total	20,837

Source: Hostels Operations Unit, Community Services Department, Municipality of Metropolitan Toronto, Statistical Package, 1 July 1987–30 June 1988.

shelter costs for an adequate and suitable dwelling available in their market area ... in the Operating Agreement'. To identify these households in core housing need, norm rent income cutoffs are matched against households by dwelling unit size. Table 1 shows these figures for 1988.

Table 1
Norm Rent Incomes, 1988

Dwelling Unit Size	Settlement Size	
	< 100,000	100,000 +
1 bedroom	$15,287	$18,177
2 bedrooms	17,580	22,463
3 + bedrooms	19,260	27,390

Norm rent incomes are the minimum incomes that households required in 1988 in order to be able to afford, in their general market areas, units of the sizes specified above, in adequate condition, without spending 30% or more for their shelter. Households are matched against appropriate norm rent incomes by the National Occupancy Standard, which assesses household composition and size to determine the size of dwelling unit required to suitably house the household. Households living in housing that does not meet norm housing standards, with incomes below those tabled above, are in core housing need.

[4]This estimate was calculated by multiplying the number of households with children in core housing need (96,000) by the average household size (3.6).

[5]All tables in this section were custom-produced by the Housing Needs Analysis Section of the Research Division of Canada Mortgage and Housing Corporation. The tables present data on households with children aged 24 or younger where the head of the household is 60 or younger, thereby excluding seniors (whose needs are quite distinct).

These waiting lists reflect the demand for public and rent supplement housing; they do not reflect the total need for assisted housing. The most commonly recognized measurement to determine need for rent-geared-to-income accommodation in the general population is 'core need' as defined above in note 4.

[7]Local housing authorities in Ontario use a priority rating system to measure an applicant's need for rent-geared-to-income housing to ensure that applicants with the greatest need are given priority in the allocation of housing. Applicants with the same number of points are housed on the basis of date of application. Need is determined not only by household income, but also by percentage of income spent on shelter costs, current accommodation suitability and condition, and critical housing requirements (notice to vacate, temporary accommodation). Social Assistance levels are used to determine income level for maximum points to be awarded under this system. To be

eligible for rent-geared-to-income housing in Ontario an applicant must be a permanent legal resident, be at least 16 years of age and a non-dependent, and be capable of living independently or with arranged assistance.

[8]Within core need the Ontario Ministry of Housing recognizes a further, needier subdivision identified as 'deep need'. Deep need is calculated on the basis of Statistics Canada poverty levels and the priority rating scale. The 1986 Non-Profit program requires that municipal and private non-profit corporations must develop projects with a minimum of 40% deep need units and co-operatives must provide at least 25% deep need units.

Glossary

Adapted housing — any housing that has been modified or renovated to suit the needs of residents with disabilities. Common modifications include exterior ramps to entrances and exits, wider doorways to accommodate wheelchairs, and grab bars in hall ways and bathtub areas.

Assisted Housing — a term used interchangeably with 'social housing' (see below).

Non-profit housing — accommodation built under several sections of the *National Housing Act* by private non-profit groups (i.e., churches, charitable groups), public non-profit developers such as municipalities, and not-for-profit co-operatives.

Public housing — accommodation built under two sections of the National Housing Act (#40943). The Public Housing Program was virtually brought to a halt in 1979.

Rent-geared-to income — a term used for situations in which renters pay a set percentage of their total income (25%-30%) as a monthly shelter cost.

Rent Supplement — a term used interchangeably with 'subsidized housing' (see below).

Retrofitted housing — a term that is used interchangeably with 'adapted housing' (see above).

Social housing — a term used by Canada Mortgage and Housing Corporation to refer to all of the accommodation built under their government-assisted programs for modest- and low-income users.

Subsidized housing — usually refers to accommodation where the rent is partially paid for by a government intervention (see rent-geared-to-income). The government money is paid to the housing sponsor through various government programs.

Tenure — a term used to describe the state of either owning or renting a home

Unit — a term used interchangeably with 'apartment' ('apartment unit').

References

Appleby, T.
1990 'Almost 90% of Homeless Youth Have Drug Problem, Survey Finds'. Results from study by Ontario's Addiction Research Foundation, reported in *Globe and Mail*, 9 June.

Bird, T.
1990 'Shelter Costs'. *Social Trends*. Statistics Canada (Spring).

Burke, M.A.
1990a 'Co-operative Housing: What the 1986 Census Tells Us'. Statistics Canada, Working Paper (July).

1990b 'Co-operative Housing: A Third Tenure Form'. *Social Trends*. Statistics Canada (Spring)

Canada Mortgage and Housing Corporation
1989a *Rental Market Survey: Toronto CMA* (October). Ottawa.

1989b *Survey of RRAP for the Disabled.* Prepared by Larsson Consulting Ltd., Ottawa.

Canada Safety Council
1987 *Accident Fatalities.* Ottawa.

Carss, B.
1985 'Foster Farm: Portrait of a Public Housing Community'. Honours Research Project, Ottawa Council for Low Income Support Services.

Community Services Council
1989 *From Gaps to Options: A Report on the Needs of People with Physical Disabilities in York Region* (10 October).

Consumer and Corporate Affairs Canada, Product Safety Branch
1989 'Canadian Accident Injury Reporting and Evaluation (CAIRE)'. Special tabulations.

Daly, G.
1988 *A Comparative Assessment of Programs Dealing with the Homeless Population in the United States, Canada and Britain.* Ottawa: Canada Mortgage and Housing Corporation.

Denton, M.A., C.K. Davis, and B.J. Nussey
1987 *Patterns of Support: the Use of Support Services among Family Public Housing Tenants in Ontario.* Toronto: Ontario Ministry of Housing.

Environics Research Group Ltd.
1989 *The Needs and Attitudes of Disabled Ontarians.* Prepared for Ontario Office for Disabled Persons (April).

Goldman, B.
1988 'Children's Health: Health of Toronto's Street Kids Disturbing, Study Reveals'. *Canadian Medical Association Journal*, 138 (1 June).

Hagey, J.N., G. Larocque, and C. McBride
1989 *Highlights of Aboriginal Conditions, 1981-2001:* Part I: *Demographic Trends*; Part II: *Social Conditions.* Ottawa: Indian and Northern Affairs Canada (October).

Hill, P.
1979 'Discussion Papers on Themes Related to International Year of the Child: Play and Recreation'. Prepared by the International Playground Association. New York.

1979 'Discussion Papers on Themes Related to International Year of the Child: Play and Recreation'. Prepared by the International Playground Association. New York.

Indian and Northern Affairs Canada
1988 *Basic Departmental Data.* Evaluation Directorate (December).

Klodawsky, F., and A. Spector
1988 'New Families, New Housing Needs, New Urban Environments: The Case for Single Parent Families'. In C. Andrew and B. Milroy (eds), *Life Spaces: Gender, Household Employment.* Vancouver: University of British Columbia Press.

McLaughlin, M.A.
1988 'Homelessness in Canada: Families'. *Transitions*, March. (Ottawa).

1989 'Homelessness in Canada: The Report of the National Inquiry'. Ottawa: Canadian Council on Social Development.

Melvin, J.
1980 *Play Spaces to Accommodate Disabled Children.* Ottawa: Canada Mortgage and Housing Corporation, Children's Environments Advisory Service, Research and Development Program.

Mihaly, L.
1989 'Beyond the Numbers: Homeless Families with Children'. Washington, DC: Children's Defence Fund, Child Welfare and Mental Health Division (April).

Muscovitch, A.
1980 *Study of the Child's Perception of the Neighbourhood.* Ottawa: Canada Mortgage and Housing Corporation, Children's Environments Advisory Service, Research and Development Program.

Offord, D.
1986 *Ontario Child Health Study: Summary of Initial Findings.* Toronto: Queen's Printer.

Ontario Ministry of Housing
1986 *A Place to Call Home: Housing Solutions for Low-Income Singles in Ontario.* Report of the Ontario Task Force on Roomers, Boarders and Lodgers to the Honourable Alvin Curling, Minister of Housing (December).

1988a *Tenant Satisfaction Survey 1988 Results.* Management Operations and Review Section.

1988b *More Than Just a Roof: Action to End Homelessness in Ontario.* Final Report of the Minister's Advisory Committee on the International Year of Shelter for the Homeless.

1989   *Tenant Satisfaction Survey 1989 Results.* Management Operations and Review Section.

Phillips, E., and H. Andrews
1982   'Residential Satisfaction and the Neighbourhood Perceptions of Young Adolescents in Public Housing', *Child in the City Report No. 15.* Center for Urban and Community Studies, University of Toronto (April).

Social Planning Council of Ottawa-Carleton
1990   'Survey on the Needs of Youth for Shelter in Ottawa-Carleton (July).

Statistics Canada
1990   *The Health and Activity Limitation Survey, Highlights: Disabled Persons in Canada.* Cat. 82-602 (March).

Wei Djao, A.
1990   *Housing Needs of Urban Native Families: A Comparative Study of Children's and Parents' Perceptions.* Ottawa: Canada Mortgage and Housing Corporation, Children's Environments Advisory Service, Research and Development Program.

Wekerle, G.R.
1988   *Women's Housing Projects in Eight Canadian Cities.* Ottawa: Canada Mortgage and Housing Corporation (April).

Wilkins, R., O. Adams, and A. Brancker
1990   'Changes in Mortality by Income in Urban Canada From 1971 to 1986'. *Health Reports*, 1 (2), Statistics Canada.

Index